Transactions of the Royal Historical Society

FIFTH SERIES

39

LONDON 1989

© Royal Historical Society

British Library Cataloguing in Publication Data

Transactions of the Royal Historical Society.
  —5th series, vol. 39 (1989)
  1. History—Periodicals
  I. Royal Historical Society
  905   D1

ISBN 0–86193–121–1

Made and printed in Great Britain by Butler & Tanner Ltd, Frome and London

CONTENTS

iii

TRANSACTIONS OF THE
ROYAL HISTORICAL SOCIETY

PRESIDENTIAL ADDRESS

By G. E. Aylmer

COLLECTIVE MENTALITIES IN MID SEVENTEENTH-CENTURY ENGLAND: IV. CROSS CURRENTS: NEUTRALS, TRIMMERS AND OTHERS

READ 18 NOVEMBER 1988

AMONG the most striking changes from the text-book generalisations of my school days is the emphasis given nowadays to those who were not committed to either side in the Civil War, those who tried and in some cases succeeded in keeping clear of the conflict altogether. Indeed so great has been the stress on neutrals and neutralism and on the general reluctance to take sides and to begin fighting at all in 1642, that we are in danger of having to explain how a mere handful of obstinate or fanatical extremists on each side contrived to drag the country down into the abyss of Civil War.[1] I have said enough in my previous addresses in this series to make my own position clear on that. Among Royalists, including the King himself, there were enough who believed that rebellion must be put down, whether they were more concerned to defend the constitutional prerogatives of the Crown, the government and liturgy of the Church, or the whole existing fabric of society. Correspondingly there were enough Parliamentarians who believed that religion, liberty and property were in deadly peril, through the design for Popery and arbitrary government. If these beliefs had been confined to a few dozen or even score of men on each side, it is not credible that a war would have begun in 1642, where fighting broke out be it noted in Lancashire, Yorkshire

---

[1] A. M. Everitt, *The Community of Kent and the Great Rebellion 1640–1660* (Leicester, 1966); J. S. Morrill, *The Revolt of the Provinces 1630–50* (revised edition, 1980); A. Fletcher, *The Outbreak of the English Civil War* (1981).

I

and Somerset before the preparations and manoeuverings of the two main armies led up to the campaign and battle of Edgehill.[2]

My purpose today is to offer a collective portrait of those who cannot be comprehended within the two camps, including those who moved—whether smoothly or uneasily—between them. In spite of the emphasis which has been put on neutrality treaties by the gentry of particular counties, which were intended to keep the war out of their respective territories, and notwithstanding attempts to analyse the actual and would-be neutrals, there was never a coherent third force in the 1640s. There was no ideology of neutralism. There were only what may be called varieties of non-alignment. I suggest that we may distinguish at least four distinct types or categories, of which two have in turn to be sub-divided.

First of all there were the ignorant, uncomprehending and apathetic masses, those incapable of grasping the issues at stake; those on whom the war might well impinge, through the physical disruption caused by the movement of armies in the fighting of battles, by conscription, requisitioning and taxation. Generally speaking these comprised the poorest, least literate and worst informed elements in the population. Much turns on how effective we believe the Uniformity Act to have been in its requirement for universal church attendance every Sunday; and following on from that, whether we think that people listened to what they heard in church and understood it. They may of course have gone to church, have heard and understood, but still have not been swayed one way or the other by the content of the prayers and sermons. In the Abstract of his Oxford D.Phil. thesis, submitted in 1955, Professor Brian Manning wrote: 'The country people over wide areas of England formed a great neutral mass'; and later: 'In 1645 the peasantry in many areas rebelled against the War and against both parties'.[3] As a description of the Club-Men movement, of which I shall say more in the course of this paper, the latter half of this statement seems much to the point, whereas the opening sentence may be potentially misleading unless by 'neutral' we understand ignorant, apathetic and indifferent. Later in the same text Manning wrote that 'the neutrals amongst the nobility and the gentry were moderate men'. Here, I would suggest, we need a slightly more systematic classification. Neuters, to use the contemporary term, might

---

[2] E. Broxap, *The Great Civil War in Lancashire (1642–1651)* (Manchester, 1910; reprinted Clifton, N.J., 1973), ch. iii; P. R. Newman, 'The Royalist Armies in Northern England 1642–45', D.Phil., Univ. of York (1978), ch. 1; D. Underdown, *Somerset in the Civil War and Interregnum* (Newton Abbot, 1973), ch. 2; S. R. Gardiner, *History of England . . . 1603–42* (10 vols., 1883–4), X, ch. cv. This excludes the King's two attempts to seize Hull, because no fighting took place involving loss of life.

[3] B. S. Manning, 'Neutrals and Neutralism in the English Civil War', D.Phil., Univ. of Oxford (1955; deposited 1957).

be motivated by self-interest, disgust with one side or both, literal inability to choose, or genuine detachment from the issues at stake. Likewise, my third category, of side-changers, can be divided between the principled, the opportunistic, and the merely disillusioned. Finally, I shall consider the reactions of the younger generation: of those too young to take sides in the Civil War years, but whose attitudes over the period down to the 1660s seem to be of particular interest.

A close reading of those speeches, sermons and tracts which purport to be neutral, or have at some time been so described, reveals several actually to be written from either a royalist or a parliamentarian standpoint. Sometimes it is the very moderation of the author's position which may mislead: in other cases an element of deliberate deception or disguise is evident.[4] The county neutrality treaties of 1642 to early 1643 reflect self-interest together with a genuine belief that there was much right and wrong on both sides. Individuals for whom there is enough reliable contemporary evidence to reconstruct their changing attitudes are few in number. There is a particular problem here for the historian: on the whole the higher men were in the social scale or the more eminent in their profession, the more likely their views are to be documented, yet at the same time the greater were the pressures on them to take sides, the more difficult it was for them to opt out. In spite of Clarendon's unflattering remarks about him, it would be fallacious to call Thomas Howard, Earl of Arundel and Surrey, a neutral because he withdrew to the continent during the war.[5] Sir Roger Twysden, the Kentish antiquary, was a neutral by choice but was treated as if he were a royalist by the parliament and its agents. A man of lower social rank and less local influence, might have held identical views to Twysden and been left unmolested. Another well known Kentish gentleman, Sir Edward Dering of Pluckley, was perhaps neutral by inclination, but a side-changer in practice. Unlike clergymen, who were often compelled to become either partisans or conformists, and of whom more later, some other professional men, notably lawyers and medics seem to have been able to continue in their careers without being forced to take sides at all. The sympathies of Matthew Hale, who held office during the 1650s and again after 1660, having changed sides successfully, are obscure before 1650. A number of his clients were royalists, even including Irish Catholics.

[4] For example: *The State of the Whole Kingdom* ... (1642), Wing S5324, royalist; [William Prynne], *A Soveraign Antidote To Prevent, Appease and Determine Our unnaturall and destructive Civill Warres and Dissensions* (1642), Wing P4086, parliamentarian; *A Miracle: An Honest Broker*... (1642), Wing M2206, parliamentarian; *A Plea for Moderation* ... (1642), Wing P2512, royalist.

[5] *History of the Rebellion* ... ed. W. D. Macray (6 vols., Oxford, 1888), i. 69–71 (Book I, paras. 118–19).

Would-be neutrals or those working for an 'accommodation', i.e. a compromise peace, were liable to be treated as side changers, even as traitors. Speaking on the scaffold when he was about to be hanged, Richard Challenor is recorded as having said:

It came from Mr. Waller under this notion, that if we could make a moderate party here in London, to stand betwixt the gappe, and in the gappe, to unite the King and the Parliament, it would be a very acceptable work, for now the three Kingdom's lay ableeding ...[6]

By contrast, his associate Nathaniel Tompkins denied that he was a Papist, but openly asserted his royalism as a servant of the king for over twenty years.[7] Edmund Waller's own position is far from clear. He was eventually received back into favour in the 1650s, but navigated the rapids of the Restoration without difficulty, his most consistent principle according to the *D.N.B.* being support for religious toleration bracketed, it seems fair to add, with self-preservation.[8] Most of the neutralist authors remain impenetrably anonymous. If Pepys's friend and rival, Thomas Povey, son of the Exchequer Auditor Justinian, were indeed 'The Moderator' of 1643, then he was in successive decades a neutral, a Cromwellian hanger on, and a court favourite under Charles II. *The Moderator expecting sudden peace or certain ruine ...* of February 1642/3 is undoubtedly one of the most eloquent neutralist tracts.[9] Moreover, an even more cogently argued pamphlet, published a few months later than this, refers favourably to the Moderator and so raises the possibility of common authorship. If both suppositions are correct, this would make Povey easily the most effective spokesman for a compromise peace and the most practical in outlining its possible bases. The second of these pamphlets raises a very fundamental

[6] [Richard] Challenor, *His Confession and Speech ...* (1643), Wing C1800, p. 4. He is mis-spelt Chaloner in the *DNB* and by Wing.

[7] *The Whole Confession and Speech ... of Mr Nathaniel Tompkins ...* (1643), Wing T1865. Clarendon says that he was Clerk of the Queen's Council (*Hist. Reb.*, Book VII, paras. 54–73); he is not in the *DNB*. For the fullest account of Waller's Plot, see still Gardiner, *History of the Great Civil War 1642–1649* (3 vols., 1888–91), chs. vii & viii.

[8] For Edmund Waller himself, see *DNB*; Introduction to *Poems*, ed. G. Thorn Drury (2 vols., 1893); W. L. Chernaik, *The poetry of limitation: a study of Edmund Waller* (New Haven, 1968); *Poems 1645 (etc.)* (Menston, Yorks, 1971), includes speeches in parliament, 1641–3; B. D. Henning (ed.), *History of Parliament. The House of Commons 1660–1690* (3 vols., 1983), iii. 653–7.

[9] On Povey, the *DNB* is quite inadequate. His career can be pieced together from D. Underdown, *Pride's Purge ...* (Oxford, 1971), pp. 104 n., 253, 383; R. Latham & W. Matthews (eds.), *Pepys' Diary* (11 vols. 1970–83), x, *Companion*, pp. 344–5. Besides secondary sources on Cromwell's 'Western Design', for the 1650s and after see *Cal. St. Papers Colonial, America and West Indies 1574–1660*, pp. 460–96; *ibid., Addenda, 1574–1674*, pp. 135, 211, etc.; British Library, Additional MS 11411, Povey's West India letter book 1655–60.

point—of relevance in any age for those who find themselves unable to take sides in some great contemporary conflict. Instead of asking, which party has more right on its side, ask yourself, whose victory will be more or less damaging to society as a whole and to the values which you most cherish. The anonymous author of 1643, Povey if it be he, puts it thus:

> ... the truth is, it is not so common nor so likely for people to rise up without cause, as for Governors to oppress without cause. Therefore there is less danger in the King yielding what appears to be too much than in the Parliament's doing so.[10]

It was one thing to coin the phrase 'the character of a moderate man', quite another to find a policy which would avoid the coming of war in 1642, or to bring about an end to it after that. For what was the basis of such a programme to be? Which side was to give way over the Church; or, failing that, could there be a return to the ideas briefly discussed in the spring of 1641 whereby bishops would share authority with diocesan committees, and the Prayer Book would be preserved but in an amended form? Who was to concede more over the militia and control of munitions supplies and fortified places, such as the Tower of London, Hull and Portsmouth? Would Parliament drop its demands in the Nineteen Propositions and perhaps some of those in the Ten Propositions of the previous year, in return for additional safeguards to prevent a recovery of royal power to its pre-1641 level? Could there be a full and unconditional pardon for the leading figures, including those regarded as extremists, on both sides? That surely should have been attainable given the basic requirement of mutual trust. As in almost all schemes for multilateral disarmament, trust between the parties was more fundamental than the specific issues at stake between them. This is not to deny the sincerity of 'moderate men' in the 1640s (nor indeed of moderate women either, except that they expressed themselves much less frequently and with greater difficulty); nor is it to controvert those modern scholars who have emphasised the extent of neutralism in the 1640s. It is simply to cast some doubt on the possibilities of an effective neutralist programme, as successive Rubicons were crossed in 1641 and 1642.

Years after the Restoration, Dr John Worthington, whom we shall meet again later this afternoon, wrote to an ex-pupil, who had been deploring current animosities among churchmen and others:

---

[10] *Queries and Conjectures* ... Wing Q165, in G. Erskine-Hill & G. Storey (eds.), *Revolutionary Prose of the English Civil War* (Cambridge, 1983), pp. 230–6, esp. p. 233.

What you add of your being grieved ... is an argument of a more moderate spirit which I have discerned in you and some others ... This spirit, had it ruled in the times, when the Long Parliament began, might have prevented all those long continued traines of sad calamities and cruelties that followed.[11]

True enough, no doubt. Once more, however, if we try to think ourselves back into the situation of contemporaries during the early 1640s, might we not fairly say that it takes two to make the concessions which are needed if 'a moderate spirit' is to prevail?

Turning now from neutrals to our third category, that of side-changers, a point of terminology needs to be got out of the way. The very name 'Trimmer' has come to have a pejorative flavour, implying someone who switches over in order to keep in with the winners, to be on the side of what Napoleon called the big battalions. It is worth remembering that when the name was introduced by the Marquis of Halifax in the 1680s, it meant almost precisely the reverse of this, being taken from the image of trimming a boat or ship which was too low in the water on one side or the other; the Trimmer as characterised by Halifax[12] puts his influence on the side of the Crown if Parliament is getting too powerful, or the reverse as the need may be. Whether any of those who changed sides between 1642 and 1660 did so in order to restore the balance by joining the weaker party, seems extremely doubtful. Self-interest appears a better explanation for the successive changes in position by James Marquis, later 1st Duke of Hamilton, between 1642 and 1647. The case of Henry Rich, Earl of Holland, may be susceptible of a more charitable interpretation—as a side-changer who fatally miscalculated both his own interests and his ability to influence events. The fact that both of them ended their days on the scaffold in February 1649 brings us to another possible distinction. Those who made only one switch of allegiance, most of them either in 1642–3 or in 1647–8 or in 1659–60, should perhaps be distinguished from those who changed twice or more often. That would for example put the Yorkshireman Sir Hugh Cholmley (1643, Parliamentarian to Royalist), Archbishop John Williams (1645, Royalist to Parliamentarian) and Edward Montague, later Earl of Sand-

---

[11] R. C. Christie (ed.), *The Diary and Correspondence of Dr John Worthington*, vol. II, Part ii (Chetham Soc., CXIV, 1886), p. 315.

[12] This is to assume that he, and not his uncle Sir William Coventry, was the author. For a brief discussion of this and an accessible version of the text, see J. P. Kenyon (ed.), *Halifax Complete Works* (Harmondsworth, 1969); the older, classic text is H. C. Foxcroft, *Life and Letters of ... Halifax* (2 vols., 1898), ii. 273 *et seq.*; also W. Raleigh (ed.), *Works of ... Halifax* (Oxford, 1912), and for more recent discussions, T. C. Faulkner, 'Halifax's *The Character of a Trimmer* and L'Estrange's Attack on Trimmers in *The Observator*', *Huntington Library Quarterly*, xxxvii (1973–4), pp. 71–81; M. N. Brown, 'Trimmers and Moderates in the Reign of Charles II', *ibid.*, pp. 311–36.

wich (1659–60, Cromwellian to Royalist) in a different category from Roger Boyle, Lord Broghill, who switched in 1647 and again in 1660, Anthony Ashley Cooper, later the 1st Earl of Shaftesbury (1643–4 and again 1659–60), Charles Howard, later 1st Earl of Carlisle (1647 and 1660) and George Monck (1647 and 1660). Perhaps we should exclude those who helped to bring about or simply accepted the Restoration and concentrate on those who switched more than once during the 1640s: the three peers who joined the King at Oxford and then rejoined the Parliament in London during the course of 1643— Bedford, Clare and Holland; Sir Thomas Savile, Earl of Sussex (1643 and 1645–6), Edward Massey—one of the ablest military commanders of the time (1642 and 1647–8). Again it seems best to put in a separate category those parliamentarians who became royalists at some point between 1647 and 1649 and remained such thereafter: such as Denzil Holles, Francis Annesley, Sir John Clotworthy, Sir William Waller, Sir John Maynard, William Prynne and others, and to distinguish them from those who had switched before 1647 (as mentioned above) or who were won back by the Protector in the mid and later 1650s, such as John Glynne and John Maynard the younger. Clearly the repeal of the Engagement Act in January 1654 altered the basis of what Professor Skinner has called the *de factoist* position.[13] Not all repeated switches over were consistently either opportunistic or principled. The well known editor and pamphleteer Marchamont Needham, appears to have become a royalist in 1647, a decision which cannot have been motivated by short-term self interest; as against this, his changes of allegiance to support the Commonwealth in 1650, then the Protectorate in 1654; and finally his attempt to resurrect his royalism in 1660, signify at least pragmatic *de factoism*, at worst sheer opportunism.[14]

It is hard to know how many, besides the ignorant and apathetic, were neutrals out of genuine detachment or inability to choose sides at all. The well-travelled and experienced diplomat, who had been twice disappointed of the Secretaryship of the State, Sir Thomas Roe might be one such; Edward, Lord Herbert of Cherbury, ex-Ambassador and amateur philosopher, another. Both were of a ripe age by 1642, as were Henry Montague, 1st Earl of Manchester (Charles I's Lord Privy Seal, who died at the end of 1642), and the compulsorily retired Secretary of State, Sir John Coke (d. 1644). The younger Sir Dudley

[13] Q. Skinner, 'Conquest and Consent: Thomas Hobbes and the Engagement Controversy' in G. E. Aylmer (ed.), *The Interregnum The Quest for Settlement 1646–1660* (1972 and paperback 1974), pp. 79–98, 208–9, 222–4, which is still in my view the best account.

[14] J. Frank, *Cromwell's Press Agent: A Critical Biography of Marchamont Nedham, 1620–1678* (Lanham, Md., 1980).

Carleton (1599–1654), nephew of Secretary Dorchester, seems a clearer case. A Clerk of the Privy Council, he simply withdrew at the outbreak of war to the Netherlands where he had acquired some property in the course of his diplomatic career; although suffering penal taxation as if he were a royalist, he made his peace with the regime and so was able to return to England before his death.[15] And there were other servants of King Charles whom it seems impossible to classify as either royalists or parliamentarians.[16]

What of those populist peasant neutrals, the Clubmen? Within the south western counties, David Underdown has offered an explanation of their leanings for, or more often against one side or the other in terms of the social geography of particular districts.[17] Whether he would wish to extend this to the Clubmen of the Welsh borders or of the West Midlands is not clear. It certainly seems that they may have had anti-royalist leaders in Monmouthshire, Worcestershire and Herefordshire and in parts of Somerset; anti-Parliamentarian ones in Dorset, Wiltshire and other parts of Somerset. Although Professor Underdown has done much more research on this than anyone else, I remain inclined to the more old-fashioned view that the Clubmen were against whichever army was on their backs at a particular time and place.[18] The Dorset and Wiltshire Clubmen's programme published in July 1645, but drafted in May of that year, would have been more awkward for the New Model Army and for Parliament's local forces, simply because by that time there were no Royalist forces left in those counties except a very few isolated garrisons which were closely besieged; none the less it is far from being a pro-Royalist manifesto. Indeed since the parliamentary army was the better paid, supplied and behaved of the two by this date, many of its demands would have been potentially more damaging to the Royalists.[19] When renewed financial crisis led to massive arrears and the taking of free quarter in 1659–60, popular anti-army feeling was to show itself again after an interval of about ten years.

I turn now to writers, thinkers and intellectuals in general. It would be flattering to be able to identify a kind of moderate, ecumenical, irenic tradition persisting through the Personal Rule of Charles I, the

[15] G. E. Aylmer, *The King's Servants . . . 1625–42* (1961; 2nd edn. 1974), p. 389.

[16] *Ibid.*, via the index, under 'Neutrals', etc.

[17] D. Underdown, 'The Chalk and the Cheese: Contrasts among the English Clubmen', *Past & Present*, lxxxv (1979), pp. 25–48.

[18] Manning, 'Thesis', ch. 6; Morrill, *Revolt of Provinces*, via index; R. Hutton, 'The Worcestershire Clubmen in the English Civil War', *Midland History*, v (1979–80) pp. 39–49; P. Gladwish, 'The Herefordshire Clubmen: a re-assessment', *ibid.*, x (1985), pp. 62–71.

[19] *The Desires and Resolutions of the Club-Men of . . . Dorset and Wilts . . .* (1645), Wing D1180, Thomason E. 292/24, dated 12 July.

Civil War, the Regicide, the Republic and the Restoration. I mean flattering less to contemporaries than to ourselves, on the grounds that most historians today are middle-of-the-road, as well as being middle-aged and middle-class. And most of us would no doubt like to regard ourselves as irenic and ecumenical. How tenable is this view historically? One of the foremost historians of our time has, with great eloquence and force of argument, traced such a tradition in European thought all the way from Erasmus through the Dutch Remonstrants, the English Arminians, the Great Tew Circle, and the Latitudinarians, to the moderate Enlightenment of the eighteenth century.[20] I am not competent to assess the validity of Lord Dacre's interpretation in its wider European context; in relation to seventeenth-century England there do seem to be some difficulties, or at least some problems to be faced before we can either agree that his case is proved or even accept that his argument is meaningfully posed. To admire the Great Tew Circle is not necessarily to assume that most of its members had much influence, either in their own time or afterwards. It is common ground that the crisis of 1640 and the coming of Civil War two years later spelt the disintegration of the group. Even to describe what happened in these terms may however indicate a misconception. For, as the author of a recent study has very pertinently reminded us: 'in writing of Great Tew we are dealing with an ethos, and not with a social unit'.[21] Thomas Hobbes, in any case a tangential and untypical member of the Circle, went abroad and returned only as the author of the great *de factoist* apology for absolutism in 1651. William Chillingworth was unhappy about the division into parties and the coming of war, but he served loyally in the King's forces, actually as a military engineer before doing so as a chaplain. His death may well have been hastened by the bullying tactics of his far less admirable puritan captor, Francis Cheynell; but Chillingworth's royalism is beyond any doubt. His masterpiece, *The Religion of Protestants*, of 1638, was first and foremost an apologia for the Church of England against Rome, a marvellous making good of his own earlier youthful indiscretion. Whether it did much to advance the course of Protestant unity either during the 1640s and 1650s or after the Restoration is another matter,

---

[20] H. R. Trevor-Roper, *Historical Essays* (1957), 'Erasmus'; *Religion, The Reformation, and Social Change* (1967), 'The Origins of the Enlightenment'; *Renaissance Essays* (1985), chs. 3, 4, 7; and most recently *Catholics, Anglicans and Puritans* (1987).

[21] J. C. Hayward, 'New Directions in Studies of the Falkland Circle', *The 17th Century*, II, i (1987), 19–48, quotation from p. 20. I am extremely grateful to Dr Hayward for lending me a copy of his Cambridge Ph.D. thesis (1982); it is a matter of regret that neither his nor two earlier theses on Great Tew have been published. I am also grateful to Dr P. Beale, the editor of *Index of English Literary Manuscripts* (1980–, in progress).

and not a question easily answered.[22] John Hales of Eton (1584–1656) was a non-combatant and died saddened by the times in which he lived; to make of him a neuter or straddler rather than a sad but sincere royalist and Anglican is a travesty of the facts. Falkland himself, host to the circle, was unhappy with many of the king's policies and practices; he may have deliberately courted death—the evidence is too thin to say more—nonetheless he died in battle on the King's side. As to the survivors, in so far as Hyde helped to save Charles II from lurching into Popery and absolutism during his years of exile, all Anglicans and monarchists must be reckoned for ever in his debt. But age, and until 1660 hardship made him rigid and unforgiving. Historians still disagree about his part in the religious settlement and legislation of 1660 to 1665. All else apart, he was at least as concerned to prevent the King from introducing toleration by prerogative action as he was to mitigate the severity of the church hierarchy and the members of the two Houses against their now defeated and defenceless enemies, the victors of the Civil War and Interregnum. Likewise Gilbert Sheldon, Warden of All Souls College from 1636 until the Puritan visitation of Oxford, may have been less illiberal as Bishop of London and then as Archbishop of Canterbury than he would have been without the pre-war influence of Great Tew; it is always difficult to prove a negative. So too with George Morley, Bishop of Worcester (1660–3) and then of Winchester (1662–83), although in his case Calvinist leanings in theology may serve to explain better his relative leniency towards Protestant dissenters. John Earle also, successively Dean of Westminster, Bishop of Worcester and then of Salisbury, was a strong royalist but not a hard-line persecutor in the 1660s. Chronology suggests that he is more likely to have been attracted to Tew and the Falkland circle because, as some of his 'character' essays show, he was a liberal-minded christian humanist, rather than having been influenced by the circle so as to become more irenic and ecumenical.[23]

John Selden, if indeed he can be counted a member, was beyond question one of the intellectual prodigies of his age. Again Great Tew cannot be said to have formed him, only to mark a phase in his long career from research assistant under Sir Robert Cotton to benefactor of the Bodleian Library. His importance as a political theorist is more

[22] The account which I have found most helpful is R. R. Orr, *Reason and Authority The Thought of William Chillingworth* (Oxford, 1967).

[23] The first edition of the *Microcosmographie* was 1628, revised *STC*, no. 7439; the earliest known MS is 1627 (Bodleian Library, English Poetry, E.112). I am not clear why in the *Addenda and Corrigenda to the DNB* Earle's authorship is denied; by whatever date in the 1630s we are to think of the Great Tew Circle as being in existence, he was already a mature scholar, having been a fellow of Merton College since 1619.

open to debate than his achievement as a historical scholar.[24] As a parliamentarian his best days were in the 1620s; during the Long Parliament he helped to prevent the Presbyterian church settlement from being more oppressive and theocratic than it might otherwise have been. Politically he withdrew into detachment, whether or not we are to call it neutralism, from the time of Pride's Purge and the Regicide.

Not only was the Great Tew circle broken up by the Civil War, its intellectual and cultural influence was deflected. Once the rebellion was seen as a fundamental challenge to authority in both church and state, the room for irenic, ecumenical policies was fatally narrowed. And it is another, quite distinct group of intellectuals who may be thought to have exemplified such values in the 1650s and after.

Much has been written on the so-called Cambridge Platonists, and it is unlikely that I can add anything of consequence. They seem on the surface to have little by way of direct links either with Tew or with the English Arminians, although Henry Moore was a boy at Eton when Hales was a Fellow.[25] Moreover their strongest ties with the Dutch Arminians were too late in date to explain the genesis of their own ideas.[26] It is, historians of the movement agree, significant that all the leading figures were brought up within the Cambridge Calvinist mould (under the baleful posthumous influence of William Perkins) and that all of them came to reject the doctrine of double predestination.[27] This is described so attractively in the subsequent autobiography of Simon Patrick, to whom we shall shortly be returning in another connection, that quotation is irresistible:

[24] See the claims made by R. Tuck in his *Natural Rights Theories: Origins and Development* (Cambridge, 1979), ch. 4. The most recent assessment of Selden's scholarship in relation to his politics, but so far only reaching *c.* 1630, is P. Christianson, 'Young John Selden and the Ancient Constitution, *ca.* 1610–18', *Proceedings of the American Philosophical Society*, vol. 128, part 4 (1984), pp. 271–315 and John Selden, the Five Knights' Case, and Discretionary Imprisonment in Early Stuart England', *Criminal Justice History*, vi (1985), pp. 65–87.

[25] M. H. Nicolson (ed.), *Conway Letters: The Correspondence of Anne, Viscountess Conway, Henry More, and their friends, 1642–1684* (1930), p. 40 & n. 5.

[26] R. L. Colie, *Light and Enlightenment A Study of the Cambridge Platonists and the Dutch Arminians* (Cambridge, 1957), esp. chs. i & ii. The suggestion that Samuel Hartlib and John Dury formed a link between the Dutch Remonstrants and the English Latitudinarians is unfortunately not pursued or documented; its relevance to Lord Dacre's argument is obvious.

[27] J. Tulloch, *Rational Theology and Christian Philosophy in England in the 17th Century* (2 vols. Edinburgh and London, 1872), vol. ii; J. A. Passmore, *Ralph Cudworth. An Interpretation* (Cambridge, 1951); Colie, *Light & Enlightenment*; G. R. Cragg (ed.), *The Cambridge Platonists* (A Library of Protestant Thought, New York, 1968); C. A. Patrides (ed.), *The Cambridge Platonists* (Stratford-upon-Avon, no. 5, London, 1969); see also D. Bush, *English Literature in the Earlier 17th Century 1600–1660* (revised edn. Oxford, 1962), pp. 340–9 and appendices. Needless to say, this note is not intended as a bibliography.

... I cannot but here acknowledge one singular blessing which I enjoyed by my conversation with Mr. Smith, which is fresh in my mind to this day, as the very place is where we were discoursing together about the doctrine of absolute Predestination; which I told him had always seemed to me very hard, and I could never answer the objections against it, but was advised by divines to silence carnal reason.

At which he fell a laughing, and told me they were good and sound reasons which I had objected against that doctrine, and made such a representation of the nature of God to me, and of His goodness to men in Christ Jesus, as quite altered my opinion, and made me take the liberty to read such authors (which were before forbidden me) as settled me in the belief that God would really have all men to be saved, of which I never after made a question, nor looked upon it as a matter of controversy, but presumed it in all my sermons.[28]

Clearly the tutorial, or as Cambridge calls it the supervision system sometimes has its uses. In the famous 1651 exchange of letters between Benjamin Whichcote, the oldest member of the group, and his Calvinist ex-tutor Anthony Tuckney, he was accused of being over familiar with the works of certain heterodox authors, including Thomas Jackson (1579–1640), President of Corpus Christi College, Oxford, latterly also Dean of Peterborough. Whichcote admits to having read some of Jackson's works (which in total are alarmingly voluminous), together with those of Richard Field, a follower of the great Hooker, and of the Anglican apologist Henry Hammond; but he asserted that it was many years since he had done so and that he had in any case read far more extensively (for his sins) in the works of Calvin, Beza and Perkins.[29] Besides being one of the leading anti-atheistical writers of the early seventeenth century, Jackson's churchmanship was Laudian in character and his theological position unmistakeably Arminian. More significant, however, for our purposes it has recently been persuasively argued that he was a Platonist, and in this sense a forerunner of the Cambridge group.[30] Another connection which has been suggested rests on the assumption that Falkland was himself a

---

[28] *The Autobiography of Symon Patrick, Bishop of Ely* (Oxford, 1839), pp. 18–19.

[29] BL, Sloane MS 1710, fo. 309 *et seq.* (late 17th or early 18th-century copies of the apparently lost originals); *Eight Letters of Dr Anthony Tuckney and Dr Benjamin Whichcote* ..., bound with S. Salter (ed.), *Moral and Religious Aphorisms ... of ... Dr Whichcote* (new edn. London, 1753); the two texts seem identical. The letters have been quoted in part by Tulloch, Cragg, Patrides (and no doubt others), but have not so far as I am aware been reprinted in full anywhere.

[30] Sarah Hutton, 'Thomas Jackson, Oxford Platonist, and William Twisse, Aristotelian', *Journal of the History of Ideas*, xl (1978), 635–52. I am very grateful to Dr Hutton for giving me copies of her articles, some in advance of publication, and for

Platonist, and that the intellectual heritage of Great Tew can be so designated. The Cambridge University Librarian of the 1650s, Thomas Smith, though not himself a Platonist was a friend of John Worthington, a peripheral member of the group. In 1660 books by Chillingworth and Falkland were actually reprinted in Cambridge, and there is other evidence of mutual regard and shared interests.[31] In spite, however, of its obvious interest, this connection seems too late in date to account for the initial reception of Platonist or neo-Platonist ideas in Cambridge by the early 1650s, or to explain their holders' political evolution.

As with Great Tew, so with the Cambridge Platonists: it remains arguable however far they were a coherent group. Whichcote was essentially a teacher and preacher, who published nothing and was in any case expelled from Cambridge at the Restoration, although he accepted the Uniformity Act and held various parish livings after this. His 'Aphorisms' are fuller of homely common sense, than the philosophy of any particular school. Thus for example no. 6:

> it is a great deal easier to commit a second sin than it was to commit the first; and a great deal harder to repent the second than it was to repent of the first.

Too true, as we should all no doubt be aware. John Smith, perhaps the most gifted writer of them all, and Nicholas Culverwell were both dead by 1652. The case for any continuing influence on the thought or the churchmanship of the later seventeenth century must turn primarily on the writings and personalities of Ralph Cudworth and Henry More. It is worth setting their Cambridge careers in a wider context from the 1640s to the 1660s. The Puritan-Parliamentarian purge of Cambridge has been admirably described and analysed in a recent article.[32] It was conducted under the personal direction of that most moderate of parliamentarian leaders, Edward Montague, 2nd Earl of Manchester; moreover overt royalism in Cambridge had been effectively crushed from as early as the autumn of 1642. So it was a more restrained, one is almost tempted to say gentlemanly affair than the purge of Oxford a few years later. In theory, subscription to the Solemn League and Covenant was the prerequisite for continuing in

---

other helpful suggestions; she is currently re-editing the correspondence of Henry More, Anne Lady Conway and their circle. On Jackson's Arminianism, see now also N. Tyacke, *Anti-Calvinists: The Rise of English Arminianism c. 1590–1640* (Oxford, 1987), via the index.

[31] Hayward, 'New Directions ...', pp. 29–30; P. Hammond, 'Thomas Smith: a beleaguered humanist of the Interregnum', *Bull. Inst. Hist. Res.*, lvi (1983), pp. 180–94.

[32] J. D. Twigg, 'The parliamentary visitation of the University of Cambridge, 1644–1645', *E.H.R.*, xcviii (1983), pp. 513–28.

post, whether as head, fellow, scholar or college chaplain. But when we are told that so palpable an Anglican and Royalist as Sancroft was not required to take the oath, it is less surprising to learn that the same may also have been true of Whichcote, Worthington, and More, though apparently not of Cudworth. Whichcote is said to have been the most uneasy about accepting a college headship under the new dispensation. He and Worthington were both to lose their positions at the Restoration, though both accepted the terms of the Uniformity Act and later held livings elsewhere. Henry More simply continued in his fellowship at Christ's under every successive regime from 1639 to his death in 1687. The contrast of all these with Cudworth is striking. He managed to retain both his headship and his chair at the Restoration, despite a much greater measure of commitment to the regimes of the previous decades. It had been Sir Henry Mildmay, M.P. a non-signing regicide and one of the less admirable one-time King's Servants, who had proposed Cudworth as a fast-sermon preacher in February 1646/7 and who was afterwards instructed by the House to express gratitude for the sermon and to request its author to publish it. At the same time the parliamentary committee on the affairs of Cambridge was instructed to settle an additional income of £150.00 a year on the Mastership of Clare Hall, to which Cudworth had been elected two years before.[33] Admittedly the famous sermon of 31 March 1647 can be read as a plea for peace and reconciliation, the kind of pronouncement which might have emanated from Great Tew if the circle had still existed, and if we can assume that its ethos had survived the Civil War.[34] But perhaps as a logical, if somewhat deferred sequel to this, Cudworth corresponded with Secretary Thurloe under the Protectorate, about finding able young men as recruits for the public service.[35] All this makes his being left unmolested after 1660 the more remarkable. The explanation may simply lie in the facts that under the college statutes of Christ's his election was not *ultra vires*, and that there was no extruded previous incumbent alive to claim back either Mastership or Professorship; whereas it was on one or both of these grounds that Whichcote and Worthington lost out.[36] Of Cudworth's subsequent influence I am tempted to say that his full-scale philosophical works are so difficult to read that their

[33] *Journals of the House of Commons* (folio, London, n.d.), 5, *1646–8*, pp. 97, 131.

[34] Wing C7469. In Cragg and Patrides (the latter without the prefatory Dedication to the House); also, for a handy reprint if obtainable, R. Cudworth, *A Sermon preached before the House of Commons March 31, 1647* (Facsimile Text Society, N.Y., 1930).

[35] G. E. Aylmer, *The State's Servants ... 1649–60* (1973), pp. 71–2.

[36] This is partly made clear in Worthington, *Diary & Correspondence* (Chetham Soc., XIII, 1847, XXXVI, 1855, CXIV, 1886), I, 202–3, 216–17, II, ii, 378. For Whichcote's case, see also J. Heywood & T. Wright, *The Ancient Laws of the 15th century, for King's College, Cambridge, and for the public school of Eton College* (1850), pp. 287–95.

impact is unlikely to have been very great. Henry More of course enjoyed a respected place in Lady Conway's circle and also had links with Lady Ranelagh and her brother Robert Boyle and the Royal Society, to which he and Cudworth were elected in 1662 on John Wilkins' recommendation.[37] He certainly wrote more clearly and cogently than Cudworth, but More's wider influence too is hard to assess.

Lest anyone should think that I am dwelling unfairly on conformism among Cambridge dons, we should remember that the ejections there in 1644–5 totalled 217, and that there was a further purge, whose victims included Sancroft, following the imposition of the Engagement under the Commonwealth. Admittedly the comparable Oxford total from 1647–8 was 370; but, if one wanted to cite a really distinguished 'Vicar of Bray', it would be Thomas Barlow (1607–91), a Fellow of Queen's, Bodley's Librarian, provost of Queen's and eventually Bishop of Lincoln, who has been described both as a trimmer and as a Calvinist. He awaits a modern biographer.[38]

Mentioning the Vicar of Bray provides an interesting example of the pitfalls in oral history. In Thomas Fuller's *Worthies* the conforming incumbent is said to have remained in post continuously from Henry VIII's reign to that of Elizabeth I, whereas in the poem the reigns spanned would appear to have run from Charles II to George I. And to cap this, according to the Victoria County History, he was not at Bray but the next door parish.[39]

The phenomenon of passive conformity, especially among the clergy, deserves more serious consideration than this. There are numerous difficulties, some more obvious than others, in the way of its assessment. Estimates have of course been made from the 17th century onwards of the numbers expelled as Anglicans or on other grounds in the 1640s and 1650s, and as puritans and nonconformists in the 1660s. The problem is to keep track of mobility (mainly due to translations and promotions) and of deaths, in trying to calculate the

[37] Nicolson, *Conway Letters*, via the index; also Kathleen M. Lynch, 'The Incomparable Lady Ranelagh', in J. Butt (ed.), *Of Books and Humankind. Essays and Poems presented to Bonamy Dobree* (1964), pp. 25–33.

[38] For these totals, see Twigg, 'Parliamentary Visitation'. The Oxford purges of the 1640s and 1660s are much the more fully documented: see *The Register of the Visitors ... 1647–58*, ed. M. Burrows (Camden Soc., new ser. xxix (1881), and *The Restoration Visitation ...*, ed. F. J. Varley (Camden 3rd ser., lxxix, 1948, Camden Miscellany, xviii). For Barlow, see *The Genuine Remaines of that learned prelate Dr Thomas Barlow* (1693), Wing B832; *DNB* and refs. in numerous other works, including histories of The Queen's College, Oxford, and the Bodleian Library.

[39] T. Fuller, *The History of the Worthies of England*, ed. P. A. Nuttall (3 vols., 1840), i.112–13; G. Grigson (ed.), *The Oxford Book of Satirical Verse* (Oxford, 1980), no. 69, pp. 158–60, and in other anthologies; Victoria County History, *Berkshire*, iii (1923), 125, 'Cookham'.

residual total of those who conformed throughout. To take one county, which is unusually well documented and with which I happen to have some familiarity, in Dorset there were about 85 extrusions from approximately 239 incumbencies during the 1640s, although taking account of curates these affected more like 100 individuals. By contrast, in 1660–62 there were about 105 extrusions, but because of pluralism or the amalgamation of livings, this involved only some 67 individuals. On my calculations, the number of clergy who retained their incumbencies without a break from 1641 to 1662 was around 40.[40] On the basis of this it would be absurd to assert that one sixth of all parish clergy were passive conformists: in the first place, Dorset may have been unrepresentative of the country as a whole in any number of possible directions, but this apart it is impossible to tell what proportion of those who conformed in the 1640s and 1650s would have done so again in the 1660s, if they had still been present and alive. More research is needed here before we can safely generalise; none the less the category of passive conformists should clearly be included in any comprehensive survey of collective mentalities.

Writing rather over 100 years ago, John Tulloch, who certainly still deserves respect as a historian of religious thought, virtually identified the Cambridge Platonists with that other elusive category, the Latitudinarians. In this he was following Bishop Gilbert Burnet. As opposed to this, the most recent study denies that the term Latitudinarian is applicable to any specific group or party and equates it with mainstream Restoration churchmanship.[41] The name itself is indeed worth pondering a little more, before we try to decide to whom if anyone it was intended to apply. In 1662 there appeared, by 'S.P. of Cambridge', *A Brief Account of the new Sect of Latitude-men Together with some reflections upon the New Philosophy. In answer to a Letter from his Friend at Oxford*. Assuming the author of this to have been Simon Patrick, future Bishop of Ely, and at this time Rector of St Paul's Covent Garden, Patrick's explanation in 1662 is in terms of age: those who are disapprovingly singled out in this way, he writes

---

[40] I have relied basically on G. D. Squibb, *Dorset Incumbents, 1542–1731*, reprinted from *Proceedings of the Dorset Natural History and Archaeological Society*, vols. 70–75 (1948–53), cross-checked against A. G. Matthews, *Calamy Revised* ... Oxford, 1934), and *Walker Revised* ... (Oxford, 1948). In the very few cases where these two distinguished authorities disagree about particular individuals, I have preferred the higher figures for extrusions and the lower for continuity, so as not to exaggerate the latter. For the most recent general treatment, see I. M. Green, 'The Persecution of "Scandalous" and "malignant" parish clergy during the English Civil War', *E.H.R.*, xciv (1979), 507–31.

[41] J. Spurr, '"Latitudinarianism" and the Restoration Church', *Histl. Jnl.*, xxxi (1988), 61–82. See G. Burnet, *History of my own time*, Part I, *The Reign of Charles II*, ed. O. Airy (2 vols., Oxford, 1897), i.331–41, esp. p. 334.

are such, whose fortune it was to be born so late, as to have their
education in the University, since the beginning of the unhappy
troubles of this Kingdom.

Hence they had ascended through the academic *cursos honorum* without
asking themselves about the validity of the titles to office of those
admitting them. 'In opposition to the hide-bound, straight-laced spirit
then prevailing, they were called Latitude-Men'. S.P. went on to
defend them against their critics 'the Narrow-Men' and to emphasise
their loyalty to the traditions of the Church. He admits their opposition to the authority of Aristotle and the Schoolmen and defends
their interest in the New Science (mentioning in the course of this
Gilbert, Galileo, Descartes, and Harvey). 'True philosophy', he con-
cludes, 'can never hurt sound Divinity'. Once the educated gentry of
England had grown acquainted with the atomical (that is, cor-
puscular) hypothesis of matter, the clergy could not remain stuck with
dockleaves and bulrushes![42]

I suggest that his generational argument fits his own age-group
extremely well. Indeed it seems broadly applicable to anyone who
had entered Cambridge after 1642 or Oxford after 1646. If we limit
ourselves only to future bishops, Patrick himself was born in 1626,
Edward Fowler in 1632, Thomas Sprat and Edward Stillingfleet in
1635, Thomas Tenison and John Tillotson in 1636. Their formative
academic years were all in the 1640s or 1650s. But it is no kind of an
explanation for the Cambridge Platonists proper: Cudworth, Culverwell, More, Smith, Whichcote, Worthington. Nor indeed would it
be for other eminent figures, who conformed in some measure during
the Interregnum but did well again after 1660, such as Edward
Reynolds, Seth Ward, and John Wilkins.

Let us return briefly to the name and my reasons for unease with
the prevailing explanation. In 1666 Samuel Parker, future Bishop of
Oxford under James II, published *A Free and Impartial Censure of the
Platonick Philosophie*, in which he described Platonism as 'an
ungrounded and Fanatick Fancy'. He attacked its adherents with
regard to their morality, logic, natural philosophy (that is science)
and above all theology. His technique of guilt by association involved
bracketing them successively with 'our late English Rosie-Crucians',
with Hobbes, with the Cabbalistic tradition and with Hermes Tres-
megistus. But of Latitude-men there is no mention.[43] The second
edition of Simon Patrick's defence appeared in 1669, and in that year
Pepys described Dr Wilkins, then Bishop of Chester, as a 'Lati-

---

[42] S.P., *A Brief Account* . . . (1662, Wing P754), pp. 4–5, 6–9, 14–15, 19–21, 24.

[43] (Oxford, 1666, Wing P 463, dedicated to Dr Bathurst, President of Trinity
College), pp. 2, 4, 34, 40, 46, 76, 87, 104, 109–10.

tudinarian'. The word is really quite a mouthful; it was used once by Patrick in 1662 and once ironically by More in 1665, but 'latitude-men' remained for some years the more common form. Another restrained defence appeared in 1670, written in the dialogue form so beloved of the time. This was entitled *The Principles and Practices, Of Certain Moderate Divines of the Church of England (greatly misunderstood) Truly Represented and Defended*. So closely did its style and content reflect the Cambridge group that Thomas Barlow at first believed it to have been written by Henry More. Only later did he learn that the author was the Oxonian future bishop, Edward Fowler. This would seem to support Gilbert Burnet's identification or, alternatively, mis-identification.[44] It seems clear, however, that the term would not have been applied to the ex-Laudians, the rising Tory high-fliers, and the future non-Jurors among the churchmen of Charles II's reign. Common sense suggests that it was indeed applied to a body of people and opinions within the church which did, if only indirectly and to a limited extent, owe something to the traditions of Great Tew, but also to the passive conformists of the 1640s and 1650s, those who had not been committed to the Puritan cause, still less to the Directory of Worship or the principle of a republic. They were no doubt themselves divided on the issue of comprehension versus toleration, with regard to Non-conformists after 1660. Thanks to external circumstances, notably the triumph of William in 1688–9, the Toleration Act was a partial victory for their cause, at least for some of those who had survived until then.

The relationship between the New Science and the political and religious issues of the time has exercised historians of greater intel-lectual penetration, as well as wider and deeper scholarship than myself. It is only the continuing disagreement among them which prompts me to say anything about it at all.[45] A direct causal link between Puritanism and the Scientific Revolution no longer seems tenable; but the reverse of this, namely that the Puritan cause was actually inimical to scientific advance, or that Anglicans, Catholics and Cavaliers at large were more positively involved than their opponents is, if anything, even less plausible. Again the identification of the New Science with moderates, neutrals, side-changers and lati-

---

[44] Latham & Matthews (eds.), *Pepys Diary*, ix.485, 16 March 1669; S.P., *A Brief Account*, p. 7; Nicolson (ed.), *Conway Letters*, p. 243; [E. Fowler], *Principles and Practices* ... (1670), Wing F1711, Bodleian 80 A 16 Linc. (I am extremely grateful to Mrs Mary Clapinson for identifying both of the manuscript annotations as being in Barlow's own hand.)

[45] For a bibliography down to the early 1980s, see Barbara J. Shapiro, *Probability and Certainty in 17th-century England: A Study of the Relationship between Natural Science, Religion, History, Law and Literature* (Princeton, 1983), notes to ch. ii, pp. 273–87, & ch. iii, n. 2, pp. 287–8.

tudinarians is tempting. In spite of the prominence of John Wilkins (1614–72) there really is not enough of the right kind of evidence. William Brouncker (1620–84) and Sir Robert Moray (1608–73) to mention the two leading figures in the establishment of the Royal Society, may have been untypical aristocrats, but their royalist commitment is clear. Two hypotheses may perhaps be ventured. The first is that because of their more obvious relevance, applied science and technology tend to be more bound up with the concerns of the state; pure mathematics and science less so. Enthusiasm for the latter is more likely to cut across political and ideological barriers. Secondly some regimes are more, some less favourable to scientific advance than others; but in a seventeenth-century English context this does not correspond to any simple antithesis between Puritan and Anglican, parliamentarian (or republican) and royalist (or monarchist).[46] Beyond this I am inclined to think that there are only random associations, although to say that will seem terrible heresy to some, and an admission of intellectual defeatism to others.

Nor should we make the Restoration more of an intellectual watershed than it was. Although the future archbishops, Tillotson and Tenison were already launched on their respective careers, the religious temper of the 1660s was emphatically not that of the 18th century. To use such a phrase as 'The Age of Enlightenment 1660–1750' as a subtitle to a book called *Reason, Ridicule and Religion*, is to risk confusing the era of Hoadley and the early deists, let alone the days of the Latitude-men and the Cambridge Platonists, with the time of Hume and Gibbon. Whether or not the anti-atheistical attacks made on Thomas Hobbes and others were justified, the mental climate of the time was very different, as indeed those very attacks perhaps testify.[47]

In my second address I referred briefly to the Civil War allegiance of English Catholics, and undertook to say something more about the non-Royalists among them. As with others of the ignorant and apathetic there is really no evidence here for the inarticulate masses. For those who are capable of expressing themselves, certainly of getting their views into print, we must remember the bitter controversies by which the English catholic community was itself riven at this

[46] The handiest and most reliable presentation of the essential data is in M. Hunter, *The Royal Society and its Fellows 1660–1700. The Morphology of an early scientific institution* (British Society for the History of Science, no. 4, Chalfont St. Giles, 1982; corrected edn. 1985). The author wisely adopts a classification of the early fellows by status and occupation, rather than by ideology.

[47] J. Redwood, *Reason, Ridicule and Religion: The Age of Enlightenment in England 1660–1750* (1976). See also D. Wootton, 'Lucien Febvre and the Problem of Unbelief in the Early Modern Period', *Jnl. of Mod. Hist.*, lx (Dec. 1988); I am grateful to Dr Wootton for letting me read this before publication.

time. Without entering into those issues, especially their ecclesiological aspects, one of them is clearly relevant to my theme today. Some Roman Catholics were much readier than others to do a deal with whoever came out on top in the Civil Wars, in order to improve the position of their own religion. The Queen herself, partly because she took such a low view of the Church of England, was prepared to contemplate a Royalist-Presbyterian or later a Royalist-Independent alliance. To controvert this or prevent it was largely the motive for Hyde's 1649 paper, in which he advocated instead a Royalist-Leveller alliance as the lesser evil. The best known individual Catholics who came nearest to being *de factoist* for the benefit of their faith were Sir Kenelm Digby and Thomas White, *alias* Blacklo. Digby was surely too cosmopolitan, too much of a virtuoso ever to have been representative of the English catholic nobility and gentry as a whole.[48] White is a more complex, and elusive figure. Most of his career until his last years were spent on the continent, much of the time studying and then teaching in catholic seminaries. His support for the Archpriest, or Bishop of Chalcedon, Richard Smith is only of consequence for our purposes because White and Digby contemplated winning limited toleration for lay recusants and even for priests at the expense of the Jesuits. Paradoxically, while White was attacked by Hobbes on account of his scientific views (although for the sage of Malmesbury with unusual restraint) it was a 'Hobbist' or *de factoist* work which led to his undoing. *The Grounds of Obedience and Government* (1655) adds little to the literature of engagement and allegiance. Considering Hobbes's almost frenzied anti-papalism, it is surprising to find a catholic priest, whose very life was at risk every time he came to England, adopting such superficially similar arguments in favour of absolutism.[49] We must, however, remember that except for Brandenburg-Prussia and the Scandinavian kingdoms, the continental monarchies which approached most nearly to Hobbes's requirements for a commonwealth were in catholic countries, while Catholic Eras-

[48] There is a voluminous bibliography, Digby having attracted numerous biographies; the most recent scholarly study is M. Foster, 'Sir Kenelm Digby (1603–65): as man of religion and thinker', Parts I & II, *The Downside Review*, (Jan. & Apr. 1988), pp. 35–38, 101–25.

[49] Among relatively recent studies see R. J. Bradley, SJ, 'Blacklo and the Counter-Reformation ...', in C. H. Carter (ed.), *From the Renaissance to the Counter-Reformation* (N.Y., 1965; London, 1966), pp. 348–70; H. W. Jones, (ed. & transl.), Thomas Hobbes, *Thomas White's De Mundo Examined* (Bradford, 1972); T. A. Birrell (ed.), R. Pugh, Blacklo's Cabal 1680 (Farnborough, 1970); H. W. Jones, 'Thomas White (or Blacklo), 1593–1676; New Data', *Notes & Queries*, 218, new ser. XX (1973), 381–8; B. C. Southgate, '"That Damned Booke": The Grounds of Obedience and Government (1655), and the downfall of Thomas White', *Recusant History*, xvii (1985), 238–53.

tianism was a powerful element in the age of the Counter-Reformation.[50]

In conclusion I should like to turn briefly to those 'unacknowledged legislators of the world', the poets. There were of course Cavalier and Puritan poets whose allegiance never wavered, even if as in Milton's case their ideas developed and the policies which they advocated changed. Among the side-changers I have already mentioned Edmund Waller. To those who switched once (although he was to switch again, at least in religion if not in politics), we may add John Dryden. The case of Andrew Marvell is more complex. This is mainly because we know so little about him between his graduation from Cambridge at the precocious age of seventeen and his appearance as tutor to Mary Fairfax some ten years later. Did he choose to travel abroad as a passive royalist like John Evelyn the diarist? It is generally agreed that his 'Horation Ode' of 1650 is deeply ambivalent in its political resonances. Its consistency can only be saved by insisting that the author's sympathies with the King are strictly personal. Marvell's official service, unlike Milton's, followed the repeal of the Engagement under the Protectorate, and he was to leave office again under the restored Commonwealth in 1659. As with other ex-Cromwellians this may have made his conformism at the Restoration less unpalatable. That it must have been acceptable to the authorities is evident in his successful intervention on Milton's behalf in December 1660. Marvell's poems may not have been read outside a small circle until much later, but his service as Assistant Latin Secretary must surely have been quite widely known. When he wrote *The Last Instructions to a Painter* in the autumn of 1667, Marvell was disgusted with the King's ministers and with the conduct of the Dutch War; the greatest danger to what he most valued at that time lay in the rising power of France. By contrast in late 1672 *The Rehearsal Transpros'd* marked a shift of front, where Samuel Parker seemed to be claiming for the bishops the powers of an ecclesiastical Leviathan. By the time of Part II, the Declaration of Indulgence, about which Marvell may well have had ambivalent feelings, had been withdrawn, and the first Test Act passed. Even more clearly than in 1672 the greatest dangers were by then not from an excess of royal prerogative but from the kind of Anglican intolerance that had led to the second Conventicle Act of 1670. When Marvell's last substantial work, *An Account Of The Growth of Popery And Arbitrary Government* appeared at the end of 1677, Danby's proposed Test Bill of 1675 had failed, but in every other respect the situation had grown worse. In particular the Pension House of

[50] A. D. Wright, *The Counter-Reformation* ... (1982), chs. 5 & 8, or via the index; J. Lynch, 'Philip II and the Papacy', *T.R.H.S.*, 5th ser. xi (1961), 23–42; among earlier works, see J. Orcibal, *Louis XIV contre Innocent XI* ...(Paris, 1949).

Commons had long since ceased to be able to play its proper role in the government of the country. Even then Marvell's monarchism like his temperate protestantism remains a fixed point of reference.[51] It is idle, if fascinating, to speculate on what role he would have taken in the crisis of 1679–81, let alone if he had survived until 1688–9. The fairest verdict may be: a Trimmer indeed, but in the meritorious, not the meretricious sense of that word.

I should like to end with a disclaimer and warning and then a modest suggestion. One fundamental difficulty applies to the subject matter of all these four addresses. To describe, then to analyse the reactions of an individual or even of a group of people to the public events of their age, is not necessarily to uncover their motives. These may be straightforward, in the sense of someone doing something for the reasons that he or she gives—no more and no less; but things may not be like that. And here we come to the limits of what is possible for any historian, however steeped in the sources, however sensitive and acute in their interpretation. In a way, when preparing these addresses I have been encouraged by the difficulties encountered by my own academic and intellectual betters. With human motivation we can, at most, deal in probabilities, never in certainties. Hence, if I may venture to say so, the advantages of a prosopographical approach. If we find that a statistically significant number of people with particular characteristics are likelier than others to have followed a certain course of action, or indeed of inaction, we have—I would submit—established at least a connection or correlation, sometimes even a matter of cause and effect.

We should not expect perfect consistency, total rectitude in the people of the past, any more than we do today. We should not judge those who lived through the upheavals of the seventeenth century more severely than we would hope (if humanity survives and if English history is still studied) to be judged in our turn 300 years or more from now.

---

[51] Besides the numerous editions of his works, older biographies and critical studies, see in particular J. M. Wallace, *Destiny His Choice: The Loyalism of Andrew Marvell* (Cambridge, 1968); D. I. B. Smith (ed.), Andrew Marvell, *The Rehearsal Transpros'd and The Rehearsal Transpros'd The Second Part* (Oxford, 1971); A. M. Patterson, *Marvell and the Civic Crown* (Princeton, 1978); H. Kelliher (comp.), *Andrew Marvell Poet and Politician 1621–78 An Exhibition to commemmorate the tercentenary of his death* (British Library Reference Division, 1978); in addition I am most grateful to Professor Caroline Robbins for copies of articles and other help, back in the 1970s. I hope that my having been an undergraduate pupil of Dr Christopher Hill and a colleague of the late C. A. Patrides may almost qualify me as an honorary Marvellian.

BURIAL AND STATUS IN THE EARLY MEDIEVAL WEST

By Edward James

READ 29 JANUARY 1988

EARLY medieval archaeology can be said to have its origins with the investigation of burial: with Otto III's opening of Charlemagne's tomb in 1000; with medieval and early modern reports of the discoveries of the graves of kings or warriors; and, most notably, with the discovery at Tournai in 1653 of the grave of an early Frankish king, Childeric.[1] And, until very recently, the study of burials dominated the subject. This is only natural. Graves are easily recognisable when discovered accidentally; often they were intended to be, and have remained, a very visible part of the landscape. Surviving royal burials are, of course, very rare. But there are over one hundred thousand excavated graves of lesser personages from the period between *c.* 450 and *c.* 1000: an astonishing mass of data which forms a significant proportion of the total available evidence for the early Middle Ages and which needs to be assessed and taken into count by any early medievalist interested in the totality of the period. And it can be argued that cemeteries offer rather more opportunity than the written sources to understand the world of those below the status of kings and bishops, and to do so without the ecclesiastical bias that the written sources have. We nevertheless have to remember that graves are not the unconscious waste products of society, like most of the data studied by an archaeologist: rubbish pits, building remains and so on. Bodies were deliberately and carefully placed in the ground, along with whatever accompanied them. Those responsible for the burial made a whole series of choices about the manner in which they carried out this action. A burial, like a written text, is a product of conscious mental activity, and subject to many of the problems of interpretation and analysis with which historians are familiar.

In what follows I want to examine one of the most common ways of analysing graves and making historical sense of them; I hope that

---

[1] See H. Beumann, 'Grab und Thron Karls des Grossen zu Aachen', in W. Braunfels and P. E. Schramm, ed. *Karl der Grosse*, IV (Dusseldorf, 1967), 9–38; P. Périn, *La Datation des Tombes Mérovingiennes* (Geneva, 1980), 5–8; M. Kazanski and P. Périn, 'Le Mobilier Funéraire de la Tombe de Childéric: Etat de la Question et Perspectives' and R. Brulet et al. 'Nouvelles Recherches à Tournai, Autour de la Sépulture de Childéric', both in *Revue Archéologique de Picardie*, no. 3–4 (1988), 13–43.

this will make the problems and potential, as well as the current archaeological debate, more familiar to historians. Some chronological and geographical limitations impose themselves, apart from the fact of my own greater familiarity with the Merovingian material from Gaul. The period from the late fifth to the early eighth century is the one in which a significant percentage of the population of Europe buried grave-goods with the dead. There are in museum cases or cardboard boxes all over England, northern France, Belgium, West Germany and Switzerland, and to a much lesser extent in Italy and Spain, considerable quantities of these grave-goods, mostly unearthed in the nineteenth century with the aim of filling those museum cases relatively cheaply. But after the eighth century grave-goods are infrequent except in eastern Europe and Scandinavia; throughout the period they are absent altogether in some parts of Europe—southern Italy and Spain, Ireland, and from those parts of Britain not settled by the Anglo-Saxons. The custom of church burial and churchyard burial, which, by the end of the period, is almost universal over most of western and northern Europe, also creates gaps in the evidence; the continuous use, and consequent archaeological disturbance, of most of these sites has destroyed much of the evidence from the early medieval period.

When the early medievalist thinks of a cemetery, he or she generally thinks of a *Reinhengräberfeld*, a row-grave cemetery of the sixth or seventh century. With their rows of individual graves, many of them equipped with grave-goods of some kind, these survive in large numbers, and are readily distinguished and dated. But outside the area of the *Reihengräberzivilisation*—south-east England, north-east France, Belgium, the Rhineland and the Upper Danube—many other cemeteries have been located. They can be defined largely by the absence of the classic *Reihengräber* features: the graves are haphazardly placed; the burials are often not in simple trenches, but in sarcophagi or in coffins made up of slabs of stone (cists); they are seldom provided with grave-goods—or, if they had once been so provided, the grave-goods have been removed in subsequent reuses of the grave. These cemeteries are much more difficult to study than the *Reihengräberfelder*: absence of grave-goods means the absence of any ready way to date individual graves and hence to plot the growth of the cemetery, its lifespan and so on. It is hardly surprising that archaeologists have concentrated on the *Reihengräberfelder*. But it is unfortunate: grave-goods, particularly the more spectacular variety, have distracted the attention of archaeologists from the cemetery itself, and encouraged them to regard it as yet another interesting collection of artefacts. And, in fact, much can be learnt from the location and disposition of grave-goodless graves in a cemetery. Few of these have been properly excavated and published, however; the rewards are not so immediate or so obvious to the excavator or to the funder.

There have been a number of ways in which early medievalists have analysed cemeteries, and used them to extend our historical knowledge. Until well after the Second World War, it was common to write the history of the Germanic invasions by assigning graves or whole cemeteries to 'German' (immigrant) or 'Roman' (indigenous). Sometimes this involved measuring skulls to see how many of the cemetery population were dolichocephalic and hence of Germanic origin; few archaeologists, and no scholars, any longer believe that this has any significance.[2] Equally discredited is the attempt to discern the racial origins of the population by other means, such as by looking at burial ritual or at grave-good types. On the Continent the distinction between a *Reihengräberfeld* and a grave-goodless cemetery of (presumed) similar period was earlier this century explained very simply in racial/national terms: *Reihengräberfelder* belonged to the Germanic invaders or immigrants, while the other cemeteries were those of the descendants of Romans. Cemeteries which combined the features of both types were regarded as the cemeteries of racially mixed communities. Even now Anglo-Saxon archaeologists still regularly assume that their *Reihengräberfelder* are the cemeteries of Germanic immigrants and their descendants. But increasingly differences in burial customs are being explained in terms of regional, chronological or social variations. There are, of course, also differences in styles of dress, dress-fastenings and jewellery, which are often revealed through the funerary evidence. Though dress fashion may be an indicator of ethnic identity, there are other factors involved, such as product availability, and regional identity must not be confused with racial identity. The racial explanation has also, of course, been undermined by historians, who would argue now that racial or national groupings were much more fluid, and much less biologically determined, than was thought even a generation ago.[3] Peoples might well distinguish themselves by particular dress; but peoples are not necessarily genetically linked groups, but were, in large part, political entities created out of the melting pot of the *Völkerwanderung*.

Hardly more plausible are attempts to determine the religious history of a community from the cemeteries.[4] In the past this has

---

[2] For some discussion of 'la mythe de la race nordique' see L. Buchet, 'Anthropologie des Francs', *Dossiers Histoire et Archéologie*, lvi (1981), 78–81.

[3] Notably since R. Wenskus, *Stammesbildung und Verfassung: Das Werden der Frühmittlelalterlichen Gentes* (Cologne and Graz, 1961).

[4] On which see above all B. K. Young, *Merovingian Funerary Rites and the Evolution of Christianity* (Ph.D Dissertation, University of Pennsylvania, 1975), summarised in 'Paganisme, Christianisme et Rites Funéraires Mérovingiens', *Archéologie Médiévale*, vii

usually been done by making assumptions about the religious meaning of a particular burial custom, or of a particular piece of iconography. One assumption in particular led, and still leads, some early medievalists to believe in the possibility of deducing religious affiliations from graves: the assumption that the deposition of grave-goods is an inherently pagan custom. Thus: 'True gifts must be regarded as conflicting with Christian ideas, as they express a belief in a bodily life after death where there would be a need for everyday objects.'[5] This implies, of course, firstly that there is only one clearly defined unchanging body of Christian belief, and secondly, that there are no other possible explanations for the deposition of grave-goods. The fact that the Franks began to deposit grave-goods for the first time in the generation in which their monarchy and aristocracy became Christian; the fact that the most lavish and elaborate of depositions in the Frankish kingdoms were made inside churches (such as Cologne Cathedral and the abbey church of St-Denis); perhaps even the negative fact that the only burial customs condemned by the early medieval church were those involving the deposition of sacred materials such as the consecrated Host: all of these things should warn us against assumptions such as these. Even more simplistic are attempts to judge the religion of the dead person by means of the artefacts themselves: an object with Christian iconography (such as the famous jug from grave 319 at Lavoye) could have had all kinds of meanings for the family which chose to bury it.[6] Other more conclusive evidence—epitaphs with religious formulae, for instance—is very rarely found in archaeological context.

Problems with these kinds of traditional enquiry have forced cemetery specialists to restrict themselves very largely to sociological speculations. Attempts along these lines began among German archaeologists in the 1920s, continued in the post-War period, and received a great boost, particularly among English-speaking archaeologists in Britain and Scandinavia, as the influence of the New Archaeology spread from the United States in the 1970s. In 1971 Lewis Binford proposed that 'a larger array of duty-status relationships (characteristic of high rank) will entitle the deceased to a larger amount of corporate involvement in the act of interment, and to a larger degree of disruption of normal community activities for the

---

(1977), 5–81. See also the comments of D. A. Bullough, 'Burial, Community and Belief in the Early Medieval West', in P. Wormald et al. ed., *Ideal and Reality in Frankish and Anglo-Saxon Society* (Oxford, 1983), esp. 186ff, and A. Dierkens, 'Cimetières Mérovingiens et Histoire du Haut Moyen Age', *Acta Historica Bruxellensia*, iv (1981), 15–70.

[5] A.-S. Gräslund, *Birka IV: The Burial Customs* (Stockholm, 1981), 84.

[6] G. Chenet, 'La Tombe 319 et la Buire Chrétienne du Cimetière Mérovingien de Lavoye (Meuse)', *Préhistoire*, iv (1935), 34–118.

mortuary ritual'.[7] Tainter argued, from ethnography, that 'variability in mortuary practices must be understood in terms of variability in the form and organisation of social systems, not in terms of normative modes of behaviour.'[8] And although Peter J. Ucko's article showing the wide range of burial practices discovered by the ethnographer is often quoted by those sceptical of finding clear explanations of the archaeological material, Ucko too regarded it as 'the most important of all the lessons to be drawn from the ethnographic material' that 'one society will undertake several different forms of burial and that these forms will often be correlated with the status of the deceased'.[9] How do these theories work when applied to the early medieval material?

Archaeologists have begun with the most obvious manifestations of status in burials: material wealth. Many *Reihengräberfelder* possess a few individual graves which are distinguished from others by the quantity and quality of their grave-goods—and both the quantity and quality frequently enable such graves to be dated fairly precisely. Often the wealthy graves appear at the beginning of a cemetery's life, or at the beginning of a new development of an earlier Gallo-Roman cemetery—as so-called 'founder-graves': a prime example would be Charleville-Mézières, where a new cemetery began in the early sixth century, separated from the Roman burial-grounds, with a number of richly furnished burials.[10] In the early sixth century on the Continent there are a number of graves, like those at Charleville-Mézières, which can plausibly be associated with the arrival of aristocratic followers of the Frankish conquerors Childeric and Clovis. Sometimes this 'aristocratic' material can be studied to see the role which that aristocratic family or families played in the development of a particular cemetery. Frequently, however, when dealing with characteristically 'aristocratic' material found in old excavations, all that can be done is to say that such material was found somewhere within a particular cemetery. Even here, however, we might draw historical conclusions. Françoise Vallet has recently looked at the distribution of 'aristocratic objects' from the classic Frankish row-grave cemeteries in Picardy, such as Caranda, Hermes, Marchélepot, Picquigny, exca-

[7] L. Binford, 'Mortuary Practices: Their Study and Their Potential', in J. A. Brown, ed., *Approaches to the Social Dimension of Mortuary Practices* (Society for American Archaeology, Memoirs 25) (1971), 17, 21, as summarised by J. A. Tainter, 'Mortuary Practices and the Study of Prehistoric Social Systems', *Advances in Archaeological Method and Theory*, i (1978), 125.

[8] Tainter, 'Mortuary Practices', 107ff.

[9] P. J. Ucko, 'Ethnography and Archaeological Interpretation of Funerary Remains', *World Archaeology*, i (1969–70), 270.

[10] B. K. Young, *Quatre Cimetières Mérovingiens de l'Est de la France: Lavoye, Dieue-sur-Meuse, Mézières-Manchester, Mazerny* (BAR International Series 208: Oxford, 1984), 78–103.

The Saint-Quentin and Augsburg grave 1 finds each had an elaborate knife-sheath, and both seem to have incorporated a pocket for a stylus. Among the clerics, of course, it was the saints who were accorded the highest status: measurable archaeologically, should we want to, in terms of the privileged position of the grave within the church.

Because recognition of a privileged grave is not dependent on grave-goods, it is possible to locate them and draw some conclusions even when a cemetery has been pillaged by treasure-hunters of the Middle Ages or later. At Krefeld-Gellep, for instance, there were a number of graves which had been emptied but had once been of enormous size: grave 2268 was the largest known from the Merovingian period, 6.5m long, 4.2m wide and 3.55m deep ($97m^3$). There were empty spaces around 2268 and another large grave, 2528: it is possible that this represents the space that was once covered by a barrow, which announced clearly the importance of the buried person. Wood which survived in tomb 2268 can be dated dendrochronologically; it was cut in 589. Between *c.* 530 and *c.* 590, therefore, some half-a-dozen important people were buried at Krefeld-Gellep, in burials set apart by their conspicuous expenditure (in terms of wealth of grave-goods or amount of man-power expended, or, originally, probably both) from the other graves in the cemetery.[18]

In 1979, I argued that the individual cemetery was the most important frame of reference for understanding burial practices and their social implications, and indeed that this might be the only possible frame of reference.[19] That, in other words, one might be able to detect aristocrats and others within an individual cemetery, because the community which used it would devise their own methods of distinguishing particular graves by means of grave-goods or other signals, but that one could never be sure that the thinking behind burial practices was necessary the same in a neighbouring community, let alone in one on the other side of the kingdom. But I was not thinking out the problem carefully enough at that time. In particular, I did not do enough to distinguish between different types of grave-goods. The deposition of various types of vessels, or possible amulets such as pebbles or shells, in a grave, or the layout of the body in the grave, or the construction of the grave itself, are practices which could clearly vary from one community to another. But the bulk of the objects that most archaeologists lump together as 'grave-goods' are probably in fact those objects which the buried person wore or carried around (even if only on special occasions) during his or her lifetime. Weapons

[18] Ament, in Duval and Picard, *Inhumation Privilégiée*, 43, drawing on the work of R. Pirling.

[19] E. James, 'Cemeteries and the problem of Frankish Settlement in Gaul', in P. H. Sawyer, ed., *Names, Words and Graves: Early Medieval Settlement* (Leeds, 1979), 55–89.

can probably be classed in this category; perhaps horses, or the horse-harness placed in the grave in lieu of the animal itself; perhaps, indeed, almost all but the vessels of ceramic or other material.[20] If social status is something that is expressed in dress and other accoutrements, then we have some possibility at least of being able to move away from the local community to analyse Frankish society as a whole, in particular its social structure.

The commonest form of such investigation has been to imagine that the different sets of personal equipment—above all, weapons—that are found in cemeteries can be equated directly with the forms of social and class status which we find in the law-codes. Thus, according to Fremersdorf, those buried with a sword were freemen; those buried with a spear and/or arrows were half-free or freedmen; those buried with no weapons at all were slaves. For Neuffer-Müller, those buried with several weapons were freemen; those buried only with a scramasax were half-free. Ross Samson has recently republished the table which Heiko Steuer published in 1982 illustrating the array of suggestions which have been made along these lines.[21] Indeed, recently Leslie Alcock has suggested such a way of reading the Anglian graves in seventh century Bernicia. Modifying his alpha, beta, gamma system in a traditional British academic fashion with added pluses and minuses, he has proposed that sword-graves be classed alpha, spear-graves (with or without a shield) beta, and graves with nothing more than a knife and perhaps belt-buckle as gamma; these correlate with the three-fold division of Anglo-Saxon society found in the con-temporary law-codes, into thegn, churl or free warrior, and unfree.[22] A similar result has been argued by Bergljot Solberg in a study of the 4629 recorded early medieval Norwegian graves; here the equation is made with the medieval laws of a somewhat later period.[23]

There are real problems posed by all these interpretations. For instance, the distinction between sword-burials and scramasax burials on the Continent may well be chronological rather than social; single-edged scramasaxes were replacing double-edged swords from the later sixth century, in graves at least, and probably in actual everyday use. Spears and axes seem to have declined as symbols of status between

[20] See the remarks of Dierkens, 'Cimetières Mérovingiens', 43–44. On horse-graves see M. Müller-Wille, 'Pferdegrab und Pferdeopfer im Frühen Mittelalter', *Bericht van de Rijksdienst voor het Oudheidkundig Bodemonderzoek* 20–21 (1970–71), 119–248.

[21] R. Samson, 'Social Structures from Reihengräber: Mirror or Mirage?', *Scottish Archaeological Review*, iv, part 2 (1987), 117; Steuer, *Sozialstrukturen*, 311.

[22] L. Alcock, 'Quality or Quantity: the Anglian Graves of Bernicia', in V. I. Evison, ed., *Angles, Saxons and Jutes* (Oxford, 1981), 168–186.

[23] B. Solberg, 'Social Status in the Merovingian and Viking Periods in Norway from Archaeological and Historical Sources', *Norwegian Archaeological Review*, xviii (1985), 61–76.

the early sixth and the late seventh centuries, or perhaps these originally high-status objects were being imitated by those lower down
the hierarchy. There is also the danger of ignoring regional differences
in suggesting these wide-scale equivalences; even though social status
may be symbolised in life by the same accoutrements, we cannot
assume that mortuary behaviour is uniform. To do so, as Steuer has
pointed out, would mean that 'the Alamannic area is largely settled
by free farmers, since the combination of spatha and sax is very
common, and the Frankish area only by small farmers or half-free,
and the Bavarian area mostly by slaves'.[24] Yet Solberg argues from
regional differences that in Norway 'the women in the coastal areas
had a higher social status than those in the inland area'.[25] Alcock too
uses his equation to make comparisons between regions: Bernicia was
'a society in which warrior-peasants were thin on the ground, and
warrior-aristocrats relatively numerous', while 'Wessex had a few
sword-bearing thegns ... (and) a large mass of yeoman-warriors'—
though he admits here that the practice of West Saxon practice of
handing swords down from generation to generation (in fact not
known historically until after the practice of burying grave-goods had
ceased) may have distorted the picture.[26] We are being asked to
envisage a culture, or range of cultures, spread from Kent up to
southern Scotland, with not only a generally accepted way of representing social distinctions but also of symbolising them in the grave.

A very similar, and earlier, attempt to characterise aristocratic
graves on a wide scale was made by Rainer Christlein, although it
does not make any such clear correlations with the low-codes; it has
proved very influential on the Continent.[27] Christlein distinguished
four main quality groups among the male graves of the period, in
terms of grave-goods and of grave-construction. He divided his bottom
group, A, into those which were without any weapons (A1) and those
which had simply a scramasax (A2); his B-graves were those provided
with a sword; his D-graves were the very small number of 'royal'
graves, as at Tournai, Cologne or Morken. It is the C-graves, which
correspond to our aristocratic graves, to which the most attention has
been given. Christlein argued that there were certain objects which

---

[24] Steuer, *Sozialstrukturen*, 314. The problem is also set out clearly in id., 'Zur
Bewaffnung und Sozialstruktur der Merowingerzeit', *Nachrichten aus Niedersachsens Urge-
schichte*, xxxvii (1968), 18–87, and J. Werner, 'Bewaffnung und Waffenbeigabe in der
Merowingerzeit', *Settimane di Studio del Centro Italiano di Studi Sull'Alto Medioevo*, xv
(Spoleto, 1968), 95–109.

[25] Solberg, 'Social Status', 75.

[26] Alcock, 'Quality or Quantity', 177.

[27] R. Christlein, 'Besitzabstufungen zur Merowingerzeit im Spiegel reicher
Grabfunde aus West- und Süddeutschland', *Jahrbuch des Römisch-Germanisches Zen-
tralmuseum, Mainz*, xx (1973), 147–80.

were likely to occur in association with each other in these graves, such as horse-bits in male graves, gold disk fibulae and gold cloisonné brooches in female graves, wide bronze bowls of Mediterranean manufacture (often called 'Coptic bowls'), wooden buckets with bronze decorations, gold rings, with the dead of either sex. The suggestion was that these items were placed in graves to symbolise or display or claim status of a particular kind. Christlein also argued that distribution of these C-graves within a cemetery may be significant: that C-graves scattered throughout a cemetery may indicate rich peasants/farmers who aspire to aristocratic status, while the grouping of C-graves in one place, whether in the centre of the cemetery or to one side, suggests the existence of a wealthy and aristocratic family. Christlein's theory assumed, like Alcock's theory, an aristocratic culture, including ideas about the expression of status via dress and mortuary behaviour, which was remarkably uniform across a large area. Heiko Steuer's criticisms of this idea have recently been strongly rebutted by Simon Burnell, who argues also in favour of Christlein's idea that the paucity of C-graves in Bavaria indicates that the aristocracy was numerically much smaller in Bavaria than in Alamannia. Significantly too he underlines one aspect of Christlein's argument that was often forgotten by his critics, and where he does differ markedly from Alcock and other modellers: that 'his model was intended to highlight only personal wealth and hence *de facto* social status and influence within a community, rather than institutionalised social rank'.[28]

The idea of trying to quantify *wealth* rather than more legal ideas of social status appealed particularly to those New Archaeologists interested in applying quantitative methods to their data. There are however problems with the elaborate or not so elaborate scoring systems which some archaeologists have devised, in which each item in a grave is given a score, and in which a woman with a fifteen-bead necklace, one point each, turns out to be as rich as a warrior with a gold-hilt long-sword.[29] In Anglo-Saxon archaeology this has led to absurdities such as the conclusion that Kentish women were richer than Kentish men: in fact, of course, this conclusion came about largely because Kentish women were more likely than Kentish men, until the 1980s at least, to wear such items as gold earrings. But even when restricting one's attention to a single sex, and not attempting comparisons between the sexes, scoring depends on rather arbitrary assignments of values to objects whose actual value in early medieval

[28] Burnell, *Merovingian to Early Carolingian Churches*, 397.
[29] As in C. Arnold. 'Wealth and Social Structure: A Matter of Life and Death', in P. Rahtz, T. Dickinson, and L. Watts, ed., *Anglo-Saxon Cemeteries 1979* (BAR British Series 82: Oxford, 1980), 81–142.

society we cannot know; this holds true even of the most sophisticated methods, such as those used by John Shephard.[30] Similar problems result from the assumption that grave-goods symbolise social status and wealth in a static way, so that, for instance, Franks can be seen to be poorer in the seventh century than they had been in the sixth: in fact by the seventh century items deposited in the grave were normally restricted to items of personal dress (the glassware, bronze bowls and so on are absent in the later period), while the richest are being buried in churches and rarely leave burials which are undisturbed.

Before we take stock of all these theories we do have to remember that we still do not know for certain *why* grave-goods were placed in the grave, or by whom. Some archaeologists talk as if the dead person carefully laid out the goods before clambering into the grave. Who *is* responsible for the ceremony of burial? Did the community have an acknowledged expert in burial customs (as in twentieth-century western culture)? Did that person allow a choice of different customs?—was there a Frankish equivalent of Evelyn Waugh's mortuary hostess, who supplied Mr Barlow with a menu? 'Embalmment of course, and after that incineration or not, according to taste ... Normal disposal is by inhumement, entombment, inurnment or immurement, but many people just lately prefer insarco-phagusment'.[31] Or was burial left to the heirs, or to the family? All these questions relate closely to the problem of the role of grave-goods in the ritual. Were they, perhaps, gifts bestowed on the dead by those present at the funeral? This would clearly affect one's social interpretation of the deposit very seriously. Were they placed in the grave by the family of the dead man in a desire to assert its social standing at a time when the death may bring that status into question? In which case rich grave-goods may be an indication of insecurity; families secure in their social status may not need to make such a gesture—and, by the mid-sixth century in Francia, or the late seventh century in England, are likely to be burying their dead under a church, and not in the row-grave cemetery. Another suggestion which has won a number of adherents since the earlier part of this century is that items closely associated with the dead could not be inherited by their heirs, and had to be disposed of in some other way: the

[30] J. Shephard, 'The Social Identity of the Individual in Isolated Barrows and Barrow Cemeteries in Anglo-Saxon England', in R. Burnham and J. Kingsbury, ed., *Space, Hierarchy and Society* (BAR Supplementary Series 59: Oxford, 1979), 47–79. (For some criticisms, see J. D. Richards, *The Significance of Form and Decoration of Anglo-Saxon Cremation Urns* (BAR British Series 166: Oxford 1987), 12–13.) Similar flexible scoring methods have been adopted by Jane Brenan in 'Assessing Social Status in the Anglo-Saxon Cemetery at Sleaford', *Institute of Archaeology Bulletin* 21–22 (1984–85), 125–131.

[31] E. Waugh, *The Loved One* (Harmondsworth, 1951), 37.

military equipment of men (*Heergewäte*) and the jewellery of women (*Gerade*) were consigned to the grave in Merovingian times, and by Carolingian times were passed to the Church. There was indeed later a portion of the goods which went to the Church, but it was *not* the *Heergewäte* or the *Gerade*, which, in later German law, was specifically assigned to the son(s) and to the daughter(s).[32] Alcock suggests there may be some relationship between the military equipment placed in the grave and that later offered to the lord as heriot upon the warrior's death; but this likewise does not help to explain the function of grave-goods.[33]

It could be that different types of grave-goods were deposited for different reasons. The vessels containing offerings of food or drink may contain a portion of the funeral feast, offered in homage to the dead, or represent some other aspect of the funerary ritual.[34] Some objects may reflect a symbolic statement of function, like the croziers buried in the graves of later medieval bishops. In one area at least I suppose we can be reasonably certain of the symbolic nature of a burial deposit: this is the case of those boys' graves provided with miniature axes or scramasaxes. Some of these could be toys, or items actually used in some way in life, either for training or for purposes of displaying status, but some were clearly quite unusable—miniature axes without a socket for the haft, for instance—and must surely have been manufactured for symbolic deposition in a grave. Boys' graves also often contain adult weapons: the best example is that of the Cologne 'prince', whose helmet would have fitted him, but whose weapons he could barely have lifted.[35] These cases are our clearest evidence for weapons as representing the free, 'aristocratic' or privileged status of the person buried. The problem, perhaps an unanswerable one, is: how generally accepted were such symbolic statements in early medieval society?

If so many of our problems with the interpretation of the burial evidence rest upon our difficulties with grave-goods, many others relate to not thinking sufficiently carefully about what 'status' means. In most of the discussion 'status' has been equivalent to 'class', which in turn has a direct link with 'wealth'. 'High status' burials differ from 'low status' burials in terms of their wealth, or what we perceive of as their wealth, measured in terms of quantity, amount of precious

---

[32] J.-P. Jacob and J.-R. Mirbeau-Fauvin, 'Heergewäte et Gerade: "Les Mots et Les Choses"', *Bulletin de Liaison de l'Association Française d'Archéologie Mérovingienne*, iii (1980), 81–85.

[33] Alcock, 'Quantity or Quality', 176.

[34] Cf. G. Behm-Blancke, 'Trinkgaben und Trinkzeremonien im Totenkult der Völkerwanderungszeit', *Alt-Thüringen*, xvi (1979), 171–227.

[35] Most conveniently seen in J. Werner, 'Frankish royal tombs in the Cathedrals of Cologne and St-Denis', *Antiquity*, xxxviii (1964), 201–16.

metals, amount of labour required. And, Christlein's reservations apart, most discussions have proceeded from the law-codes, and the knowledge that early medieval society was highly stratified, to the association of the varying levels of wealth found in the graves with the varying wergilds found in the law-codes.

All the law-codes we have from the barbarian kingdoms (except those modelled on the Theodosian Code, and intended for the Roman element) do divide the population into a fairly clear set of legal categories, marked by different wergilds. In the event of murder most of this amount is paid to the kin of the victim; the rest to the king or his representatives. In the *Pactus Legis Salicae* the average free-born Frank is given the wergild of 200 *solidi*; young girls and women past child-bearing age have the same wergild; a woman of child-bearing age ('up to the age of sixty years old who can have children' specifies a later addition to the *Pactus*) and a free-born boy under twelve, on the other hand, have wergilds of 600 solidi.[36] This high wergild is shared by a Frank who is in the king's retinue, and by a high royal official, the *grafio*. All these figures are tripled if someone is murdered in his own house, and by a group of conspirators. However, 'if anyone abducts, kills, sells or manumits another's slave' the criminal pays the set fine of 35 solidi. The freedman is likewise not regarded as having a wergild, or indeed a kin who can avenge him; his value is placed at 100 solidi, payable to his lord. *Lex Ribvaria* has almost precisely the same provisions, with one or two minor adjustments: the child-bearing age for women is taken (more realistically) as ending at forty; the cost of the murder of a slave is put at 36 solidi.

The early medieval law-codes may be particularly misleading at two ends of the social spectrum: with the slaves and with the aristocracy. The law-codes treat slaves as property, alongside cattle and cart-horses; they were separated in every way from free peasants. Yet in terms of their economic and social life there was probably little to choose between them. Both were tied to the land and to their lord and master, yet both could work their own land and had a limited amount of personal freedom—which included, perhaps, the ability to contemplate upward social mobility. In the context of weapon-burials, it is significant that Steuer is able to put together historical evidence from various parts of Europe to illustrate that it was accepted that slaves in certain circumstances could carry and use weapons.[37] Nor should we presume that the kinds of wealth revealed in the graves necessarily correlates with high legal status. We recall the eleventh-

---

[36] *Monumenta Germaniae Historica, Leges Nat. Germ.*, IV (i), ed. K. A. Eckhardt, now with a convenient translation by T. J. Rivers as *The Laws of the Salian and Ripuarian Franks* (New York, 1986).

[37] Steuer, *Sozialstrukturen*, 52–53, 329.

century Anglo-Saxon saying cited by Dorothy Whitelock: even if a churl 'thrive so that he have a helmet and coat-of-mail and a gold-plated sword, if he has not the land, he is nevertheless a churl'.[38]

Law-codes inevitably have to lay down categories and boundaries; it is likely that they give a very misleading impression of rigid strati-fication and hierarchy in societies in which so-called 'class' divisions were in fact very fluid and where individuals could be socially highly mobile. Indeed there is no reason to believe that the legal categories revealed in the codes always have much to do with social classes at all. Some examination of the categories makes this clear. The basic distinctions are three-fold in all the barbarian law-codes: there are the unfree; the ordinary freeman or freewoman; and those among the free who have extra status. Among the Franks the last group may consist of particular categories regarded as important for the people as a whole—those on royal business, women of child-bearing age and boys under twelve. The only surviving trace of wergild tariffs in the Visigothic law illustrates the same point: the death of a man between 20 and 50 is assessed at 300 solidi, but males of 10 or of 75 have a wergild of 100 solidi.[39] The distinctions in the law-codes reflect a desire on the part of the legislators (whoever they were) to categorise the social worth of individuals, not to divide them up into social classes. That social privilege and social distinctions played a part in the actual operation of the law is highly likely, but it played little part in the minds of the lawyers. With the Franks, as with the Romans, social status and wealth did not necessarily correlate with legal status: consequently, the law-codes do not provide us with much of a guide to the social divisions among the Franks. Even among other peoples we are probably not necessarily dealing with 'classes' in the law-codes at all, but with 'status-groups' of different kinds.

In barbarian societies that vague sociological term 'status' could have very varied forms, relating to age, sex, office, occupation, and so on. Indeed, occupation may be a facet of status which particular grave-goods may reveal. Christopher Scull has recently studied those Anglo-Saxons who were buried with a balance and weights. Most of the balances were unusable and were thus, he argues, 'status symbols': not, he suggests, pertaining to aristocrats or merchants, but to the reeves or *praefecti* of the seventh-century sources, whose task was to regulate trade.[40] Other manifestations of 'occupation-status' in graves

---

[38] D. Whitelock, *The Beginnings of English Society* (Harmondsworth, 1952), 85.

[39] Quoted by D. Claude, *Geschichte der Westgoten* (Stuttgart, 1970), 143 n. 115, referring to Lex Visigothorum 8.4.16.

[40] 'Balances and Weights from Early Anglo-Saxon Graves: Implications for the Contexts of Exchange', in the *Résumés des Communications* for *Peuplement et Echanges, IIIe–*

may be smiths, as at Hérouvillette (Calvados) or merchants, as at Birka.[41] As Steuer reminded us, we should not be thinking in terms of the kind of social models in which society is organised in various pyramidal structures, whether bottom heavy, with a high proportion of unfree, or middle-heavy, with a higher proportion of free peasants. Instead we ought have a much more overlapping and complex pyramidal model, or else a model which takes into account the fact that status can derive from many different aspects of social existence, where an individual can partake of status in different ways depending on context or circumstance.[42] This corresponds to the argument of Lewis Binford that the aspects of the 'social persona' of an individual which were or might be recognised in burial were age, sex, condition and location of death, social affiliation and social position. Most early medievalists, of course, have concentrated upon the last—and even that has subdivisions which may be archaeologically detectable. Thus Steuer suggests that an explanation of the fact noted by J. Werner at Bülach, that silver-damascened belt equipment was found in graves poorly equipped with weapons, may be that there is a distinction between rank (weapons) and wealth (items of clothing).[43] Other anomalies occur which can really only be explained in terms of a complex view of status: thus, Kaiseraugst and Munningen both had graves poorly equipped in terms of the usual male equipment, yet containing half a dozen or more gold coins.[44] Things are clearly more complicated than Christlein and others have argued, and clearly more variable from cemetery to cemetery. Such conclusions make Steuer's *Frühgeschichtliche Sozialstrukturen*, an investigation of the archaeology of social structure, essentially a negative and critical one: however useful these refinements derived from the historical material might be to an historian, they are extremely difficult for the archaeologist to detect and explain.

To proceed further requires this recognition that categorising grave-good assemblages into a social hierarchy is too much of an over-simplification. Social status was not necessarily the same as legal status; grave-goods did not necessarily reflect either. Status within the community could, perhaps, depend as much on the size and influence of one's family or kin-group as upon wealth: in this case the grave-goods might indeed reflect the status of an individual—particularly if

---

IXe Siècles (the 39e Symposium Saxon de l'Arbeitsgemeinschaft für Sachsenforschung [*sic*], Caen, 12–16 septembre 1988).

[41] For a smith, see James, *Franks*, 207–9; for possible 'merchant-graves', see Gräslund, *Birka*, 79–81.

[42] Steuer, *Sozialstrukturen*, figs 2–7, pp. 19–24.

[43] Ibid., 314.

[44] Ibid., 324.

we think that the family is responsible for the deposition of grave-goods—but we would be seriously misled if we interpreted the burial deposit in class terms. We have to use the grave-goods in a more subtle way. An instance of grave-goods revealing status, but not in simplistic class terms, has very recently emerged from an analysis which my research student Guy Halsall is at present undertaking as part of his work on the Merovingian *civitas* of Metz.[45] He has analysed data from the cemetery of Ennery, in Lorraine, where we are lucky enough to have skeletal data as well as the grave-goods. His initial findings suggest that there is a strong correlation between grave-goods and age. Children have few grave-goods, and they are not clearly distinguished in gender terms. The old are treated similarly, with old women losing their jewellery and old men the more specifically military items, such as sword and spear. Both have fewer grave-goods than younger adults. Women between 14 and 22, and to a lesser extent women between 22 and 40, on the other hand, precisely those who, in the law-codes are given enhanced legal status, are distinguished by the quantity and variety of the items buried with them. In the case of Ennery the dramatic increase of gender-specific artefacts for females of 14 to 22 years perhaps argues that marriageable, rather than simply child-bearing, age brought on an increase of status in the community—or is it, simply, that they were expected to dress more lavishly? It would seem that more work on distinctions of gender and age would throw much more light on these status distinctions.[46]

Other pointers to future progress are to be found in recent work on Anglo-Saxon England. Some have been inspired by structuralist ideas, such as Ellen-Jane Pader and Julian Richards. Pader argues that looking at grave-good types is not enough; one must look at how they are used and placed. The role of individuals in the community, and their links with other individuals, may be reflected in the way a corpse is laid out in the grave, or in such apparently minor features such as whether a knife is placed on the left or the right of the body.[47] Julian Richards, after a very detailed statistical analysis of Anglo-Saxon cremation urns and their contents, pointed out a number of significant correlations between the individual urn and the status of the deceased: adult males had taller and wider pots than others; females tended to be buried in pots with curvilinear decoration; miniature iron blades and shears in the cremation urns tend to be associated with children

---

[45] So far published only in summary form in *Bulletin de Liaison de l'Association Française d'Archéologie Mérovingienne*, xii (1988), 50–52.

[46] Cf. the discussion of children's graves in Burnell, *Merovingian to Early Carolingian Churches*, 450ff.

[47] E.-J. Pader, *Symbolism, Social Relations and the Interpretation of Mortuary Remains* (BAR British Series 130: Oxford, 1982).

and older adults; and so on.[48] In this sense mortuary behaviour may reflect the symbolic decoration found in other spheres of Anglo-Saxon life, if Tania Dickinson is right that the variability of decoration on saucer-brooches allowed these brooches 'to serve as subtle personal markers, representing political or social affiliations and aspirations'.[49] It is clear that archaeologists and historians have to be, at the same time, both more cautious and more ambitious in the scope of their enquiry. Simple equations of wealth and status are not enough; but more subtle interpretations of the evidence may in future suggest status gradations within a community, and across communities, that will counterbalance the oversimplifications drawn from the law-codes and other historical material. We may yet be able to write social history from the huge quantity of mortuary evidence; we have as yet hardly begun.

[48] Richards, *Significance of Form*; and id., 'Style and Symbol: Explaining Variability in Anglo-Saxon Cremation Urns', in S. T. Driscoll and M. R. Mieke, ed. *Power and Politics in Early Medieval Britain* (Edinburgh, 1988), 145–161.

[49] T. M. Dickinson, 'Material Culture as Social Expression: The Case of Saxon Saucer Brooches with Running Spiral Decoration', in the publication cited in n. 40 above.

THE HABSBURGS AND THE HUNGARIAN
PROBLEM, 1790–1848
By R. J. W. Evans
READ 4 MARCH 1988

The real source of our troubles lies in the governmental system.
... There are political arrangements which, by virtue of their
permanence, do not gain, but rather lose strength, till at length the
moment is reached ... when their long life qualifies them only to
be allowed to die.[1]

ON 4 MARCH 1848 Hungarians were excitedly debating the
devastating criticisms of their country's rulers pronounced before
assembled members of the diet the previous day by the popular
tribune, Lajos Kossuth, the culmination of a campaign of agitation
which stretched back a decade and more. Kossuth called for a
constitutional transformation, with a responsible ministry, full legal
equality, and the abolition of all privilege. The following month his
programme was conceded wholesale by the authorities, under pressure
from the sans-culottes of Budapest, and prostrate before their own
Viennese revolution—for Kossuth's speech had played a major part
in unseating Metternich there. Six months later power passed to a
fully secessionist Hungarian regime, in which Kossuth enjoyed near-
dictatorial sway. The ensuing civil war, during which the dynasty was
declared deposed, took a further year to contain; its outcome appeared
to be a complete breakdown of mutual confidence between king and
country.

Those with long memories in 1848 could recall a constitutional
crisis of similar dimensions, albeit with a less bloody outcome. On 4
March 1790 news had just been received of the death of Joseph II,
who had ruled Hungary as an authentic enlightened despot. A wave
of anti-Habsburg emotion led to the systematic burning of Joseph's
decrees, then to plotting with Prussian diplomats. The bizarre project
was even mooted of placing Karl August of Weimar on the Hungarian

---

[1] The whole speech in L. Kossuth, *Írások és beszédek 1848–1849-ből*, ed. T. Katona
(Budapest, 1987), 12–26, quoted at p. 19. Convenient summaries of succeeding events
in *Magyarország története*. Vol. VI: *1848–90*, ed. E. Kovács (2 vols., Budapest, 1979), ii.
61 ff. (by Gy. Spira); and, in English, in I. Deák, *The Lawful Revolution: Louis Kossuth
and the Hungarians, 1848–9* (New York, 1979).

throne—presumably with Goethe as his adviser.[2] Again desperate government measures, this time to forestall rather than to undo revolution, included brutal action against the radical opposition: the 'Jacobin' trials and executions of 1794–5 had repercussions throughout the political nation.[3]

There is no doubt, then, that the Habsburgs had a 'Hungarian problem'. On the one hand, Hungary, with her loosely-associated territories of Croatia and Transylvania, was structurally different from the rest of their realms, especially since more coherent policies of centralisation and consolidation had begun to be implemented by the dynasty from the 1740s. An Empire originally brought together on the basis of oligarchy and Catholic culture was turning into an Empire regulated by new institutions and precepts which seemed perforce to stop short at the river Leitha, leaving a diet, local administration, distinct legal system, and stagnant agrarian economy behind Hungary's separate customs frontier. *De jure*, and often *de facto*, most features of a 'dualism' between two halves of the same polity already stood in place.

On the other hand, however, such dualism sat uneasily—as it was to do until the very end of the Monarchy—with the broader implications of government policy, particularly with the evolution of a unitary means of defence, that *raison d'être* of the Habsburg *Gesamtstaat* as enunciated in the Pragmatic Sanction. The single Austrian army, containing Hungarian regiments within it since 1715, and liaising with Hungarian auxiliary forces outside it, paid no heed to any separate claims of the Crown of St Stephen in its organisation or operations, and as little as possible in matters of recruitment and financial provision.[4] It was the Habsburgs' bad luck that their most ungovernable realm also nursed the deepest sense of grievance.

Yet in fact the whole long period between 1790 and 1848 was characterised by a relationship between Hungary and her rulers far more pacific than the events of those terminal years would seem to imply. Eighteenth-century modernisation programmes did not lack support in Hungary; nor did the conservative monarchism inspired by experience

---

[2] H. Marczali, *Az 1790/1-diki országgyűlés* (2 vols., Budapest, 1907), *passim*; R. Gragger, *Preußen, Weimar und die ungarische Königskrone* (Berlin/Leipzig, 1923).

[3] Convenient summaries in *Magyarország története*. Vol. V: *1790–1848*, ed. Gy. Mérei (2 vols., Budapest, 1980), i. 159–212 (by K. Benda); and, in English, in E. Wangermann, *From Joseph II to the Jacobin Trials* (2nd edn., Oxford, 1968), esp. 109ff.

[4] There is no adequate study of the army for the period in question, but much may be derived from recent studies of the subsequent period: A. Schmidt-Brentano, *Die Armee in Österreich. Militär, Staat und Gesellschaft, 1848–67* (Boppard a.R., 1975); G. E. Rothenberg, *The Army of Francis Joseph* (W. Lafayette, Ind., 1976); *Die Habsburgermonarchie, 1848–1918*, ed. A. Wandruszka and P. Urbanitsch. Vol. V: *Die bewaffnete Macht* (Vienna, 1987).

of the Revolutionary and Napoleonic wars.[5] The Habsburgs provided, not only the bugbear of an absent ruler, but three widely admired and respected Palatines (viceroys)—one of them, Joseph, serving over fifty years in the office. The diet proved a focus, not only for discontent, but also for a series of grand reconciliations.

The first of these, presided over by Palatine Alexander Leopold, took place in the early 1790s, when reform commissions of the diet (so-called regnicolar deputations) hammered out proposals more harmonious and 'Josephinist' in spirit for the fact that the pressure of Joseph's personality had been removed, and the nobility greeted the French war with fervent declarations reminiscent of their *vitam et sanguinem* pledge to the young Maria Theresa.[6] From 1794 there was indeed a hiatus, with the panic, initiated by the Palatine, about a Jacobin conspiracy, and then some hard bargaining over the army. In 1805 the diet forced concessions, with the French at the gates of Vienna; two years later it raised a storm about economic issues: but by 1808 all was sweetness and light again, and in 1809 the time-honoured Hungarian *levée en masse* trundled out to defy Napoleon's blitzkrieg. Over the next fifteen years the same peripateia: a unilateral devaluation of the currency by the emperor-king revived clamorous expressions of grievance, which were compounded when Francis I added to his stony inflexibility further demands, of dubious constitutional status, for recruits and taxation. But concerted resistance and the promptings of Palatine Joseph persuaded the ruler to reconvene the diet and come to terms with the opposition.[7]

This diet of 1825–7, besides being a very important exercise in mending fences, also generated fresh tensions, as a campaign for reform began to emerge, concerted by publication of the reports of the regnicolar deputations, held over from the 1790s. The programme of material transformation and spiritual renewal associated with István Széchenyi soon gave rise to more advanced social and political

[5] Major reappraisal of the eighteenth-century evidence in D. Kosáry, *Művelődés a XVIII. századi Magyarországon* (Budapest, 1980), and E. H. Balázs, *Bécs és Pest-Buda a régi századvégeken* (Budapest, 1988). Cf. R. J. W. Evans, 'Maria Theresa and Hungary', in *'Enlightened Absolutism': Reform and Reformers in Later Eighteenth-Century Europe*, ed. H. M. Scott (1989), 189–207.

[6] In general Narczali, *1790/1-diki országgyűlés*; M. Horváth, *Magyarország történelme*, vol. viii (Budapest, 1873), 129ff., 199ff. Cf. the argument of E. Mályusz in the introduction to his edn. of *Sándor Lipót főherceg nádor iratai, 1790–5* (Budapest, 1926), esp. pp. 137–41. Graphic description of the renewed pledge in Országos Levéltár (National Archives, Budapest, hereafter 'OL'), P 1765, csomó 86, nos. 9850 seqq.

[7] Mályusz, *Sándor Lipót*, esp. 172ff., for 1794–5. S. Domanovszky, *József nádor élete* (2 vols., Budapest, 1944), for the next period, complementing E. Wertheimer, *Ausztria és Magyarország a tizenkilencedik század első tizedében* (2 vols., Budapest, 1890–2), and Horváth, *Magyarország történelme*. Still fundamental for the early 1820s: M. Horváth, *Huszonöt év Magyarország történelméből 1823-tól 1848-ig* (2 vols., Geneva, 1864), i. 3–134.

demands. The authorities' first response was again tough, and included imprisonment for the rising Kossuth; but then the fifteen-year cycle repeated itself, with the Palatine once more prominent, and the diet of 1840 seemed to achieve a substantial reconciliation. During the next decade antagonisms revived, in measurably more hectic forms, with the growth of a primitive style of party politics; the liberal opposition called for a total abolition of noble privilege. Yet even the initial stages of the 1848 crisis display significant elements of compromise, under the patronage of the young Palatine Stephen, and the April Laws were passed by the diet in traditional form. They ushered in a ministry of all the talents under Count Batthyány, whose actions were designed in part to head off the prospect of extremer movements, like the radicalism of Budapest.[8]

I shall return later to the question why the old bottle proved unable to hold new wine. But how had it been tough or capacious enough to endure so long? One answer lies in an issue whose *dénouement* exactly spanned the decades from 1790s to 1840s: for besides the accommodation of basically backward-looking material grievance couched in oppositional ideology, one crucial item of forward ideology with material implications had its place in the scheme of semi-ritualised alternate confrontation and pacification. This was the issue of language.

Voices were raised from the 1780s for Magyar as the national or mother tongue of Hungary. They constituted a reaction against Joseph II's notorious imposition of German, but also a fruit of Enlightenment interest in the vernaculars and of new literary enthusiasm.[9] The pressure of writers like Ferenc Kazinczy helped elicit a first paper provision for Magyar, mainly as a subject in schools, by the compromise package of 1792. After further government concessions the language came into widespread voluntary use from 1805. After 1830 it was made compulsory in much of the public service, besides exerting its impact through the young Academy of Sciences, whose statutes received royal sanction the following year. Between 1836 and 1845 Magyar became the language of constitutional record and dietal proceedings, while Latin was eliminated in education, its other remaining bastion.[10]

---

[8] For 1848 in its historical context see, besides the works cited above, n.1, the classic account by Horváth in *Huszonöt év*, ii.567ff., and in *Magyarország függetlenségi harcának története 1848 és 1849-ben* (3 vols., Pest, 1871–2); and the important new treatment by A. Urbán, *Batthyány Lajos miniszterelnöksége* (Budapest, 1986).

[9] D. Rapant, *K. počiatkom maď'arizácie* (2 vols., Bratislava, 1927–31), i (for background) and ii (for 1790–2); cf. R.J.W. Evans, 'Joseph II and Nationality in the Habsburg Lands' in '*Enlightened Absolutism*', ed. Scott, 209–19.

[10] Full discussion and documentation in Gy. Szekfű (ed.), *Iratok a magyar államnyelv kérdésének történetéhez, 1790–1848* (Budapest, 1926).

Four comments can readily be made about these measures. First, they were achieved by ordered transaction between Habsburgs and nation, after the crisis of 1790 and before that of 1848. Secondly, they acted thereby as a safety-valve in relations between court and country, indeed in some respects they signified a retreat of the latter from explicitly political activity (Kazinczy is a good exemplar of such a surrogate function). Yet, thirdly, they yielded from the very beginning friction inside Hungary with other nationalities (or, more precisely, with those citizens who set store by other languages and cultures); and the qualified but stubborn resistance to them from Vienna in some measure foresaw, without (so far as I can judge) welcoming, those longer-term disruptive effects.[11] Fourthly, the advance of Magyar heightened the distinctiveness, and especially the *perceived* distinctiveness, of the dominant element in Hungary vis-à-vis the rest of the Monarchy: in that way too, it built up trouble for the future.

One final, broader point, however, most concerns me here. Language, with all the national issues which it embodied, was also an administrative matter: not so much a crude question of jobs, since, objectively speaking, the traditional usage of Latin formed almost as effective a barrier against the outside world as Magyar; but a whole set of relations, internal and external, of executive authority, the more so given the rapid spread of the written word in this period. Elsewhere in the Monarchy, in the later nineteenth century, that would be obvious. In Hungary, before 1848, it may surprise, given the persuasion, common to many contemporaries as to historians, that Hungary was distinguished by an absence of bureaucracy.[12] Horsemanship, political rhetoric, hospitality, chronic indebtedness, rustic pursuits, maybe even cultural patronage: all these, and a little J.P. work, might detain her nobility; but not state service. Yet Hungary did have an administration—not just in her counties (which I shall touch on shortly), but, superior and logically prior to them, in royal agencies with extensive authority under the constitution. Moreover this central administration, I propose to argue, represented the main force for lasting stability in the country's relations with her Habsburg rulers.

Hungary had some 4,300 appointed royal officials in 1840, nearly

---

[11] I have found no evidence in Szekfu's collection, or elsewhere, of any governmental policy to favour the language laws in the hope of profiting from their divisive effects; rather there are dire predictions of their likely result. But more work would be necessary to confirm the negative hypothesis.

[12] Kossuth's comments, in his speech of 3 March 1848 (above, n. 1) are typical in identifying bureaucrats as an emanation from Vienna: 'a bécsi bürokratikus kormányrendszer ... a bécsi rendszer csontkamarájából egy sorvasztó szél fúj reánk ... a bürokratikus mozdulatlanság ama politikája, mely a bécsi státustanácsban megcsontosodott ... büro és bajonett nyomorú kapocs ...'.

1,000 of them in three central institutions.[13] The Chancellery, headed by a Cancellarius, played an advisory and mediatory role in the various divisions of business—taxes, peasant questions, military supply, trade, communications, religion, charities, education, medicine, etc.—which passed between Vienna, where it was located, and the country.[14] Chief executive powers inside Hungary rested with the Lieutenancy Council, under the Palatine, which received directives (*rescripta, decreta*) from the king, issued mandates (*normalia*) to the localities, and possessed, like the Chancellery, a lively tradition of comment and remonstrance. The Chamber, under its President, managed the fiscal and economic interests of the Crown.[15] There were, besides, high legal officers—Chief Justice (Iudex Curiae), Personalis, and judges of the Royal Curia—whose functions overlapped closely with those of the executive branch.

Indeed, one crucial qualification for senior posts in the administration was a training in Hungarian law. The other was linguistic competence, in Latin, German, and Magyar. By the early nineteenth century we find some evidence of formal preparation and competitive appointment, a structure of (mostly modest) salaries, with certain pension rights, and what appears a largely diligent response from an understaffed cadre (above all in the law courts) to the mounting volume of business. Its bureaucratic procedures evidently borrowed heavily from Austrian models,[16] but its recruitment was quite distinct: this service remained in its upper echelons overwhelmingly Hungarian—with the Chancellery as a quasi-diplomatic enclave in the Habsburg capital—and noble. The fact that some foreign experts might be infiltrated, especially into the Chamber, and that some

---

[13] E. Fényes, *Magyarország statistikája* (3 vols., Pest, 1842–3), i. 113f. Cf. *Schematismus inclyti regni Hungariae partiumque eidem annexarum pro anno 1839* (Buda, 1839), 97ff.

[14] There is no history of the Chancellery; but cf. Fényes, *Magyarország statistikája*, ii.119–24, and earlier M. Horváth [also Mihály, but not the historian], *Statistica regni Hungariae et partium eidem adnexarum* (Pozsony, 1802), pt. 3. Brief accounts of the administrative background in G. Barany, 'Ungarns Verwaltung, 1848–1918' in *Die Habsburgermonarchie*, ed. Wandruszka and Urbanitsch. Vol. II: *Verwaltung und Rechtswesen* (Vienna, 1975), 306ff.; and in A. Csizmadia, *A magyar közigazgatás fejlődése a XVIII. századtól a tanácsrendszer létrejöttéig* (Budapest, 1976), 65ff.; cf. Evans, 'Maria Theresa and Hungary', in some ways a companion article to this one.

[15] On the council, *faute de mieux*: Fényes, *Magyarország statistikája*, ii. 124–8; I. Felhő and Á. Vörös (comp.), *A helytartótanácsi levéltár* (Budapest, 1961). On the Chamber: I. Nagy, *A magyar kamara, 1686–1848* (Budapest, 1971), 288ff.; cf. Fényes, *Magyarország statistikája*, iii. 33ff.

[16] For which see, most recently, K. Megner, *Beamte. Wirtschafts- und sozialgeschichtliche Aspekte des k.k. Beamtentums* (Vienna, 1985); W. Heindl, 'Beamte, Staatsdienst und Universitätsreform ... 1780–1848', *Das achtzehnte Jahrhundert und Österreich*, iv (1987), 35–53.

capable commoners might be ennobled to climb the career ladder, did not—I t¹.ink—alter its basic ethos.

Two important riders need also to be entered. The administration, while Hungarian in background, was not necessarily Magyar. It contained goodly numbers of Germans and Croats, who with few exceptions did not associate themselves with Austrian sentiments where those might clash with Hungarian ones. At the top, Palatine Joʳeph set an example in hard-working defence of the interests of his adopted country: although dispensed *ad hominem* from the language decrees, he became surely the last secular governor anywhere whose patriotism was measured by the excellence of his Latin.[17] The corollary is that, like Joseph, government servants proved much slower than the opposition to make the great transition from *amor patriae* in its traditional territorial context to linguistic nationalism: not that many were altogether impervious to the latter as time went on; but private sympathies would be moderated by professional priorities. Moreover the administration, while noble in background, was not necessarily conservative. Mildly reformist endeavours might be stunted by the experience of 1795, when certain officials were dismissed. Yet—as elsewhere in the Monarchy—they lived on, fortified in Hungary by the rising proportion of Protestants who could now enter the service.

The crucial brokerage function of these administrators was exercised partly at the diet, where leading royal servants attended either *ex officio* or by virtue of their social status; but mainly through control of affairs, personal contacts, and networks of influence. Prominent members of the opposition could regularly be won over—an early case is that of Péter Balogh at the beginning of the 1790s—a practice which, in the hands of such as Ludwig Wirkner in the 1830s and 1840s, has frequently, but perhaps over-excitedly, been condemned as subornation.[18] The real continuity, however, was assured by familial lineages within the bureaucracy.

What sort of people are we dealing with here? Let me flesh out the general impressions with a few particulars. Some belonged to the old aristocracy, among them the two senior royal officials at the start of our period. The Chancellor in 1790 was Károly Pálffy, member of an arch-aulic family, but with a base of considerable popularity in the country. His father had served in the same post before him, till

---

[17] General characterization in Domanovszky, *József nádor élete*. Contemporary tributes by F. Kazinczy, *Művei*, ed. M. Szauder (2 vols., Budapest, 1979), ii. no. 215; Horváth, *Huszonöt év*, ii. 419–23.

[18] Examples in Horváth, *Magyarország történelme*, 248f.; id., *Huszonöt év*, i. 130, 228, 285f.; cf. S. Takáts, *Kémvilág Magyarországon* (2nd edn. Budapest, 1980). Defence by L. Wirkner, *Meine Erlebnisse. Blätter aus dem Tagebuche meines öffentlichen Wirkens vom Jahre 1825 bis 1852* (Pressburg, 1879), 69ff., 129ff.

dropped for insubordination; his nephew would do so again in the 1830s.[19] Chief Justice in 1790 was the still young, zealous, and malleable Károly Zíchy, a very effective mediator who, dismissed for a time after 1795, returned with an Austrian governmental post; his son, another Károly, became President of the Chamber.[20] The Zíchys provide a classic example of bureaucratised magnates, who can hardly have joined the administration for money—the representative side certainly seems to have run them and the Pálffys into debt in the 1790s, even though some sinecures may have lain within their grasp[21]—and who, often ensconced in Vienna, nevertheless usually remained, in some fundamental sense, Hungarians.

A more significant grouping, since most traditional aristocrats did not have a regular link with the professional administration, is the new aristocracy: a handful of families raised to great influence through their ambitious response to the fresh official opportunities opened up under Maria Theresa and Joseph II. We have another classic case in the Mailáths, the brothers József and György and their progeny, who held high financial, legal, and chancellery posts through three generations, culminating in simultaneous service as Cancellarius and Judex Curiae during the 1840s. The values they espoused found expression in the writings of almost the only Mailáth who did not accept public office: János (Johann), loyalist historian of the Habsburg Monarchy, but also an enthusiast for Hungarian legends and folklore, who impoverished himself in support of the Academy and other cultural purposes.[22] The Croatian Szécsens gained prominence at much the same time, through Sándor, President of the Chamber for eighteen years from 1790. His son and grandson followed him in the service, as did successive generations of their fellow-countrymen, the Bedekoviches.

Such recently established families shade into a further subgroup of

[19] Much of the personal information in these paragraphs rests on general compendia, especially I. Nagy, *Magyarország családai* (8 vols., Pest, 1857–68); C. Wurzbach, *Biographisches Lexikon des Kaiserthums Oesterreich* (60 vols., Vienna, 1856–91); and J. Szinnyei, *Magyar írók élete és munkái* (14 vols., Budapest, 1891–1913). Sometimes the information is discrepant. More recent sources add little. On Pálffy see also Marczali, *1790/1-diki országgyűlés*, 59f.

[20] Ibid. 6of.; Wertheimer, *Ausztria és Magyarország*, ii. 17f. and *passim* (a negative view); Mályusz, *Sándor Lipót*, 26f. and *passim*; I. Bakács (comp.), *A Zíchy család levéltára* (Budapest, 1963).

[21] Debts: OL P 708, kútfő 21, folder 3, fols. 21f.; cf. G. Felloni, *Gli investimenti finanziari genovesi in Europa tra il Seicento e la Restaurazione* (Milan, 1971), app. 3. Sinecures: Mályusz, *Sándor Lipót*, p. 508n.

[22] J. Mailáth, *Geschichte des östreichischen Kaiserstaates* (5 vols., Hamburg, 1834–50); Z. Várady, *Gróf Mailáth János szerepe a magyar irodalomban* (Máramorssziget, 1911); Kazinczy, *Művei*, ii, nos. 161, 229. There is much *passim* on György and Antal Mailáth in the literature on the 1840s cited below.

those which rose in just the decades under consideration to assume a major part in running Hungary. Here again we encounter first two personalities who, having served Joseph II with considerable loyalty but markedly declining enthusiasm as he rode roughshod over the constitution, were largely instrumental in picking up the pieces after his death. József Ürményi, the Personalis, had been the chief architect of Hungary's educational reform. Although dismissed like Zíchy in 1795, he soon returned as Chief Justice, retaining his influence into the 1820s, and his son acted as long-time governor of Fiume, Hungary's only port.[23] Alongside Ürményi in the effective campaign to reconcile the country with its ruler stood his protégé, Sándor Pászthory, son of a judge from the middling nobility. Under Joseph, Pászthory had become the brains of the Chancellery (as well as Hungarian representative on the Educational Commission in Vienna); then he too was governor of Fiume until his early death in 1798.[24]

Pásztory was an outstanding public servant. His papers suggest fluency in six languages (including English); yet he reckoned Magyar not least of them, and it was Pászthory who persuaded Joseph to his historic decree of December 1789 which for the first time summoned the diet in Hungarian as well as Latin. His cosmopolitanism, Freemasonry, and interest in foreign constitutional models clearly helped him in his shrewd management of the unruly diet proceedings of 1790.[25] At Fiume Pászthory took on a promising clerk who later married his daughter and pursued a similar career in the next generation: Zsigmond Szőgyény became successively fiscal official in Pest, youngest assessor on the Tabula Regia, financial administrator in Vienna, and Personalis back in Hungary. The Szőgyénys were a semi-loyalist family: the grandfather had served over twenty years in the Lieutenancy Council, but the father stayed in the provinces, and his letters to Zsigmond afford a fascinating glimpse into the play of conflicting pressures. 'From all this [the changes of 1795], dear son, you can learn what a great vanity it is to crave for office; how much better to follow the advice of the ancient sages.... A tranquil heart

---

[23] Kosáry, Művelődés, 388f., 410ff. passim; Mályusz, Sándor Lipót, passim, for his earlier career. S. Domanovszky, József nádor iratai, vol. i (Budapest, 1925), covers the 1795 episode.

[24] This account of Pászthory rests on his papers in OL P 643, csomó 30; on Kosáry, Művelődés, 327, 390, 444–5, 465, 473; and on the scattered references in Marczali, 1790/1-diki országgyűlés, and in L. Hajdu, II József igazgatási reformjai Magyarországon (Budapest, 1982), esp. 103ff.

[25] For Pászthory's English: OL P 643, csomó 30, fols. 312f.; L. Hajdu, A közjó szolgálatában (Budapest, 1983), 96, 109. For the language decree: Szekfű, Iratok, pp. 34ff. Freemasonry: OL, loc. cit. fols. 315ff. See also the verdict of Kazinczy, Művei, i. 272f.

makes for happiness, not fine rank or riches.' And he pleads that Zsigmond observe Hungarian manners, and wear the broad cloak or *köntös*, not the sort of attire 'which makes Magyars vomit'.[26] We must hope the elder Szőgyény was not too disappointed: Zsigmond advanced to a salary of 6,000 gulden per annum (having begun at 100), with a pension for the widow after his death from overwork in 1826; but his love for his native language seems to have survived, along with a key role as honest broker with Vienna during the early 1820s. The third generation, László Szőgyény, was Vice-Chancellor of the realm on the eve of 1848, and entered the titled nobility.[27]

From a third level of more workaday figures we may again take two examples. János Somogyi came from middling circumstances, through an unsavoury task as royal prosecutor in the 1790s, to act as Hungarian adviser on the Staatsrat, the highest deliberative body in the Monarchy. But he was no Austrian myrmidon: even Kazinczy, on whom he pronounced a death sentence (later commuted), testifies to that.[28] The survival of some of his dossiers from the 1800s shows his involvement in all manner of major decisions affecting Hungary, and his evident closeness to the Emperor, who tended to accept his opinion. Somogyi's influence extended from the diet and the noble *levée* to the most senior individual appointments, especially perhaps in the Church.[29] Dániel Kászonyi, of similar background, did not rise so high: he stuck at a chancellery secretaryship, followed by a district fiscal post. Touched by the Enlightenment in youth, he grew more conservative and somewhat snobbish later, but retained broad cultural interests. Through his papers we can penetrate further into the hybrid milieu of the new Hungarian bureaucrat and his semi-Magyar and semi-German, part urban and part landed ménage.[30]

We can only speculate why men like Somogyi and Kászonyi joined the service. The proliferation of marginal landowners, particularly in the north and west of Hungary, may have played its part; but so must the attractions of a more exciting life than that in the average manorhouse—where Theresa Kászonyi would hardly have taken up flute,

[26] Szőgyény's papers are in OL P 643, csomó 29, including (tétel 8) the anonymous *Szőgyény Zsigmond . . . élet-rajza* (Pest, 1828); details about his family ibid., tétel 1, fol. 35; letters from his father ibid., tétel 10, fols. 3, 5, 12, 14, 21, 23.

[27] OL loc. cit. tétel 4, fols. 47, 16–15; tétel 6 (salary). Kazinczy, *Művei*, ii, no. 179 (patriotism). Correspondence with Metternich and Stadion, OL loc. cit. tétel 9, esp. fols. 93ff., 151ff.; tétel 10, fols. 35–61. L. Szőgyény-Marich, *Emlékiratai* (3 vols., Budapest, 1903-18), i.

[28] C. von Hock and H. I. Bidermann, *Der österreichische Staatsrat. Eine geschichtliche Studie* (Vienna, 1879), 651; Kazinczy, *Művei*, i. 427ff, esp. 438, 450; Wertheimer, *Ausztria és Magyarország*, ii. 34 (a negative view).

[29] The dossiers are in OL P 971; cf. Kazinczy, *Művei*, i. 580.

[30] These papers are in OL P 1975. They have an intrinsic interest which I hope to be able to exploit more fully elsewhere.

clarinet, *and* cello. There were certainly compensations for the hard-pressed chancellery registrar Zmeskáll, another protégé of Pászthory, who became one of Beethoven's intimate friends (and dedicatee of one of his most challenging string quartets).[31] We may recall, in the same context, that some of the composer's closest aristocratic patrons were the descendants of Maria Theresa's Hungarian bureaucrat and counsellor, Count Brunswick.

This royal executive—whose systematic study is long overdue—created the polarity which, in the first instance, split the political life of Hungary. Members of the historic noble nation either belonged to it, in modest but increasing numbers, or they did not. The opposition, formed essentially by negative reference to it, objected to this 'foreign' growth; proclaimed its own 'liberties' with ever more libertarian trappings; represented bureaucracy as the principal impediment to national progress and its officers as 'brahmins'. Many argued like the elder Szőgyény and tried to bind their diet deputies not to accept any royal post for a specified period of years.[32] Yet the stronghold of the opposition also lay in administration, at the level of the counties. The power of these 'fifty-two republics' resided, on the one hand, in their right to send representatives to the Lower House of the diet; but on the other, precisely in their cheap, amateur, and elective functionaries who oversaw a growing number of local activities. By 1840 there were 6,000 county employees, often operating in new buildings designed for the purpose. Moreover, from 1805, they became the focus for policies of Magyarisation, as county after county resolved on a vigorous assertion of its right to conduct affairs in the native language.[33]

We have, then, the setting for a protracted contest between Hungarian crown and Hungarian country, waged through the period with intermittent ferocity and passion. Ostensibly the constitutional struggle concerned the diet: a magnate-clerical Upper House, with its dissident minority, versus a gentry-dominated Commons, with its considerable proportion of loyalists. But at a deeper level it was a battle between the two administrations. The crown sought to implement its will from above; country *parlementaires* to frustrate it, by remonstrance,

---

[31] Mentions of music in Kászonyi's accounts, OL loc. cit. fols. 275–86. K. Vörös, 'Zmeskáll Miklós udvari titkár élete és pályafutása', *Levéltári Közlemények*, xliv-xlv (1974), 615–31. The quartet in question is that in F minor, opus 95.

[32] Horváth, *Huszonöt év*, i. 307–11, ii. 492f.; L. Révész, *Die Anfänge des ungarischen Parlamentarismus* (Munich, 1968), 148ff.

[33] Fényes, *Magyarország statistikája*, i. 113f., ii. 128ff. (numbers and tasks). The buildings are described in Gy. Antalffy, *Reformkori magyar városrajzok* (Budapest, 1982), *passim*. Much evidence of Magyarizing intent in D. Rapant, *Ilegálna maďarizácia, 1790–1840* (Turčiansky Svätý Martin, 1947) though the results were not always commensurate: cf. Szekfű, *Iratok*, 133ff., 170ff.; Zs. Kemény, *Változatok a történelemre*, ed. Gy. Tóth (Budapest, 1982), 504.

fortified with the vital element of inter-county correspondence, by mandating their delegates (with the sanction of recall if they exceeded instructions), and by unofficial pre-dietal sessions—like that which Kossuth addressed on 3 March 1848. The opposition sought to promote reforms from below, in a fashion which the central authorities branded as insubordinate and anarchic.[34]

The strategy of high officials from one generation to the next was to turn the resultant impasse. They had a *point d'appui* in the shrievalty of each county, a nominated post to which the king could appoint from the ranks of reasonably docile magnates, or select in lieu a so-called administrator from among his career bureaucrats. Pászthory and others prepared a detailed blueprint for Joseph II on ways to gradually purge the constitution of its voluntaristic excesses, with strong men to deploy the full powers of the sheriff and engineer favourable elections to a suitably managed diet. These plans were refurbished in the early 1790s, and contemplated again in the years after 1800. Much the same course was attempted during the early 1820s, when Szőgyény figured prominently.[35] It was the government's Hungarian advisers who experimented with counting rather than weighing votes in the local assemblies; who backed the summoning of a diet and a return to the work of the old regnicolar deputations; who saw to the installation of a popular Chancellor in the self-made and honourable Revitzky. By the 1840s county elections and proceedings became tumultuous and sometimes violent, with each side blaming the other. Now the regime once more reverted to expedients strikingly similar to those first tabled in the 1780s: the energetic young Vice-Chancellor Apponyi, supported by the Mailáths and Wirkner, sponsored official lobbying and attempts to split the opposition in the localities, and undertook a more concerted drive to impose well-paid administrators on the recalcitrant county organisations.[36]

---

[34] In general, and on mandates: Révész, *Anfänge*. On instructions: A. Degré, 'Zala megye reformkori követutasításai', *Levéltári Közlemények*, xliv-xlv (1974), 143–60. On the unofficial meetings (*kerületi ülések*): Takács, *Kémvilág*, 150ff.; K. Kecskeméti, 'La séance circulaire de la diète hongroise à la fin de l'ancien régime', *Parliaments, Estates and Representation*, vi (1986), 135–47.

[35] 1780s: Hajdu, *II József*, 103ff. Early 1790s: OL P 643, csomó 30, fols. 310f., 413f., 451–3. 1800s: Wertheimer, *Ausztria és Magyarország*, ii. 75ff. 1820s: Szőgyény papers as above, n. 27; Horváth, *Huszonöt év*, i. 24ff.; H. Haselsteiner, 'Herrscherrecht und Konstitutionalismus in Ungarn: der Widerstand des Komitates Abaúj gegen das Rekrutierungsdekret von König Franz vom 4.4.1821', *Österreichische Osthefte*, xvii (1975), 233–40.

[36] For the violence: Horváth, *Huszonöt év*, ii. 3ff., 178ff., etc.; Révész, *Anfänge*, 120ff. For the *modus operandi* (though they leave crucial questions unanswered): J. Varga, 'A kormányszervek előkészületei az 1843. évi diétára', *Századok*, cxiv (1980), 727–48; A. Molnár, 'Deák Ferenc és a zalai liberális ellenzék megbuktatása az 1843-as követválasztáson', *Levéltári Szemle*, xxxvii (1987), 2, 47–59. Most historians from Horváth on

The point is that these inter-Hungarian disputes concerned means rather than ends. In fact we find substantial overlap in the actual policies formulated. Both sides proclaimed the need for an elimination of feudalism and backwardness. Officials as well as liberals looked to commercial and industrial advance, from projectors like Pászthory and György Mailáth in the 1790s to those who drafted the massive legislation of 1840 on bills of exchange and bankruptcy.[37] Improved communications by land and water were almost universally regarded as a desideratum. There was widespread backing for legal reform, with greater equality, abolition of *aviticitas* (which prevented free trade in land), and rationalisation of the intricate and clogged system of seventeen existing jurisdictions. Tax reform, with a relaxation of peasant burdens, and full religious toleration, removing disabilities on non-Catholics, likewise commanded a broad measure of support.[38] Even over Magyarisation, most patriots came to seek the same ultimate solution as nationalists. Their relation to Hungarian, the mother tongue of most, the working tongue of almost all, certainly by the 1830s, might be more relaxed and pluralist; but it was hardly less positive, for all their rejection of the rhetoric of the opposition, precisely because of its source, and their retention of Pászthory's watchword: 'absit coactio'.[39]

Moreover, neither side evinced much solidarity, or a consistent front for antagonism. The royal administration and its judicial personnel certainly looked more embattled by the 1840s, their remaining enlightened traditions increasingly devalued. They were now outflanked by—and to some extent subsumed within—a more authentically reform-conservative grouping, which marched under the banner of 'cautious advance' and was lent rather spurious ideological

---

have given these endeavours a bad press; contrast the vindications by Wirkner, *Erlebnisse*, and by Szőgyény-Marich, *Emlékiratai*.

[37] Much evidence in M. Horváth, *Az ipar és kereskedés története Magyarországon* (Buda, 1840), 321ff. The two 1840 laws, which must be far the longest in the annals of the Hungarian diet, are printed in *Magyar törvénytár: 1836–68 évi törvénycikkek*, ed. D. Márkus *et al.* (Budapest, 1896), 109–45, 160–74; cf. Wirkner, *Erlebnisse*, 113ff.

[38] On all this see Horváth, *Huszonöt év*, ii. 140ff. and *passim*; Gy. Miskolczy, *A kamarilla a reformkorszakban* (Budapest, 1938), 107ff. For legal reform: B. Sarlós, *Deák és Vukovics, két igazságügy-miniszter* (Budapest, 1970); for the existing legal structure: Fényes, *Magyarország statistikája*, iii. 104–28.

[39] Szekfű, *Iratok*, doct. 19 (Pászthory). By the 1840s the last generation of Hungarian, as opposed to Magyar, patriots was rapidly dying out: prominent ones are discussed in V. Jankovič, *Ján Caplovič, život, osobnost', dielo* (Turčiansky Svätý Martin, 1945); in J. Tibenský's introduction to A. Mednyanský, *Malebná cesta dolu Váhom* (Bratislava, 1981); in I. Fried, 'Rumy Károly György a kultúrközvetítő, 1828–47', *Filológiai Közlöny*, ix (1963), 204–18; and in the autobiography of J. L. Pyrker, *Mein Leben, 1772–1847*, ed. A. P. Czigler (Vienna, 1966).

trappings by the writings of the 'Hungarian Gentz', Aurél Dessewffy.[40] Meanwhile, serious inconsistencies within the opposition came to the fore, and threatened the anyway slender majority which it could usually command in the Lower House. Some liberals, especially Eötvös and Kemény, were fiercely critical of county corruption. Religion also created divisions; and while numerous Catholics rallied to the grievances over mixed marriages (an issue which, often overlooked by historians, aroused some of the bitterest passions of the Hungarian *Vormärz*), loyalist elements among the Protestants mistrusted much of the reform programme. Urban patriciates were very wary of the implications of the enhanced constitutional voice being demanded on behalf of their towns. In the background lurked a deeper malaise: the intrinsic paradox of a campaign to extend civil rights and the suffrage, which feared it might threaten the hegemony of Magyardom in the counties and ultimately in the country as a whole; of a movement which identified individual liberties so surely with one nationality in the state as to drastically limit their validity and alienate even progressives who valued minority cultures.[41]

Let me recapitulate the argument so far. Hungary's political stagnation resulted from an impasse between two more or less equally matched parties, both seeking dominance, one from above, the other from below. But the sides actually shared many objectives, and the battle-lines were by no means clearly drawn. Could they not have been reconciled before time ran out for the grand experiment of a renewal of Hungary in reasonably favourable circumstances? A sense of this mission, and the urge to fulfil it, lay at the root of Széchenyi's greatness; just as its failure weighed more heavily upon him than upon anyone else.

Count István (Stephen) Széchenyi's father had been a leading public servant of Joseph II, as well as an outstanding patriot (founder of the Hungarian National Museum and Library). Later, disillusioned with progressive ideas, he lived mainly in Vienna amid a coterie of ultramontane Catholics. His son moved in the opposite direction. He began with intimate Austrian connections and a cosmopolitanism fostered by service in the army. He maintained close links too with

---

[40] Horváth, *Huszonöt év*, i. 541ff., ii. 67ff.; J. Varga, *Kereszttűzben a Pesti Hirlap: az ellenzéki és a középutas liberalizmus elválása 1841–42–ben* (Budapest, 1983), 101ff.; I. Z. Dénes, 'The Political Role of Hungary's Nineteenth-Century Conservatives and How They Saw Themselves', *Historical Journal*, xxvi (1983), 845–65, at 849ff.

[41] Classic texts are J. Eötvös, *Reform* (Leipzig, 1846), and Zs. Kemény, 'Korteskedés és ellenszerei' (1843) reprinted in *Változatok*, 7–180. On the vulnerability of the diet opposition, Kecskeméti, 'Séance circulaire', 146f., conveniently brings together some statistics. Horváth, no friend of the government, nevertheless saw 1844–5 as a real missed opportunity for it: *Huszonöt év*, ii. 283–7, 304ff.

senior royal administrators, being—for example—related to the Zíchys by three separate bonds of wedlock. Yet he felt increasingly impelled to further the cause of his homeland openly, not least through the encouragement of Crescence, wife of the younger Károly Zíchy, whom he married after the latter's death. Széchenyi took two famous initiatives: offering a year's revenue to endow a national Academy; and publishing a treatise in Magyar on what the author called 'Credit', but we should describe as economic growth. Neither represented an overtly political gesture—though they were arranged to coincide with the diets of 1825 and 1830. Széchenyi's programme envisaged national regeneration by practical activity (what Polish reformers would come to call 'organic work'): agrarian improvement, modern communications, banks and savings, self-help through publicity, clubs, and societies. He held aloof from oppositional demands for major constitutional change; at the same time he long kept his distance from state institutions. Although wooed by both sides, he sought through strict neutrality to act like a bridge (we might say, recalling his most celebrated project) between the Buda of the royal hirelings and the Pest of the budding revolutionaries, as the mutual stereotypes had it.[42]

During the 1840s it became clear that Széchenyi could not sustain this role. Increasingly frightened at the unrest which he saw being unleashed by the agitation of the left, he rounded on Kossuth; temporised on social reforms designed to liberate the peasantry, abolish privilege, and admit commoners to full political participation; and denounced much of the administrative Magyarisation now in full swing.[43] At the same time, while loosely associated with the central authorities from 1845 as director of a state scheme for regulating the river Tisza, another brainchild of his, Széchenyi remained an awkward bedfellow as an independent-minded *grand seigneur*, and one whose attack on chauvinism concerned only the *modus operandi*. No one could trump him in the urgency of his underlying commitment to the Magyar character of the self-sufficient Hungarian state to which he aspired: it is typical that his roundest castigation of nationalist

[42] The bibliography on Széchenyi is enormous, and I cannot begin to do justice to it here. A very helpful introduction in English to his earlier career is G. Barany, *Stephen Széchenyi and the Awakening of Hungarian Nationalism, 1791–1841* (Princeton, 1968). The classic account of Széchenyi as reform conservative is Gy. Szekfű, *Három nemzedék. Egy hanyatló kor története* (2nd edn., Budapest, 1922), 59ff. Perceptive contemporary observers are Horváth, *Huszonöt év,* i. 194ff.; Zs. Kemény, 'Gróf Széchenyi István', in *Összes művei,* vol. ix, ed. P. Gyulai (Budapest, 1907), 143–303; and, in English, J. Paget, *Hungary and Transylvania* (2 vols., London, 1839), i. 204–28.

[43] On the *querelle:* Varga, *Kereszttűzben;* id., *Helyét kereső Magyarország* (Budapest, 1982), retailing much of the same information. I. Széchenyi, *A Magyar Akadémia körül,* ed. G. Szigethy (Budapest, 1981).

hotheads was expressed in a presidential address to the Academy which neither he nor any other member imagined should embrace the interests of the non-Magyar cultures of Hungary.[44]

A good deal of the blame for failing to harmonise the various shades of reformist patriotism must rest with Széchenyi himself. Precisely because he was so identified with the movement for change, he held himself directly responsible for its direction and pursued deviants with venom. One has only to read his brilliant, visionary, but tortured prose, in its tempestuous prolixity, clothing the most everyday objectives with real or contrived ethical tension, to perceive the workings of a deep psychological instability. Yet this is much more than just the personal tragedy of a man driven to madness and eventual suicide. For Széchenyi's published writings, struggling for self-expression in the language with which he felt a complete emotional association, alongside the diary entries, where he expresses his inmost doubts and fears in his German mother tongue, are together emblematic of that flawed co-operation between Hungary and Austria on which his whole scheme of gradual national fulfilment had been predicated. The 'mixed marriage'; the two parties 'united in travail by God in His wrath': Széchenyi coined his *bons mots* precisely because he was the completest embodiment of the contradiction.[45]

Let us therefore turn back to the larger Habsburg context, bracketed out thus far in order that we might clarify the domestic issues. I have argued that the main agencies with responsibility for Hungary were native, not alien growths. Yet, of course, Hungary possessed essentially a royal administration, not a royal government; fundamental decisions were taken across the Austrian frontier, with an eye to the needs of the Empire as a whole. That was not *terra incognita* for Hungarians: we find them in the rest of the Monarchy in increasing numbers by the early nineteenth century (their experiences cry out for serious investigation). Some must simply have been assimilated, wholly or partly, especially those who entered the army. Diplomats who served abroad could cultivate an amphibious persona, marrying Magyar panache with conventional loyalty to the Ballhausplatz. What matters for present purposes is that few Hungarians joined the Austrian administration. There were, indeed, certain prominent ones. Several of the Josephinist generation moved on to posts abroad: Mailáth in Galicia and Venice, Ürményi in Galicia, above all the

---

[44] Examples of Széchenyi's national ardour in his *Világ, vagy is felvilágosító töredékek* (Pest, 1831), 63ff., 8off; *A kelet népe* (Pozsony, 1841), 42ff.; *Magyar Akadémia*, 41ff.

[45] The diaries are published as *Gróf Széchenyi István összes munkái*, vols. x–xv = *Naplói*, ed. Gy. Viszota (6 vols., Budapest, 1925–39). Cf. the argument of R. J. W. Evans, 'Hungary and the Habsburg Monarchy, 1840–67: A Study in Perceptions', *Etudes Danubiennes*, ii (1986), 18–30, at p. 30.

ubiquitous Zíchy, who rose through the treasury and the war ministry to become chairman of the highest policy-making body, the Staats-und Konferenzrat. One of Zíchy's successors at the Hofkammer was Mihály Nádasdy, and Reviczky (the later Chancellor) worked there too, as well as in the Austrian provinces. Obscurer officials, like Gervay, could sometimes be found in high places; and it is a nice irony that Venice was lost in March 1848 by a Pálffy and a Zíchy, as civil and military governor. Yet on the whole Hungarian nationals seem conspicuous by their rarity.[46]

So far so good, for—as we have seen—constitutional and practical constraints made it even harder for Austrians to serve in Hungary. But the near-hermetic sealing of the two administrations had potentially disastrous implications for Hungary, since the highest *gesamtmonarchisch* bodies stood at the apex of the Austrian system only. Potential turned into actual disaster because of a further crucial asymmetry: the loyalty of Hungarian officials to the essential structures of Austrian govern-ment was not reciprocated by their opposite numbers, who frequently showed themselves scathing about Hungary and actively subversive of her constitution.

Austrian perceptions of Hungary had evolved with the reform programme of Maria Theresa and Joseph II. The new Staatsrat excoriated her backwardness and obscurantism, her oppressive seign-eurs and noble exemptions (now abolished across the Leitha), which led to an alleged underpayment of taxes; while the very density and comparative efficiency of Austrian administration contributed to a dislike of the Hungarian management of business. Kaunitz was a spokesman for this position; so was Joseph, who dismissed conciliatory memoranda from the Chancellery (when he read them at all) as 'rubbish' (*Quark*) or 'soap-bubbles', resting on 'Hunnish principles'. By the 1790s the Staatsrat gained one Hungarian representative; but the first of these, Izdenczy, turned out to be a very rare example of the totally unpatriotic Magyar. Later advisers, like Somogyi, showed more national spirit; yet the body was progressively downgraded, while the newer Staats-und Konferenzrat proved (despite Zíchy) not much better.[47] Baldacci was viciously anti-Hungarian all the time, the Archduke Charles on occasion. A general lack of sympathy, usually compounded by ignorance and misconception, pervaded these coun-sels, and the distaste for manners, dress, or language could quickly

[46] Here again, as so often, Wurzbach, *Biographisches Lexikon*, forms the prime source, for all its vagaries. Cf. Evans, 'Hungary and the Habsburg Monarchy', 21 ff.

[47] Hock and Bidermann, *Staatsrat*, 143f. (quoted) and *passim*; Evans, 'Maria Theresa and Hungary' (Kaunitz); F. Strada, *Izdenczy József, az Államtanács első magyar tagja* (Budapest, 1943, reprinted from *A Bécsi Magyar Történeti Intézet Évkönyve*, x).

pass into overt hostility, accompanied by propaganda (as in the 1780s and the years around 1815).[48]

Those latter years also saw the emergence of the two most notorious pillars of the *Vormärz* Monarchy. One was the secret police, inherited from the 1790s and directed from Vienna, which used local informers and censors, but proved almost as mistrustful of loyalists as of the opposition.[49] Its antics automatically appeared more grotesque in Hungary for being more ineffectual there; but they highlighted a further imbalance between the two halves of the Empire. In Hungary, anti-Austrian sentiments derived from the opposition and were fairly freely expressed, as befitted an essentially open society. In fact criticism was directed primarily at the censorship and at other manifestations of real or supposed external influence within the country—contrast a marked restraint (before the opening of Pandora's box in 1848) on the nature of Austrian absolutism—and it was partly offset by a certain attractiveness exercised by the city and culture of Vienna, even upon its enemies. In Austria, however, anti-Hungarian sentiments emanated from those closest to the crown, and found expression within the corridors of a much more secretive establishment. Thus Hungarian parochialism, by non-interference, worked to Habsburg advantage; whereas Austrian parochialism meddled devastatingly in Hungary's affairs.

The other pillar, and an arch-meddler, was Metternich, who began by knowing precious little about Hungary at all. That could be an advantage, since he tended to learn through his contacts with the Zíchy family—he nursed a grand platonic relationship with the wife of Károly senior and later married the latter's temperamental grand-daughter, Melanie.[50] Certainly Metternich gave Hungary much attention; it formed anyway a kind of quasi-foreign political issue which allowed him scope to do so. Certainly he played with the idea, floated by the Palatine Joseph, of more estates' representation *à la hongroise* elsewhere in the Monarchy, and favoured calling the 1825 diet.[51]

[48] Baldacci etc.: Szekfű, *Iratok*, nos. 44–5, 49; B. Hóman and Gy. Szekfű, *Magyar történet* (3rd edn. 5 vols., Budapest, 1935–6), v. 177f. A good example of 1780s propaganda is F. R. Grossing, *Ius publicum Hungariae* (Halle, 1786); for the 1810s see A. Springer, *Geschichte Oesterreichs seit dem Wiener Frieden* (2 vols., Leipzig, 1863–5), i. 178ff.

[49] Takáts, *Kémvilág*. For the overall workings of the police: I. Beidtel, *Geschichte der österreichischen Staatsverwaltung, 1740–1848*, ed. A. Huber (2 vols., Innsbruck, 1896–8), ii. 77ff.; D. E. Emerson, *Metternich and the Political Police: Security and Subversion in the Hapsburg Monarchy, 1815–30* (The Hague, 1968).

[50] OL P 708, kútfő 21, folder 3, fols. 90–100; H. von Srbik, *Metternich, der Staatsmann und der Mensch* (3 vols., Munich, 1925–54), i. 238f., 244ff.

[51] For Metternich's 'constitutionalism': A. G. Haas, *Metternich: Reorganization and Nationality, 1813–18* (Wiesbaden, 1963); E. Radvany, *Metternich's Projects for Reform in*

Yet Metternich's constitutionalism amounted only to the conservation of an ancient monument: 'Let the edifice stand, but immure the national firebrands within it.'[52] He became paranoid about change, and myopic about patriots as well as nationalists. In Metternich's mind too, stealth and patience were required for 'the great work of trying to civilise Hungary' under Austrian auspices. He committed a fatal misjudgment in the 1830s, spurning Széchenyi, whom he knew well socially (and with whom he, of course, became related through the Zíchys) as a 'Decembrist', then encouraging the razzia against young radicals. Eventually, in 1844, he shifted his tack, forcing acceptance by his governmental colleagues of the Apponyi–Wirkner *démarche*, on the grounds that 'we cannot allow the stomach to think, while the head merely digests'. But that head remained thoroughly Viennese-centralist.[53]

Those who have tried to exonerate Metternich from this, as from other failings of the *Vormärz* regime, have tended to locate anti-Hungarian sentiment among a Bohemian clique around his rival, Kolovrat. Such historiography rested largely on a misconception (fanned by inter-war prejudice) about 'Czech' influence, and on a reification of personality squabbles in the Staatskonferenz.[54] But it does encapsulate the truth that Austria's administrators *were* predominantly Bohemian, and that Kolovrat's own roots, like those of Kübeck, and even of the chief of police, Sedlnitzky, lay deep in Josephinist traditions there. More serious was probably the rise of German national sentiment, in bureaucratic guise, while Austria's constitutional liberalism—which would, by contrast, seek allies in Hungary—still lay only on the horizon.

One final comment on these Austrian attitudes: they represented a general reluctance to see any Hungarian point of view. It is frequently asserted that the Habsburgs indulged a tactic of divide and rule over the nationality frictions in Hungary before 1848. Despite a vague awareness of the possibility as a *topos* traceable back at least as far as Kaunitz, there is very little real sign of it. Metternich and his col-

---

Austria (The Hague, 1971). Apposite criticisms in Szekfű, *Iratok*, 105ff.; E. Andics, *Metternich und die Frage Ungarns* (Budapest, 1973), chs. 1 and 2.

[52] Horváth, *Huszonöt év*, i. 38–41; Andics, *Metternich*, ch. 3 (quoted).

[53] Quoted from Srbik, *Metternich*, i. 436f.; cf. ibid. 465–71; Horváth, *Huszonöt év*, ii. 274–83; Wirkner, *Erlebnisse*, 146ff.; Szekfű, *Iratok*, 109ff., and docts. nos. 144 seqq.; Andics, *Metternich*, 219f. and chs. 8–10.

[54] H. Schlitter, 'Die Wiener Regierung und die ungarische Opposition im Jahre 1845', *Beiträge zur neueren Geschichte Österreichs*, iv (Vienna, 1908), 241–95; id., *Aus Österreichs Vormärz* (4 vols., Zurich etc., 1920), iii; Szekfű, *Iratok*, 65ff., 106ff.; Miskolczy, *Kamarilla*. Metternich encouraged this view himself: 'Der Tschechismus wie der Magyarismus hatten sich bereits verkörpert; der erstere auf dem Wege landjähriger Caressen von oben, der andere durch ein Erheben von unten', *Metternich—Hartig: ein Briefwechsel des Staatskanzlers aus dem Exil, 1848–51*, ed. F. Hartig (Vienna/Leipzig, 1923), 45.

leagues engaged in a brief flirtation with the Croats, returned a dusty answer to the Slovaks, ignored the Rumanians, alienated many local Germans, and so on.[55] The indiscriminately unforthcoming stance of Vienna's *ancien régime* appears more damning than any belated backing for ethnic groups whose main grievance was the very language legislation which—hesitantly but inexorably—it had conceded.

Hungary's misfortune on the eve of revolution thus lay not only in the domestic impasse between reformers from within the system and from without, which frustrated vital measures and favoured only the advance of the Magyar tongue, that wasting and two-edged asset; but also in the asymmetry whereby the loyalty of Hungarian officials went unrequited, and their Austrian counterparts could undermine it by ensuring that concessions on all fronts came too little, too late. Nonetheless the revolutionary outcome was still extremely remote in November 1847, as the noble diet convened for what proved to be the very last time. The Apponyi initiative, clumsily handled, seemed to have failed; yet the whole conservative programme already went further than had the liberal one earlier, and the personable new Palatine Stephen might still be the man to reactivate a broadened administration, while the Kossuthist opposition apparently lacked impetus in the face of inconclusive debates and still thin Lower House majorities.[56] Even the dramatic events of March–April 1848 may be claimed (as was suggested before) to display important elements of a grand compromise, much of it—apart from the responsible ministry—already on the table, and sealed by a bureaucracy which, formally superseded, actually proved crucial to its implementation.[57]

Then followed Vienna's second profound disservice: unyielding hostility to change suddenly crumbled into a ministry too weak to prevent contagious disorder in Austria, yet heir to most of the anti-Hungarian prejudices of the counsellors it had displaced. Now the military question came home to roost, not so much because of the international situation (for foreign conflict tended also to draw Austria and Hungary together), but because nationalist ferment threatened the stability of the new regime in Budapest; whereas during the

[55] Mályusz, *Sándor Lipót*, 52 n., 387 n. (Kaunitz). I cannot enter here into this subject, where traditional Magyar (and some foreign) suspicion has been much exaggerated; but see, briefly and accessibly on the most pressing and stormiest issue, E. M. Despalatović, *Ljudevit Gaj and the Illyrian Movement* (Boulder, Colo., 1975); and, for the fullest case-study, D. Rapant, *Slovenský prestolný prosbopis z roku 1842* (2 vols. Liptovsky Svätý Mikuláš, 1943).

[56] Horváth, *Huszonöt év*, ii. 503f., 512, and *passim*; Kemény, *Változatok*, esp. 264, 271f., 277ff., 402ff.; Schlitter, *Vormärz*, 55ff.; I. Szabó, *Jobbágyok-parasztok: értekezések a magyar parasztság történetéből*, ed. L. Für (Budapest, 1976), 272ff.

[57] Urbán, *Batthyány Lajos*, 248. A prosopography of the 1848 administration is still lacking.

whole period since 1790 this potentially most disruptive aspect of the Hungarian problem had lain largely dormant, surfacing only in intermittent friction over recruits, training, and frontier guards.[58] And the response of the nationalities derived extra bitterness from another ill-fated contingency: for the Batthyány government came on the scene at the moment of maximum discontent over the language issue, when the full Magyar package had just been granted, but no chance had yet been given to palliate and balance its effects with other social and political measures.

The revolutionary upshot in 1848–9 proved a traumatic shock which etched more deeply the existing presumptions on both sides of the river Leitha. In that respect particularly its results are still with us. Austrian historiography has remained ever since a fair reflection of those contemporary perceptions; and its claim that Hungary was reformable only by Austrian methods and personnel possesses a grain of truth, as the large strides made towards modernisation in the neo-absolutist 1850s demonstrate.[59] Most Hungarian historiography, likewise taking a contemporary perception as its starting-point, has concentrated on the liberal and radical opposition, and seen national salvation to reside in fully autonomous representative institutions. That is a better-directed and more serious assertion. Arguably, however, mid-nineteenth-century Hungary was not really a very liberal place—the insights of a sobered Eötvös and Kemény in the 1850s have much to commend them.[60] Perhaps only the accidental survival of an ancient constitution conditioned the priorities of the *Vormärz*.

The events of 1848 may have swept along many of the younger generation, like the son of Dániel Kászonyi, who became one of the extremest radicals of the day.[61] Yet the settlement of the 1860s—and the Compromise is surely the last of the grandiose reconciliations which we have followed since 1790—was made possible by members of that generation: by a regrouping either of cautiously reformist officials like Apponyi, Mailáth, Bedekovich, Szécsen and Szőgyény, or of moderate liberals touched, however much they might have

[58] Marczali, *1790/1-diki országgyűlés*, ii. 75–132; Horváth, *Magyarország történelme*, 231ff., 309ff.; id., *Huszonöt év*, i. 468–70 and *passim*; Fényes, *Magyarország statistikája*, ii. 145ff., iii. 53–5.

[59] The massive contemporary self-congratulation by C. von Czoernig, *Oesterreichs Neugestaltung, 1848–58* (Stuttgart/Augsburg, 1858), needs to be balanced by the yet more massive modern evaluation by H.-H. Brandt, *Der österreichische Neoabsolutismus: Staatsfinanzen und Politik, 1848–60* (2 vols., Göttingen, 1978).

[60] See particularly [J. Eötvös], *Die Garantien der Macht und Einheit Oesterreichs* (Leipzig, 1859), esp. 43ff., 138ff.; and Kemény's 'Forradalom után' and 'Még egy szó a forradalom után', in *Változatok*, 181–559.

[61] D. Kászonyi [junior], *Magyarhon négy korszakai*, ed. D. Kosáry (Budapest, 1977).

sought to emancipate themselves from it, by the accommodating patriotism of their fathers. Eötvös, after all, was the son of a thoroughly loyal Vice-President of the Chamber; Kálmán Tisza of one of the toughest county administrators of the 1840s.[62]

Subsequent Hungarian governments continued to act in the spirit of conservative reform with constitutional trimmings. They proceeded to construct a neo-Josephinist bureaucratic edifice much indebted to Austrian models ('administrative centralization in Hungary is second to none', declared an informed observer in 1914);[63] they remained fatefully wedded to the old noble ethos of *ancien régime* officialdom; they faced the same insubordination from parliamentary deputies and the counties which in the end István Tisza, taking a leaf from his grandfather's book, sought to root out through decree and manipulation. By the stormy years of that second *Vormärz* before 1914, the Hungarian authorities were as embattled as their early nineteenth-century predecessors, and almost as vulnerable to Austrian subversion, even if their share in running the *Gesamtstaat* had become much larger. It is a quaint detail with which to conclude that when loyalism faced the last great challenge to its vision, the last great choice of options, at the coming of the First World War, the Austro-Hungarian ambassador in Paris was another Szécsen, and in Berlin another Szőgyény.

[62] Latest on Eötvös's background is I. Schlett, *Eötvös István* (Budapest, 1987), 10ff. There appears to be nothing of substance on Lajos Tisza; but Horváth, *Huszonöt év*, ii. 327ff., outlines his machinations, if such they were. For a shrewd interpretation of the 1867 Compromise as a product of traditional 'transaction', see L. Péter, 'The Dualist Character of the 1867 Hungarian Settlement', in *Hungarian History—World History*, ed. Gy. Ránki (Budapest, 1984), 85–164.

[63] Barany, 'Ungarns Verwaltung', 311 (quoting the president of the Administrative Court) and *passim*.

CENSORSHIP, PROPAGANDA AND PUBLIC OPINION: THE CASE OF THE KATYN GRAVES, 1943.*

By P. M. H. Bell

READ 22 APRIL 1988

THE SUBJECT of this paper is not the sombre story of the mass graves at Katyn, filled with the corpses of murdered Polish officers; nor will it deal directly with the question of who killed those officers.[1] I approach these events in the course of research on the relationship between public opinion and foreign policy in Britain during the Second World War, and on the closely related matters of censorship and propaganda as practised by the British government in that period.[2] The diplomatic crisis produced by the affair of the Katyn graves was one in which publicity was freely used as an instrument of policy—indeed sometimes policy and publicity were indistinguishable. Those who controlled British censorship and propaganda, and attempted to guide public opinion, were faced with acute and wide-ranging problems. It is the object of this paper to analyse those problems, to see how the government tried to cope with them, and to trace the reactions of the press and public opinion, as a case study in the extent and limitations of government influence in such matters.

On 12 April 1943 the German news agency Transocean announced that German troops had discovered mass graves in the Katyn forest, some twelve miles west of Smolensk, containing the bodies of about 10,000 murdered Polish officers. Berlin radio broadcast the story on 13 April, and during the next few days the press and radio across Europe—Axis, occupied and neutral—took up the tale. The various reports contained a number of elaborations and inconsistencies, notably concerning the number and condition of the corpses (the

---

* I acknowledge with gratitude a research grant from the Nuffield Foundation which enabled me to carry out wide-ranging research on public opinion in wartime, and a further grant from the British Academy for specific work on this paper.

[1] See J. K. Zawodny, *Death in the Forest: the story of the Katyn forest massacre* (London, 1971), and compare the discussion of the evidence in two despatches by the British Ambassador to the Polish government, O'Malley to Eden, 24 May 1943 and 11 Feb. 1944, both in Public Record Office, PREM 3/353. The evidence indicates overwhelmingly that the officers were killed by the Soviets.

[2] Cf. P. M. H. Bell, 'War, foreign policy and public opinion: Britain and the Darlan affair, November–December 1942', *Journal of Strategic Studies*, v, 1982, No. 3, 393–415.

number eventually proved to be between 4,100 and 4,500); but all agreed that the men had been shot in the back of the neck, and that the killings had been carried out by the Russians in the spring of 1940. The accounts were accompanied by lists of names of the dead, compiled from papers found on the corpses.[3]

The Soviet government issued a denial of the German stories on 15 April, claiming that some Polish prisoners of war had been captured by the Germans near Smolensk in 1941. The Germans had evidently shot these men, and were now trying to cover up their crime.[4]

On 16 April the Polish government in London issued a statement setting out in some detail a story of which it had long been aware. Since 1941, when a Polish army began to be formed in Russia from released prisoners of war, it had become apparent that about 15,000 troops, including over 8,000 officers, were missing. The Poles had made great efforts to trace these men, without success; and the Soviet authorities had given conflicting accounts of their whereabouts: for example, that all officers had in fact been released, or on the other hand that 15,000 prisoners had escaped to Manchuria in 1941. The statement concluded by saying that the Poles were accustomed to the lies of German propaganda and understood the purpose of these revelations, but in view of the details which they contained it was necessary for the graves to be investigated and the facts verified. The Polish government had therefore approached the International Red Cross at Geneva to send a delegation to the site to verify the facts. On 17 April a further statement repeated that the Polish government had asked the IRC to conduct an enquiry, but changed the emphasis by listing German crimes against the Polish people and denying the Germans any claim to use crimes attributed to others as arguments in their own defence.[5]

Any Red Cross investigation would have been limited to identifying the bodies; but the Poles hoped for some advantage even from this. In the event, however, the Polish appeal played into the hands of their enemies. The German government seized the opportunity to announce (on 17 April) that they too had asked the Red Cross to

[3] The Political Warfare Executive (PWE) prepared (29 April 1943) an analysis of Axis reports, with a note on discrepancies between them: PRO, FO 371/34565, C4889/258/55. Collections of newspaper reports from several countries may be found in the Chatham House press cuttings collection, British Library Newspaper Library, and at the Polish Institute in London.

[4] The denial was published in English in *Soviet War News*, 17 April 1943, and published or summarised in the British press on the same date. It may also be found in General Sikorski Historical Institute, *Documents on Polish-Soviet Relations, 1939–1945* (*DPSR*), i (London, 1961), No. 306.

[5] Texts of the two statements, in English, *DPSR*, I, Nos. 307, 308. They appeared in the British press, 17 and 19 April.

intervene. On 19 and 20 April a leading article in *Pravda* and a *communiqué* by Tass asserted that the simultaneous approaches to the Red Cross by the Polish and German governments showed that the two were working in collusion. Following this accusation, the Soviet government broke off diplomatic relations with the Polish government, by a note delivered on 25 April and published on the 26th.[6]

Publicity was thus the essence of the Katyn affair. Each of the three governments principally involved created or sought public attention. The Germans produced a propaganda *coup* designed to sow dissension among their enemies, making a strong appeal to anti-Communist sentiment. Bolshevism was a regime of murderers, and in the event of a Communist victory in Europe the same thing would happen in France as had happened to the Poles at Katyn; yet it was to this regime that the British and Americans were giving their full support.[7]

The Polish government for its part faced the grim evidence of the list of names, which tallied with names on their own rolls of those missing in Russia. Already, through diplomatic channels, by direct appeal to Stalin, and by the tireless investigations of Captain Czapski, the Poles had done all they could by private enquiry to trace their missing officers. They now had to face the reaction of General Anders' army in Iraq, which had only recently left the Soviet Union and in which these officers were known as comrades in arms and fellow prisoners. There were already ominous reports from the British authorities in the Middle East that Anders' troops were losing confidence in the Polish government; and the Foreign Office believed that, with the news of Katyn, there was danger of serious trouble among these troops. These warnings were known to the Polish government.[8] Recent reports reaching London from Poland indicated that any concessions by the Polish government to the Soviet Union would mean that it no longer represented the nation: these referred to territorial questions, but were likely to apply equally strongly to the Katyn graves.[9] In Britain, General Sikorski, the Prime Minister, was already under attack from those who claimed that he was unduly compliant towards the Russians. In these circumstances the Polish government had to be

---

[6] Soviet note, in English, *DPSR*, I, No. 313; published in the British press, 27 April.

[7] For the German propaganda effort, see Michael Balfour, *Propaganda in War, 1939–1945* (London, 1979), 332–4; for references to France, see e.g. *Le petit Parisien*, 17–18 April 1943.

[8] FO 371/34593, C3375/335/55, Hopkinson to Strang, 17 March 1943, and attached papers; C3583/335/55, Minister of State, Cairo, to FO, 31 March 1943; C3623/335/55, same to same, 1 April; C3742/335/55, FO to Washington, 20 April. Count Edward Raczynski, *In Allied London* (London, 1962), 133.

[9] FO 371/34383, C 3345/50/62, BBC Survey of European Audiences: S-E Europe, 10 March 1943. The Germans used loudspeakers in the streets of Warsaw to broadcast the news of Katyn.

seen to be taking action to investigate the stories about Katyn. Inquiries behind the scenes would not do. So the Poles acted publicly, rapidly and independently.

The Soviet government had to issue a denial of the German stories, because silence would be taken as assent. Its action in breaking off relations with the Polish Government, however, might have been kept quiet for a time. Churchill appealed to Stalin to refrain from making the decision public, 'at any rate till every other plan has been tried'. The British Ambassador in Moscow, Sir Archibald Clark Kerr, tried hard to persuade Molotov to defer publication. Both failed. Stalin wrote to Churchill on 25 April that the note had been delivered and publication could not be avoided, giving reasons which were themselves in the public domain—attacks on the Soviet Union by Polish papers in Britain, and the reaction of public opinion in Russia, indignant at the ingratitude and treachery of the Polish government.[10] Whatever the real reason, the Soviet government moved swiftly to publish a decision which could have been kept quiet for a time, to give British diplomacy a chance to find a way out of this phase of the Soviet-Polish problem.

The three governments all used publicity as a weapon, and the British were caught in the crossfire of statements and accusations. Their problem was very public, and its handling had to be a matter of publicity.

To appreciate the nature of the British government's difficulty, we must examine its main elements: the question of Polish-Soviet relations, including recent public skirmishes; the machinery of censorship and propaganda available to the British authorities; and the range of public opinions which were involved in the Katyn affair.

Polish-Soviet relations early in 1943 were very difficult, partly through the legacy of several centuries of history, and partly as a consequence of the events of the previous four years. In September 1939 Germany and the Soviet Union partitioned Poland between them. The Red Army occupied about half the country, taking 230,000 prisoners of war in the process; and at the end of October the USSR annexed these territories. In the next eighteen months, somewhere between a million and a million-and-a-half people were deported from eastern Poland to the Soviet Union. After the German attack on the Soviet Union in June 1941, British mediation helped in the negotiation of an agreement (30 July 1941) which restored diplomatic relations between the Polish and Soviet governments; but this agreement made no specific reference to the frontier between the two states.

[10] Churchill to Stalin, 24 April 1943, and Stalin to Churchill, 25 April, Warren F. Kimball, ed., *Churchill and Roosevelt: the complete correspondence* (Princeton, 1984), ii 193–6; Kerr to Eden, 26 April, FO 371/34569, C4646/258/55.

The Soviet government continued to insist on the boundaries of June 1941, while the Poles held to those of August 1939. These events thus left two major sources of friction between the two governments: the frontier question, and the fate of the Poles (prisoners of war and deportees) in the Soviet Union.[11]

The British Government stood uneasily between the Poles and the Soviets. In 1939 Britain had committed itself to maintain the independence (though not the territorial integrity) of Poland; and in 1940, after the fall of France, General Sikorski's government had been welcomed to London. Polish airmen fought with courage and dash in the Battle of Britain, and substantial land and naval forces served alongside the British. On the other hand, since June 1941 the Soviet Union had borne the brunt of the war, and was clearly going to play a crucial role in the peace settlement. Both Poland and the Soviet Union were now allies of Great Britain. Poland was the older ally, but the Soviet Union was by far the stronger. Moreover, the British government was dubious about both the ethnic basis and the practicality of Polish claims to territories in the east of inter-war Poland. By early 1943 opinion in the Foreign Office was moving towards the idea of Poland accepting losses in the east (probably to the so-called Curzon Line proposed in 1920) in return for compensation in the west; though Eden warned of the danger that Sikorski's government might be repudiated by the underground movement in Poland if it accepted such a loss of territory.[12]

In January and February 1943 the Polish-Soviet frontier conflict was again emerging into the open, with an exchange of public statements between the two governments about the status of the disputed territories and their inhabitants. The British government tried to limit the damage done by this verbal duel by preventing discussion in the British press and foreign newspapers published in Britain. A Ministry of Information guidance memorandum of 2 March 1943, issued at the behest of the Foreign Office, requested the press to use no material on the frontier problem other than that provided by British government sources. The Ministry of Information thought this would not work, and it was indeed only partially successful.[13] Polish-language papers independent of the Polish government published articles on the frontier question, and British Catholic journals vigorously supported the Polish case. On the other side, the London *Evening Standard*

---

[11] On the background of Soviet-Polish relations, see Antony Polonsky, *The Great Powers and the Polish Question, 1941–45* (London, 1976), especially 13–23.

[12] Polonsky, 24, 121–2; CAB 66/34, WP(43)69, note by Eden for War Cabinet, 17 Feb. 1943.

[13] Guidance memo., FO 371/34566, C2905/258/55; MOI Executive Board minutes, 2 March 1943, INF 1/73.

(4 March) published a cartoon by Low attacking 'Polish Irre-sponsibles', and on 10 March *The Times* first leader (by E. H. Carr) took the striking line that 'If Britain's frontier is on the Rhine, it might just as pertinently be said ... that Russia's frontier is on the Oder, and in the same sense.' The Communist *Daily Worker* reprinted articles from *Soviet War News*, published by the Soviet Embassy in London, bitterly critical of the Polish government. The Polish and Soviet Ambassadors both complained to the Foreign Office; but the Con-troller of Censorship at the Ministry of Information only lamented that he could do no more than write to offending newspapers to remind them that they had disregarded the guidance memorandum, whose effect had been to curb comment by those who observed it, leaving the field free for those who did not.[14] It was a salutary illustration of the limitations of the British system of censorship and guidance.

The legal basis of censorship lay in Defence Regulations. No. 3 prohibited the publication of information useful to an enemy, and No. 2D empowered the Home Secretary to suppress a newspaper which systematically published matter calculated to foment opposition to the prosecution of the war. The censorship thus imposed on the press was 'voluntary', in that there was no compulsory censorship before publication; but submission of material to the censor conferred immunity from subsequent prosecution. In addition to censorship under the Defence Regulations there was the long-established system of Defence Notices, which throughout the war included an 'obser-vation' that it would be a disservice to the country to publish discussion of 'matters prejudicial to the good relations between ourselves and any neutral or allied country'. D Notices were for guidance only, as were the Ministry of Information 'guidance memoranda', instituted in 1941. Censorship of broadcasting was dealt with separately from that of the press, and was much more rigorous, with every word scrutinised in advance on grounds of both security and policy, and switch censors standing by to cut off any unauthorised changes.[15]

Censorship represented the negative side of the government control of press and radio. The positive side, in terms of government pro-motion of news or opinion, took the form of guidance and propaganda. There were well-tried arrangements for briefing the press, which most

[14] The Catholic journals were *Catholic Times*, 4 March, *Catholic Herald*, 5 March, and *The Tablet* 6 March. Chief Censor's remarks in FO 371/34565, C2509/258/55, minute by Nash, 10 March 1943.

[15] Defence Regulations are set out in CAB 66/12, WP(40)402, 8 Oct. 1940, and CAB 66/19, WP(41)268, 12 Nov. 1941. Three sets of D Notices for the wartime period are in BBC Written Archives, R61 (Censorship), along with the rules on broadcasting censorship.

journalists and editors were very willing to accept. For broadcasting, the government installed in the BBC (February 1941) two Advisers (Home and Foreign), whose advice was most certainly to be followed. Propaganda abroad was controlled by the Political Warfare Executive, under whose direction the European Services of the BBC operated. When the government had a line which it wished to be followed, there was no shortage of means by which that line could be propagated.

Yet there was a strong sense among those who administered the system that the machinery of censorship and propaganda was in practice limited in its effectiveness. A. P. Ryan, the government-appointed Home Adviser to the BBC, wrote in June 1941 that 'The Ministry of Information is a sop to Cerberus, and the history of animal management contains no more dismal record of failure. No dog has been stopped barking by the Ministry of Information.'[16] Like many *bons mots*, this was an exaggeration, but its substance was correct. Most of the dogs could be restrained for most of the time, but when they chose to bark, as some did about the Polish frontier question, they could not be stopped. The graves at Katyn posed questions which were both sharper and more profound than those raised by the frontier problem. There had recently been much public discussion of Nazi war crimes, drawing heavily on evidence from Poland, and the question of responsibility for a massacre of the kind reported from Katyn would be expected, in most circumstances, to engage the zealous attention of the press and public opinion, with potentially disastrous effects. If one of Britain's allies was responsible for murdering several thousand officers in the army of another ally, who could foresee the consequences? The British government faced an acute problem in the management of news and opinion, with instruments of control which were formidable in appearance but defective in operation.

The problem was compounded by the number and variety of forms of public opinion which were involved. With British home opinion, the reputation of the Soviet Union stood high. The battle of Stalingrad, which ended in February 1943, brought admiration for Soviet fighting power to its height, and its public apotheosis was marked by the celebration of Red Army Day up and down the country on 23 February. Gallup polls taken in March and April 1943 placed Russia first for both effort and achievement in the war, ahead even of Britain, and with the USA an also-ran.

---

[16] Ryan to Monckton, 4 June 1941, BBC Written Archives, 830/37; cf. Asa Briggs, *History of Broadcasting in the United Kingdom*, iii, *The War of Words* (London, 1970), 32.

March 1943   Considering what each of these countries could do, which one do you think is trying hardest to win the war: Russia, China, USA or Britain?

Russia 60; China 5; USA 2; Britain 33.

April 1943   Which country of the United Nations do you think has so far made the greatest single contribution towards winning the war?

Russia 50; China 5; USA 3; Britain 42.[17]

The degree of popularity enjoyed by the Soviet Union early in 1943 was such that the British government would have found it hard to take a public stance against the USSR, even if it had wished to do so. Yet there were also doubts, and a lingering opposition, which might be stimulated by serious accusations against the Soviets. In January and February 1943 the Home Intelligence Reports prepared by the Ministry of Information indicated some anxiety about Russian ambitions at the end of the war. From Scotland, where Polish troops were stationed, some people were reported as saying that the Poles had been neighbours of the Russians for so long that they might know better about Russia than the BBC did. Such opinions were only those of a minority, but Gallup polls showed reservations of a more extensive kind, with substantial proportions preferring a post-war alliance with the USA, and expecting better relations with the Americans than with the Russians when the war was over.[18] There was a group of Conservative MPs who supported Polish interests; and Catholic opinion, led by Cardinal Hinsley and the Catholic press, was strongly sympathetic to the Polish cause. There was scope for anti-Soviet opinion to develop, and a public debate about Katyn and the NKVD was an unwelcome prospect for the British government.

As well as British opinion, there were the various centres of Polish opinion in Poland itself, in Britain and the Middle East, and among Polish-Americans in the United States. The Poles were naturally profoundly moved by the news of Katyn, and the reactions might well be severe enough to damage further the morale of General Anders' army and endanger the stability of General Sikorski's government. The British authorities were also conscious of an ill-defined but sig-

[17] Home Intelligence, *British Public Feeling about America*, q.25; Gallup archives, BIPO Survey 98.

[18] INF 1/292, Home Intelligence Reports 120–123; BIPO Survey 94; *British Public Feeling about America*, q.58. The Gallup poll questions were:

Dec. 1942. If after this war you HAD to choose between an alliance with Russia or with America which would you choose? Russia 32; America 46; Don't Know 22.

March 1943. Which country do you think it will be easier for us to get on with after the war: USA or Russia? USA 46; Russia 22; Same 17; Don't Know 15.

nificant public opinion in occupied Europe. In eastern Europe, where the prospect of Soviet occupation was beginning to loom, the Katyn graves cast a chilling shadow; while in the west, where relations between the Communists and other resistance groups remained uneasy, old fears and doubts were likely to be revived. The British, who had undertaken a prominent propaganda role through the European broadcasts of the BBC, had to say something to their listening public across the continent. Indeed, the British government had to cope with the news about Katyn for all its different constituencies, and what it said to one could not differ markedly from what it said to another. It was a hard nut to crack.

Before looking at how the British dealt with this problem, we must ask what the policy-makers believed about Katyn at the time. With varying degrees of certainty, Churchill, Cadogan and Roberts in the Foreign Office, and Clark Kerr in Moscow all concluded that the Soviet Union was responsible for the massacre. Eden appears to have left no written opinion, but there is no sign that he disagreed.[19] On 24 May the British Ambassador to the Polish government, O'Malley, analysed the evidence in what was rightly described as 'a brilliant, unorthodox and disquieting despatch', which makes painful reading even now. His conclusion was that Soviet guilt was a near, though not an absolute, certainty. The minutes on this despatch within the Foreign Office, while criticising some points in its style and approach, did not dissent from its conclusions. It was given very restricted circulation, to members of the War Cabinet and the King; and Churchill sent a copy to Roosevelt. All this implied acceptance.[20] This in turn meant that British senior ministers and the Foreign Office, in their handling of this matter in terms of news and propaganda, were consciously engaged in deception, or in later jargon, a 'cover-up'.

British ministers who were acquainted with the evidence believed that the Soviets had carried out the massacre, but they could not allow this to affect their policy. British policy in the immediate crisis was simply to prevent Katyn from damaging Anglo-Soviet relations and to keep the way open for a Polish-Soviet reconciliation. Churchill assured Stalin on 24 April that Britain would oppose any investigation by the Red Cross, which in territory under German control would be a fraud. Moreover, he wrote, 'we should never approve of any parley

---

[19] For Churchill, see FO 371/34568, C4230/258/55; Raczynski, *In Allied London*, 141; cf. Elisabeth Barker, *Churchill and Eden at War* (London, 1978), 249. For Cadogan, see David Dilks, ed. *The Diaries of Sir Alexander Cadogan, 1938–1945* (London, 1971), 523. For Roberts, see FO 371/34569, C4464/258/55. For Kerr, see Clark Kerr to FO, 21 April 1943, FO 371/34569, C4464/258/55.

[20] O'Malley to Eden, 24 May 1943, and accompanying minutes, FO 371/34577, C6160/258/55. Cf. Louis Fitzgibbon, *Katyn Massacre* (London, 1977), 193–213, where the despatch and minutes are printed.

with the Germans or contact with them of any kind whatever'. Eden persuaded Sikorski to regard the appeal to the IRC as having lapsed, though neither he nor Cadogan could induce the Poles to withdraw it.[21]

Little more could be done behind the scenes. Publicity continued to dominate the Katyn affair, and it was clear that one of the main things the British government had to do was to devise a policy for the public domain, using its instruments of censorship, propaganda and guidance. What could it do?

Censorship, in the sense of preventing the story of the Katyn graves being given any circulation in Britain or British-controlled areas, proved impossible. On 13 April, the day after the first German reports, the semi-official Polish daily, *Dziennik Polski*, proposed to publish the story and approached the British press censor, who said that there was no legal power to stop it. The Foreign Office News Department then persuaded the editor to hold the story up for twenty-four hours, but they could do no more. The Polish Embassy rightly pointed out that the news was already widely known among Poles in Britain—its telephone had been ringing constantly. If *Dziennik Polski* did not print it, other papers certainly would, and official silence would do more harm than good. In effect, though a Foreign Office official grumbled about the censorship selling the pass, there was no pass to sell. The censors had no power to stop the story of the graves, and if they had it would have served little purpose, with the news all over the European radio stations. There was a suggestion in the Foreign Office for at least a voluntary truce on public *comment*, with the Polish press and *Soviet War News* agreeing to keep quiet, and the British restraining the papers which might act as champions for the two sides. But, as Roberts observed, 'Since the Germans are speaking to the world, we cannot expect the Russians and Poles to keep quiet'. If the Poles did not take a firm line in public, he doubted if there would soon be a Polish government at all; and since the *Soviet War News* had not accepted British guidance on the frontier question, it could not be expected to do so on Katyn.[22] The idea of a truce was rapidly given up.

The Middle East, a particularly sensitive area because of the presence of General Anders' army, seemed to offer rather more scope for censorship. Certainly the British military and civil authorities had greater freedom of action than the government at home, and sometimes they could act effectively. On 18 April Anders issued an Order

[21] Churchill to Stalin, 24 April 1943, Kimball, ii. 193–4; Sikorski's record of conversation with Eden, 24 April, *DPSR*, II, 696–702; FO 371/34573, C4919/258/55, minute by Cadogan, 30 April.

[22] FO 371/34569, C4478/258/55, minutes by Lancaster and Roberts, 13, 14 and 15 April 1943; FO 371/34570, C4664/258/55, minutes by Ridsdale and Roberts, 21 April.

of the Day instructing all units to celebrate a requiem mass for the souls of their comrades who had been prisoners of war in the camps at Kozielsk, Starobielsk and Ostashkov (from which officers had been transferred to Katyn); for all those who had died in Soviet prisons and labour camps, or who had been deported and died of hunger, cold and disease; and for all who had died in the struggle against the Germans. Maisky, the Soviet Ambassador in London, speedily protested to Eden, and the British Commander-in-Chief in the Middle East, General Wilson, went to see Anders and ordered him to restrain all 'hot-headed talk', and to ensure that nothing critical of the Soviet Union appeared in writing. Anders accepted what Wilson insisted was a direct order, and his next formal Order of the Day, referring to the Soviet breach of diplomatic relations with Poland, was moderate in tone, emphasising the need to keep up the struggle against Germany. The British also imposed censorship on the Polish troops' internal army newspaper—though they could not stop the soldiers talking among themselves and with others.[23] In Persia, the British Minister in Teheran, Sir Reader Bullard, instructed the British censors (20 April) not to release any message about the Katyn graves, but two days later he reported that Tass statements on the subject were circulating freely, infuriating the Poles, who were prevented from replying by the censorship stop. If anything effective was to be done, he concluded, it must be at a higher level.[24] But when, on 21 April, the Minister of State in Cairo, Richard Casey, proposed to issue a censorship stop for the whole Middle East area, forbidding any mention in the press or on the radio of either the Katyn graves or the frontier question, the Foreign Office told him that the story had gone too far to be hushed up, and that to bottle up all news would only encourage rumour.[25] This was true. Wilson could assert his military authority over Anders, but it was impossible to insulate the whole area from the Katyn story. Even in apparently favourable circumstances, censorship was of little avail.

Turning to propaganda, the problems were almost as severe. A propaganda line of some kind had to be produced for the Political Warfare Executive (PWE) Directives for Europe, and the closely linked BBC European News Directives. On Polish-Soviet relations just before the Katyn story began, the stance to be adopted was

---

[23] Minbranch Bagdad to Minister of State, Cairo, 29 April and 2 May 1943, FO 371/34571, C4828/258/55 and 34572, C4897/258/55; Minister of State, Cairo, to FO, 29 April, FO 371/34570, C4743/258/55. M. Josef Czapski, who edited the newspaper for Anders' army, said in an interview in May 1987 that the British excluded comments on Katyn from that paper, though the main effect of this was merely to anger the troops.

[24] Bullard to FO, 20 and 22 April 1943, FO 371/34569, C4383 and 4458/258/55.

[25] Casey to FO, 21 April 1943, and attached papers, FO 371/34569, C4458/258/55.

already a matter of great delicacy. One directive laid down that broadcasters should say nothing to offend the Russians, nothing to cause despair in Poland, nothing to arouse discontent among Polish troops—indeed, if at all possible, to say nothing. However, behind the tact the main position was clear: Britain had decided unequivocally to collaborate with Russia during and after the war. 'The Red bogey is a red herring', played up only by Germans and traitors—this was the PWE line, and a joint PWE and Ministry of Information committee agreed in March that the German propaganda campaign to exploit the Bolshevik danger was reaching a crescendo.[26]

When the Katyn story emerged, the line was thus largely prejudged. The expected crescendo had arrived. The PWE Central Directive of 21 April laid down that the story of the graves was part of a German political counter-offensive to offset Allied military successes. PWE must not get involved in controversy, but treat the affair as an attempt to revive the Bolshevik bogey and split the alliance. The BBC Polish services were instructed to adhere rigidly to the Central Directive— 'Silence is the Golden Rule'. News of the Polish appeal to the Red Cross was to be broadcast only in Polish government air time, and on no other service.[27] With the breach in Soviet-Polish relations, this policy of near-silence began to appear unrealistic and unprofitable, and at the BBC Newsome tried to produce a more subtle approach in his European News Directives. He argued that listeners could be divided into three categories: (1) those whose sole concern was to get rid of the Germans, and who feared that the Soviet-Polish rift would lead to a more dangerous split between the western allies and Russia; (2) those who saw the affair as a test case for British attitudes as between smaller states and the USSR; and (3) those who hoped the rift might save Germany from defeat. The main task of broadcasters was to reassure the first category—there would be no split between the allies; this would also disappoint the third, pro-German group. The middle category would have to go unreassured. This was if anything rather too subtle; but its main tenor was clearly pro-Soviet. PWE continued to elaborate its existing line about German propaganda, comparing the Katyn story to that of the Reichstag fire, i.e. a case of the Germans blaming others for what they had done themselves. 'It is our job', stated the Directive of 28 April, 'to help to ensure that history will record the Katyn Forest incident as a futile

<hr>

[26] PWE Central Directives, 3 and 24 Feb. 1943, FO 371/34381, C907/50/62 and C1884/50/62; PWE Weekly Directive for BBC Polish Services, 26 Feb., FO 371/34555, C195/129/55. Special Issues Committee, 15 March, FO 371/34383, C3686/50/62.

[27] PWE Central Directive, 21 April 1943, and Directive for Polish Services, 22 April, FO 371/34555, C3119/129/55; European News Directive, 17 April, BBC Written Archives, OS 137B.

attempt by Germany to postpone defeat by political methods.' On 4 May a special European News Directive declared that the supreme political crisis of the war had been passed, and the main task now was to ram home the failure of the German attempt to split the alliance.[28] This was one of many occasions when a forced optimism was the duty of the propagandist.

In dealing with home opinion, there was less urgency to produce a directly propagandist line, but the double issue of the Katyn graves and the Soviet-Polish breach was sensitive and dangerous, and it was also an area in which both the Soviets and the Poles were keenly alive to any slights which appeared in the press. The British authorities had to devise guidance for the press. The main lines were the same as those used in Europe. On Katyn, Foreign Office advice was that the story should be treated as a German attempt to undermine allied solidarity, and that nothing was to be gained by going into the rights and wrongs of the matter. When the breach in Polish-Soviet relations came about, the Foreign Office urged the press (26 April) not to get excited about it or lend it too much importance: Britain would work to bring the two sides together again, as she had done in 1941. As to the graves, no impartial investigation was possible while the Germans were in control of the area.[29]

The War Cabinet discussed the question on 27 April, and agreed that the Minister of Information, Brendan Bracken, should ask the British press 'not to canvass the Russo-Polish quarrel or to take sides in it'. Bracken pointed out that the Soviet Ambassador was likely to influence some papers in one direction, while the Polish press took another; so it was also decided that Eden should urge restraint upon Maisky, while the Foreign Office and Ministry of Information together should prepare new rules to control foreign language papers.[30] The British government thus resolved on a three-pronged attack on its publicity problem, dealing with the Poles, the Soviet Embassy and its satellites, and the main body of the British press.

Churchill spoke sternly about the Polish press in the War Cabinet on 27 April and he telegraphed to Stalin in firm language:

> The Cabinet here is determined to have proper discipline in the Polish press in Great Britain. Even miserable rags attacking Sikorski can say things which the German broadcast repeats open-mouthed

---

[28] PWE Directive, FO 371/34384, C4287/50/62; European News Directive, BBC Written Archives, OS 137E.

[29] FO to Minister of State, Cairo, 26 April 1943, FO 371/34570, C4665/258/55; minute by Allen, 8 June 1943, FO 371/34578, C6424/258/55.

[30] CAB 65/34, WM(43)59th Conclusions.

to the world to our joint detriment. This must be stopped and it will be stopped.[31]

This was easier said than done. Official Polish government statements could usually, though not always, be controlled—for example, Sikorski had to change a reference to the German 'revelations' about Katyn to 'allegations'.[32] An official at the British Embassy with the Polish government tried to keep an eye on the wide range of Polish papers published in Britain, of which the Foreign Office had a list of 39. Some of these were in effect private news-letters, and it was in practice almost impossible for the British to keep track of them.[33] In terms of law, the government accepted that it could not exercise more rigid control over the Polish press than over the British, which meant that there was a good deal of leeway for the papers concerned. In terms of administrative power, there was talk of using the system of licences for the distribution of newsprint to cut off supplies to a recalcitrant journal; but it was ruefully acknowledged that a small paper could always find a supplier somewhere.[34] The review of policy on the foreign-language press ordered by the War Cabinet on 27 April was not completed until 17 June, and then proved to be a very damp squib. Security censorship was already applied in the same way as to the British press, and it was not proposed to change it. Political censorship, said the report, would be an enormous task, even simply in terms of reading the material; and it would have the undesirable effect of making the British government responsible for everything that appeared—when it had no control, it could at least disclaim liability. The final recommendation was only that the foreign language press should be warned that the government required restraint (for example, in matters likely to prejudice good relations with an ally), and that failure to practise it might be punished by withdrawing the paper ration or the licence to publish. This was accepted by the War Cabinet on 21 June, but was a complete anti-climax after Churchill's stern talk about disciplining the Polish press.[35] In effect, the tone of the Polish papers seems to have been generally moderate in May and June; but that was due to diplomacy and self-restraint, not to new regulations.

[31] Churchill to Stalin, 28 April 1943, Kimball, II, 199–200.

[32] Fo 371/34604, C5032/1389/55, draft broadcast by Sikorski for Polish National Day.

[33] FO 371/34556, C5339/129/55. One enterprising Pole in Edinburgh published two occasional newsletters, in one of which he proposed to run a competition for personal reminiscences on life under Soviet occupation.

[34] FO 371/34556, C5352/129/55, minute by Allen, 8 May 1943.

[35] CAB 66/37, WP(43)249, 17 June 1943; CAB 65/34, WM(43) 87th Conclusions, 21 June.

Another object of British attention was *Soviet War News*, the weekly paper published by the Soviet Embassy, whose contents were habitually taken up by the *Daily Worker* and sometimes by other sympathetic papers. The line of *Soviet War News* was to attack the Polish government as 'accomplices of the cannibal Hitler', unrepresentative of the Polish people and unwilling to lead them in the struggle against the Germans. The *Daily Worker* reproduced and embroidered these accusations, and urged that supplies of paper to the Polish press should be cut off.[36] The Polish government complained about these articles, and found the British sympathetic—Cadogan wrote of Maisky 'disseminating poison'. First Eden, then Churchill himself, sent for the Soviet Ambassador and reproved him—Cadogan noted in his diary that 'we kicked Maisky all round the room, and it went v. well.'[37] This doubtless cheered Cadogan up temporarily, but it had little effect on the recipient. *Soviet War News* continued to publish matter which the Poles found offensive. Churchill told Eden that Maisky should be warned of the dangers of stirring up the *Daily Worker*, and that the paper itself should be told that if it did not 'lay off mischief-making' it would be suppressed again. The War Cabinet twice discussed the matter (on 10 and 17 May), and twice concluded (in the delicate wording of the minutes) that 'it would be inexpedient to offer any advice to the *Daily Worker*'.[38] The British used up a good deal of energy on this issue, but to little practical effect.

What of the response of the British press to its government's guidance? In the early stages of the crisis, between the release of the German stories about Katyn and the breach of Polish-Soviet relations, the press in general followed the lead of the Foreign Office and confined itself to printing summaries of the German claims and the various Polish and Soviet statements. There was very little comment. The *Catholic Herald* (22 April) quoted with approval opinions published in *Dziennik Polski*; the *Spectator* (23 April) wrote that, while the story looked like a German invention, the officers had disappeared and needed to be accounted for. The *Scotsman* (23 April) published a letter from a Pole who had been a prisoner at Kozielsk in April 1940: his fellow-prisoners had been removed by the Soviets at that time, and never been heard of since. There was no formal editorial comment, but the very appearance of this bald and pregnant statement was

[36] *Soviet War News*, 20 and 28 April 1943; *Daily Worker* between 20 April and 4 May, when there was a long article on 'The Polish Plot', by Ivor Montagu.

[37] FO 371/34571, C4778/258/55, Eden to Kerr, 29 April 1943; FO 371/34574, C5136/258/55, minute by Churchill, 30 April; *Cadogan Diaries*, 525.

[38] PREM 3/354/9, Churchill to Eden, 16 May 1943; CAB 65/34, WM(43) 10 and 17 May 1943. Bracken did make a statement in the Commons (20 May) that the existing ban on the export of the *Daily Worker* remained in force.

comment enough. On the other hand, *Tribune* (23 April) reproved the Poles for appealing to the Red Cross—'a slap in the face of an ally who has suffered untold agonies in a common cause'.

Given the nature of the story, this represented a success for government guidance, and indicated that the press were in sympathy with it. On 26 April, however, the breach of relations between the Soviet Union and Poland meant that comment could no longer be avoided. Foreign Office guidance was that the break was a success for German propaganda, which had set out to sow discord, and that Britain must work to heal the rift, as in 1941. Diplomatic correspondents and leader-writers reproduced these sentiments faithfully and even cheerfully. The *Daily Herald* (28 April) struck a nice balance by agreeing that the Poles had a duty to inquire into the German charges, but the Russians were right to claim that an inquiry under German control would be useless. The *Sunday Times* (2 May) produced a near-parody of earnest goodwill: we must aim at repair, not criticism; Goebbels had fished in troubled waters and got a bite from both Polish and Russian fish; we must make a fresh start. Optimism was the order of the day. On 28 April almost the whole press seized avidly on a Moscow Radio broadcast saying that relations with Poland were 'suspended', rather than severed. This proved to be of no significance, but on 6 May *The Times* found fresh hope in answers by Stalin to questions put by its special correspondent. Stalin reaffirmed that his government wished to see a strong and independent Poland after the war, in solid and neighbourly relations with the USSR. This was widely welcomed in the press, with the encouragement of official blessing—it was 'regarded in British quarters as helpful and constructive'.[39] Unhappily it was followed within a day by a harsh public statement by Vyshinsky, accusing Polish relief workers of spying for the Germans and asserting that the Polish government would not allow its troops to fight on the eastern front.[40]

There was some dissent. The Polish case attracted strong sympathy in the *Scotsman*, which on 27 April published a long leading article pointing out that some one-and-a-half million Poles had been carried off to concentration camps in Russia, because Stalin did not want them in his new territories. The whereabouts of most of them, and of 10,000 officers, remained unknown. While this article attributed no specific responsibility for Katyn, its inference was unmistakeable; and it also strongly supported the Polish case on the frontier question. The *Scotsman* published other articles in support of the Polish government, and (apparently alone among the daily press) opened its columns to

---

[39] *Daily Telegraph* diplomatic correspondent, 7 May 1943.
[40] *The Times* and other papers, 8 May 1943.

letters from Poles and their friends. The *Glasgow Herald*, though in less forthright terms, also defended the Poles against charges of collusion with the Nazis and referred to the Polish deportees in Russia.[41] This sympathy north of the border was a mark of the links forged by the Polish Corps stationed in Scotland, and doubtless also a tribute to the work of the Scottish office of the Polish Ministry of Information, which produced a well-prepared news-letter for the Scottish press.[42]

In England, the *Manchester Guardian* was cautiously protective of the Poles: the appeal to the Red Cross was ill-advised, but had been made out of duty to the relatives of the missing men and in response to Polish opinion. The *Spectator* drew attention to the long search for the missing officers.[43] The Catholic press, while acknowledging the need to maintain Allied unity, was outspoken in its support for the Poles. The *Catholic Times* held that the Polish government had had no choice but to ask for an inquiry; *The Tablet* analysed the weaknesses of the Russian case, and emphasised the moral issue: 'We have obligations to truth and justice which must take precedence of politic calculations or the desire to say pleasant things.'[44] In *The Nineteenth Century*, F. A. Voigt produced a closely reasoned discussion of the Polish case, and emphasised that the Polish government in London did not exist 'merely to save the Foreign Office from bother or to placate the Russian Embassy. It exists to carry out, as far as possible, the will of the Polish nation.'[45]

On the other side, the *News Chronicle* took a strong pro-Soviet line, notably in articles by A. J. Cummings, who wrote that the Poles had acted most reprehensibly by appealing to the Red Cross. The Russians were angry, and so was the British government—'I should think so!'[46] *Tribune* wrote sympathetically of Polish suffering and heroism, but quoted Jefferson to the effect that some innocent men must fall in the cause of liberty. The *New Statesman* condemned the folly of the Poles in appealing to the Red Cross, and went on: 'this is not to say that many Polish officers may not have been shot or relegated to Siberia by the GPU ... the Soviet Government, often with reason, would

---

[41] *Scotsman*, 28, 29 April, 3 May 1943; *Glasgow Herald*, 27 April, 7 May.

[42] A set of these news-letters (which began in April 1943) is in the Polish Institute Archives, A 9 III 2d/10. There is no sign that a similar effort was made south of the border.

[43] *Manchester Guardian*, diplomatic correspondent, 1 May 1943; *Spectator*, 30 April, 397, 14 May, 441.

[44] *Catholic Times*, 30 April 1943, and cf. *Universe* and *Catholic Herald*, same date; *The Tablet*, 24 April and 1 May 1943.

[45] 'Poland, Russia and Great Britain', *The Nineteenth Century and After*, June 1943, 241–259.

[46] *News Chronicle*, 27, 30 April, 7 May 1943.

regard the landed aristocracy and the officer class of Poland in the light of Fascists and class enemies.'[47]

This chilling comment illustrates a striking fact about the general attitude of the British press: the almost complete absence of a moral stance. This was in sharp contrast to the treatment of the deal with Admiral Darlan a few months earlier, when the press wrote freely of honour and dishonour, of the ideals for which the Allies were fighting and how they were tarnished by association with a quisling. On Katyn and Polish-Soviet relations, on the other hand, the press spoke the stern language of realism and power politics. The *News Chronicle* wrote (27 April) that 'whatever the rights and wrongs' of the dispute, the over-riding consideration must be the defeat of Germany. The *News Chronicle*, the *New Statesman* and *The Times* all wrote of the necessity and the stabilising value of a Soviet sphere of influence in eastern Europe.[48] Other papers were less forthright, but outside the *Scotsman*, the *Nineteenth Century*, and the Catholic press there was almost no concern to inquiry into the truth about Katyn or to raise questions of justice. It is said that the British press is subject to periodic fits of morality, sometimes induced by stories of massacres. On this occasion there was a concentrated attack of *Realpolitik*. In the midst of a long and desperate war, this may not be surprising; but it is interesting that there was so marked a contrast with the Darlan affair. The major difference appears to be that, while the Darlan deal had offered strategic gains, these were less fundamental and far-reaching than those involved in the Soviet alliance, and so allowed more scope for the play of moral scruples and political principles. In the Foreign Office, supposedly the home of *Realpolitik*, there was serious discussion of the moral issues; but officials were doubtless glad to see that in the press their guidance was heeded, and the issue was damped down.

It remains to enquire how far we can trace the reactions of the British people to these events. Organised, or pressure group, opinion appears to have been largely pro-Soviet. The Foreign Office files retain sixty-one resolutions, letters and telegrams from trade union branches, shop stewards' committees, the Russia Today Society, and branches of the Communist Party. All castigated the Polish government for taking up the Hitlerite lies, making mischievous allegations against our Soviet allies, and so forth. Many appear to draw on a common source, though they doubtless represented the views of those

---

[47] *Tribune*, leading article, 7 May 1943, article 'Bisons and Hooligans', 21 May; *New Statesman*, leading article, 1 May.

[48] *News Chronicle* and *New Statesman*, 1 May 1943. The leading articles in *The Times* by E. H. Carr, and the despatches from Moscow by Ralph Parker, who was deeply sympathetic to the Soviet point of view, consistently advocated the acceptance of a Soviet sphere in eastern Europe as the only realistic outcome of the war.

who sent them. The Polish government also received similar communications (one, from a branch of the Amalgamated Engineering Union, was charitably inscribed 'Yours in unity'); and also a few letters of support from private individuals.[49] In the House of Commons there was the making of another pressure group, of MPs sympathetic to the Poles, but they made no move except in private, at a meeting of the Commons Foreign Affairs Committee on 11 May, when half-a-dozen members protested that the Poles were not being allowed to state their case about Katyn fairly.[50]

For the public at large, our best source is the weekly Home Intelligence report prepared for the Ministry of Information. The first reports, during the week of 13–20 April, indicated that the German stories about the Katyn graves were usually not believed, though in Scotland they were causing bitter discussion and ill-feeling. By the following week, the Katyn question was linked with the rupture of diplomatic relations, and the two issues tended to merge until interest in both died away during the last week in May. Home Intelligence made a detailed analysis of reactions, finding the most common to be that the breach in Soviet-Polish relations was a success for German propaganda, and the next the hope that the British and Americans could mediate. (These reflected precisely the line taken by the Foreign Office and most of the press.) There was criticism of the Poles for being pro-German rather than pro-Russian, and for an over-hasty appeal to the Red Cross; but also anxiety about Soviet ambitions, and unfavourable comment on Soviet speed in breaking off relations. Working-class opinion was said to favour Russia; Scotland and Northern Ireland showed strong currents of opinion supporting the Poles. The reports indicated a widespread disinclination to take sides, because people felt they did not know enough about what had happened; among those who did take sides, the balance of opinion favoured Russia, mainly on the ground that the war could not be won without her. On the issue of the graves, the reports noted specifically that it was the effects which caused most concern: 'Few people appear to worry very much about the truth or falsehood of the allegations; it is the possible results that worry them.'[51] In general, these reactions were very close to those in the press; though there appears to have been more doubt about the Soviet position among the public than in the public prints; in Scotland, the influence of contacts with Polish troops was clearly important.

[49] FO 371/34572, C4910/258/55; FO 371/34576, C5834/258/55; Polish Institute Archives, A 12.49/WB/Sow/4A.

[50] FO 371/34578, C6424/258/55, Wardlaw-Milne to Cadogan, 2 June 1943.

[51] INF 3/292, Home Intelligence Reports 133–139, 13 April–1 June 1943; the detailed analysis is in 135.

The diplomatic crisis brought about by Katyn was one of publicity. The Germans, Soviets and Poles all used publicity to achieve a political end, with some measure of success. The Germans did not succeed in splitting the alliance against them, but they raised an element of friction within it. The Soviets broke off relations with the London Poles in favourable public circumstances, and so paved the way for the creation of a Polish government under their own influence. Some Polish ministers regretted their appeal to the Red Cross as a failure in foreign policy terms, but in terms of maintaining the government's reputation with its own people, in Poland and elsewhere, the move was necessary and successful.

The British government was in a different situation from these three. It found itself in a position where policy and publicity could not be separated, and where any diplomatic move behind the scenes was liable to be thwarted by a public statement or press article. Its instruments of censorship, guidance and propaganda, formidable in appearance, were of limited practical assistance. Censorship was a broken reed: nothing could stop the story of the graves being discussed, though some restrictions could be imposed where British military control was strong. Guidance was respected by those who wished to follow it, including most of the British press, which like the government wished to preserve the Soviet alliance as crucial to the winning of the war. When political commitment or powerful sentiment pulled in another direction, as in the case of the *Daily Worker*, the Polish press, and some Catholic and Scottish journals, government guidance was disregarded and editors went their own way. As for propaganda, PWE was reduced to saying almost nothing. In these circumstances, the British government could only adopt the simple and well-tried expedient of sitting tight and waiting for things to blow over. It may have been the only feasible course, but it was far removed from sophisticated theories of political warfare, and not commensurate with representations of a government controlling all the levers of publicity and the shaping of opinion.

Did the crisis affect public opinion, and did public opinion affect policy? The Katyn story appears to have had little effect on British opinion about the Soviet Union. There were already doubts and anxieties set against the general popularity of the USSR, which were sharpened by Katyn, but only partially brought into the open: only a few elements in the press raised public questions, and MPs remained quiet. The public impact of the story was limited, though it was not forgotten. As for British policy, that was more affected by the use of publicity by other governments than by its own public opinion. The British government was determined not to allow the main lines of its policy to be disturbed: the Soviet alliance had to be maintained, and to that end discussion of Katyn must be damped down. There was some speculation as to whether a different line would pay more dividends. From Moscow Clark Kerr telegraphed on 29 April: 'We know M. Stalin sets great store by public opinion in the United Kingdom, and that he sometimes fails to gauge it aright ...' Kerr thought that Stalin should be made to feel that he had gone a little too far, and had given public opinion a severe jolt. A few weeks later, Roberts wondered whether a strong press reaction against the Soviet breach of relations might not have had salutary results on Soviet policy.[52] But these remained speculations; and we may reasonably doubt whether Stalin set so much store by British public opinion. Damping down remained the order of the day, and indeed the crisis passed, as most crises do. In the long run, however, damping down was not so easy. Katyn reappeared in 1944; then at the Nuremberg trials; and later still in the question of a memorial to its dead. The story of censorship, propaganda and public opinion in relation to Katyn has not ended yet.

[52] FO 371/34572, C4909/258/55, Kerr to Eden, 29 April 1943; FO 371/34578, C6424/258/55, minute by Roberts, 9 June.

THE ENGLISH CAMPAIGN AGAINST LUTHER
IN THE 1520s

The Alexander Prize Essay

By Richard Rex

READ 20 MAY 1988

SINCE the days of John Foxe, ecclesiastical historians of the 1520s have concentrated on the Odysseys and Passions of the earliest English Protestants. Their Catholic opponents, with the notable exceptions of John Fisher and Thomas More, have been largely ignored. The object of this essay is to redress the balance by examining the English commitment to orthodoxy in the 1520s, a commitment made primarily by the secular and ecclesiastical authorities, but seconded enthusiastically by the academic community. It aims not to rewrite the entire ecclesiastical history of the decade, but merely to draw attention to an important though neglected element in the story. Nevertheless, it hopes to be a contribution to the reassessment of the English Reformation that has been carried out in much recent research.[1] The essay is primarily an investigation of polemics, rather than of politics or of popular religion. Beginning with Henry VIII's decision early in 1521 to take up the pen personally against Luther, it draws out the connection of this with the promulgation in England of *Exsurge Domine*, the Papal condemnation of Luther, and suggests a solution to the vexed question of the 'real' authorship of Henry's *Assertio Septem Sacramentorum*. It investigates the continuation of this polemical assault on Luther by English scholars; and examines its international dimension, gathering evidence of the patronage and co-operation extended to Luther's continental opponents by the English authorities. In conclusion it proposes that the strongly orthodox commitment of the English authorities in the 1520s ebbed away only as

---

[1] The current debate about the English Reformation has been pursued in general accounts such as J. J. Scarisbrick's *The Reformation and the English People* (Oxford, 1985), local studies such as M. Bowker, *The Henrician Reformation: the Diocese of Lincoln under John Longland 1520–1547* (Cambridge, 1981), and essays such as *The Reformation Revised*, ed. C. Haigh (Cambridge, 1987). It is summarised in R. O'Day's *The Debate on the English Reformation* (1986). It remains to be seen whether A. G. Dickens's magisterial survey, 'The Early Expansion of Protestantism in England 1520–1558', *Archiv für Reformationsgeschichte*, lxxviii (1987), 187–222, represents a truce, or merely a new phase in hostilities.

the pressing needs of the 'King's Great Matter' occasioned competing, and ultimately conflicting, intellectual priorities.

Our story begins with Cuthbert Tunstall's report of 21 January 1521 from the Diet of Worms, describing Luther's *De Babylonica Captivitate*, and recommending that this and similar works be kept out of England.[2] This report probably led to Wolsey's ban on the sale and possession of Luther's books early that year,[3] and brought to Henry VIII's attention for the first time the work which he chose to refute. Henry was at work on his *Assertio* by April 1521,[4] and the project was obviously known to Warham by 3 April, when he wrote to Wolsey extolling their king's devotion to orthodoxy, and arranging a meeting at Lambeth on 11 April to discuss further action against Luther.[5] This meeting led to the promulgation of *Exsurge Domine* on Sunday 12 May, the public commencement of the English campaign. While a bonfire gave material expression to the condemnation, John Fisher, at Wolsey's command, gave the intellectual justification in a sermon (remarkable for its penetrative account of Luther's ideas) during which he made the first public announcement of the king's decision to refute Luther. As he did so, Wolsey waved a copy of the unfinished book to the assembled crowds.[6] In the days following the bookburning, Wolsey despatched copies of the bull to the diocesan bishops,[7] and there were bonfires at Oxford and Cambridge as it was promulgated there.[8]

[2] *Calendar of Letters and Papers, Foreign and Domestic, of the Reign of Henry VIII* (henceforth *LP*), ed. J. S. Brewer, J. Gairdner and R. H. Brodie (1862–1932), iii, pt. 1, appendix to the preface, pp. ccccxxxviii–ix.

[3] This is known only by hearsay as the proclamation itself does not survive. But it cannot have been issued when Tunstall left for Germany in September 1520 (*LP* iii, pt. 1, 973); nor yet, perhaps, when John Dorne of Oxford sold two books of Luther's in December. However, the interrogatories put to Humphrey Monmouth in 1528 show that the ban was common knowledge by April 1521 (*LP* iv, pt. 2, 4260). A letter from Leo X to Wolsey expressing thanks for the ban, dated 17 March 1521, allows us to propose a date in January or early February (*LP* iii, pt. 1, 1234).

[4] *LP* iii, pt. 1, 1220 and 1233, Pace to Wolsey, 7 and 16 April.

[5] *LP* iii, pt. 1, 1218.

[6] *The sermon of John*, in *The English Works of John Fisher*, pt. 1, ed. J. E. B. Mayor (Early English Text Society, extra ser. xxvii, 1876), 327, 'the kynges grace our souerayne lorde in his owne persone hath with his pen so substauncyally foghten agaynst Martyn luther'. See the Venetian ambassador's report of 13 May 1521 in *I Diarii di Marino Sanuto*, ed. F. Stefani, G. Berchet, and N. Barozzi (58 vols., Venice, 1879–1903), xxx. 315.

[7] *The Register of Charles Bothe, Bishop of Hereford (1516–35)*, ed. A. T. Bannister, Cantilupe Society (Hereford, 1921), 102, records its arrival at Hereford between 6 June and 28 July 1521. J. Rouschausse, *La vie et l'oeuvre de Jean Fisher* (Nieuwkoop, 1972), 137, notes its arrival in Rochester on 4 June.

[8] At Cambridge Dr Nicholas (the deputy vice-chancellor) was reimbursed 'pro potu et aliis expensis circa combustionem librorum Martini lutheri'. See *Grace Book B, Part II*, ed. M. Bateson (Cambridge, 1905), 93. In Oxford the bull was fixed to the dial in St Mary's churchyard, and Luther's books were burned. See A. Wood, *The History and Antiquities of the University of Oxford*, ed. J. Gutch (2 vols., Oxford, 1792–6), ii. 19.

The involvement of the universities is one of the most interesting things about the promulgation of *Exsurge Domine* and the composition of the *Assertio*. In April 1521 both universities nominated senior theologians to attend a conference about Luther convened by Wolsey in London. Though the evidence about this commission is scattered and fragmentary, an intriguing picture of its duration, membership and activities can nevertheless be reconstructed. Its chronological limits are fixed by the election of the Oxford delegates on 21 April;[9] and the return home of the Cambridge delegates by early June. The *Grace Book* gives no exact date for this, but the Cambridge men were reimbursed on or shortly after 1 June; and a dedication from one of them, Henry Bullock, to Nicholas West, dated Cambridge, 5 June 1521, shows that they had returned by this time.[10] The commission therefore met only during May, although John Clerk was later to claim that Wolsey had maintained the scholars at his own expense for several months.[11] The delegates themselves were the pick of England's theologians, combining humanist and scholastic learning. The Oxford delegation included a Dominican, John de Coloribus, who had studied at Lille and Paris before coming to Oxford; and a Franciscan, John Kington, who had been praelector in theology at Magdalen, and later became Lady Margaret reader of divinity. The first Lady Margaret reader, John Roper, also came; as did Thomas Brinknell, who held the lectureship in theology founded by Cardinal Wolsey himself. Two non-resident members accompanied them: Richard Kidderminster, abbot of Winchcombe, a well-known Benedictine scholar, and Edward Powell, canon of Salisbury, who in 1540 died a traitor's or a martyr's death for refusing the royal supremacy.[12] The Cambridge representatives remind us that sympathy with humanism did not necessarily entail sympathy with the Reformation. Three of them, Henry Bullock, Humphrey Walkden, and John Watson, were friends and correspondents of Erasmus, and had studied Greek under him in the early 1510s. Their careers offer ample evidence of their humanist

[9] *Epistolae Academicae*, ed. W. A. Mitchell (Oxford Historical Society, new ser. xxvi, 1980), 380.
[10] *Grace Book B II*, 92, records reimbursement 'pro expensis londini circa examinacionem lutheri ad mandatum domini Cardinalis'. H. Bullock's *Lepidissimum Opusculum Luciani* (Cambridge, 1521) sig. A3v, 'quam [viz. academia] iamdudum in nobis cum eramus Londini eius [viz. Wolsey] nomine, multis beneficiis ornavit, nunquam satis laudata benignitas tua'. The gifts to West on 1 June (*Grace Book B II,* 92) were presumably in return for those favours.
[11] Presenting the *Assertio* to Leo X, Clerk claimed 'Coetum virorum undecumque doctissimorum quo in hunc [viz. Luther] scriberent, convocavit: eosque suis impensis, mensibus aliquot aluit', *Assertio Septem Sacramentorum* (1522), sig. B1r.
[12] A. B. Emden's *Biographical Register of the University of Oxford to 1500* (3 vols., Oxford, 1957–59; henceforth *BRUO*) summarises their careers at pp. 268, 470, 1047, 1053, 1510, and 1590.

inclinations. The fourth man, Robert Ridley, was a friend of Polydore Vergil, and became secretary to Cuthbert Tunstall.[13] Although Walkden died soon afterwards, the other three men remained firm opponents of Lutheranism throughout their lives. Ridley and Bullock both owned copies of John Fisher's refutation of Luther,[14] while Ridley and Watson took an enthusiastic part in the prosecution of heresy in the ensuing decade.

No direct evidence survives about the work of this commission, but it is most likely that its first task was to examine the bull *Exsurge Domine* prior to its promulgation in England. A parallel for this can be found at Louvain, where the theologians had been similarly convoked for such a purpose by Jerome Aleander the previous year.[15] Of greater significance is the probable involvement of Wolsey's commission in the composition or at least the revision of Henry's book against Luther. The timing alone argues strongly for this. Henry began writing in April, Wolsey had a copy of the as yet unfinished work by 12 May, and Pynson had printed it by the middle of June. Thus, the theologians convened in May were ideally placed to assist. There is some circumstantial evidence for this. Scarisbrick's documentation of Henry's wayward, spasmodic, and idiosyncratic theologising of the 1530s casts considerable doubt on his ability to complete a work of sustained, coherent, and orthodox argument at all, much less in a couple of months.[16] Even the dedicatory verses to Leo X, inscribed in Henry's own hand on the presentation copy, were only chosen by him from a selection procured by Wolsey.[17] Although it is clear that Henry began the task unaided, contemporary rumour supports the theory that he received a considerable amount of help. After its official presentation to Leo X, the Imperial ambassador at Rome wrote to his master, 'It is said that all the learned men of England had a part in its composition'.[18] Thomas More's famous remark that his minor role in the production of the *Assertio* was undertaken only 'by his graces appointment and consent of the makers

---

[13] *De Calamitate Excidio & Conquestu Britanniae*, ed. P. Virgil (1525), dedication to Tunstall.

[14] *Assertionis Lutheranae Confutatio* (Antwerp, 1523). Ridley also owned John Dietenberger's *De Votis Monasticis* (Cologne, 1524). See A. B. Emden, *Biographical Register of the University of Cambridge to 1500* (Cambridge, 1963, henceforth *BRUC*), pp. 105, 481, and 681. For Walkden and Watson see pp. 611 and 622.

[15] É. de Moreau SJ, 'Luther et l'Université de Louvain', *Nouvelle Revue Theologique*, liv (1927), 401–35, esp. 416–19. The bull had arrived in England towards the end of March, and was published on 12 May, which suggests there was some connection with the commission.

[16] *Henry VIII* (1968), 403–20.

[17] *LP* iii, pt. 1. 1450, Wolsey to Henry, c. July 1521.

[18] *Calendar of State Papers, Spanish*, ii. 363, Juan Manuel to Charles V, 17 October 1521.

of the same' offers convincing proof that the *Assertio* was not the result of Henry's unaided efforts.[19] Moreover, there certainly was some contact between Henry and the commission. He ordered Wolsey to arrange for him to address them,[20] and in a letter to Leo X of 21 May he took the credit for convoking them.[21] It is certain that Henry was assisted in his work, and there is no more probable source for such assistance than a group of professional theologians in the right place at the right time.

After the theologians had finished their labours in London, they were asked to return to their universities and write individually against Luther. Of the Cambridge men, only Bullock is known to have fulfilled this request, though his effort is unfortunately lost.[22] The Oxford theologians threw themselves into the task. Richard Kidderminster was said by the university to have written ably on indulgences, and Kington, Roper, Brinknell, and de Coloribus were also commended: best of all was the work of Edward Powell, who had written on the papacy, and on the eucharist and the other sacraments. His was the only work recommended for publication.[23] None of the others survives. But this was only the start of the university's reaction against Luther. The local ordinary, John Longland, bishop of Lincoln, was keen in the struggle, taking pains to seek out Lutheranism and Lollardy in his visitations.[24] As the king's confessor he was involved in the plans for the heresy purge in 1525–26,[25] and he preached against Luther in 1527.[26] There is no doubt of course that heretical doctrines surfaced in Oxford. In 1526–27 a nest of Lutherans was unearthed in the new Cardinal's College. But the response was firm. In February 1527 the university wrote to Warham asking him to see that Fisher or Tunstall provided them with a list of Lutheran books for censorship.[27] The

---

[19] W. Roper, *The Lyfe of Sir Thomas Moore, knyghte,* ed. E. V. Hitchcock (Early English Text Society, original ser. cxcvii, 1935), 67.

[20] *LP* iii, pt. 1, 1233, Pace to Wolsey, 16 April 1521.

[21] *LP* iii, pt. 1, 1297.

[22] John Bale, *Scriptorum Illustrium Maioris Brytanniae Catalogus* (2 vols., Basel, 1557), 707.

[23] *Epistolae Academicae,* letters 89 and 90, pp. 111–14: Oxford University to Henry and Wolsey, 17 February 1522. Edward Powell's book was *Propugnaculum Summi Sacerdotii Evangelici* (1523).

[24] Bowker, *Hentician Reformation*, 57–64.

[25] *LP* iv. pt. 1. 995, Longland to Wolsey, 5 Jan. 1525. This clearly belongs to 1526.

[26] J. Longland, *Tres Conciones* (1528), fo. 35r. The sermon was delivered on 27 November, at the start of the proceedings against Bilney and Arthur.

[27] *LP* iii. pt. 1. 1193, Warham to Wolsey, 8 March, reports the contents of the letter from Oxford. Warham's letter is printed by H. Ellis in *Original Letters, Illustrative of the English Reformation* (11 vols., 1825–46), 3rd. ser., i. 239. *LP* follows Ellis in dating it to 1521, but Warham's claim that the Lutheran infection had been contracted from Cambridge (p. 241), and his advice that only the ringleaders be summoned to London,

Lutherans were made to recant, and Dr Richard Maudlyn preached at the ceremony.[28] Another Oxford theologian, John Holyman, who became bishop of Chester under Mary, preached against heresy at St Paul's twice in 1530.[29] Opposition to heresy continued into the 1530s, as conservatives attempted to put academic and financial pressure on evangelicals;[30] and it overlapped noticeably with opposition to Henry VIII's divorce. Several men educated at Oxford in the 1520s later became prominent in these ways—although most accepted, perhaps with reservations, the Henrician settlement. Edward Powell was one of Catherine's theological counsel during the divorce controversy. John Roper, Richard Maudlyn and John Holyman stood against the divorce, as did John Moreman of Exeter College, William Mortimer, Robert Aldridge, Robert Cooke, the Franciscan Thomas Kirkham, and the Dominican Thomas Charnock.[31] Charnock was in trouble in 1534 for writing in favour of papal supremacy, although he was soon persuaded to conform.[32] The Franciscan Kirkham was involved that same year in a pulpit controversy with John Bale at Doncaster.[33] Richard Smyth preached at Oxford in defence of purgatory and other Catholic beliefs in 1536.[34] Away from Oxford itself, Edward Powell, William Hubbardine and Roger Edgeworth were among those who preached against Latimer at Bristol in the 1530s.[35] Later in Henry's reign, Edgeworth was inhibited from preaching, a penalty renewed under Edward. He returned to favour only under Mary, when he published his collected sermons, which included several attacks on

---

while the small fry be dealt with at Oxford (p. 242), clearly refer to the Cardinal's College affair.

[28] Wood, *History*, ii. 32.

[29] *Epistolae Academicae*, ep. 188, pp. 262–4: Hugh, abbot of Reading, to Oxford Univ., 4 Dec. 1530; and the reply, ep. 190, 265–6.

[30] *LP* viii. 799, deposition against Robert Croft, fellow of New College, relating to comments made around 19 May 1535, to the effect that college funds would not be available to radicals. See also *LP* vii. 308, Michael Drome to William Marshall, 9 March 1534.

[31] Wood, *History*, ii. 45–6, and 48.

[32] *LP* vii. 259.

[33] A. G. Dickens, *Lollards and Protestants in the Diocese of York 1509–1558* (Oxford, 1959), 141.

[34] *LP* x. 950. G. R. Elton, *Policy and Police* (Cambridge, 1972), 25, notes that Smyth also attacked the Lutheran doctrine of justification. It is not clear whether this is to be identified with the sermon Smyth preached that year at the recantation of a heretic (Wood, *History*, ii. 65). Further light should be cast on Smyth's intriguing career by Colin Armstrong, of Trinity College, Cambridge, who is currently researching into religious conservatism in the later years of Henry VIII.

[35] *The Works of Hugh Latimer*, ed. G. E. Corrie (2 vols., Parker Society, 1844–5), ii. 225, lists Powell, Hubbardine, the master prior of St John's, master Goodryche, and the Dominican John Hilsey as Latimer's early Bristol opponents.

Luther.[36] The prominent humanist Thomas Robertson of Magdalen, a chaplain of Longland's, was a conservative under Henry; was far from content with the doctrinal innovations under Edward; and under Mary contributed a dedicatory ode to Alban Langdaile's refutation of Nicholas Ridley.[37] Other scholars, such as Moreman, Smyth, Hugh Weston and Nicholas Harpsfield, were put under considerable pressure in Edward's reign, and some preferred exile to compromise.[38]

To turn now to the other university, we are all familiar with the early progress of the Reformation in Cambridge. The White Horse has been flogged almost to death. Yet even though there were ripples of Lutheranism in the Cam, there was a wave of opposition to Protestant ideas which historians have generally overlooked. John Foxe's account of Latimer's escapades, for example, uncovers considerable zeal for orthodoxy. He gives a lengthy list of those who preached against Latimer: Bullock, Watson, Nicholas Metcalf, Robert Buckenham, and Doctors Venetus, Buckmaster, Nateres, Philo, Blythe, Cliffe, Downes and Palms, mostly heads of colleges; four fellows of St John's, Ralph Baynes, John Rud, Thomas Greenwood, and John Brickenden; and a fellow of King's Hall, Thomas Tyrell; as well as Nicholas West himself, the bishop of Ely.[39] Another Cambridge man, Dr Shirwood, criticised Latimer's ideas on ecclesiastical authority a few years later.[40] Latimer at this stage was still far short of outright Protestantism, so we can deduce quite safely that his opponents had little time for Luther. Other names can be added to the roll of Luther's early Cambridge opponents. Robert Wakefield, fellow of St John's, criticised Luther in his inaugural lecture as reader of Hebrew in 1524.[41] And as late as 1534, by which time he was

---

[36] *Sermons very fruitful* (1557). See fos. 19r, 37v and 165v for criticisms of Luther.

[37] *Catholica Confutatio* (Paris, 1556), fo. 2r. Robertson was deprived of his preferments under Elizabeth.

[38] For Edgeworth, Harpsfield, Hubbardine, Moreman, Robertson, Smyth, and Weston, see A. B. Emden, *Biographical Register of the University of Oxford, AD 1501–1540* (Oxford, 1974), 184–5, 268–9, 308, 400, 487–8, 524–6, and 616–7. Weston's few years in gaol under Edward VI are missed by Emden, but are attested by Weston himself in the records of the 1554 disputation with Latimer (*Works*, ii, 265).

[39] J. Foxe, *Acts and Monuments*, ed. G. Townsend (8 vols., 1843–9), vii. 437 and 451–452. Despite the obvious conflation of Latimer's Christmas Sermon of 1525 with his Sermons on the Card of 1529, there is no reason to doubt the names, although some of the heads of houses may merely have signed some written censure of Latimer.

[40] Latimer, *Works*, ii. 309–17, for Latimer's reply. Shirwood, a royal chaplain (*LP* v. p. 315) and court preacher (*LP* v. p. 324), was a noted hebraist (see his *Ecclesiastes*, Antwerp, 1523) who studied much abroad. He incorporated DD at Cambridge in 1526, and can probably be identified with the Shirwood who had graduated BA in 1508 and MA in 1511. See J. and J. A. Venn, *Alumni Cantabrigienses* (10 vols., Cambridge, 1922–54), part 1, vol. iv, p. 65.

[41] *Oratio de Laudibus* (n.d.), sigs. N4v to O3r. Though the sermon is dated 1524, internal evidence shows that it was revised before being published circa 1528–9.

probably a chaplain to Cranmer, he sniped at Luther in the course of a defence of Henry VIII's divorce.[42] George Day (also of St John's, and later university orator) contributed two odes against Luther to John Fisher's *Assertionis Lutheranae Confutatio*.[43] The William Dynham whose epigram against Luther appears in Powell's *Propugnaculum* may perhaps be the Johnian pupil of Richard Croke and Henry Gold.[44] Another fellow of St John's, Nicholas Daryngton, wrote to Gold from Louvain in 1522 enclosing articles of recantation sworn by an Augustinian friar—he felt that Watson, Pareus, Farman, and Latimer would all be interested.[45] Before his conversion by Bilney, Latimer himself had been a keen opponent of Lutheranism, attacking Melanchthon in his BD disputation, and owning a copy of Powell's *Propugnaculum*.[46] John Addison, a fellow of Pembroke, who became Fisher's chaplain in 1522, supervised the publication of the *Confutatio*.[47] John Cheesewright of Pembroke (d. 1537) was an avid collector, and perhaps reader, of anti-Lutheran polemic. His library included works by Cochlaeus, Dietenberger, Eck, Erasmus, Fisher, More, and Radinus.[48] Another Pembroke man, Robert Cronkar, spoke out in the 1530s against Henry's divorce, the break with Rome, and heresy, claiming to have received revelations of dire perils should the kingdom not repent.[49] A fellow of Michaelhouse, Nicholas Wilson, provided the preface to a Latin translation of Fisher's 1521 sermon,[50] and has left notes for a sermon against justification by faith alone.[51] It may fairly be observed that this list locates orthodoxy in the obvious places—the ruling authorities, and John Fisher's own college—but this does not make it any less significant. Besides, the presence of three men from Pembroke, supposedly riddled with Protestantism, should warn us against stereotyping colleges.[52] And the presence of such

---

[42] *Kotser Codicis* (n.d., but c. 1534), sig. F.ii.v.

[43] *Confutatio* (Antwerp, 1523), sig. a2r-v.

[44] Powell, *Propugnaculum*, fo. lv. See also *LP* iv. pt. 1. 1143, Croke to Gold, no date.

[45] *LP* iii. pt. 2. 2052. Latimer certainly, and Farman allegedly, later developed Protestant sympathies. I have been unable to identify 'Pareus'.

[46] Latimer, *Works*, i. 334. His copy of *Propugnaculum* is Cambridge University Library F.9.55.

[47] *Confutatio*, title page verso, letters under the Privy Seal granting the royal privilege to Addison in publishing the book.

[48] M. H. Smith, 'Some Humanist Libraries in Early Tudor Cambridge', *Sixteenth Century Journal*, v, pt. i (1974), 15–34.

[49] He also owned the *Evangelicae Veritatis Homiliae Centuriae Tres* (Cologne, 1532) of Friedrich Nausea, a leading Catholic reformer, which he annotated favourably. His copy is O.2.29 in the library of Emmanuel College, Cambridge.

[50] *Contio quam Anglice habuit* (Cambridge, 1522), title page verso to sig. B3r, dated 1 Jan. 1521 (i.e. 1522).

[51] *LP* viii, 452, no. 1.

[52] P. Collinson, though properly cautious, perhaps makes a little too much of Pem-

scholars as Baynes, Bullock, Shirwood, Wakefield and Watson should make us beware of assuming that Cambridge's militant tendency had any monopoly on humanism.

The role of St. John's in the opposition to Lutheranism is hardly surprising since John Fisher was in effect the college's founder. Nevertheless, it has generally been overlooked.[53] In the later versions of the college statutes, Fisher placed the defence of the orthodox faith among the reasons for the college's existence,[54] and the first generation of Johnians did not entirely let him down. Many examples show how, as at Oxford, resistance to heresy was often bound up with opposition to Latimer, Henry VIII's divorce, and the royal supremacy. Henry Gold was to be executed for his part in the Nun of Kent's treasonable revelations. John Ainsworth died for repudiating the royal supremacy.[55] Ralph Baynes argued against the divorce, and left England for Paris at a very timely moment, shortly before Fisher's arrest in 1534.[56] Dr Richard Hillyard, after urging several northern religious houses against surrendering to Henry VIII, fled to Scotland in 1539.[57] John Rud, having moved to Christ's College, was imprisoned in March 1534 for having preached too mildly on the Nun of Kent. It took a personal interview with Cranmer to persuade him to abandon his opposition to the divorce and the supremacy.[58] St John's

broke Protestantism in the 1520s in *Archbishop Grindal 1519–1583* (1979), 38–9. The evidence for the Protestantism of George Stafford or Stavert is decidedly flimsy. His will is traditional in form, though his bequests of his Greek and Hebrew scriptures confirm his reputation as an Erasmian humanist. Cambridge University Library, University Archives, Vice-chancellor's Probate, Register of Wills, I, fo. 49v.

[53] H. C. Porter is only interested in the college's later history as one of the 'notorious strongholds of factious Calvinist Puritanism': *Reformation and Reaction in Tudor Cambridge* (Cambridge, 1958), 3.

[54] *The Early Statutes of St John's College, Cambridge*, ed. J. E. B. Mayor (Cambridge, 1858), 88.

[55] Elton, *Policy and Police*, 21–2.

[56] *LP* ix. 52, Simon Heynes to Cromwell, 2 October 1535, reported that Baynes had left England for Paris before Fisher's execution. Accounts in St John's College, Cambridge show that he had ceased to draw his salary as reader in Hebrew there in 1534 (Cambridge, St John's College, Muniments D106.6, fo. 65v last mentions him receiving payment on Lady Day 1534). He was still in Paris in 1538 (*LP* xiii. pt. 1. 1169, Richard Brandisby to his brother Peter, 11 June 1538). Fisher was interrogated about his activities in 1534 (*LP* viii. 859, questions 23 and 37). Baynes may have returned to England in the 1540s, as his rectory at Hardwick was vacant through resignation in 1544 (Cambridge University Library, Ely Diocesan Records G/I/7, Registers of West and Goodrich, fo. 72v). But he had not been resident there, and he was certainly abroad again by 1548.

[57] *LP* xiv. pt. 2. 684, Sir W. Eure to the Council of the North, 14 Dec. 1539. Hillyard was elected fellow of St John's College, Cambridge, in 1524. He graduated BD in 1530 and DD in 1532.

[58] *LP* vii. 303, Rud to Roland Lee, 8 March 1534. This was probably also the occasion of the letter dated 11 February (no year) from the Master of Christ's to Cromwell,

as a body sent messages of support to Fisher in the Tower, and, after his execution, for a time at least even celebrated his exequies.[59] It is no wonder that the master of the college, Nicholas Metcalfe, was summoned to London for a menacing interview with Thomas Cromwell in the aftermath of the Pilgrimage of Grace, and was forced to resign his headship.[60] Even so, the college embarrassed Henry by attempting to elect in his stead not the royal candidate George Day, but Nicholas Wilson, who had spent several years in the Tower for refusing the oath to the succession, before eventually conforming.[61] And it may be more than coincidence that two other old friends of Fisher's, John Watson and Robert Shorton, had resigned respectively from the masterships of Christ's College around 1530, and Pembroke Hall in 1534. Both were opponents of the divorce and of heresy, and Shorton had been master, and Watson a fellow, of St. John's. Of course most Johnians accepted the royal supremacy. However, many of them baulked at Protestantism. In 1545, even William Cecil, later the architect of the Elizabethan settlement, seems to have donated to the University Library a copy of Fisher's *De Veritate Corporis et Sanguinis Christi in Eucharistia*, with an enthusiastic manuscript dedicated suggestive of conservative opinions about the sacrament.[62] An orthodox

---

calendared at *LP* v. 798. See also Cranmer to Cromwell, 28 April 1534, *Cranmer's Remains* (Parker Society, 1846), 287. Rud's subsequent career was that of a 'Vicar of Bray', Venn, *Alumni Cantabrigienses*, part 1, vol. 3, p. 496.

[59] A fifteenth-century Wells calendar that passed into the possession of John Cheke and then William Cecil (British Library, Additional MS 6059) has in Cheke's hand the entry 'Exequie Roffensis in Collegio Joannis, iiis iiiid.' to which Cecil added the date 22–23 June. See J. Armitage Robinson, 'Somerset Mediaeval Calendars', in *Muchelney Memoranda*, ed. B. Schofield, Somerset Record Society, xlii (1927), 143–83, esp. 145–6.

[60] R. F. Scott, 'Notes from the College Records', *The Eagle* xxxi (1910), 332, deposition by Thomas Watson, 15 October 1565. 'Doctor Metcalf after the aforesaid visitation ... was in trooble before ... Lord Crumwell, and shortly after I was present in the Colledge Chaple when he returnyng home dyd in the presence of all the fellows resygne the Maystershippe, saying that he was commaunded to do so, whych he dyd with weepyng tears'.

[61] T. Baker, *History of the College of St John the Evangelist, Cambridge*, ed. J. E. B. Mayor (2 vols., Cambridge, 1869), i. 110–11. Wilson was elected on the first ballot, but wisely declined the honour. Day was then elected by majority.

[62] *De Veritate* (Cologne, 1527), Cambridge University Library Rel. d. 52. 17, facing title page, in italic script, 'G. C. Lectori. Quanquam opus hoc grande tibi videri possit Lector consultum tamen tibi velim ut in perlegendo non disistas. Nam si hunc assecutus fueris satis strenuum ac armatum fore adversus impias sacramentariorum sycophantias spero. Vale & Spartam quam nactus es hanc adorna. 1545'. On the title page is written 'Gulielmus Cicyll'. Professor Sir Geoffrey Elton has pointed out to me that the dedication is not in Cecil's familiar hand, and that Cecil is not known to have written an italic hand. But no other William Cecil can be identified at either Oxford or Cambridge at this time. There is no impossibility in his owning Fisher's book at this date. Sir William Petre bought a copy in 1547. See F. G. Emmison, *Tudor Secretary*

treatise on justification was dedicated to Henry VIII in the 1540s by John Redman.[63] Thomas Vavasour disputed at Cambridge in 1549, before going into exile. Having graduated in medicine in Italy, he returned to practise at York under Mary, and was gaoled for recusancy under Ellizabeth.[64] George Bullock, a fellow from 1538, fled to France in 1551. He returned under Mary and became Master, only to flee again under Elizabeth.[65] As J. K. McConica has observed, St. John's also provided several leaders of the Marian reaction, including four bishops—Baynes, Day, Thomas Watson, and John Christopherson—as well as the fiercely orthodox John Young, Master of Pembroke under Mary, and imprisoned recusant under Elizabeth. Thomas Watson and Alban Langdaile published tracts in defence of the real presence. Richard Croke was the first witness for the prosecution at the trial of Cranmer. John Seton, the leading Tudor dialectician, conformed under Henry, broke with the Edwardian settlement over the eucharist, welcomed Mary enthusiastically, and fled to Rome under Elizabeth.[66] Although it must not be forgotten that St John's provided an impressive number of the Marian exiles (21 out of 76 who can be assigned to a Cambridge college),[67] the college clearly had a strong Catholic party as well.

Official encouragement in the struggle against Luther was not confined to the resident theologians of Oxford and Cambridge. The best-known English opponent of Luther at that time was John Fisher, bishop of Rochester and chancellor of Cambridge, a man who already enjoyed a European reputation as a scholar. The sermon which he preached in May 1521 was followed by the monumental *Assertionis Lutheranae Confutatio*, the nearest thing to a complete refutation of Luther then available, and one of the most popular attacks on Luther of the decade. Fisher, like the other English opponents of Luther, was probably obeying a royal command. His *Confutatio* carried on the reverse of the title page a privy seal warrant addressed to John Addison which, besides conferring the royal privilege, commended the book's contents and author. Fisher's remaining polemics, which were like

---

(1961), 220 (a reference I owe to Colin Armstrong). However, though I am inclined to think Cecil did own the book, it cannot be regarded as certain.

[63] *De Iustificatione,* ed. C. Tunstall (Antwerp, 1555). Under Edward VI Redman came to doubt transubstantiation and to regret his work on justification.

[64] Dickens, *Lollards and Protestants,* 218–19. Venn, *Alumni,* Part 1, vol. iv, p. 297. C. H. and T. Cooper, *Athenae Cantabrigienses,* 2 vols. (Cambridge, 1858–61), vol. i, p. 327.

[65] G. Bullock, *Oeconomia Methodica Concordantiarum Scripturae Sacrae* (Antwerp, 1572), dedications, sigs. +3r–+4v.

[66] See Langdaile's *Confutatio,* fo. 2v, for a poem by Seton in praise of that work. Seton himself wrote a pamphlet of verses in praise of Mary, and in defence of the eucharist, upon Mary's accession: *Panegyrici in victoriam illustrissimae D. Mariae reginae* (1553).

[67] Porter, *Reformation and Reaction,* 95–6.

this one published on the continent, all carried the royal coat of arms—which perhaps indicates a degree of official sanction. It seems safe to assume that his *Defensio Regiae Assertionis* (a reply to Luther's attack on Henry) was, like Thomas More's *Responsio*, written at Henry's behest. This more theological reply was largely completed by the middle of 1523, but publication was delayed until June 1525— according to Fisher, because there were rumours or hopes of Luther's recanting.[68] In the meantime, Fisher also replied to Luther's *De Abroganda Missa Privata* with his *Sacri Sacerdotii Defensio*, which appeared on the same date as the *Defensio Regiae*.[69] Fisher's final polemical publications were a second sermon, preached at Henry VIII's request on the recantation of Robert Barnes in February 1526,[70] and a massive defence against Oecolampadius of Catholic eucharistic doctrine, the *De Veritate Corporis et Sanguinis Christi in Eucharistia* (Cologne, 1527).

Fisher did not produce these works without assistance and encouragement. His most active collaborator was Cuthbert Tunstall, who contributed to at least four of his major anti-Protestant polemics. Tunstall's assistance and advice in composing the *Confutatio* were acknowledged in the most generous terms.[71] And he brought to Fisher's attention, and thus ensured that Fisher would refute, a book which had recently appeared under the name of Ulrich Velenus, whose thesis was that St Peter had never been to Rome. Aghast at its catastrophic implications for papal primacy, Fisher immediately replied with the *Convulsio Calumniarum*.[72] Later, Tunstall was to receive the dedication of the *Sacri Sacerdotii*, in which Fisher thanked him for his help with that work too.[73] Finally, in the *De Veritate*, Fisher acknowledged Tunstall's loan of a Greek edition of the liturgies of Basil and Chrysostom.[74] Since the eucharist was to be the subject of one of Tunstall's own polemical publications,[75] it seems unlikely that his contribution was limited to lending sources. The two men also cooperated in other fields, such as the censorship of books. In 1524, Wolsey, Warham, Fisher, and Tunstall were constituted official censors of the book trade.[76] The fact that, as we have seen, Oxford

---

[68] J. Fisher, *Defensio Regiae Assertionis* (Cologne, 1525), dedication to Nicholas West, sixth leaf recto.

[69] The two books were clearly revised for simultaneous publication, as each referred to the other as already written. Fisher, *Defensio,* fo. LXVIr; *Sacri Sacerdotii,* fo. XLIIIv.

[70] *LP* iv. pt. 1. 995, Longland to Wolsey, 5 Jan. 1525 (really 1526).

[71] *Sacri Sacerdotii,* sig. a4r.

[72] *Convulsio Calumniarum* (Antwerp, 1522), sig. A2r.

[73] *Sacri Sacerdotii,* sig. a4r.

[74] *De Veritate,* fo. LXIIIr.

[75] *De Veritate Corporis et Sanguinis Domini Nostri Iesu Christi in Eucharistia* (Paris, 1554).

[76] E. Surtz, *The Works and Days of John Fisher* (Harvard, 1967), 97.

University later sought via Warham the advice of Tunstall and Fisher on censorship[77] suggests that those two did most of the work. When Clement VII was considering convoking a small council in Rome to reform the Church, Fisher and Tunstall were the delegates whom he requested from England.[78] Tunstall himself preached at the burning of Tyndale's first New Testament some time in 1526, and his secretary was none other than Robert Ridley, who was involved in the examination of that translation for heresy. Another scholar to whom Fisher turned for comment was Nicholas West, who was prominent with him and Tunstall in the Protestant 'show-trials' of the 1520s. Fisher was indebted to him for help with the *Defensio Regiae*, and gave him the dedication.[79] Fisher's official correspondence reveals that he was careful to obtain the comments of other learned men,[80] and not only Englishmen. A letter he wrote to a friend of Erasmus, Herman Lethmaet of Utrecht, shows the bishop accepting an amendment from him even while the *Confutatio* was going through the press.[81] And it seems as though John Eck had access to the *Defensio Regiae* before its publication in 1525.[82]

Tunstall was, with Henry VIII, responsible for bringing England's best-known literary figure, Thomas More, into the polemical arena. The *Responsio ad Lutherum* of 1524 was the fruit of a royal request or command, as was More's reply to Bugenhagen's *Epistola ad Sanctos in Anglia*.[83] His subsequent campaign against Tyndale began with the official sanction of a licence from Tunstall to read heretical books.[84] Another leading English humanist, Sir Thomas Elyot, also joined the fray, at least if he really is to be identified with the 'Papyrius Geminus Eliates' who wrote the preface to Edward Powell's *Propugnaculum*.[85] Edward Lee was said to have written against Luther, and to have persuaded the Carthusian John Batemanson to do likewise.[86] John

---

[77] *LP* iii. pt. 1. 1193, Warham to Wolsey, 8 March 1522 (misplaced from 1527).

[78] *LP* iv. pt. 1. 435, Clement VII to Wolsey, 20 June 1524.

[79] *Defensio Regiae*, sixth leaf recto.

[80] R. Sharpe to N. Metcalfe, 1 July (1522), St John's College, Muniments D105.43. Transcribed by G. J. Gray, 'Letters of Bishop Fisher, 1521–3', *The Library*, 3rd ser., xv (1913), 142–5.

[81] Gemeentelijke Archiefdienst, Gouda, MS 959, pp. 15–23. Printed in J. Fisher, *Opera Omnia* (Würzburg, 1597), 1704–07. For Lethmaet see *Contemporaries of Erasmus*, ed. P. G. Bietenholz and T. B. Deutscher (3 vols., Toronto, 1985–7), ii. 327–8.

[82] *Enchiridion Locorum Communum*, ed. P. Fraenkel (Corpus Catholicorum xxxiv, Münster, 1979), p. 24*.

[83] R. Marius, *Thomas More: a biography* (New York, 1984), 326.

[84] *LP* iv. pt. 2. 4028.

[85] C. M. Bouck argued convincingly for this in 'On the Identity of Papyrius Geminus Eleates', *Transactions of the Cambridge Bibliographical Society*, ii (1958), 352–8.

[86] *Erasmi Epistolae*, (*EE*), ed. P. S. Allen, (12 vols., Oxford, 1906–17), iv letter (ep.) 1064, to Oecolampadius, c. 5 Feb. 1520, 'Eduuardo, qui et in sex positiones Lutheri

Fisher informs us that, among others, his former Cambridge tutor, William Melton, had written some as yet unpublished tracts against Luther.[87] Melton's interest in polemical theology is confirmed by the inventory of his library, which included Fisher's *Confutatio*, *Sacri Sacerdotii*, and *De Veritate*, as well as another tract against Luther which cannot be certainly identified.[88] Queen Catherine's Spanish confessor, the Observant Franciscan Alphonsus de Villasancta, published treatises against Luther on indulgences, and against Melanchthon on free will.[89] The satirist John Skelton reproved the unorthodox tendencies of some of the younger members of the universities in his *A replycacion agaynst certayne yong scolers* (c. 1528). Even Richard Pace, the king's secretary, played his part, with a Latin translation of Fisher's sermon against Luther, which he sent to Leo X on 1 June 1521.[90] This translation was subsequently published at the Cambridge press of John Siberch in January 1522. Siberch published another book (with a dedication to Nicholas West) which fits into the polemical campaign of those years, a sermon on the eucharist (*De Sacramento Altaris*, Cambridge, 1521) by the thirteenth-century archbishop Baldwin of Canterbury, upholding transubstantiation, the sacrifice of the mass, and the special priesthood.

As early as 1521 the English campaign against Luther had had an international dimension. Copies of the latest anti-Lutheran works printed in Rome were sent to England for Henry, Wolsey, and their scholars to consider. In March, Giglis sent an unnamed polemic against Luther,[91] and on 12 July Ghinucci presented Wolsey with Cajetan's *Responsiones*, which he had received from de' Medici.[92] Tunstall's mission to the Diet of Worms was of course overshadowed by the Lutheran question. In the following years, there was much contact between England and Europe, in both the polemical and the political spheres, in the struggle against Lutheranism. Henry's *Assertio* played a major role in establishing this contact, and in creating for England a reputation of commitment to orthodoxy. As a Latin work, it was aimed at a European readership, and it enjoyed considerable early

---

scripsit'. Bale, *Catalogus* i. 709. L. E. Whatmore claims there is a copy of Batemanson's book, printed at Paris in 1538, in the Bodleian Library (see *The Carthusians under King Henry VIII*, Analecta Cartusiana cix (Salzburg, 1983, p. 12)), but I have found no trace of it.

[87] *De Veritate*, sig. BB4r, 'Guillielmus Meltonus Eboracensis ecclesiae Cancellarius, theologus eximius, qui de quibusdam capitibus haeresum Lutheri scripsit. Sed liber eius haud dum praelo commissus est, sicut nec aliorum plurimi'.

[88] *Testamenta Eboracensia V* (Surtees Society lxxix, 1884), 258–9. The vaguely entitled 'Disputacio contra Lutherum' could well be Henry's *Assertio*.

[89] *De Libero Arbitrio* (1523); and *Problema Indulgentiarum* (1523).

[90] *Monumenta Reformationis Germaniae*, ed. P. Balan (Berlin, 1883), letter 98.

[91] *LP* iii. pt. 1. 1204, Giglis to Pace, 29 March 1521.

[92] *LP* iii. pt. 1. 1411.

success. It was the first widely selling book against Luther, running in a short time to ten editions, and soon appearing in German translations by Thomas Murner and Jerome Emser. Luther's reply, the *Contra Henricum Regem Angliae* (Wittenberg, 1522), elicited from Henry a letter to the German princes, urging them to redoubled efforts against Luther, and castigating the antimonarchical sentiments which he thought underlay Luther's attack on him.[93]

The *Contra Henricum* spurred a number of Catholic polemicists to Henry's defence. Among them was Thomas Murner, who visited England in August 1522 to present his work to Henry in person.[94] He was suitably rewarded with a gift of a hundred pounds on the instructions of Henry, who was anxious that he should return to Germany as soon as possible to continue his labours.[95] Murner travelled back with the embassy of Henry Parker (Lord Morley) and Edward Lee (the king's almoner),[96] and all three were entertained by Fisher at Rochester on their outward journey.[97] Murner was a great admirer of Fisher's work, and in his defence of the mass drew heavily on the *Confutatio*, as was pointed out by Martin Bucer in a subsequent reply.[98] The embassy with which Murner returned to Germany was carrying royal patronage for another continental opponent of Luther. This author, Johannes Fabri (vicar-general of Constance), whose *Malleus Haeresim Lutheri* had appeared earlier that year at Rome, was rewarded with a royal chaplaincy (although there may also have been diplomatic motives behind this generosity, as he was a close adviser to Ferdinand of Hungary).[99] Some years later, in 1527, Fabri came to England as leader of an embassy from Ferdinand, to urge Henry to go on crusade. During his visit, he received a copy of a sermon against the worship of saints which Oecolampadius had preached on All Saints, 1526. This sermon was filled with invective against Fabri, who had engaged Oecolampadius in disputation shortly before. He therefore composed a reply, dated London, 1 April 1527, in which he praised the orthodoxy of his English hosts.[100] Other minor European polemicists who received English patronage in these years included the scholastic Jacob Latomus, who wrote against the *Oeconomica Christiana* at the instigation of his former pupil at Louvain, Oliver Pole,

---

[93] *LP* iv. pt. 1. 40, misplaced in 1524.

[94] *Ob der Kunig us Engelland ein Lugner sey oder der Luther* (Strasburg, 1522).

[95] *LP* iii. pt. 2. 3270, More to Wolsey, 26 Aug. 1523.

[96] *LP* iii. pt. 2. 3390, Morley to Wolsey, 4 Oct. 1523.

[97] *LP* iii. pt. 2. 3373, Morley to Wolsey, Sept. 1523.

[98] *De Caena Dominica*, in *Martini Buceri Opera Latina*, volume I, ed. C. Augustijn, P. Fraenkel and M. Lienhard. (Studies in Medieval and Reformation Thought, xxx, Leiden, 1976), 6, 10, and 17.

[99] *LP* iii. pt. 2. 3630, Fabri to Henry, 12 Dec. 1523, a letter of thanks.

[100] *De Intercessione Sanctorum*, in *Opuscula* (Leipzig, 1538).

archdeacon of Lewes;[101] and the humanist George Witzel, an early revert from Lutheranism, who received financial assistance from Edward Lee in 1534.[102]

The linchpin of the English response to Luther's attack on Henry was Erasmus. In 1523, Erasmus's English correspondents all sang the same tune, presumably one called by the court. Tunstall's letter of 5 June 1523 told him of the king's relief that he had wholly disowned Luther's vitriolic reply; and urged upon him Henry's anxiety that he should make public his opposition to Luther. This letter touched on Luther's denial of free will, and may have given Erasmus the idea of treating this subject.[103] By early 1524 Erasmus had completed a draft of his *De Libero Arbitrio Diatriba* against Luther. Perhaps aware of the co-operative nature of the English campaign, he sent a copy to Henry 'for you and other scholars to consider' before publication.[104] When the *Diatriba* was published at Basel in September, he sent out two special batches, one to Rome, the other to England. In a letter to Gianmatteo Giberti, he mentioned that he had contemplated dedicating the book to Wolsey (in fact, there was no dedication).[105] Erasmus clearly regarded Rome and England as the places it was most important to satisfy about his orthodoxy.

Erasmus was by no means the only major continental scholar who enjoyed English patronage or encouragement in writing against Luther. Another was John Eck, one of Luther's earliest opponents. He too had published a defence of Henry VIII against Luther,[106] and in August 1525 he left Ingolstadt accompanied only by his dog[107] for a tour of the Lower Rhine and England, in order to see for himself how well or ill orthodoxy was faring in those regions. In England he was introduced to Henry VIII, Fisher, More, and Polydore Vergil,

---

[101] Latomus, *De Fide et Operibus, et De Institutis Monasticis*, dedication to the reader, 6 June 1530. See his *Opera Omnia* (Louvain, 1550), fo. 133r.

[102] Cochlaeus to Aleander, 23 April 1534, printed in W. Friedensburg, 'Beisträge zum Briefwechsel der Katholischen Gelehrten Deutschlands im Reformationszeitalter,' *Zeitschrift für Kirchengeschichte* xviii (1898), 247–8.

[103] *EE*, v. ep. 1367, pp. 290–3, esp. 292.

[104] *EE* v. ep. 1430, pp. 417–18. 'Si gustus operis probabitur maiestati tuae caeterisque doctis, absoluemus et alicubi excudiendum curabimus'.

[105] *EE* v. 1481, 2 Sept. 1524. See also eps. 1482 to Aleander, and 1483 to Hezius. For the English batch, see eps. 1486, to Wolsey (2 Sept.); 1487, to Tunstall; 1488, to Warham; and 1489, to Fisher (all of 4 Sept.); and 1493, to Henry (6 Sept.).

[106] *Asseritur hic invictissimi Angliae regis liber de sacramentis* (Rome, 1523).

[107] William Hay of King's College, Aberdeen, recorded that Eck made his journey disguised with lay clothes and a thick beard (because he wished to pass through Reformed territories), and accompanied by his dog. See J. C. Barry, 'William Hay of Aberdeen: A Sixteenth Century Scottish Theologian and Canonist', *The Innes Review* ii (1951), p. 96. I owe this curious reference to Colin Armstrong.

and his welcome led him to outstay his schedule.[108] Fisher wrote to his lord, Duke William of Bavaria, apologising for keeping Eck in England longer than had been planned.[109] More gave him a copy of his *Responsio*, letting him into the secret of its authorship, and Henry gave him twenty pounds.[110] Eck's chief claim to fame was the single best-selling book against Luther of the 1520s (and indeed of the whole century), the *Enchiridion Locorum Communum* of 1525. The *Enchiridion*, which ran for more than 100 editions, was a hand-book of scriptural and patristic citations and pithy knock-down arguments to be used in controversies. The first edition was dedicated to Henry himself, who took pride of place in the list of sources from whom Eck had derived his material. Fisher came third on this list, and calculations based on the recent critical edition of Eck's work suggest that he might have taken as much as a fifth of his material from Henry and Fisher.[111] Although little further evidence of Eck's connections with England survives, it is known that his nephew Severinus came to study under Fisher at Rochester, and died there in the 'sweat' of 1528. Fisher wrote a letter of condolence to his uncle.[112] It is also interesting to note that an edition of the *Enchiridion* was published by an English bookseller, Henry Pepwell, who payed for its printing by Hillenius of Antwerp,[113] and that the book continued to circulate in England even after the break with Rome.[114]

In the few years after 1521, the problem of Lutheranism seemed to be under control in England. Because of the language barrier, Lutheranism was mostly confined to the German merchants and to the academic or clerical classes. The book-burnings of 1521 and the strong opposition to Lutheranism in the academic sphere seem to have prevented it making great headway. But in late 1525 circumstances conspired to give the English government the impression that a Lutheran plot to subvert the realm was under way. On 1 September, Luther himself, misinformed by the king of Denmark that Henry was becoming favourable to his ideas, wrote to Henry apologising for the bitterness of his reply to the *Assertio*. At about the same time, one of Luther's lieutenants, John Bugenhagen, wrote his *Epistola ad Sanctos in Anglia*, urging English Lutherans to bear up and hope for deliverance. The picture was further blackened for the English authorities

---

[108] Eck to Clement VII (17 Sept. 1525), ep. 255 in Balan, *Monumenta*, 538–40, describes his tour.

[109] T. E. Bridgett, *Blessed John Fisher* (1888), 114–16.

[110] H. S. Herbrüggen, 'A Letter of Dr Johann Eck to Thomas More,' *Moreana*, ii, no. 8 (1965), 51–8, esp. p. 53.

[111] J. Eck, *Enchiridion*, p. 2. This critical edition attempts to identify Eck's sources.

[112] *Enchiridion*, p. 300.

[113] *Enchiridion Locorum Communum* (Antwerp, 1531), title page.

[114] *LP* vii. 1307; viii, 799 and ix. 846.

by the sermons preached in Cambridge that Christmas by Barnes and Latimer. Most importantly of all, news came from Cologne that two Englishmen were preparing an English translation of the New Testament. Rumours of this reached Edward Lee, then at Bordeaux on his way to Spain, in December 1525. He wrote home recommending firm and prompt action.[115] Wolsey decided to carry out a thorough purge, which is outlined in a letter from Longland to Wolsey of 5 January 1526.[116] The premises of the Hanse merchants were to be raided; proclamations against heretical books were to be renewed; and there was to be a book-burning at St Paul's. The book-burning was held on 26 February, when Barnes publicly recanted his heresy. At Henry's suggestion, Fisher preached the sermon, which was subsequently printed (*A sermon had at Paulis*, n.d.). But it was also felt necessary to respond to this Lutheran conspiracy on the theological level. Thomas More composed a reply to the letter of Bugenhagen,[117] and Cochlaeus published his own reply to it at Cologne in February 1526.[118] A reply to Luther seems to have been commissioned from Juan Luis Vives, who sent a draft to Henry from Bruges on 13 July 1526.[119] In August Wolsey was arranging to have this sent to various foreign princes.[120] He insisted on sending with it copies of Luther's original letter, which therefore had to be retrieved from Thomas More.[121] The letters were despatched on 31 October to the duke of Saxony, the archbishop of Mainz, and the pope.[122] Duke Georg received his in December, and generously forwarded a copy to Luther in time for Christmas.[123] Both the archbishop and the pope ordered Henry's reply to be printed.[124]

The episode of Tyndale's New Testament sealed English connections with one of Luther's most prolific opponents, John Cochlaeus,

---

[115] *LP* iv. pt. 1. 1802 and 1803, Lee to Henry VIII and Wolsey, 2 Dec. 1525.

[116] *LP* iv. pt. 1. 995.

[117] Marius, *Thomas More*, 326.

[118] *Epistola Iohannis Bugenhagii Pomeranii ad Anglos. Responsio Iohannis Cochlaei* (n.p., 1526).

[119] *LP* iv. pt. 2. 3261, Vives to Henry VIII. *LP* dates this to 1527, but P. Smith argued convincingly for 1526 in 'Luther and Henry VIII,' *E.H.R.*, xxv (1910), 656–69, esp. p. 663. See also D. Birch, *Early Reformation English Polemics* (Salzburg, 1983) p. 27.

[120] *LP* iv. pt. 2. 2371, Wolsey to Henry VIII, 4 Aug. 1526.

[121] *LP* iv. pt. 2. 2420, Knight to Wolsey, 21 Aug. 1526.

[122] *LP* iv. pt. 2. 2668, John Wallop to Wolsey from Cologne, reported forwarding the copies for Saxony and Mainz.

[123] *LP* iv. pt. 2. 3697, Duke Georg to Henry, 27 Dec. 1526 (misplaced in 1527).

[124] *LP* iv. pt. 2. 2776, Albert of Mainz to Henry, 3 Jan. 1527; and 3031, Campeggio to Henry, 10 April 1527. It ran to eleven editions. See W. Klaiber, *Katholische Kontroverstheologen und Reformer des 16. Jahrhunderts* (Reformationsgeschichtliche Studien und Texte 116), 136.

a minor humanist,[125] a tireless polemicist, and a letter-writer on an almost Erasmian scale. His original interest in English affairs had been inspired by Henry's *Assertio*, of which he had written a defence (although this was never published).[126] The opportunity to establish good relations with England came in 1525, when he went to Cologne to work with Peter Quentell (the leading Catholic printer and publisher of the decade) on a complete edition of the scriptural commentaries of Rupert of Deutz, a twelfth-century Benedictine who had been claimed temerariously as a proto-Protestant. This project brought him into contact with the printers and booksellers of Cologne, from whom he heard of a clandestine plot to 'turn England Lutheran willy-nilly'.[127] Judicious generosity with wine enabled him to discover that an edition of 3000 copies of an English New Testament was being produced. Cochlaeus took his information to Herman Rinke, a City father, and a supporter of English political interests in the Empire. Rinke and the City Council tried to track down the press, but only succeeded in driving it from the city.[128] Nevertheless, Rinke and Cochlaeus wrote to warn the English authorities, who, as we have seen, acted promptly on the information.[129] Cochlaeus then set out to capitalise on this connection, dedicating various volumes of his Rupert edition to Henry, Wolsey, Fisher, Tunstall, and West—central figures in the campaign against Luther.[130] The first batch were forwarded on 30 September 1526, by Sir John Wallop, the English representative in Cologne, to Henry, Wolsey, and Fisher.[131] Cochlaeus probably

---

[125] For a sympathetic account of Cochlaeus, see R. Bäumer, 'Johannes Cochlaeus (1479–1552),' *Katholische Theologen der Reformationszeit*, ed. E. Iserloh (2 vols., Münster, 1984), i. 73–81. For a less sympathetic treatment, G. Wiedermann, 'Cochlaeus as Polemicist,' *Seven-Headed Luther* ed. P. N. Brooks (Oxford, 1983), 195–205.

[126] Letter to Henry VIII, 26 Aug. 1529, in J. H. Pollen, 'Johannes Cochläus an König Heinrich VIII von England und Thomas Morus,' *Römische Quartalschrift*, xiii (1899), 43–9, esp. p. 44.

[127] J. Cochlaeus, *Commentaria ... de actis et scriptis Martini Lutheri* (Mainz, 1549), p. 134, tells the story, noting the Lutheran boast, 'Velint Nolint Rex et Cardinalis Angliae, totam Angliam brevi fore Lutheranam'.

[128] This explodes the common misconception that Tyndale's translation was being printed by (of all people!) Peter Quentell. J. N. Bakhuisen van den Brink names Quentell as the printer in his 'Ratramn's Eucharistic Doctrine and its Influence in Sixteenth-Century England', *Studies in Church History*, ii (1965), 65, without giving any authority, but the error goes back at least to 1870. Its ultimate origin was doubtless a careless reading of Cochlaeus. The notion that these events took place in 1524 also has no basis in the records.

[129] Cochlaeus, *Commentaria*, 134.

[130] The various works of Rupert included: *In Apocalypsim Johannis*, dedicated to Henry VIII; *De Glorificatione Trinitatis*, to Fisher; *In Cantica Canticorum*, to Tunstall, from Henry Abbot of Deutz (all Cologne, 1526); *De Operibus Sanctae Trinitatis* (Cologne, 1528), to Wolsey, from Franz Birckmann; and *De Victoria Verbi Dei* (Cologne, 1529), to West.

[131] British Library Cottonian MS Vitellius B. xxi. fo. 11. See *LP* iv. part 2. 2530.

came into contact with Tunstall and Robert Ridley at this time. He heard that Tunstall had delivered the sermon at a conflagration of more than 2000 copies of the Tyndale New Testament,[132] and we know that Ridley also was concerned in this affair.[133] Ridley was to receive two dedications from Cochlaeus. The first was *Aliquot Articulis* (n.p., 1527), a refutation of Anabaptist errors;[134] the other was an edition of Isidore of Seville's *De Ecclesiasticis Officiis*. In this latter work, Cochlaeus testified to a regular correspondence with Ridley.[135] Although it is notoriously difficult to argue from printed dedications to personal relationships, we may do so legitimately in this case not only because of the sheer number of dedications to English patrons— fourteen—but because of the tantalising references they contain to a mostly lost correspondence.

Cochlaeus's closest friend in England was John Fisher. Their connection originated with Fisher's *Confutatio*. Impressed beyond measure by the work, Cochlaeus immediately published some of its articles in a German translation,[136] and would have translated the whole book could he have found a publisher. The following year, Cochlaeus made contact with Fisher by dedicating to him a reply to Luther's attack on the peasants.[137] The two men became regular correspondents, and a few fragments of their letters survive. Cochlaeus kept Fisher informed about progress on his edition of Rupert,[138] and presumably also on the spread of Lutheranism. He may have been responsible for persuading Fisher to write against Oecolampadius, for he was certainly in correspondence with him about the Swiss Reformer in 1526. He exchanged several letters with the Lutheran Bilibald Pirckheimer on this subject, reporting to Pirckheimer that Fisher was at work on a refutation of Oecolampadius, and sending Fisher a copy of Pirckheimer's similar effort. He later told Pirckheimer of Fisher's opinion that it was good 'in so far as it is Catholic'[139]—a thrust at the Lutheran's rejection of transubstantiation. Cochlaeus's interest in Fisher's *De Veritate* bore fruit in 1528, when he translated its five lengthy prefaces

---

[132] Cochlaeus, *Commentaria*, p. 135.

[133] BL Cotton MS Cleopatra E. v. fo. 392. See *LP* iv. part 2. 3960.

[134] The preface of this very rare book is reprinted in Cochlaeus's *Commentaria*, 172–4.

[135] *Beati Isidori ... De Ecclesiasticis Officiis* (Leipzig, 1534), dedication to Ridley (sigs. A1v to A2v).

[136] *Von dem hochgelehrten geistlichen bischoff Jo von Roffen uss Engelland, seines grosen nutzichen buchs zwei artickeln verteutscht von Doctor Jo. Cochleus* (Strasbourg, 1524).

[137] *Adversus Latrocinantes et Raptorias Cohortes Rusticorum. Responsio Johannis Cochlaei Wendelstini* (Cologne, Sept. 1525). Title page verso.

[138] In his dedication to Henry of *In Apocalypsim*, Cochlaeus cited a letter from Fisher looking forward to the editions of Rupert on John's Gospel and Revelations (title page verso).

[139] Cochlaeus to Pirckheimer, 15 September 1526, cited in Surtz, *Works and Days*, 337.

into German. That same year, he was urging Fisher to write against the Anabaptists,[140] and he was still trying to persuade Fisher to join in controversies in 1531, when he wrote to More that he hoped Rossaeus or Fisher would deal with Melanchthon as he deserved.[141] These later efforts were in vain. Fisher told Cochlaeus that he had decided to retire from theological controversy.[142] The reason for his decision was probably his preoccupation with 'the King's Great Matter', on which he had been consulted in mid-1527, and to which he devoted more attention (he later claimed) than he had ever done to any other subject.[143]

The controversy over Henry's marriage to Catherine marked a change not only in Fisher's intellectual priorities, but in those of the kingdom as a whole. Henceforth the interest of the English government in foreign and domestic scholars was to have their judgment on the marriage, not on Luther.[144] It is no coincidence that the one man who found plenty of time to write against heresy over the next seven years was the one who stood aside from the marriage question— Thomas More. Henry's search for intellectual support for his divorce led him to compromise his zeal against Lutheranism. He even made advances to Wittenberg. At home, proceedings against the radical Latimer were hampered by royal intervention because of his known support for the divorce. Advanced ideas were tolerated at court, even in the circles closest to the king, for much the same reason. The idle talk of Norfolk and Boleyn against papal supremacy around 1530 was a far cry from the papalism of the *Assertio Septem Sacramentorum*—which Henry was soon to disown as something the bishops had tricked him into undertaking.[145] Of course, heresy continued to be attacked in these years. Bishops such as Longland, Stokesley and Lee continued to investigate heresy in their dioceses. But the patronage of the intellectual attack on reformed ideas disappeared. Once Wolsey had gone, those who had been most active against heresy tended to be found among the opposition. Tunstall, Fisher, West, and Ridley were among Catherine's twelve advisers, and Doctors Powell, Watson, and Wilson were active in her support. Nobody would suggest that the divorce,

---

[140] *EE* vii. ep. 1928, from Cochlaeus, 8 Jan. 1528, 288, 'Rogo igitur ... ut scribas contra hanc diram sectam; ... Itidem rogabo reuerendissimum dominum Roffensem'.

[141] Letter to More, 29 June 1531, Pollen, 'Cochläus an Heinrich VIII', 48, 'Utinam Rosseus vester aut R. D. Episcopus Roffensis hunc rhetorem digne pro meritis excipiat'.

[142] J. Cochlaeus, *Fasciculus Calumniarum* (Leipzig, 1529), sig. A. i. v, dedication to Fisher, dated 5 July 1529, 'Quod in Lutherum nihil amplius aedis aut scribere intendis, meo quidem judicio recte facis'.

[143] *LP* viii. 859, p. 336, no. 8.

[144] M. Dowling draws attention to the effect of the marriage crisis in disturbing the peace of English humanism in her *Humanism in the Age of Henry VIII* (1986), 44.

[145] *LP* vii. 152, Chapuys to Charles V, 4 Feb. 1534.

or the concomitant break with Rome, turned England Protestant overnight. But it did blur certain issues. Doctrinal confusion came to be the mark of the Henrician Church, from the top down. Henry showed himself more than willing to enter into negotiations with foreign Lutherans, yet continued to burn native Protestants. Among his people—to his intense annoyance—doctrinal debate became the stuff of alehouse dispute. The English campaign against Luther was over. The battle for the soul of England had begun.

ANGLO-SCOTTISH UNION AND THE COURT OF JAMES I, 1603–1625

The Alexander Prize Essay proxime accessit

By Neil Cuddy

WHEN in 1629–30 Rubens gave James I his conventional apotheosis on the Banqueting House ceiling, he also, more originally, depicted his reign's major achievements. Two stood out: the general benefits of James's rule, peace and plenty; and, given pride of place, the Union of England and Scotland.[1]

Rubens' vision may surprise those more accustomed to viewing the period through the eyes of twentieth-century historians. Their picture centres on the total parliamentary failure, between 1604 and 1607, of a legislative programme of Union: in its stead, the king had to make do with limited judicial and prerogative measures, effecting a mere dynastic association of the two still separate kingdoms. With that failure and those meagre measures, the question disappeared between 1608 and the achievement of real Union under Queen Anne: if James I's scheme was an impractical 'idea before its time', by 1707 full parliamentary Union merely tidied up a basically uncontentious question.[2] The magnitude of the disparity between the two pictures— between what was significant then and what seems so now—is our starting point. It calls for a thorough investigation of precisely what sort of Union James achieved. Dr Galloway rightly observed that calling the situation after 1603 a 'Union of Crowns' merely begs the question of what James's English accession actually meant.[3] The central purpose of this essay is to assess the practicalities of the achievement so eloquently witnessed on the Banqueting House ceiling.

From Wyatt's rebellion and the Dutch revolt, to Bohemia in 1618, the Bishops' Wars, and Spain's problems in the 1640s, the century

---

[1] G. Parry, *The Golden Age Restor'd: The Culture of the Stuart Court, 1603–42* (Manchester, 1981), 32–7.

[2] B. Galloway, *The Union of England and Scotland, 1603–1608* (Edinburgh, 1986); C. Russell, 'Parliamentary History in Perspective, 1604–1629', *History*, lxi (1976), 1–27, esp. 5; B. P. Levack, 'Towards a more Perfect Union: England, Scotland and the Constitution', in B. Malament (ed.), *After the Reformation: Essays in Honour of J. H. Hexter* (Manchester, 1980), 57–74; D. H. Willson, 'King James I and Anglo-Scottish Unity', in W. A. Aiken and B. D. Henning (eds.), *Conflict in Stuart England: Essays in Honour of Wallace Notestein* (1960), 41–55.

[3] Galloway, *Union of England and Scotland*, 1.

after 1550 was hostile to dynastic empires; now as never before, new religious and national allegiances strained those more traditional bonds of loyalty.[4] Therefore James's first and highest priority was an attempt to legislate his fragile personal union of crowns into a more permanent one of institutions, laws and peoples. And if in 1607 it failed, the attempt was no idle whim; its seriousness is shown by the massive repercussions of its failure, from which stemmed much of the politics of the rest of the reign. If we turn our attention to where the revisionists direct it, away from parliament to the court, we immediately see Anglo-Scottish Union not as a unique, inconsequential and purely legislative failure, but as a central political preoccupation throughout the reign. First, the Union of the crowns was above all expressed in the accession settlement of the court; second, the court was then used by the king to further his plans for Union in parliament, but itself became a prime sticking-point and the trigger of both spontaneous and factional opposition to those plans; third, after failure in parliament, the court and Bedchamber functioned over the rest of the reign both as a continuing symbol of Union, and as its main structural expression. And fourth, James's use of his court to promote Union fits intelligibly into a wider chronological and European context. In consequence, the shape of the political narrative of his reign will be seen to require re-adjustment.

The Union, in short, needs to be seen as practical, flesh-and-blood politics rather than as an abstract constitutional failure. The Union of Crowns began in constitutional theory at the moment Elizabeth I's 'natural' body died, when the monarch's second 'public' body instantly transmigrated to the thirty-seven-year-old frame of James Stuart at Holyrood; in political practice, it began less mystically with the Union of the two Courts. This was a hard driven political bargain, still open when the king left Edinburgh on 5 April, haggled over while the King moved south in stages, partially settled at York and Theobalds, and finally put into effect when he took up residence at the Tower of London in mid-May 1603.

James in Scotland had lived in a court whose keynote, like the French court upon which it was based, was open access to and populous intimacy with the king in his Chamber. From this intimacy stemmed political influence: the Chamber was the power base both of James's Lord Treasurer and chief favourite Sir George Home (later Earl of Dunbar), reportedly in 1600 'the only man of all other most inward with the king', and also of his supporters, tagged by observers

[4] T. Aston, ed., *Crisis in Europe 1560–1660* (1965), esp. 107–9, 115–16; G. Parker and L. M. Smith (eds.), *The General Crisis of the Seventeenth Century* (1978), esp. 17, 57–73.

the 'Chamber faction'.[5] The political centrality of the Chamber was thus clear to all observers. Accordingly, for the English in the crucial months before Elizabeth's death, the Scottish Chamber became the focus of political ambition. Brothers to the earls of Pembroke, Northumberland, and Worcester, sons to lords Eure and Hunsdon, Cecil's nephew, and such substantial gentlemen as Sir Henry Bromley, Sir Oliver Cromwell and Sir John Holles were sworn into the Scots chamber, either in Edinburgh or on the journey south. They represented some of the great families of Tudor England.[6]

James's reversionary court, waiting on Elizabeth's death, was also co-operating with the Elizabethan political establishment; it therefore operated by proxy, containing not the principals, but the brothers, relatives and friends of those presently in (or excluded from) power under Elizabeth. But in opening his Chamber to both English and Scots, James was also beginning the political organisation that would be necessary for a real Union of the Crowns. The future king of England unilaterally began to divide his entourage evenly between the two nations before he left Edinburgh.

Cecil and Northampton anxiously rode ahead to meet the king at York, and successfully persuaded James against Raleigh, Cobham, and Northumberland by suggesting (among other things) that they opposed James's retaining any Scots advisers in England. But they themselves hoped that draconian limits could be placed on the Scots; the main business of the first official Council messengers to reach James had evidently been to confirm that no Scots would get offices or places on the Council. At York, however, their disappointment began: James insisted that two of his Scottish Gentlemen Ushers be sworn as partners to the English ones who met him there to organise his journey south: as soon as the king met the advance party of his new English court, he began splitting its offices between the nations.[7]

At Theobalds—Cecil's private house—on 3 and 4 May, the new English Privy Council was organised. James forced five Scots onto it: Sir George Home, Lord Treasurer of Scotland, became Chancellor of

---

[5] *Register of the Privy Council of Scotland*, iii (1578–85), 322–3; vi (1599–1604), 203, 207–8; *Calendar of State Papers Scottish*, xiii (1597–1603), 723, and index *sub* 'Chamber faction'. Cf. the last adult male to rule before James, and the political importance of his entourage; e.g. David Starkey, *The Reign of Henry VIII: Personalities and Politics* (1985).

[6] *The Letters of Philip Gawdy*, ed. I. H. Jeayes (Roxburghe Club, 1906), 130–1; H.M.C., *Salisbury*, xv (1603), 10, 19, 28; H.M.C., *Portland*, ix. 129. Public Record Office, Lord Steward's Dept. LS 13/168, fo. 57r.

[7] Raleigh and Sir John Fortescue lost their offices to Scotsmen for having advocated their exclusion. R. C. Munden, 'The Defeat of Sir John Fortescue: Court *versus* Country at the Hustings?', *E.H.R.*, xciii (1978), 811–16, esp. 814 n.; Public Record Office French Transcripts, P.R.O. 31/3/35, Beaumont to Henri IV (1 and 8 Apr., 1603); LS 13/168, fo. 49r, 16 Apr.

the Exchequer; and Lord Kinloss became Master of the Rolls in Chancery. At a stroke the top jobs in the key financial and legal departments were split between English and Scots.[8] And James evidently intended to go further: he proposed to give Cecil 'a Scottish partner' in the Secretaryship; while revival was rumoured of the Lord Presidency of the Council for the duke of Lennox (perhaps to offset the English majority there). But neither intention came to anything.[9] James, though without surrendering totally, had so compromised with the guarantors of his succession that the new conciliar régime closely resembled the old.

At the Tower of London, however, a new court was formed, about 11–13 May, which represented less of a compromise for the king. A new Privy Chamber was created, consisting of 24 English and 24 Scots Gentlemen, divided into four groups of twelve (split six to six by nationality) each on duty for three months. All of the Scots and most of the English were in fact those who had been paired in and were now expelled from James's original Scottish Chamber, now abolished.[10] Such symbolic 'equal partition' was thus fully in line with James's actions: in admitting English to his Scottish Chamber in Edinburgh; in splitting equally the key offices of his outer chamber at York; and more modestly in altering Council, Exchequer and Chancery at Theobalds.

But here James drew the line. If the Outer and Privy Chambers were to be visible embodiments of even-handed Union,[11] James's new Bedchamber, also created at the Tower, which now took over the whole of the king's practical body service and turned the formerly important English Privy Chamber into an outer reception room, was to be an entirely Scottish preserve. The Scots who transferred from the Edinburgh Chamber to the London Bedchamber were all James's trusted agents and familiar companions. Cecil and the English who had organised the succession were now accused of having sold out the rest of the English to the Scots.[12]

Their Bedchamber monopoly was of great, and hitherto neglected,

[8] Both Lord Chancellor and Lord Treasurer now had Scots second-in-commands. B.L. Add. MS 11, 402, fo. 88: *Acts of the Privy Council*, xxxii (1601–04), 497. Galloway, *Union of England and Scotland*, 17–18.

[9] P.R.O. 31/3/35, Beaumont to Villeroy, 7 May 1603; *Calendar of State Papers Venetian*, x (1603–07), 33; cf. Galloway, *Union of England and Scotland*, 18.

[10] *Letters of Gawdy*, ed. Jeayes, 130–1; *The Memoirs of Robert Carey*, ed. F. H. Mares (Oxford, 1972), 65–6.

[11] The places of the 50 Gentlemen Pensioners (who waited quarterly in the Presence Chamber) were also to be split between the nations as vacancies occurred among the existing band.

[12] P.R.O. 31/3/35, Beaumont to Villeroy, 17 May 1603; *CSP Venetian*, x (1603–07), 33.

importance. Its value has been underestimated because James's English court has conventionally been seen as disorderly, affording easy and widely-available access to the king. 'It is strange', wrote D. H. Willson, 'that a man who loved privacy as [James] did could not have handled matters better.'[13] The strangeness stems from our lack of precise understanding. Bacon's first impression was that James was open and accessible, but that 'his virtue of access is rather because he is much abroad and in press, than that he giveth easy audience'.[14] James did nothing to alter the rigid control of access traditional to the English court; so, approachable and easy-going James might appear at first, but to see him meant an audience. And that applied to everyone who needed to see the king—including the Privy Council. They had to wait in the Withdrawing Chamber (outside the Bedchamber) to 'conferre together, and attend [James's] pleasure to be Caled in to our Inner lodginges when we shall Comaunde'.[15] If Councillors were treated thus, their inferiors were still more tightly excluded. James indeed enforced his own court regulations. In February 1621, he himself told some unauthorised Lords in his Withdrawing Chamber 'that there was a Presence and a Privy Chamber for them'.[16] The Bedchamber alone escaped these restrictions on access; indeed their own monopoly of access was guaranteed by them. And Professor Stone's figures for crown patronage, 1558–1641, dramatically illustrate the massive opportunities for profit that flowed from this.[17] Against this background, the worries of the English about the Scots make political sense. Those worries first crystallised around the issue of Union when it was put before parliament.

James's plans for Union envisaged parliamentary legislation from the very first. Since the accession settlement left Council and great offices largely in Elizabethan hands, James concentrated his own preparatory efforts in areas where he exercised most personal influence. The Borders were to serve as a model in microcosm of Anglo-Scottish co-operation and its benefits.[18] And the court was similarly used as a model to encourage the programme in parliament. If James's Bedchamber was initially wholly Scottish, the equal division between the nations of Privy Chamber and outer court was a signal of his

[13] D. H. Willson, *James VI and I* (1956), 195.

[14] Lucy Aikin, *Memoirs of the Court of King James I* (2 vols., 1822), i. 111.

[15] B.L., Harley MS 589, fo. 197v, §2; cf. E. Lodge, *The Life of Sir Julius Caesar ...* (1827), 23 for Caesar's valuation on access to the Withdrawing Chamber.

[16] P.R.O., State Papers Domestic, SP14/119/99, Locke to Carleton, 16 Feb. 1621.

[17] L. Stone, *The Crisis of the Aristocracy 1558–1641* (Oxford, 1965), 470–6, 774–6. Of 29 individuals receiving 75% of all crown patronage in his period, 10 were Gentlemen of James's Bedchamber: of 9 receiving 45% of it all, 6 were of the Bedchamber.

[18] S.J. and Susan J. Watts, *From Border to Middle Shire: Northumberland 1586–1625* (Leicester, 1975), 133–4, 148–9; Galloway, *Union of England and Scotland*, 15–16, 84–6.

intention to encourage real Union. In June 1603 the dual re-admission to the Bedchamber of an Englishman (Philip Herbert, soon earl of Montgomery) and a Scot (Sir James Hay) now began to redress the evidently deliberate imbalance there. James probably had an eye to the coming parliament with this even-handedness.[19] But Herbert was the last English appointment to the Bedchamber until April 1615. The probable explanation for the continuing exclusion was that the first admission of an Englishman brought no corresponding compromise from the English: instead problems began virtually from the moment parliament began.

All that was required in 1604 was the change of name of the two kingdoms to Britain, and the nomination of English commissioners, who would put detailed legislation to the next session.[20] These were modest proposals; yet the name change was rejected, and there was even foot-dragging on the nomination of Commissioners. If the historian finds this difficult to explain, James found it quite incredible. He told the Commons: 'I am not ashamed of my project[;] neither have I deferred it ... out of a liking of the Judges reasons, or yours.' Instead he blamed the 'few giddy heads' who had led the House astray.[21] In other words, James saw stubborn, offensive, but largely spontaneous opposition.

But was the leadership in 1604 as spontaneous as James initially thought? Dr Munden has indeed pointed to two indications that faction inspired that leadership. The Venetian ambassador thought that the Union was as opposed in the Lords as in the Commons, and that the Lords 'privately urge the Commons to stand firm, and furnish them with arguments'. Sir John Holles complained that though both Houses' attitude to Union had been the same, the Lords had voiced theirs 'like statesmen, more covertly', so that 'they clad angel-like were received into Abraham's bosom while we [the Commons] fried in the furnace of the king's displeasure'.[22] These comments can be tied more closely into the politics of the accession and the king's policy towards his Bedchamber.

Sir Edwin Sandys was the inspiration behind opposition to the

---

[19] *Memoirs of Carey*, ed. Mares, 66, a dual appointment at the Queen's suit soon after her arrival (in late June). It was uncertain in June that parliament would not be able to meet that winter (due to plague); arrangements for the coronation were only finalised on 6 July. It was usual for a new monarch to meet parliament as soon as possible. G. P. V. Akrigg, *Jacobean Pageant* (1962), 23, 29.

[20] Galloway, *Union of England and Scotland*, 20.

[21] W. Notestein, *The House of Commons, 1604–1610* (New Haven, 1971), 79–85 (quotation from p. 85).

[22] R. Munden, 'James I and "the growth of mutual distrust": King, Commons and Reform, 1603–1604', in K. Sharpe, ed., *Faction and Parliament* (Oxford, 1978), 71, citing *CSP Venetian*, x (1603–07), 151; H.M.C., *Portland*, ix. 11–13.

Union in 1604. At the outset he recognised that even changing the name of England and Scotland to Britain was 'the weightiest possible cause', and that it was necessary to 'proceed with a leaden foot'. He distracted debate on nominating English members of the Union Commission by calling for guarantees that only Englishmen would hold office under the English crown. Throughout April 1604 he refuted the official line put forward by Bacon.[23]

Sandys's predominance as a Commons opposition spokesman is suggestive taken together with observers' allegations of factional conspiracy between Lords and Commons. A clue to the likely identity of his collaborator in the Lords is his participation later in the reign in a by then well-established double-act. The political collaboration of Sandys and the earl of Southampton was evident to all observers by 1614; but there are signs that Sandys was also collaborating in the earlier part of the reign with Southampton, the man (twelve years his junior) he later claimed to have converted from youthful Catholicism.[24]

It is unlikely that Sandys's opposition to these modest, generalised measures was ranged against ideas pure and simple. As Dr Munden suggested, the attack on James's scheme for a name change in 1604 'was little more than a thinly veiled attack on the general [Union] scheme'. And opposition to the scheme was in turn unlikely to arise simply from general anti-Scottish prejudices—but rather, given the risks involved, from real, political fears and prejudices about actual Scots—in fact, the Bedchamber.[25] But since kings had always been notoriously sensitive about attacks on those closest to them, opposition to the Union served the more politically sophisticated as a means of 'coded' attack on the king's Scottish entourage.

The strongest indication of this came near the end of the first session of parliament in 1604. The earl of Southampton was arrested on Sunday 24 June by order of the king and council, together with lord Danvers and Sir Henry Neville, fellow former Essex conspirators; their papers were seized and the suspects interrogated, but they were released next day after 'several examinations'. The Venetian ambassador later gave the reason for the arrest—Southampton had 'been rumoured by his enemies to be plotting to slay several Scots much

---

[23] Notestein, *House of Commons*, 79–85, esp. 79, 81, 82—but cf. Galloway, *Union*, 20, 22; B. P. Levack, 'The Proposed Union of English and Scottish Law in the Seventeenth Century', *Juridical Review*, xx (1975), 100; Munden in Sharpe (ed.), *Faction and Parliament*, 62–5.

[24] Cf. T. K. Rabb, 'Sir Edwin Sandys and the Parliament of 1604', *American Historical Review*, lxix (1964), 646–70. L. Stone, *Family and Fortune* (Oxford, 1972), 214–15 on *c.* 1605 as a possible date for his conversion; respective entries in *D.N.B.* on their common early involvement with Virginia.

[25] Munden in Sharpe (ed.), *Faction and Parliament*, 64.

about the person of the king'. Allegedly his first intended victim was James's chief confidant, Sir George Home.[26] That such slanders were apparently believed says much about what Southampton's views on the Scots were perceived to be.

Southampton must have been dissatisfied with the accession settlement. Although James sweetened some survivors of the defeated Essex faction with considerable patronage, he thereafter gave them neither office nor influence.[27] The king could not afford wholly to ignore their leader Southampton. But the favours he received—lodging at court, sporadic attendance at the hunt, royal visits—were minor.[28] The most significant office he gained was the Mastership of Queen Anne's Game: he was left off the Privy Council until 1619, and personally distrusted by the king throughout the reign.[29] Southampton's treatment at court is the best explanation for the suspicions entertained of him as an oppositionist both in June 1604 and (as we shall see) later.

When the Union Commissioners' legislation was put to parliament in February 1607—after delays because of the sensitivity of the issue[30]—immediately a mysterious outburst by Sir Christopher Piggott explicitly denounced Scots courtiers in the context of the proposed naturalisation measures. The unspeakable spoken, at the time the speech was 'with a general amazement, neglected, without tax or censure'; but after the Commons themselves had dutifully sent Piggott to the Tower, Bacon replied officially to his outburst. Apart from 'some persons of quality about His Majesty's person here at court',

[26] *CSP Venetian*, x (1603–07), 165, 168 (26 June/6 July, 4/14 July 1604); H.M.C., *Gawdy*, 92–3, 7 (?*rectior* 27) June 1604. G. P. V. Akrigg, *Shakespeare and the Earl of Southampton* (Cambridge, Mass., 1968), 140–2. Lionel Sharpe, once chaplain to Essex and now to the king, was sufficiently concerned, not least to distance himself from his former patrons, that on the 26th—after Southampton's release—he organised gentlemen about London to band together to protect the king's person, and give their names to Sir Thomas Erskine, Groom of the Stool and Captain of the Guard, in the interests of Anglo-Scottish brotherhood. Sharpe was himself examined. *CSP Domestic*, xii (Additional 1580–1625), 482–6; H.M.C., *Salisbury*, xvi (1604), 157, 30 June 1604.

[27] L. Stone, *Family and Fortune*, 219–22 and *Crisis of the Aristocracy*, 475. Southampton's restored lands explain the apparent size of his gains; other patronage probably reflected his financial need—wealthier Essexians like Rutland received nothing. H. R. Trevor-Roper, *The Gentry* (*Ec.H.R.* Supplement No. 1, London, 1953), 35, exaggerates how far former Essexians were taken on board at James's accession by the 'Cecilians' and the 'Scots'.

[28] P.R.O. LS 13/168, fos. 77r–79r, fo. 102r; *CSP Venetian*, xi (1607–10), 206; B.L. Egerton MS 2026, fo. 23. Hunting: Hatfield MSS 278/3 [British Library microfilm], *sub* 14 Feb. 1604; P.R.O. SP14/13/8 (1605); H.M.C., *Salisbury*, xviii (1606), 270. Akrigg, *Shakespeare and Southampton*, 144–5.

[29] B.L. Add MS 38, 139, fo. 104v, Queen Anne's Council; fo. 186v gives his fee, £10 p.a.; S. R. Gardiner, *The History of England from the Accession of James I to the Outbreak of the Civil War* (10 vols., 1883–4), iii. 68–9.

[30] Notestein, *House of Commons 1604–1610*, 180–1; Galloway, *Union of England and Scotland*, 79–81, 94–6.

Bacon claimed, the number of Scots families resident in England was 'extremely small'. This ducked the charge that these 'some persons' enjoyed a wholly disproportionate share of both political power and royal patronage.[31] And the whole exchange had broken the parliamentary code of silence.

If Piggott had gone too far, Sir Edwin Sandys's opposition to the scheme was both more indirect and more successful. Against James's compromise proposals, Sandys (together with Alford and others) proposed a 'perfect union', totally subjugating Scots to English law: apparently a stratagem to kill the king's moderate proposals by replacing them with impractical extremism, which the Scots would certainly reject.[32] But if Sandys's attack was more subtle, his target was the same as Piggott's. James saw this: if in 1604 he had been disposed to blame the giddy heads of the Commons, by 1607 he saw things differently. Sandys had once again led the Commons, but now James sensed faction at work, preying on Commons xenophobia for its own ends. Departing for Royston in May, James took leave of a group of nobles in his Bedchamber. Advised to excuse the Commons, he now instead accused certain Lords. The reproaches began with Southampton, and proceeded to his brother-in-law lord Arundel and the ex-Essexian Mounteagle. They above all had been responsible for directly opposing James's wishes on the Union. Again, Southampton as prime suspect in the Lords and Sandys as prime mover in the Commons suggests that the exclusion of the old Essex faction from meaningful influence at court—at the hands largely of the Scots Bedchamber and the hated Cecilians—was triggering opposition in parliament to the more abstract Union measures.[33]

James's response to the 1606–07 Union session signalled his hardline reaction to failure. Border legislation had failed: James therefore put Dunbar at the head of a new commission there, with powers of life and death over Englishmen.[34] And at court, in March 1607, just after the attacks on the Scots in the Commons, Dunbar's protégé and fellow Scot Robert Carr publicly came to favour at the Accession

---

[31] *Journals of the House of Commons* (1803), i. 333; J. Spedding (ed.), *The Letters and Life of Sir Francis Bacon* (7 vols., 1861–74), iii. 306–7, 311; Galloway, *Union of England and Scotland*, 104–5.

[32] Levack, 'Towards a more Perfect Union', in Malament (ed.), *After the Reformation*, 66, 68. Notestein, *House of Commons*, 231–5; Galloway, *Union of England and Scotland*, 112–13—Sandys was abetted in the scheme by Southampton's other great Commons collaborator Sir Henry Neville.

[33] *Ambassades de Monsieur de la Boderie en Angleterre, 1606–1611* (5 vols., Paris, 1750), ii. 199–200 (de la Boderie to de Puisieux, 2 May 1607); Boderie also said James reproached Pembroke and the Scot lord Balfour of Burley; Galloway, *Union of England and Scotland*, 105.

[34] Galloway, *Union of England and Scotland*, 142–3.

Day Tilt, swiftly supplanting the Englishman Montgomery as king's 'favourite'. By December Carr was a Gentleman of the Bedchamber, and in the next year James was directing £20,000 of land to him as yet one more 'left unprovided for ... according to the rank whereunto I have promoted him'. Carr's promotion, by actually bolstering the Scots' domination of the Bedchamber, gave the Commons an unambiguous signal of the king's attitude to their obstruction of his union measures.[35]

Plans for another parliamentary session devoted to Union were actively pursued until December 1607, and there were further rumours in the next year. But prerogative and judicial measures could do some, though far from all, of what James had wanted from parliament, and James was persuaded to drop the scheme.[36] But if Union legislation disappeared from the agenda after 1608, the Bedchamber, the Union at court and the nationality question in general would not go away as parliamentary issues. Bedchamber patronage gains had been a central cause of distrust over the more abstract Union measures. In early 1607 the grant of £44,000 to pay the debts of the Bedchamber Scots Hay and Haddington—and also of Montgomery—was widely known of only a week before Piggott's outburst in the Commons.[37] In 1610 when parliament met again after the Union debacle, its main concern was supply. James tried to head off criticism in March by claiming that 'yee will find, that I have dealt twice as much among English men as I haue done to Scottishmen'.[38] But in February, Sir John Holles (a prominent opponent of Union in 1607) had already put up a grievance in the House which identified the court as 'the cause of all': the Scots monopolised the Bedchamber, uniquely placed to get patronage for themselves and to take a cut of whatever else was going. He asked that the

Bedchamber may be shared as well to those of our nation as to them ... and that the same chamber may have the same brotherly partition which all the other inferior forms of the court, the Presence and Privy Chamber have.

[35] P.R.O., Declared Account of the Treasurer of the Chamber, E351/543, memb. 174r; Speech of 31 Mar. 1607 in James's *Workes* (1616), 514–15, when James plainly told the Commons that all his Scots had now been promoted and provided for; H.M.C., *Salisbury*, xx (1608), 269, James to Salisbury, 23 Nov. 1608.

[36] Levack, 'Proposed Union of English and Scots Law', *Juridical Review*, xx (1975), 108–9; Galloway, *Union of England and Scotland*, 150; *CSP Venetian*, xi (1607–10), 137. Cf. E. R. Foster, *Proceedings in Parliament, 1610* (2 vols., New Haven, 1966), ii. 4–5.

[37] *The Letters of John Chamberlain*, ed. N. E. McLure (2 vols., Philadelphia, 1939), i. 238 (11 Nov. 1606), 241 (6 Feb. 1607).

[38] Speech of 21 Mar. 1610, in *Workes* (1616), 540, 542.

Not only would this stop the drain on the royal finances; it would also encourage both parliamentary supply and Anglo-Scottish amity.[39] Holles's grievance voiced what many were thinking, but it was never put to the House. Instead, similar ideas less artfully put caused James to dissolve parliament for fear that a petition was imminent to send his Scots home.[40]

James's anger after the 1610 dissolution demonstrated what in 1607 he had called his ability 'within ... my Prerogative' to 'hurt this Nation, by partiality to the Scots'.[41] In January 1611 most of the Bedchamber had their debts paid off again from the Exchequer, to the tune of £34,000 (exaggerated by observers to £40,000).[42] But the issue did not stop there. In 1614, the grievance arose again, just as that of Impositions carried over from one parliament to the next. James dissolved parliament in anger when John Hoskins demanded the Bedchamber Scots be sent home, like Canute's Danes when that other foreigner became king of England; otherwise there was a danger of another Sicilian Vespers, a massacre of the aliens.[43] James's reaction was by now predictable: far from sending home his Scottish favourite Somerset, he appointed him in July to the Lord Chamberlaincy—the highest English office so far achieved by a Scot.

Clearly, all this was disastrous. Far from being the symbol of Union, the court had become a prime grievance which triggered opposition to Union: far from the Scots Bedchamber monopoly giving the king leverage, it apparently outraged the English beyond the point of all political coherence. The early years of James's reign have been described as witnessing the 'growth of mutual distrust' between king and Commons; that, it seems on the evidence we have surveyed, is to say the least of it. Between 1604 and 1610 a parliamentary group centred on the earl of Southampton defeated the king's plans for Union, opposed the presence of the Scots in the Bedchamber, and forcefully opposed supply while that situation continued. Having demonstrated their power to destroy, they now offered to create—on their terms. In 1611 Southampton and his 'dear Damon' Sir Henry Neville put forward their 'undertaking'; the latter was to become Secretary of State, and at last given office, their faction would lead the Commons, not into opposition, but towards supply and positive

---

[39] H.M.C., *Portland*, ix. 113.

[40] Foster, *Proceedings in Parliament, 1610*, ii. 344 (23 Nov. 1610); cf. H.M.C., *Salisbury*, xxi (1609–12), 265, James to Salisbury, 6 Dec. 1610.

[41] Speech of 31 Mar. 1607, in *Workes* (1616), 519.

[42] *Calendar of State Papers Domestic*, ix (1611–18), 5; H.M.C., *Downshire*, iii. 20.

[43] P.R.O. SP14/77/42, 22 June 1614, Sir Charles Cornwallis to James; cf. /43. His speech formed the basis for Hoskins's: he explained that he had wanted no Scots removed, but rather English taken in gradually as replacements to level the numbers. T. L. Moir, *The Addled Parliament of 1614* (Oxford, 1958), 138.

parliamentary results. It was a scheme that sought not to co-operate with the *status quo*, but rather to replace in the king's counsels the 'sell-out' alliance of Cecil and the Bedchamber Scots with exclusively English bureaucrats and parliamentary spokesmen; or, in eighteenth-century terminology, to force the king's closet.[44]

James's attitudes were the all-important other half of the relationship of 'mutual distrust'. The closing of James's mind took some time; Dr Munden convincingly stressed his willingness to innovate and reform at his accession, of which the Union scheme itself was the most striking example. Even after 1610, James was still willing at least to consider a variety of alternative measures. But the killing of his cherished Union scheme, and the Commons' speeches about his Scots, alienated him profoundly. After much wavering, in 1610 James ditched Salisbury and his Great Contract to reform the finances, on the arch-conservative grounds that he would not throw away the 'imperial prerogatives and flowers of the crown', almost certainly on the advice of his chief Scottish confidant Dunbar. It seems unlikely that James's hardening prejudices ever permitted him seriously to consider the Southampton group's proposals. Late in 1610 his clerk reported he could not understand the actions of the Commons leaders 'except any had a design to lay the foundations of a popular state'; in 1612 he explicitly let it be known that he 'would not have a secretarie imposed on him by parlement'; in 1613 his Groom of the Stool still observed that 'it stiks in his stomake, this last [1604–10] Parlement'.[45]

But James was never one to let appearances tell the whole truth; he kept Southampton guessing, and his own options open, for almost three years. He did so by using his favourite Robert Carr as a screen. James may have abandoned parliamentary Union: but he was not prepared to renounce the general idea and demonstration of it. The early career of Robert Carr was an unmistakable affirmation to the English of James's determination to keep Scotland and the Scots at the front of the English political scene. Carr confirmed the primacy in the king's counsels of Dunbar, between 1607 (when Dunbar was seen as 'the chief cause why Salisbury is maintained in ... power') and January 1611, when Dunbar died. Carr then stepped forward as the great patronage broker of the court, which was 'displeasing to the English; all the same, everybody is endeavouring to secure his favour

---

[44] C. Roberts and O. Duncan, 'The Parliamentary Undertaking of 1614', *E.H.R.*, xciii (1978), esp. 483.

[45] Munden in Sharpe (ed.), *Faction and Parliament, passim:* G. Goodman, *The Court of King James I*, ed. J. S. Brewer (2 vols., 1839), i. 21, 40–1; *Letters of Chamberlain*, i. 259; *Parliamentary Debates in 1610*, ed. S. R. Gardiner (Camden 1st ser. lxxxi, 1862), 167: P.R.O. SP14/58/26, Lake to Salisbury, 21 Nov. 1610; *Letters of Chamberlain*, i. 358–9 (17 June 1612); H.M.C., *Mar & Kellie Supplement*, 55 (27 Oct. 1613).

and goodwill'. And the Southampton group were at first the most anxious of all the English to deal with him, and through him the king.[46]

Carr between 1610 and 1614 personified, under the king's direction, a negative solution to the nationality problem. He did so as a Scot by cultivating an almost exclusively English following (of which the chief member was Sir Thomas Overbury) and by affecting 'utterly [to] dislike the bold carriage and importunity' of his countrymen. Through Overbury, Carr was led to advocate Southampton and Neville's parliamentary 'undertaking' in 1612–13. But James swiftly rejected it, and then steered Carr (probably unwillingly at first) towards alliance with the more conservative English faction led by the Howard earls of Northampton and Suffolk. When Carr followed (and abandoned Overbury), James's reward was to re-assemble in his hands Dunbar's old offices and territorial influence on the borders and in Scotland: in December 1613 Carr became Lord Treasurer of Scotland; before that, James had been preparing Durham and the borders for him to step into the shoes of the extinct Neville earls of Westmorland.[47]

James's attempt to make Carr into a favourite in both kingdoms at once was a failure. It provoked intense national hatred. The threatened Sicilian Vespers almost came to pass at the Croydon races in 1612. Duels between English and Scots proliferated. And the rest of the Scots Bedchamber moved against Carr as swiftly as he tried to suppress his Scottishness and ally with the English. The parliamentary disaster of 1614 was the fatal stroke: it at once clarified to James that his favourite's English contacts could neither defuse the nationality issue, nor provide an adequate basis of support for a successful parliament. On both scores, the king by early 1615 '[knew] his mind better'; his solution to the impasse was the promotion of George Villiers to the Bedchamber, the second Englishman in the department and the first appointed since 1603.[48]

Villiers was quite clearly intended from the first to be a favourite with patronage power, standing at the king's side to manage the business of government and the tide of faction. Unlike Carr, he gained offices and influence within a year of his promotion, with a

[46] CSP Venetian, xi (1607–10), 125; xii (1610–13), 135.

[47] Goodman, Court of King James I, i. 215; Roberts and Duncan, 'Parliamentary Undertaking of 1614', E.H.R., xciii (1978), 485–8; Mervyn James, Family, Lineage and Civil Society: A Study of Society, Politics and Mentality in the Durham Region, 1500–1640 (Oxford, 1974), 67–8. The government of Scotland from the English court in general hinged on Dunbar between 1603 and 1611; thereafter, it seems that Carr's power has been undervalued. M. Lee, Government by Pen (Urbana, Illinois, 1980), esp. 121, 147.

[48] Akrigg, Jacobean Pageant, 51–4; Crisis of the Aristocracy, 247, 249–50 on duels; Letters of Chamberlain, i. 597, 599 on the Scots' solidarity against Somerset; H.M.C., Mar & Kellie Supplement, 60 (19 Apr. 1615).

deliberateness that reflected James's political reasoning rather than his simple personal favour. And it is equally clear that his promotion as an English favourite was originally intended to balance out Carr's position, now in reaction to the 1614 fiasco, as a largely Scottish one: both Fenton and the French Ambassador reported this, while Carr seems to have claimed that he suggested such a scheme to James.[49] Since Villiers's most prominent initial backers had been Southampton and Pembroke, his promotion also made some show—it remained mere show while James lived—of compromise with the attitudes of those determined opponents of James's most cherished schemes.

Carr's fall, predictable only after late summer 1615, spoiled the smooth implementation of the plan for dual favourites. James, however, could at least demonstrate his even-handedness, when the Englishman Pembroke took the Lord Chamberlaincy, by reviving the superior post of Lord Steward for Lennox. And James's deliberate search for a new Scottish favourite to replace Carr was to be a short one. On his Scottish journey in April 1617 he found his man, the twenty-eight-year-old Marquis of Hamilton. James was delighted: he 'so much rejoiced at the conquest I have made in drawing this man to wayte upon me ...., that I assure myself his service will repaye my liberallitie with a double interest'. Hamilton indeed amassed the by now customarily massive patronage gains; in 1620 he graduated from noble in residence to the Bedchamber 'without the privity of the Marquis of Buckingham'; in 1622 his marriage settlement with Buckingham's kin merely reinforced his tight grip on Scottish patronage and appointments to major offices; and when Lennox died in 1624, he replaced him as Lord Steward, at the head of James's court.[50] James at last had the dual English and Scottish favourites that the exigencies of British kingship apparently required.

Such delegation may explain the king's apparent loss of grip on affairs at the very end of his reign. But more immediately, it worked: dual favourites enabled James to co-ordinate the government of his two kingdoms; and the Scots vanished as an issue both from the day-to-day life of the court and from the English parliaments of the 1620s.[51]

What was the overall meaning of James's policy? Between 1603 and 1615, the all-Scottish Bedchamber was the ubiquitous cause of parliamentary failure to settle the vital issues of Union and finance,

[49] R. Lockyer, *Buckingham: The Life and Political Career of George Villiers, First Duke of Buckingham, 1592–1628* (1981), 16–17; Gardiner, *History of England ...*, ii. 318.

[50] H.M.C., *Mar & Kellie*, 84, James to Mar, 16 May 1618; Stone, *Crisis of the Aristocracy*, 475–6; *Letters of Chamberlain*, ii. 297, 441–2; Lee, *Government by Pen*, 212–13; H.M.C., *Mar & Kellie Supplement*, 193.

[51] On Buckingham's power in England, Lockyer, *Buckingham*, chs. i–vi; and see his procurement of the royal signature in P.R.O., Signet Office Registers of King's Bills, S.O. 3/6–3/8, *passim*.

and the trigger issue of two tactically disastrous dissolutions. Why did the king allow his Bedchamber to assume such importance, and apparently to wreck some of his most important plans?

The simple answer is that his policy of reserving the Bedchamber was a point of principle that was a central part of James's wider plans; not an inconsequential, accidental personal obstacle to them. James on arrival had done something to widen the Elizabethan establishment, which had become in practice a clique composed of a handful of families. But it was little enough: and English administration had seen so many decades of sclerosis that even an established monarch would have found it very difficult to purge the bureaucracy or create new offices in pursuit of policies.[52] So the court was to be James's breathing-space amid this stifling conservatism. The Bedchamber and Privy Chamber were new departments, the only such innovations James achieved. How did he use them, and what did he hope to achieve by manipulating their membership? To answer that, we must put his use of the court into a wider perspective.

We have examined in some detail the accession settlement of the court, and the 'equal partition' that was applied in the Outer and Privy Chambers. There were many precedents for such use of a court to promote unity between different territories, united only in the person of their ruler. Philip II in England had retained a guard of 400 split evenly into English, Spanish, German and Swiss quarters; his predecessors, the fifteenth-century dukes of Burgundy organised their *chambellans ordinaires*, drawn from their scattered territories, into quarterly shifts to institutionalise the connections back and forth between the duke and each diverse locality.[53] With fewer such problems, Edward IV's stated aim in the *Black Book* of his household ordinances was to bring representatives of the most important families from all over England to his court.[54] Tudor institutions like the Gentlemen Pensioners functioned similarly: their Captain wrote to James in 1603 that the 50 Gentlemen, waiting quarterly, were 'chosen out of the best and auncientest families of England, ... specially

[52] P. Williams, *The Tudor Régime* (Oxford, 1979), 427, 454–6. Cf. *Commons Journals*, i. 309 (15 May 1606); G. E. Aylmer, 'Office Holding as a Factor in English History', *History*, xliv (1959), 232, 240 and *The King's Servants: The Civil Service of Charles I, 1625–1642* (1974), ch. 3 and p. 159.

[53] S. Pegge, *Curialia* (5 Parts, London, 1782–1806), Pt. iii. 28; G. Huydts, 'Le Premier Chambellan des Ducs de Bourgogne', in *Mélanges d'Histoires offerts à Henri Pirenne* (2 vols., Brussels, 1926), i. 263–70; C. A. J. Armstrong, 'The Golden Age of Burgundy', in A. G. Dickens (ed.), *The Courts of Europe* (1977), 61, 63, 70.

[54] A. R. Myers (ed.), *The Household of Edward IV* (Manchester, 1959), 108, 127 on Knights and Esquires of the Household; David Starkey, 'The Age of the Household', in S. Medcalf (ed.), *The Later Middle Ages* (1981), 263, and *passim*.

recommended for their worthiness and sufficiency'.[55] James's aim was to preside over such a representative court: in 1607 he pointed with satisfaction to the 'Irish, Scottish, Welsh and English, divers in Nation, yet all walking as subjects and servants within my Court'.[56] In dividing most of his court equally between English and Scots, James was thus seeking a rather radical effect by entirely traditional means.

If this was the wider role of the court, there was a particular role for the chivalric orders established by rulers of dispersed territories in Western Europe in the fourteenth and fifteenth centuries. James practised here too his visible, symbolic even-handedness. A succession of paired Englishmen and Scotsmen were admitted to the Order of the Garter, beginning in 1603 with Lennox and Southampton. When in 1608 the earls of Dunbar and Montgomery rode off together in procession to Windsor, the Venetian ambassador reported that James thought 'that nothing can more contribute to the Union than the idea and demonstration of an equality of rank between the two nations'.[57]

Moreover, there was something about this somewhat mechanistic, numerical even-handedness which appealed to James personally. The simple composition by rank of the Bedchamber reveals symmetry for which only the king can have been responsible, who alone directed both ennoblement and Bedchamber appointment. Between 1603 and 1615 the department consisted of a duke, two earls, two viscounts, two barons and a knight. The elevation of the dual English and Scottish favourites Buckingham and Hamilton (both Marquises between 1618 and 1623) was the last and most sweeping expression of such balance; they ranked below Lennox and above six earls. James once expressed with relish his responsibility to call up and down the individual worth of his subjects just as he determined the value of his coin.[58]

Given the precedents, the context, and the personal satisfaction James evidently derived from these symmetries, why did James keep the English out of his Bedchamber for so long? One obvious answer is his concern for his own security. Dark talk of another Sicilian Vespers occurred repeatedly between 1603 and 1614.[59] James's reaction to the Gunpowder plot reflected such fears (as the motives of some of the conspirators—Guy Fawkes especially—had been partly

---

[55] J. Nichols, *The Progresses, Processions and Magnificent Festivities of King James I* ... (4 vols., 1828), i. 125–6.

[56] *Workes* (1616), 517.

[57] *CSP Venetian*, xi (1607–10), 137, 4 June 1608; xii (1610–13), 142, 4 May 1611, Arundel and Rochester; *Letters of Chamberlain*, i. 597, 599 for Knollys and Fenton in 1615.

[58] Speech of 21 Mar. 1610 in *Workes* (1616), 529.

[59] E.g. P.R.O. 31/3/35, Beaumont to Villeroy, n.d., follows letter of 24 May 1603 in vol.; *Ambassades de Monsieur de la Boderie en Angleterre*, v. 510–11 (9 Dec. 1610).

anti-Scottish): his immediate distrust for the English led, in the after-math of the plot, to him living 'in the innermost rooms with only Scots about him'.[60] But for all the play made by historians of the king's physical cowardice, James subordinated personal fear to policy. In 1605 his understanding of English annoyance at his apparent lack of trust indeed led him to refuse Edinburgh's offer of a special Scots bodyguard.[61] In excluding the English, therefore, it is probable that considerations of security merely coincided with those of policy. For all James's preference for being surrounded, in a worryingly xenophobic country, by old friends whom he could trust, there was above all political calculation in his keeping the English at arm's length.

How precise was that calculation? James may have overplayed his hand in insisting on maintaining the Scots Bedchamber monopoly, granting them massive patronage, and at the same time expecting Union legislation from an English parliament. James indeed was surprised at the ferocity of the resulting opposition; he concluded that it was for the moment unmanageable, and after 1614 ceased to press measures. If James's reputation as a man of compromise has revived recently, that should not obscure his refusal to budge on certain key issues: and his ability to choose his own entourage was one such issue. But James's insistence on this, as we have seen, was a comprehensible political stance, not a facet of an alleged character defect.[62] Since his parliamentary scheme failed, there can be little doubt that James's achievement fell short of what he had hoped for at his accession. But Rubens, for all his talents as a propagandist, was not wasting paint, five years after James's death, on celebrating the sterile constitutional failure which the twentieth century predominantly sees. Rubens celebrated James's practical victory. Indeed the early intensity of opposition which ditched his parliamentary schemes makes all the more impressive James's practical achievement in keeping his king-doms together—and to arrive at that conclusion, it is not necessary to measure James's success against his son Charles's disastrous failure. The Stuart Age was a long one, and the problem of keeping England and Scotland in step recurrent, even as late as 1745. James's achieve-ment grows in stature on the long view.

The nature and scope of the crown had been changed by James's very accession; but the institutions of government could not be changed to take account of this. It is little wonder that James relied so heavily on prerogative measures; from the first, the English parliament

---

[60] *CSP Venetian*, x (1603–07), 293, 11/21 Nov. 1605. J. Wormald, 'Gunpowder, Treason, and Scots', *Journal of British Studies*, xxiv (1985), 141–68.

[61] *CSP Venetian*, x (1603–07), 304, 22 Dec. 1605.

[62] J. Wormald, 'James VI and I—Two Kings or One?', *History*, lxviii (1983), *passim*; cf. Willson, *James VI and I*, 250–7.

had denied him more conventional means to deal with his extra-ordinary dual inheritance. Hence the use of the court, the Bedchamber and the Bedchamber favourites to express the Union. His solution to the problem was ingenious and very successful: nowhere is the inventiveness and originality of James's approach to kingship clearer. If the 'favourite' was a common phenomenon among the early seventeenth-century monarchies of Europe, James's use of two of them to deal with the business of his various realms was quite unique, and indeed unprecedented earlier in his own reign; it stemmed not from aping continental absolutism, but from managing the peculiar prejudices of English politics.[63] And our appreciation of this practical achievement means that Union needs to regain a central place in our political history of the reign of James I; the very place Rubens gave it in his own achievement on the Banqueting House ceiling.

[63] Cf. C. Russell, *Parliaments and English Politics, 1621–1629* (Oxford, 1979), 10 and n. 3. The question suggests itself whether Spanish government might not have benefited from more than one *valido* to deal with the king's various dominions (particularly Portugal before 1640).

VICTORIAN HISTORIANS AND THE ROYAL HISTORICAL SOCIETY

By J. W. Burrow

READ 6 JULY 1988

SUPERFICIALLY regarded, the foundation of the Royal Historical Society a hundred and twenty years ago belongs to that spate of foundations of academic societies and specialised disciplinary journals, on the continent and in the United States as well as in Britain, which occurred in the concluding decades of the last century and around the beginning of this. Indeed if mere date of foundation were all that counted the Society is considerably more venerable than, for example, the Royal Economic Society, which, even under its earlier title as the British Economic Association, will not celebrate its centenary until 1900,[1] and the British Academy which will not do so for two years beyond that. The Royal Anthropological Institute is three years younger than ourselves, though admittedly it represented an amalgamation of two earlier societies, the Anthropological Society of London which enjoyed a somewhat notorious existence through the eighteen sixties and the still older Ethnological Society.[2] Our *Transactions* had been published, albeit intermittently, for fifteen years before the first issue of the *English Historical Review* in 1886.[3] They had not, it has to be admitted, been fifteen glorious years. Although by the mid-'eighties matters were beginning to improve and the names of some notable historians, Acton, Creighton, Seeley, appear on the membership rolls, the productions of the Society and much of its membership were far from distinguished and it still had some way to go to establish itself as a respected institution.

Various moments, in fact, can with different kinds of justification be taken as those at which the Society became serious and established itself: the mid-'eighties, when some eminent historians were for the first time persuaded to join if not to take an active part; the 'nineties, when, as R. A. Humphreys rightly pointed out in his centenary study of the Society published twenty years ago, the quality of papers printed

---

[1] A. W. Coats, 'The Origins and Early Development of the Royal Economic Society', *The Economic Journal*, lxxviii (1868), 349–71.

[2] J. W. Burrow, *Evolution and Society* (Cambridge, 1966), 118–36.

[3] The early publishing history of the *Transactions* is given in A. T. Milne, *A Centenary Guide to the Publications of the Royal Historical Society 1868–1968* (1968).

really began to improve;[4] the presidencies of Adolphus Ward and
George Prothero from 1899 to 1905, when the earlier, and in the first
case purely nominal, reigns of the public men and men of letters, Lord
John Russell, Lord Aberdare and Sir M. E. Grant Duff, gave way to
that of the working historians; Prothero indeed has been spoken of,
notably by Tout, as the Society's second founder.[5] Professor Kenyon
would even postpone the date of the Society's 'final rehabilitation' to
the opening of the fourth series of *Transactions* in 1918.[6]

The connection, in fact, of the Society in its later form with the
Society as founded in 1868 for the conducting of 'Historical, Biographical and Ethnological investigations', at the instigation of
Charles Rogers, Scottish antiquary, genealogist, former bankrupt and
inveterate founder and joiner of learned and antiquarian societies,
though formally continuous, is also tenuous.[7] The Society's history in
its first thirty years of existence is marked by a very noticeable change
of character and by an active membership which exhibits not so much
a Burkean continuity in the succession of generations as successive
waves of conquest in which the earlier inhabitants are all but exter-
minated and are replaced by strangers of another culture.

R. A. Humphreys traced in his centenary study the decidedly murky
history of the first decade, and there is no need for me to follow in his
footsteps in detail.[8] It was the decade in which Rogers dominated the
Society and made the *Transactions* a vehicle for his own writings; in
which a subservient Council voted him ever larger increases in salary
as the Society's paid 'historiographer', built him a house and sub-
sidised the publication of his genealogical works. If the most obvious
definition of a professional is being paid, Rogers was certainly no
amateur. Inevitably there was growing criticism of the financial management of the Society, as well as of the poor quality and erratic
appearance of its publications, leading to a palace revolution in 1881
in which, at a stormy meeting, Rogers' appointment was not renewed
and after which he departed to launch verbal thunderbolts at his
supplanters. After this there was an improvement in management and
respectability, if not in the quality of the *Transactions*, and a second
wave of contributors appears more and more frequently in them. It
is fairly easy to trace this because at this period it was quite common,

[4] R. A. Humphreys, *The Royal Historical Society 1868–1968* (1969), 20.

[5] T. F. Tout in his Presidential Address, *Transactions of the Royal Historical Society*, 4th
ser., ix (1926), 21.

[6] J. P. Kenyon, *The History Men* (1983), 195.

[7] For Rogers (1825–1890) see *D.N.B.* and Charles Rogers, *Leaves from my Autobiography*
(1876).
   Biographical information for early members of the *R.H.S.* given here is the *D.N.B.*
unless otherwise stated.

[8] Humphreys, *Royal Historical Society*, 1–19.

and in the early 'eighties became still more so, for the same contributors to appear in each or virtually each successive issue, either producing instalments of a continuous work or writing on different though allied subjects. A relatively few names dominate the *Transactions* of the late 'seventies and early and mid-'eighties. This generation was in turn to disappear, by death or marginalisation, in the latter part of the 'eighties, while the same period sees the first emergence—it is tempting to use the now established political term 'entryism'—of the university teachers of history, as authors of papers and later members of Council, even though the list of contributors was to remain for a good while less distinguished than that of the contributors to the *English Historical Review*. There were no tests for admission; the Society resembled in a good many respects the publishing societies which had flourished since the eighteen forties,[9] which in a sense it partially was and, with the amalgamation with the Camden Society in 1897, actually became.[10] In the 'seventies and 'eighties the membership in general seems not to have differed in any significant way from that of other antiquarian and printing societies, making allowance for the fact that many of the latter were locally based.[11] Humphreys describes the early members fairly as 'clergymen and physicians, army officers and civil servants, barristers and solicitors, bank managers, journalists, engineers, teachers',[12] with a sprinkling of peers and country gentlemen. Women were admitted from the outset and became prominent in the *Transactions*, particularly as winners of the Alexander Prize, in the first decade of this century.[13]

But in the early years of the Royal Historical Society—'Royal', thanks to the offices of Lord John Russell, from 1872, though Rogers had impudently made a bid for the title from the outset[14]—noteworthy historians are as far to seek as prominent women. The first historian in the academic or professional sense to figure as a contributor to the *Transactions* was Oscar Browning, in 1885, with papers on the Triple Alliance of 1788 and another on the Anglo-French Commercial Treaty of 1786.[15] In the following year he was joined in the *Transactions* by his fellow Cambridge lecturer in history and a future President of

---

[9] See particularly Philippa Levine, *The Amateur and the Professional. Antiquarians, Historians and Archaeologists in Victorian England 1838–1886* (Cambridge, 1986), chs. 2 and 3, and F.J. Levy, 'The Founding of the Camden Society', *Victorian Studies*, vii, no. 3 (1964), 295–305.

[10] Humphreys, *Royal Historical Society*, 26 and Appendix (by Charles Johnson).

[11] On the typical membership of such societies see Levine, *The Amateur and the Professional*, Appendix I.

[12] Humphreys, *Royal Historical Society*, 11–12.

[13] The prize was founded in 1898. By 1908, five of its winners had been women.

[14] Humphreys, *Royal Historical Society*, 3, 10–11.

[15] *Transactions*, N.S., ii (1885), 77–96 and 349–64.

the Society, William Cunningham, with a paper on 'The foundation and decay of craft guilds'.[16] Cunningham's is now, of course, much the more distinguished name in the history of historiography, as a pioneer, along with Thorold Rogers and W. J. Ashley, of economic history, and an eyebrow may be raised at the designation of Browning so unequivocally as an historian, since his reputation today, so far as it endures, is so much more as a Cambridge personality and educationalist. But it would be anachronistic to separate the two men on these grounds at this point. Browning would have been no less an academic historian in the eyes of contemporaries; both were recently appointed Cambridge University Lecturers in History, teachers of the new (1885) reformed Tripos, and Browning, along with Prothero, was responsible in this period for making Kings *the* Cambridge college for history.[17]

Indeed the titles of Browning's early papers to the Society, with their references to high politics and foreign affairs and their professional kind of specificity, focussed without being arbitrarily minute, proclaim a departure from the Society's *ancien régime* which Cunningham's, to the casual eye, would not have done. Guilds were very much more the kind of thing the Society was accustomed to. Titles of articles veered wildly between the grandiosely general and the randomly detailed. In the earliest numbers, for example, in 1871 and 1872, we find papers on early charters of Bristol, the chronology of the Christian era, 'An official inaccuracy respecting the death of Princess Mary, daughter of James I', the Jacquerie, 'The personal expenses of Charles II in the city of Worcester', and 'Tudor prices in Kent chiefly in 1577'.[18] Cunningham's subject would not have seemed at all out of place—a reminder that the 'new' subject of economic history was in a sense more smoothly continuous with the antiquarian interests of many of the early members than was the preoccupation with high politics among both the older 'literary' historians and the new academic teachers, which had figured hardly at all among the Society's concerns. New conceptions of research transformed old subjects and the use of sources hitherto considered essentially as 'curious', in what J. B. Bury was to call 'a new kind of critical antiquarianism'.[19] Browning's papers would have looked more in place in the new *English Historical Review*, with its emphasis on politics and the state, which

[16] *Transactions*, N.S., iii (1886), 371–92. Browning's contribution was an article on the flight to Varennes.

[17] On this see Peter R. H. Slee, *Learning and a Liberal Education. The Study of Modern History in the Universities of Oxford, Cambridge and Manchester, 1800–1914* (Manchester, 1986), 68–73, 127, 150.

[18] *Transactions*, O.S., i, 2nd ed. (1875) originally issued as *Transactions of the Historical Society of Great Britain*, Volume i, Part 1 (1871) and Part 2 (1872).

[19] Quoted in Slee, *Learning and a Liberal Education*, 134.

made it, in that sense if no other, heir to the traditions of 'literary', narrative history. Talk of 'amateur' and 'professional', in fact, although the most obvious and indispensable way to approach the membership of the Royal Historical Society in the late 'eighties, elides important distinctions and obscures important continuities.

For all that, it is of course impossible to speak of what was happening to the Society from the late 'eighties to the early nineteen hundreds without using the blanket term 'professionalisation'. As Humphreys said, rather prematurely perhaps of the later eighteen nineties, 'the age of the dilletanti had ended'.[20] Victory sometimes prompted a kind of retrospective indulgence to their unprofessional forbears, as when Tout said in his 1926 Presidential Address that 'we must not be too severe on the amateurish character of the infant Society. There was as yet hardly a class of professional historians in the country.'[21] Professionalism was debatable territory in the last years of the nineteenth century and the Royal Historical Society, with its antiquarian as well as somewhat disreputable origins, was in a sense a battlefield. Dr Philippa Levine, in her valuable study of nineteenth-century antiquarian societies, remarks that the Society in the eighteen-eighties was 'caught uncomfortably between the amateur tradition and a desire to emulate the rigour of the new professionals'.[22] This expresses a truth, though Dr Levine's language here is holistic; we need to look, as she herself has done elsewhere, at the motives and sense of identity of individuals. We considered earlier Tout's indulgent 1926 reference to the infant Society's amateurism. Closer to the *mêlée*, in 1906, in the well-known paper he gave at Newnham College on 'Schools of History', he was less kindly: 'The Royal Historical Society has cast off the threatened domination of the amateur, has absorbed one of our oldest publishing societies, and has transformed its direction from the hands of persons of general eminence to those of professional historians.'[23] Tout spoke for the winning side, yet, from a safer distance, we have to wonder who had the better right to speak of 'threat'; who, after all, was there first? Dr Levine speaks more appositely when she refers to the 'marginalisation' of antiquarianism by the rise of professional history.[24] Unlike the *English Historical Review*, the Royal Historical Society was not an organ of the new professionalism from the outset. It was rather the victim of a successful takeover, and we can only guess how many of the earlier members may have lamented the old easy-going days when, as one of them happily wrote, 'The object of

[20] Humphreys, *Royal Historical Society*, 26.
[21] *Transactions*, 4th ser., ix (1926), 8.
[22] Levine, *The Amateur and the Professional*, 173.
[23] *The Collected Papers of Thomas Frederick Tout* (3 vols., Manchester, 1935), i. 95.
[24] Levine, *The Amateur and the Professional*, 72.

the Historical Society was to unite together instruction and enter-tainment.'[25] The professional takeover may have saved the Society for ourselves and eventually made it what it had never been before, distinguished, but from another point of view the professionals were the cuckoos in the antiquarians' and autodidacts' nest; it was they, not amateurism, that represented the 'threat'. What it was they supplanted and why one or two of them initially chose to colonise such an apparently unpromising concern are questions worth asking. It is tempting to speculate that the greatest prize, the fruit of Rogers' *hubris*, was the name, though direct evidence is lacking. Had it had a regionally-inspired title, like so many of the printing clubs, like for example Rogers' earlier foundation, the Grampian Club, on which its rules were based, there could have been little attraction. The Society was at least national, even before it was royal, in the sense that antiquarians with local interests and access to local, often borough, archives, could find an audience outside their locality, and the name embodied that claim to generality.

Yet the territory, if appropriately named for the professionals' purposes, was also inhabited. One thing that seems clear is that the takeover, as represented, for example, by membership of Council, was very rapid. The Council of 1886, for example, under Browning's chairmanship, which included Acton, Cunningham and Creighton, was not merely a new Council but a Council of new members; Brown-ing's name appears first on the Fellowship list in 1878, but his mem-bership lapsed and he had not been a Fellow at all in 1882, while none of the others appears on the Fellowship lists until the mid-'eighties. 1886 was also the year in which Prothero became a Fellow. Before we consider this further, however, it is worth looking at what they replaced. The leading spirits of the later 'seventies and early 'eighties, easily identifiable by the number of their papers as well as membership of Council, are a distinct generation, distinguishable both from Rogers and his cronies before the *coup d'état*, and from the new professionals. Compared with Rogers' clique their interests are less readily described as antiquarian, while the prevalence of the genea-logical interest declines perceptibly after his departure. His successors were a more mixed lot. The same names appear over and over again: George Harris, Henry Howorth,[26] most readily described as an archaeologist, Hyde Clark, a member of the Anthropological Insti-tute, who spoke indefatigably on ethnographical subjects, Cornelius Walford, Albert Wratislaw and Gustavus George Zerffi. Their dis-appearance from the *Transactions*, by death or discouragement, from

---

[25] George Harris, proposing the toast of the Royal Historical Society at its annual dinner on 15 Feb. 1875. *The Autobiography of George Harris* (London, 1888), 429.

[26] On Howorth see Levine, *The Amateur and the Professional*, 168, 169, 171.

the mid-'eighties (none of them published after 1886), rather than the ousting of Rogers in 1881, marks the fundamental change in the Society's character, even if for some years afterwards the quality of papers remained indifferent; they were the natives edged out by the incomers. The last of them, Zerffi, was still clinging on as a member of Council until 1891, but his last paper ('The Tchōng-Yông of Confucius, edited by his grandson Tchhing-Tsé') was in 1885, significantly, around the time of the transition of power on Council.

As a group their leading characteristic is idiosyncrasy. George Harris (1809–1890), for example, who first appears in the second volume of the *Transactions* (1873), and who from then onward contributed to every volume of the Old Series, until 1882, a sequence, in chronological order, of flimsy articles on the history of 'domestic everyday life, manners and customs', is really better described as a polymath and autodidact than antiquary. For much of his life he was a briefless barrister and a man of grandiose though thwarted ambition who became an indefatigable itinerant lecturer on a wide variety of subjects; the Society was merely one of his numerous audiences—numerous at least in the sense that there were a large number of them. Harris was the son of a solicitor in Rugby and entered Rugby School in 1820, where he was apparently bullied. Displaying what seems an irrepressible talent for stepping from frying pans into fires, he left Rugby for a midshipman's birth on H.M.S. *Spartiate*, but the navy did not agree with his health. Harris' autobiography, which is essentially a journal, presents a picture of a restless, difficult man whose didacticism and membership of numerous societies seem a compensation for lack of more solid achievements. He tried the bar and journalism without success, and published works on an immense variety of subjects, including law, painting and psychic phenomena. His *Life of Lord Chancellor Hardwicke* (1847) brought him neither sales nor patronage, but it drew his attention to the question of access to historical manuscripts, and the paper he wrote on this in 1857 and presented to the Social Science Association (one of his numerous affiliations) drew the notice of Lord Brougham. Harris led the deputation on the subject to Palmerston in 1859 but got no further.[27]

He became a *protégé* of Brougham, however, and after years of insecurity and even penury obtained a post as a Deputy County Court Judge and, from 1862, a Registrar in Bankruptcy; the latter seems a case of incipient poacher turned gamekeeper just in time. He obtained a pension in 1868 and became a member of the Royal Historical Society in 1872. His references to the reception of his papers are invariably complacent, perhaps not unjustifiably: he also records that

[27] For his own account of his relation to the Manuscripts Commission see *The Autobiography of George Harris*, ch. xvii.

on 15 February 1875 the Society was addressed by Rabindranath Tagore, to whom Harris was drawn by his interest in psychical research, and afterwards he and Tagore and two friends held a séance.[28] Harris' life's work, his *Philosophical Treatise on the Nature and Constitution of Man*, published in 1876, is unkindly described in the *D.N.B.* as showing 'a singular tendency to revert to the principles and terminology of the medieval schoolmen'. It is certainly a work of some eccentricity, in which Galen and Origen are cited as authorities and correspondences are eagerly traced between the seven decades of life, the seven days of the week ('Saturday is the period from sixty to seventy, the latter part or afternoon of which is by most spent as a time of relaxation') and, rather less exactly, with the times of day.[29] There is something decidedly pathetic in Harris' attempts, before its publication, to solicit criticisms of his masterwork from eminent contemporaries, whose responses, or lack of them, are duly recorded; Darwin pleaded illness, Huxley and Lubbock pressure of work;[30] Gladstone was also approached and Maudsley was helpful, but Huxley, in a later letter, delivered a stinging rebuff to Harris' appeal to the authority of his patron and idol; Huxley would have none of Lord Brougham's 'valueless scientific and philosophical opinions'.[31] It is tempting to say that we hear the polymath and autodidact given his dismissal by the new professionalism.

Another recidivist contributor to the *Transactions* in the early 'eighties was Cornelius Walford (1827–1885). Walford had been one of Rogers' chief antagonists. Also qualified as a barrister, he was a director of insurance companies, a writer on insurance matters and a member of the Statistical Society. He wrote works on the history of guilds (published posthumously in 1888), on *Fairs Past and Present* (1883), and a statistical chronology of plagues and pestilences. He was a serious antiquary in whose writings, evidently inspired by his professional interests, institutional and actuarial questions overlapped.

A more exotic figure, by origin at least, was Albert Henry Wratislaw (1822–1892). He, like Harris, was a Rugbeian, and in fact their families must have been acquainted for Wratislaw's father, who claimed descent from a noble Bohemian family, was, like Harris's, a Rugby solicitor and involved in the affairs of the School.[32] It is

[28] *Ibid.*, 416.

[29] George Harris, *A Philosophical Treatise on the Nature and Constitution of Man* (2 vols., London, 1876), i. 168–9.

[30] *Autobiography*, 409, 413, 416–17.

[31] *Ibid.*, 424–5.

[32] He had become a *cause célèbre* while a schoolboy when his father took legal action to compel Arnold to provide adequately for the education of local boys as prescribed by the school's foundation. See T. W. Bamford, *Thomas Arnold* (1960), 113–15, 130–4, 140. Harris' father was clerk to the school's trustees. Harris himself claimed to have

tempting to postulate a 'Rugby connection' in the history of the Society, but Harris' autobiography gives no direct support to this. Wratislaw had a smoother and more scholarly career than Harris; up to Christ's, Cambridge, in 1842, he graduated 3rd classic and became a Fellow and Tutor of Christ's until 1850, when he became headmaster first of Felsted's, and then, in 1855, of Bury St Edmunds Grammar School, where he succeeded the distinguished but controversial philologist and Biblical critic J. W. Donaldson.[33] Wratislaw's academic career touched or just failed to touch those of two distinguished professional historians of the new generation; he left Christ's just before Seeley arrived and A. W. Ward left Bury Grammar School the year Wratislaw took over. In the *Transactions* Wratislaw wrote on Bohemian and Slavonic topics; building on his heritage he had made himself a considerable Slavonic scholar, editing Czech works and translating medieval Slavonic poems. He died in 1892 but his last paper to the Society was published in 1881.

Finally there was the Society's intellectual historian, George Gustavus Zerffi, who produced an interminable if easy-going history of philosophical ideas in successive issues between 1874 and 1880, under the general title 'The historical development of idealism and realism', before going on to oriental wisdom in the mid-'eighties. He was obviously exercised by Darwinist materialism. He was a Hungarian who emigrated after the revolution of 1848 and managed to find a post in the Department of Art at South Kensington.[34] He published works on art, science, religion, philosophy, universal history and the Irish Question. His interests overlap to some extent with Harris's. Both wrote on art, universal history and spiritualism. Zerffi's work on the latter, published in 1871, was on spiritualism and animal magnetism and was apparently inspired by Schopenhauer.

Does it tell us much to call these men amateurs—an eccentric polymath, a statistician, a scholar, a Romantic exile? In relation to the new University teachers of history they were all amateurs only in the sense that all foreigners are foreigners; certainly they were very different kinds of amateur from those feared as potential intruders by the founders of the *English Historical Review*, 'the Stanleys and the Kingsleys', as J. R. Green, himself hardly the archetypal professional,

---

often had constitutional and philosophical discussions with Arnold while he was working in his father's practice in 1835. *Autobiography*, 43.

[33] On Donaldson, see J. W. Burrow, 'The Uses of Philology in Victorian England', in R. Robson (ed.), *Ideas and Institutions of Victorian Britain. Essays in honour of George Kitson Clark* (Cambridge, 1967), 192–3.

[34] The Council of the R.H.S. sponsored a course of lectures by Zerffi on the science of history given at South Kensington. See Humphreys, *Royal Historical Society*, 14.

called them.[35] Wratislaw was a scholar with an esoteric interest and hence, presumably, without a ready-made audience.[36] Walford was a specialist of another kind, a statistician whose work contained an historical interest. Harris's and Zerffi's interests were closest: both had had somewhat picaresque careers; both were polymaths, interested in politics and spiritualism; both were indefatigable lecturers;[37] in Zerffi's case the status involved in being a Fellow may well have mattered. It is tempting to speak of both as charlatans, which Walford and Wratislaw definitely were not. If Harris was one he was clearly unaware of it and took himself with complete and almost megalomaniac seriousness; about Zerffi it is hard to be so sure, for among his eclectic interests Zerffi was, it seems, a spy.[38] The other two most regular contributors, Howorth and Hyde Clarke, were archaeologists and ethnologists, drawn in, presumably, by the reference in the Society's title to ethnology.

Other contributors, the men of one paper, seem often to have been local men with access to a particular set of records. There were also Public Record officials,[39] whom Dr Levine has called the first real historical professionals, and a sprinkling of men rooted in older scholarly traditions such as Biblical criticism. Overlapping interests and careers, though hardly enough to establish a firm intellectual identity, may have played a part in recruitment; reading Rogers' fulsome tribute to the role in the Society's foundation played by his 'friend' Sir John Bowring,[40] it is tempting to speculate on their common interest in hymnology: another early contributor, William Irons, well

---

[35] Green to E. A. Freeman, 28 January 1867, in Leslie Stephen (ed.), *Letters of John Richard Green* (1902), 173.

[36] According to the *D.N.B.* he was invited to give a course of lectures on Slavonic literature at the Taylorian Institute in 1877.

[37] In his Presidential Address printed in 1881, 'The Science of History', Zerffi told the Society that 'I have had the satisfaction of lecturing during the last six years to, at least, 45,576 persons'. *Transactions*, O.S., ix (1881), 1.

[38] Evidence of Zerffi's activities as a spy, which appear to have extended from 1850 to 1865 (and therefore to have been long past by the time of his Presidency of the R.H.S.) is given in Tibor Franck, *The British Image of Hungary 1865–1870* (Budapest, 1976), 275–6, where Zerffi is described as 'one of the most prominent Austrian secret agents in Britain'. The same author has published a full-length study of Zerffi (Budapest, 1985) in Hungarian. I am indebted for these references and for drawing my attention to this aspect of Zerffi to the kindness of Paul Smith, and regret my inability to read Professor Franck's study of Zerffi in the original.

[39] Levine, *The Amateur and the Professional*, 2. The recruitment of Hubert Hall and H. E. Malden were important steps in the Society's advance to respectability. Malden first published in the *Transactions* in 1880 and Hall in 1886. Hall was to be the Society's Literary Director from 1891 to 1938, and its Hon. Secretary from 1894–1903. Malden followed him as Secretary and held the post for twenty-eight years.

[40] Rogers, *Autobiography*, 349. Bowring contributed an article on 'Borrowings of modern from ancient poets' to *Transactions*, O.S., ii (1873).

known as a respondent to *Essays and Reviews*, translated the *Dies Irae*, while yet another devoted himself to translating English hymns into Latin; with what object appears to be unrecorded.[41]

These, divided among the two 'generations', of Rogers and post-Rogers, were the men who died off, were edged aside and failed, so to speak, notably to replicate themselves from the mid-'eighties onwards. 1885 seems the crucial year; Walford died and Harris, according to the Report of Council, was obliged to resign from Council by failing health. The way was open to the infiltration (rather more than that on Council, though more gradually in the *Transactions*) of the university teachers, the Cambridge men.

The first cuckoo, so to speak, was clearly Oscar Browning. He was not the earliest 'professional' member; that honour seems to belong to Adolphus Ward, but his early membership, like Browning's own, lapsed without leaving any noticeable sign in the 'seventies.[42] Browning is the first of the new dispensation in the mid-'eighties; Fellow and member of Council in 1884, under Zerffi's chairmanship; Chairman in 1885 with his Cambridge colleagues Cunningham and Bass Mullinger[43] as members. By 1886, as we have seen, Browning presided over a Council which included Acton and Creighton, both new Fellows, and the Society had also been joined by Browning's colleague at Kings, Prothero, and by Seeley as Vice-President. Tout has left, for a slightly later date, a description of Browning's methods of recruitment. In 1926, as President, he recalled that his membership began in 1894, when 'I fell a coy, but not an unwilling, victim to the blandishments of Mr. Oscar Browning, who used to the full the opportunities of a mountain holiday in the Engadine to preach the sound doctrine that no historian fulfilled the duties of his station unless he enlisted under the Society's banner'.[44] It was, to be ponderous about it, clearly an appeal to a sense of professional responsibility. Tout gave a paper in 1894; he had been preceded in the *Transactions* by two other Oxford men, Montagu Burrows and Charles Oman, two

---

[41] This was Charles Buchanan Pearson, who contributed 'Some account of ancient churchwarden accounts of St Michael's, Bath' (*Transactions*, O.S., vii (1878)). Irons contributed to the same volume an article on 'The transition from heathen to Christian civilization'. Both appear also in volume viii (1880).

[42] Ward first became a member in 1870 and remained one, though apparently inactive, in the early 'seventies. Browning appears first in the list of Fellows in 1878, and renewed his membership in 1884.

[43] James Bass Mullinger (1834–1917), a Fellow of St John's, was a teacher in the History of Education (a link with Browning) from 1885 to 1895 and Lecturer in History, 1894–1909. A man of legendary irascibility, he was sent to prison as a young man for an attack on his sister-in-law with a carving knife (J. A. Venn, *A Alumnae Cantabridgienses*). It seems possible that he is the only member of Council to have served a prison sentence.

[44] Presidential Address, *Transactions*, 4th ser., ix (1926), 1.

years earlier. But in the later 'eighties it was clearly Cambridge men, or rather, one suspects, Browning, who made the running. There was from 1886 onwards a Cambridge Branch, with Seeley as Chairman and Browning Secretary, which included Cunningham, Bass Mullinger, Prothero and A. P. Ropes, all teachers for the newly revised Historical Tripos and three of them, Browning, Prothero and Ropes, Kingsmen. Ropes was, after Browning and Cunningham, the earliest 'professional' contributor to the *Transactions*, with a paper published in 1886 and two more shortly afterwards. He was a Fellow of Kings, having taken the History Tripos and graduated in 1883; he must have been taught by Browning and Prothero.[45] The facility which won him the Chancellor's medal for English verse in 1881 was eventually, however, fatal to his career as an historian. He turned to writing for the musical comedy stage and under the pseudonym Adrian Ross was responsible for 'The Quaker Girl' and similar productions. According to the *Dictionary of National Biography* the knowledge of German he acquired to lecture on Frederick the Great 'was of immense help to him in adapting Viennese operettas'. The Fellow of the Royal Historical Society had not been useless to the adaptor of 'The Count of Luxemburg', but Ropes' academic career petered out and, remembering the interest of some of the earlier members in hymnology, it has to be said that in that respect at least standards seem to have been declining.

But to return to Browning. The motives which impelled him into the Society as the harbinger of the new professionals are intelligible in terms of his interests and the point his career had reached. He had returned to Kings from Eton in 1876, after a notable scandal, ejected from his housemastership by the Headmaster, Hornby, amid a blaze of publicity. The real, though not the ostensible, cause, seems to have been the excessive amount of interest he was displaying in a boy from another house, the fifteen-year-old George Nathaniel Curzon.[46] In the early 'eighties he was a man who needed to rehabilitate himself and to find a role and the Society seems to have figured in this. Indeed, if its foundation was in part the result of Rogers' need to recuperate his fortunes after bankruptcy, its professionalisation may owe a good deal, indirectly, to Browning's over-enthusiastic interest in his young Etonian pupils.[47] Browning was fortunate in the period of his return to Cambridge; standards in history were not, could not be, too exacting, but there were opportunities given by the newly independent

---

[45] Venn, *Alumnae Cantabridgienses* and *D.N.B.* Ropes' papers to the R.H.S. were on eighteenth-century German diplomatic subjects; Browning's influence seems apparent.

[46] Ian Anstruther, *Oscar Browning. A Biography* (1983), chs. V and VI.

[47] 'The world owes some of its greatest debts to men from whose very memory it recoils.' W. Stubbs, *The Constitutional History of England* (3 vols., Oxford, 1873), i, p. iv.

Tripos. He obtained a college lectureship at Kings in 1880, four years after Prothero, and a university one in 1884, just at the point when he begins to play a part in the affairs of the Society; he was, as it were, ripe for the insignia of professionalism.

But one impulse which seems to have constituted part of Browning's hopes for the Society dated from further back, to his thwarted career as a schoolteacher. He had early taken up the cause of professionalism in education, of teacher training, and devoted much of the latter part of his life to it, as Secretary of the Cambridge Teachers Training Syndicate, a post he held for thirty years from 1879, as well as writing about it copiously. It seems that Browning thought of himself as not so much a professional historian as a professional educator, and in the conflicts over the Tripos he was predictably for Seeley and against Ward and Prothero and the ideal of research.[48] As a young master at Eton he had formed one of a circle of young Public School masters attempting to educate themselves in their profession, known colloquially as the 'United Ushers'.[49] In the sense that it brought together masters from different schools it can be seen as an inevitably much less coherent and influential counterpart to the body of history tutors from different colleges which was formed at Oxford in the same period, the Modern History Association.[50] Associations of teachers preceded associations for research, except insofar as the older antiquarian societies of which the Royal Historical Society was one may be said to have been such. It seems likely that Browning was thinking more of the former than of the latter when he joined the Society and recruited colleagues; his hand is certainly evident in the Society's first initiative other than printing, the conference, chaired by Creighton with Browning as Secretary, organised in 1887 for the promotion of history teaching in schools[51]—the first portent of the Historical Association. It was, Humphreys says, 'a tribute to the energy and enthusiasm of Oscar Browning'.[52]

In the short term the initiative bore no fruit, and of course the idea of teacher training was only one aspect of professionalisation. Ward and Prothero, at the beginning of this century, were to throw their weight behind the notion of a school of advanced historical training in the techniques of research, which was eventually to be achieved

[48] Slee, *Learning and a Liberal Education*, ch. 5.

[49] H. E. Wortham, *Victorian Eton and Cambridge. Being the Life and Times of Oscar Browning* (new ed. 1956), 47. Browning gave his own account of the development of his educational theories while at Eton and their fruition in Cambridge in Oscar Browning, *Memories of Sixty Years at Eton, Cambridge and Elsewhere* (2nd ed. 1910), 123–4, 179, 258–65.

[50] Slee, *Learning and a Liberal Education*, 89.

[51] See *Transactions*, N.S., iv (1889), 67–84.

[52] Humphreys, *Royal Historical Society*, 22.

with the foundation of the Institute of Historical Research.[53] The Society's Presidents from 1899 onwards, including Ward, Prothero, Firth, Oman and Tout, were to be on the whole those who were identified with the new ideal of a research-based professionalism and of 'pure' history rather than the pedagogical ideas and cultivation of a 'science of politics' of Browning and Seeley. That a learned society should promote the ideal of research was obviously appropriate; it was in a sense congruous with its initial character as an antiquarian and printing club; the absorption of the Camden Society in 1897 was more consistent with the Society's original aims and character than Browning's for the time being abortive pedagogical initiatives in the late 'eighties. Attending only to Browning and rather over-dramatising the contrast, one might say that the Society was colonised on behalf of one version of professionalisation to be saved for another. The processes of professionalisation and the ideals to which it gave rise were complex and these are in some measure reflected in the Society. Just as there were different sorts of 'amateur', so there were different professionalisms. Antiquarians and scholars like Toulmin Smith, Thorold Rogers and J. H. Round[54] had more in common with the new ideal of historical research than had many of the new university history tutors, who might be unproductive or indifferent scholars, like Browning himself. The work of a number of modern historians, Piet Blaas,[55] Doris Goldstein,[56] Rosemary Jann,[57] Philippa Levine and Peter Slee has recently made us aware that the process of the professionalisation of history in this country and the associated claims for it as a 'science' exhibit complexities which defy simple characterisation. Philippa Levine has claimed that the first professional historians were not the university teachers but the Public Record Office archivists. Rosemary Jann and Peter Slee have argued in different ways for under-recognised continuities between older conceptions and the new professionalism, in terms of persisting notions of humane letters, or a liberal education, and the cultivation of 'judgement' rather than simply technique, while Blaas has stressed

---

[53] E.g., Prothero's Presidential Address. *Transactions*, N.S., xvii (1903), vii–viii.

[54] Round appears in the *Transactions* in 1894 (N.S., viii), with an article on the executions of Sir Charles Lucas and Sir George Lisle.

[55] P. B. M. Blaas, *Continuity and Anachronism: Parliamentary and Constitutional Development in Whig Historiography and the Anti-Whig Reaction between 1890 and 1930* (The Hague, 1978).

[56] Doris Goldstein, 'The Organizational Development of the British Historical Profession, 1884–1921', *Bulletin of the Institute of Historical Research*, lv (1982), 180–93, and 'The Professionalisation of History in Britain in the late Nineteenth and early Twentieth Centuries', *History of Historiography*, iii (1983), 3–26.

[57] Rosemary Jann, *The Art and Science of Victorian History* (Columbus, Ohio, 1985), esp. Epilogue.

the connections between the rhetoric of professionalism and the political cult of 'national efficiency' around the turn of the century.

The latter is a connection very evident in Prothero's Presidential Address to the Society in 1903, in which, calling for a school of advanced historical training and the compilation of a British historical bibliography, he advocated co-operative work and state-sponsorship and denounced British individualism as a source of amateurism and muddling through.[58] A later President, Tout, also invoked the common contrast with France and Germany but, indisputable professional and unimpeachable upholder of the research ideal as he was, he was prepared to argue in 1906 that 'our national deification of the amateur is by no means an unmixed evil' and to qualify his approval of specialisation and his calls for proper training with references to the wider view.[59] In his Presidential Address to the Society in 1929 he spoke again of specialisation, making, in passing, a surprisingly inaccurate and idealised reference to the Society's early history: 'we have no reason to complain of them [the processes of specialisation]. This Society is itself the result of them. It came into existence because, more than a generation ago, historians began to believe that history was a definite branch of knowledge to be studied by itself for its own sake.'[60] It came into existence for no such reason, and Tout himself knew it, but for the moment the rhetoric of professionalisation had taken over, only to be followed by the qualification: 'The movement towards specialisation continued long in full force ... But a more recent age has begun to realise that specialisation by itself is not enough.'[61] It was not a new thought for him but an abiding one. As early as 1892, in his *Manchester Guardian* obituary of Freeman, he had recognised some of the ironies of professionalisation. The terms of reference had changed, and Freeman was now denigrated for what he had once been thought to exemplify to excess. Thirty years before he had been considered 'the type of the specialist, the minute and pedantic lover of detail', while it might be that 'a generation hence an age wearied of minute specialists will turn back to Freeman's width of historical nature with admiration and envy'.[62]

I am not sure that the latter has quite happened, but the notion of losses as well as gains continues to breed gadflies. Debates over the nature and purpose of historical research, writing and education remain remarkably similar to those conducted in the later nineteenth and early twentieth centuries when history was establishing itself as a

---

[58] *Transactions*, N.S., xvii (1903), xi–xii.
[59] 'Schools of History' (1906), in *Collected Papers*, i. 105–7.
[60] Reprinted in *Collected Papers*, i. 112.
[61] *Ibid.*
[62] *Collected Papers*, i. 132.

discipline and a profession: antiquarianism *versus* literature, research techniques and historical perspectives, short periods and long, truth-for-its-own-sake and a liberal education. One then fruitful source of confusion, it is true, the term 'science', seems blessedly to have disappeared from our polemical vocabulary. A more positive if perhaps peripheral contribution to clarity might be to bear fully in mind the multiple strands which have been woven together in the term 'professional'. There has really been no single tradition and therefore no threats of deviation, no betrayals of 'its' integrity, either by pedantry or amateurism. Or, one might choose instead to say, such betrayals are endemic, constitutive of the history of history as a pursuit and a discipline. Of that multiplicity the Royal Historical Society shows the marks at different points in its history. Because 'professionalism' has come to seem in some respects a misleadingly blanket description, though an inescapable one, it no longer seems quite sufficient to see the early history of the Society simply as the triumph over amateurism, the ending of dilettantism, the growth of seriousness, or as 'rehabilitation' (we have at least to quibble at the appropriateness of the prefix). It demands rather to be seen as part of a complex process, taking place in the later nineteenth and early twentieth centuries throughout Europe and on both sides of the Atlantic, varying from country to country, subject to subject, and institution to institution. To speak of it in such large terms is, as I am very well aware, only to underline the modesty of the contribution this lecture has been able to make to depicting it.

LORD GEORGE BENTINCK AND THE PROTECTIONISTS: A LOST CAUSE?

By Angus Macintyre

READ 14 OCTOBER 1988

IN THE processes by which a political cause is defeated, there are significant, sometimes unexpected achievements. This proposition is as true of protectionism before and after the repeal of the corn laws as it is for example of Jacobitism or Gladstonian Home Rule. But while the supporters and fellow-travellers of free trade have had abundant attention, the protectionists have suffered from historical neglect redeemed in recent years only by the distinguished contributions of Robert Stewart and Travis Crosby.[1] A certain absence both of historical sympathy and of interest in the arguments of the enemies of free trade has produced a widely-held view of the protectionists as mere *révanchistes* and political untouchables, 'wild men of the right' who had to be 'dragged kicking and screaming from their last ditches' while others made proper preparations for 'a generation of bourgeois prosperity'.[2] Norman Gash, the doyen of 'the age of Peel', while keenly aware of the mixed motives—intellectual, political and economic—which influenced men's conduct in 1845–6 and beyond, writes of the protectionists as 'the dead weight' of the conservative party: their cause was too monolithic, too representative of 'a latent hostility to the other great interests of the country', to form the basis of a national party; and their leader Lord George Bentinck was principally and destructively inspired by revenge.[3]

There may be room for an appraisal of the protectionist movement and party (here considered only in the early years) and of Bentinck's short but curiously influential career. The survival and vigorous existence after 1846 of a party rejecting Peelism and for some years the

---

[1] Robert Stewart, *The Politics of Protection. Lord Derby and the Protectionist Party 1841–1852* (Cambridge, 1971), and *The Foundation of the Conservative Party 1830–1867* (1978); Travis L. Crosby, *English Farmers and the Politics of Protection 1815–1852* (Hassocks, Sussex, 1977). Derek Walker-Smith, *The Protectionist Case in the 1840s* (Oxford, 1933), is still of value for its analysis of protectionist economic arguments.

[2] Eric J. Evans, *The Forging of the Modern State. Early industrial Britain 1783–1870* (1983), 269.

[3] N. Gash, *Reaction and Reconstruction in English Politics, 1832–52* (Oxford, 1965), 47–9, 137–8, 150. For his view of Bentinck, see his *Sir Robert Peel. The Life of Sir Robert Peel after 1830* (1972), 578–9, 583, and *Aristocracy and People. Britain 1815–1865* (1979), 240–1.

label of 'conservative' were victories against the form-book of British politics which from the late 1820s to the late 1850s hatched numerous 'parties' or factions but was hostile to their long-term independent life: relative success was as fatal to them as outright failure.[4] The party aspect is bound up with a more interesting question. It may or may not be right to see protectionism as an ideology of social stasis and nostalgia; what is certain is that it offered a powerful challenge to that flexible liberal conservatism, Peelite and whig, the success of which is generally relied upon to explain both the adaptation of British society to an industrialising economy and the prolonged political dominance of the landowning classes. By the 'liberal conservative' thesis, protectionism should never have happened. But it did. Its history must be related to these phenomena of social adaptation and landed ascendancy.

The foundations of the future party were laid by the sudden emergence in 1843–4 of a truly formidable movement in defence of the interests of agriculture in loose tandem with those of shipping and West Indian sugar producers. The organisation and activities of the rightly-called 'Anti-League' are well charted.[5] Their significance has been less fully recognised. More decentralised and much less theatrical than Cobden's agitation, the Anti-League was a more important fact of national politics than the Anti-Corn Law League, and in functional terms undeniably more effective. Originally a tenant-farmers' movement centred on the eastern and southern counties, it was quickly and wisely taken over and financed by peers and gentlemen stung into action by the Cobdenites' incessant attacks on landlordism and aristocratic dominance. The duke of Richmond's Central Protection Society, the co-ordinating machine by March 1844 for nearly a hundred local bodies, included all those M.P.s—George Bankes, William and Philip Miles, Augustus Stafford O'Brien, G.J. Heathcote, Charles Newdegate and Edward Cayley—who provided a collective front in the Commons before Bentinck assumed the leadership in April 1846.

The Anti-League served two vital purposes. First, it swung the bulk of the agriculturists, graziers as well as cereal growers, firmly behind protection which united the landed interest where possible tax changes

[4] The fortunes of the protestant Ultras, Cobbettite, Philosophic, and Cobdenite radicals, the 'Derby Dilly', O'Connell's Irish party and the 'Pope's Brass Band', administrative reformers and the Peelites support this contention.

[5] See Crosby, *English Farmers*, ch. v; Mary Lawson-Tancred, 'The Anti-League and the Corn Law crisis of 1846', *Historical Journal*, iii. 2 (1960), 162–83; Stewart, *Politics of Protection*, 56–8, and *Foundation of the Conservative Party*, 206–12. Important treatments of protectionism in its local contexts are R. W. Davis, *Political Change and Continuity 1760–1885; a Buckinghamshire study* (Newton Abbot, 1972), and R. J. Olney, *Lincolnshire Politics, 1832–1885* (Oxford, 1973).

such as relief from malt, salt and hop taxes might have divided it. Officially non-partisan in order to shelter whig protectionists, the movement was almost wholly conservative in its politics. In supporting Peel's protectionism (reaffirmed in June 1844) and his corn law of 1842 against the common radical enemy, the movement served a second important purpose as a necessary focus of unity between government and parliamentary party. Mutinies over Ten Hours and sugar in 1844 and the severe bruising of Ultra protestant and anti-Irish susceptibilities with the Maynooth grant and Peel's new course in Irish policy in 1845 had undoubtedly affected the party's cohesion and morale. But the damage was not irreparable: Maynooth had not opened the road to ruin. The party's stomach for unpalatable medicine was a measure of its toughness, and it was still Peel's natural instrument of government. He did not intend to break his party; even after he moved for substantive repeal of the corn laws, he did not expect more than another murmurous, unproductive mutiny. This miscalculation, partly the result of Peel's underestimate of the Anti-League, nonetheless reveals his continuing if battered faith in the party. Its aims remained those for which he had constructed it: the defence of established institutions in church and state, the preservation of 'the territorial constitution', i.e. the governing dynamic of a landed nobility and gentry; it was, as Goulburn reminded him, 'the only barrier ... against the revolutionary effects of the Reform Bill'.[6] The protectionists also learnt Peel's lesson, and in this crucial sense, he had not failed to educate his party. When he justified his course in 1846 by fusing high notions of the responsibility of the executive and of the sovereignty of an existing parliament, his protectionist opponents acted consistently with his own theory of party in moving against him. The extent of the rebellion, involving two-thirds of the party in the Commons, is proof of the attractions of this doctrine of party and its relationship with the practice of 'parliamentary government' which Disraeli brilliantly expounded in several speeches between 1845 and 1848, and which, in certain moods, perhaps fundamentally, Peel himself shared; it also reflects the power of the protectionist movement 'out of doors'. Far from being handicapped by landowners' fears of 'democratic' politics, the Anti-League used exactly those techniques: matching the Cobdenites' registration campaign in 1845, drumming up support in 1845–6 by a great rash of meetings, pressing M.P.s to

[6] Goulburn to Peel, 30 Nov. 1845, *Memoirs by the Right Hon. Sir Robert Peel*, ed. Earl Stanhope and E. Cardwell (2 vols., 1857–8), ii. 203. For Peel's gradualist strategy for handling the corn law question before Ireland got in the way, see Prince Albert, memo. 25 Dec. 1845, *The Letters of Queen Victoria*, ed. A. C. Benson and Viscount Esher (First series, 3 vols., 1908), ii. 65–6. Stewart, *Foundation of the Conservative Party*, 187–95, and Gash, *Peel*, ch. 13, take more pessimistic views of government/party relations.

renew or take pledges to maintain protection, forcing bye-elections (and, by Crosby's tally, winning 16 out of 24 in the first half of 1846) and calling for a plebiscitary election on protection against free trade. Peel's fast footwork brought on and carried repeal too soon for Cobden's electoral tactics, as John Prest has convincingly argued, and for his broader political aims as Cobden himself later thought.[7] It did not come too soon for the protectionists. Well before Peel's plan was known, Bentinck told his father in early January that 'the cry of "No Surrender" seems very general'.[8] A rebellion was certain. Without Bentinck's leadership, it would not have ended in Peel's deposition, the proscription of the Peelites and the continued existence of an independent protectionist party.

The lack of a modern or complete biography suggests that Bentinck has proved an awkward, almost embarrassing subject. In Disraeli's 'political biography' published in December 1851, he is movingly entombed as 'an ENGLISH WORTHY', representative of a 'traditionary' politics which Disraeli matches approvingly against the politics of 'progress', but also of a protectionism which Disraeli was trying at the time to ditch as the party's policy.[9] The book, despite its calculated taciturnities on, for example, Stanley's leadership, the savagery of Bentinck's attacks on the Peelites and Disraeli's own prominence, is an indispensable source for high protectionist politics before 1848, and the sections on Peel, on Ireland and on the Jews are of compelling interest. For Bentinck's personality and motives, the result is less satisfactory: Disraeli's neo-Carlylean portrait of his virtually flawless hero lacks the colour and truth of life. By contrast there is Norman Gash's recent account which while conceding that in courage, self-reliance and moral convictions Bentinck and Peel were well matched, argues that it was not the coolly professional Disraeli but Bentinck who acted in 1846 'more in the style of a political bravo': with methods and language derived from his 'sporting world', he

[7] See John Prest, *Politics in the Age of Cobden* (1977), 103–24; and for Cobden's regrets, D. A. Hamer, *The Politics of Electoral Pressure. A Study in the History of Victorian Reform Agitations* (Hassocks, Sussex, 1977), 87–9.

[8] Bentinck to the duke of Portland, 2 Jan. 1846, Portland Papers, Nottingham University Library, PwH, fo. 193.

[9] B. Disraeli, *Lord George Bentinck. A Political Biography* (1905 edn.), 379, 382. For the political message intended by Disraeli in a work aimed optimistically at readers of 'all classes', see W. F. Monypenny and G. E. Buckle, *The Life of Benjamin Disraeli, Earl of Beaconsfield* (6 vols., 1910–20), iii. 318–30. Disraeli was sent in 1850 'two immense chests' of Bentinck's papers. Much of this collection was 'probably' destroyed subsequently by the duke of Portland, though he kept some of his son's letters to him: see *The Croker Papers*, ed. L. J. Jennings (3 vols., 1884), iii. 116 n.; and *ibid.*, 127–66, for the most extensive printed sequence of Bentinck's letters (1846–8). Several of Bentinck's friends regretted that Disraeli printed relatively few of Bentinck's letters.

brought 'a new and degrading element' into the arts of parliamentary leadership.[10]

Bentinck was far from being an Ultra or high tory, and Disraeli's view of him as a whig of 1688 modified by modern experience is more fanciful than helpful. He was successively and consistently a Canningite who supported Catholic emancipation and (more critically) the Reform Bill, a follower of Stanley and an active occupant of the 'Derby Dilly', then a recruit in Stanley's wake to the conservative party.[11] Refusals of office from Grey in 1830 and Peel in 1841 made him a back-bencher by choice: as such he served the landed interest in 1845 by his effective work on the select committee on the game laws, that almost wholly unsuccessful attempt by Bright, with whom Bentinck crossed swords frequently during the hearings, to drive a wedge between farmers and landlords. Until the corn law crisis, he was completely loyal to Peel's leadership. That suddenly betrayed loyalty, his view of the purposes and commitments of the party and his rigid adherence to a code of aristocratic honour were the springs of his reaction to Peel's conduct. For him, the conservatives' victory in 1841 had been a decisive verdict against 'the cry of Cheap Bread', as he told Lord Lincoln at the time: it followed for him that conservative M.P.s were still in 1846 committed, as he told his father, by 'distinct or ... implied Pledges to maintain Protection to Agriculture'. The 1842 Corn Law was a 'Treaty', a 'compromise', a 'contract' between Peel and the agricultural interest:

> ... we have a right to insist upon his fulfilling his Contract ... I hold that in honour Sir Robert Peel can not either break that bargain or throw up the Government on the grounds that the Agricultural Interest by their votes refuse to release him from his Engagements to them ... If he refuses he should be treated as all other treacherous Guides are,—made to march with a musket at his head & should he prove false he should be shot or hanged.[12]

The case was reasonable, the language (and the early threat of retribution, later a demand for Peel and his colleagues to make 'atonement' for the dishonour brought on Parliament and the treachery

[10] N. Gash, 'Lord George Bentinck and his Sporting World', in *Pillars of Government and Other Essays on State and Society c. 1770–c. 1880* (1986), 162–75.

[11] After 1846, he called himself a disciple of Pitt, whom he evidently regarded as far from holding 'the cold blooded Philosophy of the Political Economists': Bentinck to C. Eastland de Michele, 19 Oct. 1847, De Michele Papers, Bodleian Library, Ms Eng. lett. c. 667, fos. 173–8. The claim to being a Pittite was reasonable for one who was Canning's nephew by marriage and his private secretary. It must have had the powerful additional attraction of reaching back beyond Peel.

[12] Bentinck to Lincoln, 6 July 1841, quoted in Stewart, *Politics of Protection*, 5; to Portland, 17 Jan. 1846, Portland Papers, PwH, fo. 198.

towards the constituencies) menacing.[13] For Bentinck, the legitimacy
of aristocratic rule in the eyes of people just as important as his own
order was at stake: if a section of the aristocracy went in for wholesale
'political lying and pledge-breaking', 'the most damning fact of the
whole of this bad business will be the shock ... given to the mind of
the Middle Classes ...' To Peel's 'new principles' and his dictation by
which 'a great Majority of the Parliament should be coerced into
doing that which is dishonourable', Bentinck opposed the party's
right and duty to coerce him into 'running honest'.[14] A dogmatically
contractarian outlook, the demands of political consistency and a
passionate belief in the morality of an aristocracy—its pride in its
'chastity', in his own phrase—were the explosive imperatives of his
politics. This is the gloss to be put on the celebrated reported remark
that although 'they' told him that he would personally save £1,500
a year by free trade, he could not bear 'to be sold'.

The assets which he brought to his party were his high station as
the second son of the retiring but much respected 4th duke of Portland,
a tall, impressive figure, transparent political honesty, considerable
energy, tenacity and formidable powers of work (though these were
put under a strain which, as he recognised, damaged his health) and
his reputation as, in Charles Greville's phrase, 'the Leviathan of the
turf'. This is not the place to delve into his remarkable racing career
and his activities as a reformer of the turf. The evidence as to his own
questionable practices, to which Gash refers severely, needs weighing
carefully.[15] It comes from hostile sources, most pertinently from
Greville, his cousin and former racing partner with whom he had
quarrelled bitterly. Greville's long *de mortuis* account of Bentinck, a
blend of circumstantial evidence, perceptive judgments and long-
cherished venom, raises serious enough questions, but his criticisms of
Bentinck's subterfuges and 'peculiar code' of conduct must be read in
the light of Greville's own guilt about his love of racing ('vile pursuits,
vilely pursued'); he never made public what he alleges he knew about

---

[13] *Hansard's Parliamentary Debates*, 3rd ser., lxxxvii. 183–4, 8 June 1846. For Boyd
Hilton's brilliant analysis of the place of atonement in Peel's career, see 'Peel: A
Reappraisal', *H.J.*, xxii. 3 (1979), 585–614, and in much wider intellectual and political
terms, his *The Age of Atonement. The Influence of Evangelicalism on Social and Economic
Thought, 1795–1865* (Oxford, 1988).
[14] Bentinck to Stanley, 20 Jan. 1846, Derby MSS, quoted in Stewart, *Politics of
Protection*, 58; to Portland, 20 Jan. 1846, Portland Papers, PwH, fo. 200.
[15] Gash, 'Bentinck', esp. 169–71. See also Michael Seth-Smith, *Lord Paramount of the
Turf. Lord George Bentinck 1802–1848* (1971). Gash's tone towards Bentinck has moderated
somewhat over the years (cf. *Peel*, 595, 598). Robert Blake is generally more sympathetic, while attributing Bentinck's conduct in 1846 to 'some strange psychological
upheaval which there is now no means of understanding': *The Conservative Party from
Peel to Thatcher* (1985), 60–5.

Bentinck's malpractices.[16] It is likely that Bentinck applied standards to his villainous opponents which he did not apply so stringently to himself, likely too that his undoubted ability was channelled after an unsatisfying peacetime military career into activities which brought out the flaws in his character. The fact remains that on the two occasions when opponents accused him of bringing into politics the disreputable methods of the turf—Lyndhurst in August 1846, Lord John Russell in June 1848—Bentinck's probity and reforming reputation were entirely confirmed. Russell's petulant charge, part of which he tried at once to retract, was badly received by the House and effectively answered. Against Lyndhurst's more savage attack when he compared Bentinck with Napoleon ('nothing was too great for his malignity, or too small for his rapacity') Bentinck successfully defended the honour of men of the turf. Lyndhurst, he said, had the skill to use the rapier; Bentinck admitted to wielding the broad sword and the bayonet.[17] This military figure is a fairer guide to his political style than references to racing. (He could certainly handle statistics, doing so not merely because he was used to calculating odds but because he wanted to convince in a statistical age.) Nor is he the only man vulnerable to Gash's line of indictment. There is the matter of Cobden's language about Peel and others. Commenting on Peel's fulsome tribute to Cobden on 29 June 1846, Gladstone deplored in his diary Cobden's 'most harsh' tone and his incessant 'imputation of bad & vile motives to honourable men'.[18]

Bentinck was evidently authoritarian, unpredictably hot-tempered and at times vindictive. The impact of his personality is well conveyed by Lord John Manners, a devoted follower who was so alarmed by Bentinck's 'stern vehemence' that, as he says, 'I never ventured to argue out a question with him'.[19] His lack of formal education, putting him at a serious disadvantage with his main opponents, may partly account for the bouts of violent language. Inexperience, impatience, and an almost obsessively serious sense of responsibility made him take too much upon himself, while the ferocity of some of his speeches led some less than friendly (viz. Peelite) observers to doubt his mental

[16] *The Greville Memoirs, 1814–1860*, ed. L. Strachey and R. Fulford (7 vols., 1938), v. 93–4 (6 June 1843); v. 185 (5 July 1844); v. 303 (1 Mar. 1846), and esp. vi. 105–22 (28 Sept. 1848).

[17] John Prest, *Lord John Russell* (1972), 283; Disraeli, *Bentinck*, 352–5; *Hansard*, lxxxviii. 943–4, 21 Aug. 1846 (Bentinck).

[18] *The Gladstone Diaries, 1840–1847*, ed. M. R. D. Foot and H. C. G. Matthew (Oxford, 1974), iii. 547 (20 June 1846).

[19] Manners to Disraeli, 12 Oct. 1850, Disraeli Papers, Bodl. Lib., Box 106, BXX, fos. 67–70, an interesting account of Bentinck praising his 'boldness of conception' and administrative powers ('a mind of the first order'). It ends by describing him as 'the Strafford of the 19th Century'.

balance. This was not seriously in question, any more than it was in the case of Gladstone whose features during a speech on Disraeli's budget in 1852 were described by the young Stanley as unforgettably 'livid and distorted with passion'.[20] Recurrent attacks of influenza left Bentinck temporarily depressed, and he took quinine to help his voice, with encouraging results. His inexperience was made up for by readiness to take advice, particularly from Disraeli but also from J. C. Herries, Thomas Baring and 'King' Hudson, and by his use of expert commercial and political information supplied by Richard Burn of Manchester, editor of *The Commercial Glance*, and by H. C. Chapman, a Liverpool merchant and leading local protectionist. It was not inexperience but his conception of his dominant political role which led to serious clashes and misunderstandings with Stanley and with the whips (Major William Beresford, a hard-bitten and bigoted Irishman, and Charles Newdegate, no less protestant but a more interesting man), neither of whom had been chosen by Bentinck.[21] His surviving letters, almost all taken up with business, are revealing as to his modern-mindedness, width of general knowledge and interests,[22] but they throw next to no light on his inner mental life.[23] It seems impossible to establish his exact religious views, although no doubt truly he told Manners, defeated in 1847 at Liverpool on account of his tract-

[20] *Disraeli, Derby and the Conservative Party. Journals and Memoirs of Henry Edward, Lord Stanley 1849–1869*, ed. John Vincent (Hassocks, Sussex, 1978), 90 (16 Dec. 1852).

[21] See Stewart, *Politics of Protection*, 98–102; *Foundation of the Conservative Party*, 225–8, 232. For Newdegate's views and his published critiques (1849–52) of the statistics on which free traders relied, see Walter L. Arnstein, *Protestant versus Catholic in Mid-Victorian England. Mr. Newdegate and the Nuns* (1982), 27–9. Beresford's chief claim to fame is that technically he refounded the 'Conservative' party by sending out circulars on his own initiative and under that heading in Feb. 1848, to the fury of many, including Bentinck and Manners, who continued to call themselves 'protectionists'.

[22] Apart from the unmatched scale and modernity of his training and racing operations, Bentinck's interests included railway development, particularly in connection with his estate in Ayrshire and his father's properties there and in Nottinghamshire, extensive enclosure, navigation and draining schemes for King's Lynn and the Fens, agricultural improvements and hunting. The links between sport and politics in this period will bear further investigation. It was out hunting that Sir John Trollope remarked to Bentinck in Dec. 1845 that farmers and gentlemen were unanimous in their view of Peel: 'Was there ever such a Rascal!!!': Bentinck to Portland, 17 Dec. 1845, Portland Papers, PwH, fo. 188. Greville's account (*Memoirs*, vi. 290–1, 10 Apr. 1851), of Stanley at Newmarket—the 'statesman' in uproarious spirits surrounded by a crowd of 'loose characters of every description'—is worth bearing in mind in thinking about populist conservatism.

[23] He never married and is said, on Greville's unconfirmed testimony, to have cherished a pure and unselfish love for the duchess of Richmond. His scathing attitude to immoral behaviour or failure to pay debts makes him part of the increasingly decorous not to say puritanical face of the aristocracy discerned by David Spring, 'Aristocracy, social structure and religion in the early Victorian period', *Victorian Studies*, vi (1962–3), 263–80.

arian connections, that 'I never read or mean to read a tract in all my life, Puseyite or other'.[24] With a faint touch of disapproval, Disraeli says that his hero supported an establishment 'and no more', and that he disliked 'priestly domination' of all kinds. There was never any doubt as to his religious liberalism or his disgust at 'the artificial zeal' for religion fomented (so he thought) by the whips and the *Morning Herald* in the general election of 1847. As for the furore among his followers about Baron Lionel de Rothschild and the Jewish Disabilities Bill, this was the 'tea table twaddling' of 'a pack of Old Maids' when 'the greatest Commercial Empire of the World is engaged in a life & death struggle for existence'.[25] Consistency with his past votes and loyalty to Disraeli led to his speech and vote for the bill and his resignation of the leadership in December 1847 in response to the outraged feelings of a section of the party. Stanley rather promptly congratulated 'the "wild Bird"' on regaining its freedom.[26] But Bentinck, however temporarily disillusioned by the protectionists' degeneration into 'a "No Popery", "No Jew" Party', retained a considerable body of support in the party, some fifty members described by Manners as 'the flower of the bucolic flock'; and Disraeli, seeing him as 'the only head of decision and real native sagacity, that we possess', discerned increasing maturity as a politician.[27] Given the difficulties in replacing him, he might well have been recalled as leader but for his sudden death at the age of 46 from a heart attack on 21 September 1848.

Bentinck's impact on his party and the course of politics may be assessed first in terms of strategy. By taking the position in his first major speech of 27 February 1846 that Peel's policies amounted to 'a great commercial revolution' affecting the entire range of domestic industry and the system of colonial preference as well as agriculture, he tied his party to defending protection on the broadest grounds. This strategy, a natural response to Peel's own comprehensive plans, was also forced on the protectionists by the clamour of threatened interests and, more important, by their conviction that protection was a coherent and viable system which worked in the national interest and for the benefit of consumers and producers, colonial and domestic, who must stand or fall together. In their different ways Bentinck and Stanley shared this conviction. Unlike Disraeli who at this time stood

---

[24] Quoted in Charles Whibley, *Lord John Manners and His Friends* (1925), i. 241.

[25] Bentinck to Disraeli, 14 Nov. 1847, Disraeli Papers, Box 89, BXX, fo. 42.

[26] Stanley to Bentinck, 26 Dec. 1847, Derby MSS, quoted in Stewart, *Politics of Protection*, 125.

[27] Bentinck to Croker, 26 Dec. 1847, *Croker Papers*, iii. 157; Manners to Disraeli, 5 Jan. 1848, Disraeli Papers, Box 106, BXX, fo. 19; Disraeli to Manners, 16 Nov., 26 Dec. 1847, Monypenny and Buckle, iii. 29, 81. See also Disraeli, *Bentinck*, 361–3.

for little more than his own genius, they were nationally representative and responsible figures: it was not open to them to indulge in a great scrap over agricultural protection in 1846 and then drop the cause, as Disraeli wanted. It may be argued that the protectionist assault on free trade in the late 1840s and early 1850s impeded conservative reunion and provided an emerging liberal party with a firm basis in dogmatic free trade ideology. But these consequences could hardly have been foreseen in 1846, when Disraelian adventurism was no substitute for strongly-held beliefs and for the hope that electoral success would in due course bring an unwise experiment to an end. The comprehensive strategy had some immediate advantages: it placed obstacles in the way of the free trade juggernaut (there was plenty for Gladstone still to do in his budgets after 1859), and it bought time for endangered interests to prepare for the new terms of trade. Without this strategy the long subsequent battles over sugar duties in 1846 and 1848 and over the remaining navigation laws in 1848–9 would not have occurred, nor would the limited gains have been obtained: the bargain (in large part the result of Bentinck's effective chairmanship of the select committee on sugar and coffee plantations) struck with Russell over colonial sugar in 1848, the postponement of repeal of the navigation laws for a year.[28]

Bentinck's individual contributions to the comprehensive strategy are worth notice. The first was his search for a viable fiscal policy based on the assumption that the exact *status quo ante*-1846 was un-realisable. The search took its boldest form in a plan, outlined in his 1847 election manifesto, to abolish excise duties and replace them with revenue duties on foreign agricultural and manufactured products while allowing free colonial imports; he would also deal with 'the mischievous and absurd restrictions' of Peel's Bank Charter Act which prevented the Bank from assisting 'legitimate trade' and limited the means of transacting commercial business when the latter was plainly increasing.[29] Bentinck assumed correctly, as the general election of 1847 confirmed,[30] that the agricultural heartland was solidly pro-tectionist, but he was convinced that a reservoir of support was waiting to be tapped in the commercial, urban worlds. In cruder form, his calls in 1847 for 'a revision and equalization of taxation' as an alternative to the previous protective system and as a means of placing the over-taxed agriculturist 'on a fair footing with the Manchester manu-

[28] See Disraeli, *Bentinck*, 209–15, 339–57; Prest, *Russell*, 282–3, 298–300.

[29] *Times*, 27 July 1847, Bentinck to the Electors of King's Lynn, 24 July 1847.

[30] See Gash, *Reaction and Reconstruction*, 192, n. 1; and Stewart, *Politics of Protection*, 106–14, for the 1847 general election, when the protectionists won 42 of the 48 'agricultural' and 47 of the 59 'mixed' county seats. With 225–30 members they had more than held their own.

facturer' foreshadowed Disraeli's ingenious proposals from 1849 onwards, to which Dr Offer has drawn attention: these were designed to appeal both to urban ratepayers (shopkeepers and home capitalists, the middle and lower-middle echelons of the middle class as distinct from the urban patriciate) and to agriculturists shouldering special tax burdens.[31] It seems that Disraeli owed more to his close friendship with Bentinck than his political advance under the latter's warm patronage and the trappings of landownership at Hughenden supplied by Bentinck and his family.

Bentinck's programme for Ireland, centring on his ambitious railways scheme of February 1847 but including endowment of the Roman Catholic church, tenants' compensation and taxes on absentee landlords, was a remarkable essay in constructive Unionism and social engineering. The railway plan, by which treasury loans of up to £16,000,000 repayable over thirty years were to be made to railway companies, was designed both to give immediate employment to over a fifth of those half a million people currently employed on 'unproductive' public works and to provide Ireland with a modern transport system as a necessary stimulus to English capital investment.[32] These social and economic objectives were linked to broader political considerations. The Union with Ireland and the political dominance of landownership in England were to be buttressed by identification with a thriving Irish economy reinvigorated in its social base and hooked into the British market: as the peroration of his speech on 4 February makes clear, he saw the massive railway scheme and further state support for Irish 'enterprise' as prophylactics against revolution. More immediately, signs that Irish political divisions were giving way to cross-party unity in the face of the Famine opened up a real prospect of alliance between Bentinck's protectionists and the so-called 'Irish party' of whigs, tories and repealers brought together in the Reproductive Works Committee of December 1846. Although Bentinck received the warm initial support of most Irish M.P.s and peers, including the protectionist-minded William Smith O'Brien and the Young Irelanders, it was soon clear that he had built too much on insecure foundations. His plan was wrecked by the collapse of a fragile Irish unity, the incoherence of Irish protectionism, whig and

[31] *Times,* 27 July 1847; Avner Offer, *Property and Politics 1870–1914. Landownership, Law, Ideology and Urban Development in England* (Cambridge, 1981), 167–70.

[32] *Hansard,* lxxxix. 773–802, 4 Feb. 1847. Both the Whately and Devon Commissions had recommended state assistance for Irish railways. For the genesis of Bentinck's plan, for which he received advice from 'King' Hudson, George Stephenson and Samuel Laing, and his general views on policy towards the Famine, see Disraeli, *Bentinck,* 89–90, 216–66; and R.J. Montague, 'Relief and Reconstruction in Ireland 1845–1849. A Study of Public Policy during the Great Famine' (unpublished D.Phil. thesis, Oxford Univ. 1976), esp. 130ff.

Peelite economic orthodoxy and the fears of many of his own followers at the consequences of defeating the whig government. Although Bentinck put forward his railway scheme as non-partisan, 'a great private Bill', Russell was right to make it an issue of confidence. It was a question, as Bentinck told his father, of 'whether Lord John Russell or I were to govern Ireland'.[33]

His skills as a tactician are evident in his relentless exposure of the weaknesses in Peel's original case that the Irish subsistence crisis required repeal of the corn laws, in his insistence that Ireland provided a mere pretext for Peel's wider objectives and in his argument that Irish agriculture would be an early victim of free imports (a point taken by Peel, though he never said what he would do about it). Bentinck was able to cast serious doubts on Peel's judgment and on the government's competence, at least in protectionist eyes.[34] In the complex preparations for and administration of the *coup de grâce* to Peel's ministry on the Irish Preservation of Life Bill, he scarcely put a foot wrong: in refusing Disraeli's advice to move *ab initio* against the bill and in holding the government to the alleged urgency of the measure, he put the irreconcilable band of protectionists in as strong a moral position as was possible. Revenge was by now certainly not the only consideration. He genuinely feared that unless the ministry were forced out of power, Peel might dissolve and appeal to the country: 'The great object was to get the dissolution out of [Peel's] hands,' so he told his father, in order to prevent 'a terrible division of the Conservative ranks ... Peel as First Minister would have all the shabbiness & baseness of Mankind (which I fear constitutes a majority thereof) with him. Out of office I think for a long time he will be nobody.'[35] The fall of Peel is often seen as a joint operation in which Disraeli's philippics complemented Bentinck's influence on the rank and file. In reality Bentinck was throughout the dominant partner without whom the job might well not have been done.

It is clear that Bentinck set out not only to match himself against Peel, replying deliberately and, in the view of Stanley and J. W. Croker, successfully,[36] to the arguments and statistics in Peel's Tamworth apologia of 1847 with his own King's Lynn manifesto, but to

[33] Bentinck to Portland, 19 Feb. 1847, Portland Papers, PwH, fo. 225. For the Irish contexts and consequences, see Kevin B. Nowlan, *The Politics of Repeal* (1965), 93–144.

[34] Other examples of his tactical flexibility are his overtures to Russell and his part in the negotiations in Apr.–May 1846 for a moderately protectionist whig government until the plan was killed by Russell's firmness; he was then already opening up lines to Smith O'Brien and other Irish non-conservatives sympathetic to protection: Prest, *Russell*, 212–16; Stewart, *Politics of Protection*, 65–6; Nowlan, *Politics of Repeal*, 103.

[35] Disraeli, *Bentinck*, 156–69, 187–96; Bentinck to Disraeli, 5 June 1846, Disraeli Papers, Box 89, BXX, fo. 3; to Portland, 9 June 1846, Portland Papers, PwH, fo. 220.

[36] Stanley to Croker, 12 Sept. 1847, *Croker Papers*, iii. 133–4.

present himself as unlike all other political leaders, including Stanley. Instead of equivocal public statements there would be clear commitments of policy. Opposition would not involve a reactive 'governing in opposition' or Stanley's subtle equivocation and passivity: it would propose and press policies—a line which Stanley deplored but could not prevent. The virulent personal attacks on Peel (most notoriously the charge of having contributed to Canning's early death) and on the 'janissaries' and 'renegades' were not purposeless: when accepted by his followers they had the effect of implicating the protectionists in Bentinck's political antipathy to 'the Arch Traitor' and of perpetuating the schism among the conservatives. Stanley's attempts to moderate Bentinck's acerbic and active leadership produced only explosive protests, and he was powerless to stop the brutal scotching of every attempt at reconciliation.[37]

Whatever its crudities and mistakes, Bentinck's leadership gave his party a necessary sense of purpose and of the future which stood it in good stead in the strange currents of the 1847 election. In his own fashion he was trying to find a remedy for the serious political demoralisation inflicted by the corn law crisis. He was supplying one side of what Gladstone later called the 'old *binary* organization' of parliament; he certainly personified the clear conflicts, 'strong attachments', 'unwavering confidence' and 'warm devotion', the 'intelligible' if unprofound politics which Gladstone admired of the years before 1846 and which he hankered after in 1856.[38] For Bentinck, as the *Standard* remarked on his death, opposition was the only means of 'purifying' a party. That was his detonating, essentially moral mission. Acknowledging the formidable character of his activities in opposition, *The Times* indeed saw him as 'a political moralist, not as a statesman'. For the *Evening Sun*, deploring his views and 'the indecorous rage of his personalities' while emphasising his gallantry and 'manliness', chivalry was the theme of his career: he was 'the knight-errant of Protection'.[39] To his friends his death was a martyrdom: 'I cannot doubt,' Manners assured Disraeli, 'that it was his single-minded devo-

[37] See their correspondence in Jan. 1847, quoted in Stewart, *Politics of Protection*, 99–101. For Bentinck's attacks on Lyndhurst, an early proponent of reconciliation, and on Ripon for an allegedly corrupt barter of patronage (an affair in which Gladstone, accused by Bentinck of having affirmed with '*malice prepense*' what he knew to be untrue, became painfully involved), see *Hansard*, lxxxviii. 849–54, 18 Aug. 1846; John Morley, *Life of William Ewart Gladstone* (1905), i. 302.

[38] Gladstone to Northcote, 5 Mar. 1855, quoted in Richard Shannon, *Gladstone, I, 1809–1865* (1982), 308; and Gladstone's 1856 *Quarterly Review* article on 'The declining efficiency of parliament', quoted in Hilton, *Age of Atonement*, 353.

[39] *Standard*, 23 Sept.; *Times*, 23 Sept. (leader); *Evening Sun*, 25 Sept. 1848. For the Scots protectionist William Aytoun, reviewing Disraeli's work, Bentinck stood for 'active public virtue': 'Lord George Bentinck', *Blackwood's Edinburgh Magazine*, lxxi (Jan. 1852), 121–34. Intriguing links exist between the protectionist mentality and the

tion to his new and glorious, yet how fatal!, course of life that has killed him.'[40]

What was Bentinckian protectionism about? Lulled into security by the electoral triumph of 1841 and by Peel's policies which represented a working balance between protection and tariff reform, the protectionists had to resurrect their arguments hurriedly in and after 1846. Inevitably, they appealed primarily to historical experience and practical observation. For Archibald Alison, the Scottish, staunchly anti-Malthusian lawyer and historian, protectionism dealt not with 'the imaginary communities of the political economist' but with 'the different nations of flesh and blood . . . planted by the hand of nature'.[41] Protectionists saw themselves as the heirs of those whom Stanley called 'the most liberal commercial Ministers': Chatham, Pitt and Huskisson, Liverpool, Canning and Grey, in his line of succession, to which he might have added the pre-1846 Peel.[42] This tradition stood for a responsive executive which managed the economy, and, in its handling of taxation and tariffs, arbitrated between the needs of government and of society. By distributing the national income between the various classes and interests, it had ensured their 'inter-dependence'. The system was thus class-integrating; and by ensuring balanced economic growth, it had solved the economists' problem of an inherent conflict between the interests of agriculture and manufacturing industry. In November 1847, with the country reeling in commercial crisis, Bentinck compared the 'prosperity, growing wealth, [and] full employment' of 1845 under 'the old trade winds of national and colonial protection' with the calamitous present under 'victorious free trade'.[43]

---

contemporary revival of interest in chivalry and medievalism. Those upper-class, radically-minded men such as Edward Bulwer Lytton, Charles Tennyson d'Eyncourt and Col. Thomas Wildman identified by Mark Girouard, *The Return to Camelot. Chivalry and the English Gentleman* (1981), 69–86, as prime exemplars of his theme all ended up as protectionists, as were the writers of *Fraser's Magazine*. Manners was heavily influenced by Kenelm Digby's *The Broad Stone of Honour*, one of the sources of the revival. In addition, Eglinton (of the Tournament) became a diligent protectionist whip in the Lords. He was a friend of William Aytoun.

[40] Manners to Disraeli, 26 Sept. 1848, Disraeli Papers, Box 106, BXX, fo. 33. For Disraeli, it was 'the greatest sorrow I have ever experienced': Monypenny and Buckle, iii. 112–13.

[41] [Archibald Alison], 'Free Trade and Protection', *Blackwood's*, lv (Feb. 1844), 259. His *History of Europe* is described by Mr Rigby in *Coningsby* as proving that Providence was on the side of the Tories. His baronetcy from Derby in 1852 was reasonable reward for political and literary services.

[42] *Hansard*, lxxxvi. 1128–9, 25 May 1846.

[43] *Hansard*, xcv. 176–7, 24 Nov. 1847. Neither Stanley nor Bentinck was a high tory, but they certainly shared the 'managerial philosophy' which Boyd Hilton has associated with high toryism, and which he distinguishes from the more mechanistic liberal tory view: 'Peel', *loc. cit.*, 607.

As to the corn laws, it did not need much theory to argue that they had indeed been relevant. In the swirling fog of official statistics and supposition mathematics, nobody knew by how much they enhanced domestic prices. Protectionists continued to believe, like Peel in 1842, that the addition was small, a premium paid by the consumer in 'the interest of all classes' to establish 'a security and an insurance' against dependence on foreign supplies. The stimulus given by the corn laws to domestic production had ensured that general self-sufficiency in food supply which, to protectionists, was the bulwark of national independence. Hence, patriotic concern for the primacy of domestic supply sat comfortably with the profits to be garnered from meeting the voracious urban appetite for wheat, and with the argument, advanced at length first by Bentinck on 27 February 1846, that domestic production had kept pace with the growth of population. Marginal deficiencies in bad years as well as foreign competition could be dealt with by the sliding scale of 1842 which had worked well (to Cobden's dismay) and produced steady prices below Peel's 're-munerating' price. Farmers had learnt to live with gradual but con-siderable overall price falls under the 1828 and 1842 corn laws by using better, lower-cost methods, perhaps cushioned in the 1840s by landlords' exaction of lower rents. God's bounty, *alias* the weather, was incalculable, just as confidence was unquantifiable. Yet if the corn laws boosted agriculturists' confidence at a time of rapid social change when the passivity of their labourers could not be taken for granted, they performed a vital service: in the case of the farmers, their muscular protectionist politics was fuelled by rising expectations as much as by a defensive mentality. Confidence generated improve-ments, their metaphor Bentinck's calculations about increased yields from applying guano (as to whose quality as an organic fertiliser before the coming of superphosphates he was right). It has yet to be shown that protectionist landowners such as Portland, Newcastle, Manvers, Richmond, Rutland, R. A. Christopher and above all Philip Pusey were any less active in promoting improvement on their own estates and more generally than those who supported repeal in a drive, as D. C. Moore has argued, for growth based on high farming.[44] (Those like Lord Essex who thought farming was only for 'capitalists' were seen by Bentinck, as keen as anyone on improvement, as 'heart-less doctrinaires' ready to sacrifice 'all little men' with their 'barbarous & odious policy that goes upon the principle that none but Capitalists are henceforth to be allowed to live as farmers'.)[45] Finally, those who

[44] D. C. Moore, 'The Corn Laws and High Farming', *Ec.H.R.*, 2nd ser., xviii (1965), 544–61. For Pusey, see the masterly account by David Spring, *The English Landed Estate in the Nineteenth Century; Its Administration* (Baltimore, 1963), 139–51, 167.

[45] Bentinck to Disraeli, 15 April 1846, Disraeli Papers, Box 89, BXX, fo. 2.

defended the 1842 Law did not have the benefit of hindsight as to the effects of foreign competition on domestic prices; and in the agriculturally depressed years after 1847–8 it was natural for men to blame declining prices in a period of generally inferior domestic harvests on foreign grain imports. No more complex economic argument is needed to explain the farmers' continued attachment to protection.[46]

The protectionist case entailed belief in a subsistence theory of wages, giving ample scope for attacks on Cobden's (and subsequently Peel's) market version as a clever mask by the manufacturers of 'the Anti-Labour League' for cost-cutting and increased exploitation: 'If they [the working classes] *buy bread at Polish prices,*' said Croker in the *Quarterly Review,* 'they must be prepared to *work at Polish wages.*'[47] The rhetorical crudity of this formula and the prevailing confusion over the relationship between wages and corn prices ought not to obscure the protectionists' conviction that their system had protected domestic labour by increasing the people's purchasing power. Protectionist authors denied the applicability of the Ricardian theory of comparative advantage and deplored unilateral free trade on Britain's part. Alison assailed these and other targets with empirical, developmental and historical arguments. Differentiating between 'old' (e.g. Britain) and 'young' or 'rising' states (e.g. Poland), he discerned a 'permanent and indelible distinction', 'a fundamental law of nature', between the different effects of progress on agriculture and manufactures in such states: 'the old [state] can always undersell the young one in manufactures, but it is everlastingly undersold by them in agriculture'. Applying 'the delusive doctrines of free trade' would simply produce a 'RECIPROCITY OF EVIL'. Protection, apart from providing security against the consequences of international conflicts and war, was essential both to shelter the infant industry of

---

[46] But cf. the powerful arguments and conclusions of Susan Fairlie, 'The Nineteenth Century Corn Law Reconsidered', *Ec.H.R.,* xviii (1965), 562–73, amounting to a defence of Peel's course in 1846. Some of her statistics in 'The Corn Laws and British Wheat Production, 1829–76', *Ec.H.R.,* xxii (1969), 88–113, e.g. those for increasing domestic wheat production to 1846 and for *per capita* wheat consumption (higher under the corn laws than by estimates for 1909) support a case for the success of protection. Her figures show the increase in wheat imports from 1847–8, but do not prove that demand could not have been met under the 1842 Law. It is clear that successive corn laws worked to reduce and to steady prices. See also Wray Vamplew, 'The Protection of English Cereal Producers: the Corn Laws reassessed', *Ec.H.R.,* xxxiii (1980), 382–95, for a picture of an increasingly effective system as between consumers and producers (and dealers) which nonetheless afforded 'a significant degree of protection' to producers before 1846.

[47] See John Almack, jun., *Character, Motives, and Proceedings of the Anti-Corn Law Leaguers* (1843), esp. 40, and his *Cheap Bread and Low Wages* (1844); [Croker], 'The Budget and the Dissolution', *Quarterly Review,* lxviii (June–Sept. 1841), 265.

'young' states and the long-established agriculture of the 'old'. British unilateral free trade would not prevent an entirely natural protectionism on the part of foreigners: Russia and Prussia, he pointed out, had like Britain the capacity to create economies based on 'the inter-mixture of commerce and agriculture', and they would be wise to do so since this balance provided the best security for 'social happiness'.[48] Alison shared the universal protectionist emphasis on the importance and potential of the home and colonial markets for British manufacturers as against export-led growth dependent on foreign markets.[49]

Alison was a leading member of the team of protectionist writers associated with *Blackwood's Magazine* which included the lawyer Charles Neaves (later solicitor-general for Scotland), William Aytoun, another lawyer as well as a gifted poet, spiritual Jacobite and professor of rhetoric and *belles-lettres* at Edinburgh University, and J. B. Johnson, a Liverpool journalist. F. W. Fetter has indicated how this group pointed cogently in verse and prose to the possible consequences of free trade: a costly transfer of resources from agriculture to industry, the uncertainty of foreign markets, the effects on agricultural employment of the deflationary consequences of gold drains to pay for food imports, the dangers of reliance on foreign grain supplies.[50] The protectionists doubtless fail a Schumpeterian test of theoretical originality. By another, more practical test, their numerous metropolitan and provincial newspapers, with the intellectual spearheads of *Blackwood's*, the staider and less extreme *Quarterly* under Croker's editorship and the lively *Fraser's*, impress by the sheer volume of sustained propaganda and polemic. Until this mass of material is further investigated, we will not know how widely diffused protectionist ideas and values were, nor how broad was the evident gap between those who accepted and those who rejected free trade.[51] It might be a mistake

[48] [Alison], 'Free Trade and Protection', *Blackwood's*, lv (1844), 266–7, 385–400. Writing anonymously, he cited his own *History of Europe* as being the first to trace the decline of Rome to a free trade in grain. See also his *Free Trade and a Fettered Currency* (1847) in which he adopted the currency views of the Birmingham 'school', a position at variance with that of the protectionist leaders who were convertibility men, however strongly they criticised the restrictive effects of Peel's Bank Charter Act.

[49] For Bentinck's views on colonial preference and revenue-producing duties, and his critique of Peel's tariff reductions and of the argument that imports governed exports, see *Croker Papers*, iii. 130–2, 134–6.

[50] F. W. Fetter, 'The Economic Articles in *Blackwood's Edinburgh Magazine*, and their Authors, 1817–1853', *Scottish Journal of Political Economy*, vii (1960), 85–107, 213–31; see also his 'The Economic Articles in the *Quarterly Review*, and their Authors, 1809–1852', *Journal of Political Economy*, lxvi (1958), 47–64, 154–70.

[51] See Donald Read, *Peel and the Victorians* (Oxford, 1987), 186–241, 257–63, for an analysis of the newspapers' reactions to Peel, repeal of the corn laws and subsequent measures.

to regard J. S. Mill's *Principles of Political Economy* (1848) as far more influential at the time than John Byles's *Sophisms of Free Trade and Popular Political Economy Examined* (1849), an acutely-argued and readable assault on all the main propositions of classical economics as flawed in principle, practice and experience: it put forward something like a programme of necessary reforms for England and Ireland, and went through eight editions soon after its publication.[52] There was clearly a large and hungry audience for a polemic which demoticised and simplified economic debate and which was directed primarily not against market theory as a body of doctrine but at the social and political costs of its application. These were conveyed as to rural society by Aytoun, whose sharp wit and lighter touch effectively complemented Alison's rather portentous gravity:

> Barley from Mecklenburg, grain from Polonia,
> Butter from Holland, American cheese;
> Bacon gratuitous,
> Cargoes fortuitous,
> Float to our coasts with each prosperous breeze.
> What need we care though a desperate peasantry
> Prowl round the stackyards with tinder and match?
> Blandly we'll smile at such practical pleasantry:
> Downing Street is not surmounted by thatch.
> We're not prohibiting
> Some gentle gibbeting
> When the poor starving delinquents you catch.[53]

The threat to traditional aristocratic dominance was seen by *Blackwood's* in 1846 in terms reminiscent of Carlyle's alarming message in his *Chartism* (1839): if 'the future position of Britain were to be that of one mighty workshop, from which the whole world was to be supplied', there would be 'a commonalty of cotton, calico, and iron, with a Birmingham and Manchester aristocracy'.[54] Protectionist satire, particularly eloquent in *Fraser's*, reminded the landowners of their duties and of the perils of evading them. Powerful resonances of this tradition are evident in the biting social criticism of Surtees (who knew about and strongly sympathised with the problems of Durham farmers after repeal), as for example in the great humbug Mr Jawleyford in *Mr. Sponge's Sporting Tour,* one of 'the rather numerous race of paper-

[52] John Byles (1810–84), later Sir John, a unitarian appointed justice of common pleas in 1858, was one of the lawyers whom Bentinck thought of bringing into parliament to present the protectionist case on his behalf.

[53] 'Britain's Prosperity', *Blackwood's*, lxvii (April 1850), 390. In quite different vein, see his 'British agriculture and foreign competition', *Blackwood's*, lxvii (Jan.–Feb. 1850), 94–136, 222–48.

[54] 'The late and the present ministry', *Blackwood's*, lx (Aug. 1846), 251.

booted, pen and ink landowners' who is surprised that his guest Sponge is not reading Dizzy's life of Bentinck (as he himself is pretending to) but that 'much more useful' work, *Mogg's Ten Thousand Cab Fares*.

The protectionist leaders hardly needed much reminding about the governing mission of a landed aristocracy. This mission was memorably expounded by Stanley in his speech in the Lords on 25 May 1846, when he defined the 'aristocracy' broadly as 'the great body of the landed proprietors', the centres of 'locality', men 'who have the *prestige* of old associations attached to their names' and who conducted local business, influenced opinion, exercised hospitality and presided over their tenantry. Faced with inevitable economic crisis, it would be rational for farmers to end improvements and drive their discharged labourers into the already over-stocked manufacturing districts, and for landlords to reduce establishments, evict smaller tenants and create large farms. Stanley promised that landowners would not follow these policies and thus adopt 'the cold and selfish and calculating doctrines of political economy and free trade'. For him, the 'proud aristocracy' which Peel found such difficulty in handling was 'the firmest breakwater and the safest barrier' between the limited monarchy and 'that spirit of democracy which is fitly represented in the reformed House of Commons'.[55] Such views on the social and political duties of landownership, clustering on the ideal image of the estate run on paternalist lines, socially protective of tenants and labourers and linked with the agencies of the Church, were far from being a monopoly of the protectionists. They were shared by serious whigs such as Morpeth and of course by the Peelites: as Sidney Herbert remarked in 1845, writing of his own call to public duty, 'an aristocracy of ease and quiet and retirement would be soon upset in this country and ... would deserve to be upset'.[56] Doubtless there were some like Trollope's Mr Thorne in *Barchester Towers*, so shocked by betrayal at the hands of men whom he had regarded as 'the only saviours of his country' that he gave up politics and his duties as a J.P. for some years, consoling himself in defeat with a sense of Cato-like righteousness. The high level of protectionist political activity seems to prove him exceptional. With its agrarian base, protectionist politics exactly fitted the practice of an aristocratic governing mission, much assisted by what J. S. Mill noted in 1866 though he deplored it as 'a grovelling superstition': the widely-accepted 'axiom that human society exists for the sake of property in land'.[57]

[55] *Hansard*, lxxxvi. 1128–76, esp. 1161–4.

[56] Herbert to the Countess Bruce, 22 Jan. 1845, Lord Stanmore, *Sidney Herbert, Lord Herbert of Lea. A Memoir* (2 vols., 1906), i. 34.

[57] Quoted in R. J. Olney, 'The Politics of Land', in *The Victorian Countryside*, ed. G. E. Mingay (2 vols., 1981), i. 59.

Protectionists, Gladstone's former audience of the late-1830s, shared his organicist view of the state as well as his notion (a 'most striking' one, in Colin Matthew's words) that nationality conditioned a state's religion.[58] Unlike him, they allowed none of the holes by which, in Matthew's analysis, utilitarianism and religious pluralism could threaten the organic ideal: hence the raucous, by no means unpopular No Popery campaigns of 1847 and beyond by which protectionists expressed the identity of protestantism with British nationality which was a central feature of their mentality. Against a radical free trade ideology seen as individualist and Mammon-worshipping, pacifist, decolonising and anti-aristocratic, protectionism offered an integral nationalism under aristocratic leadership, what the Limehouse ship-yard owner G. F. Young writing in the *Quarterly* called 'a lofty and ennobling patriotism' in place of 'a vague and impracticable cosmo-politanism'. In his manifesto of 1847, Bentinck characteristically attri-buted national success to the special English qualities of 'good faith, honour, and truth', and contrasted past 'moral strength and grandeur' with the 'new morality' of Peelite free trade.[59] This brand of national-ism, no doubt partly a means by which a class under threat asserted its interests, was geared to transcend class and to work for class-integration alongside prescribed economic management. Carlyle's and Disraeli's 'Two Nations' would be made one. If Palmerston was the first beneficiary of these attitudes, the foundations of the popular appeal of Disraelian conservatism and of its successors were already being laid in the late-1840s.

What protectionism did not preach was an increased role for the state in social policy. The advocacy by Michael Thomas Sadler, from beyond the grave and through the *Memoirs of His Life and Writings* put together in 1842 by the evangelical publisher R. B. Seeley, of a 'Protective State' and a 'Paternal System' found few responses among protectionist politicians. Although Newdegate told his electors in North Warwickshire in 1847 of his belief in the principle that 'the condition of the subject's allegiance is, that his life, property, and interests be cared for by the state', they and he were probably more interested in his support of national protection, cheap money and protestantism.[60] Early Victorian paternalism was in general not for consumption by the state: it was essentially a private ethic much influenced by individual religious values and the ownership of prop-erty; it was the highest expression of aristocratic individualism and antipathetic to *dirigiste* centralisation. (It was thus perfectly acceptable

[58] H. C. G. Matthew, *Gladstone 1809–1874* (Oxford, 1986), 61–5.
[59] *Quarterly Review*, lxxxvi (Dec. 1849–Mar. 1850), 183; *The Times*, 27 July 1847.
[60] Arnstein, *Protestant versus Catholic*, 23.

to Carlyle's 'new' aristocracy. The '*moral economy* of manufactures', Léon Faucher's description of Greg & Co.'s management of their factory at Quarry Bank, was in the same order of things as the duke of Richmond's active autocracy and the earl of Chichester's search for 'God's moral economy' on his estates in Sussex.)[61] Virtually solid protectionist support for Fielden's Ten Hours Bill of 1847 and its successors was motivated as much by a rolling class reaction against manufacturers as by evangelical and tractarian humanitarianism. As to the Church's interests, the decisive defeat by the protestant dissenters of the education clauses of Graham's Factory Bill in 1843 meant that it was no longer practical politics to promote anglican concerns by an active statist policy. The crucial test came with the Public Health Bills of 1847 and 1848. Protectionists formed the bulk of the opposition to Morpeth's and Chadwick's alleged centralisation. Nearly all those who have been identified as members of the historicist school of paternalism, including Newdegate, Colonel Sibthorp and David Urquhart, rose in passionate defence of local autonomy.[62] The upshot was the mutilated half-measure of 1848. Against what Peter Mandler has seen as the sharply interventionist aims of Russell and Morpeth in the face of the 'Condition of England Question', protectionists and middle-class radicals were at one in preferring voluntarism both for themselves and the working classes.[63]

Protectionists believed not in a tutelary state but in individual aristocratic example working through or occasionally outside established institutions. One case in point is the continued interest in 'Young Englandism' after the ginger group had broken up, and in its truest exponent Lord John Manners who had acquired his neo-feudal interests and organic idealism, a heady mixture of Clarendonian royalism and Bolingbroke's patriotism with tractarianism and admiration for Gladstone, some time before his friendship with Disraeli. Manners was held up by *Fraser's* in 1847 as a unique type of social reformer hostile both to traditional constitutional notions and to contemporary economic doctrines; critical of 'a tyranny of the purse' on the part of manufacturers and of a failure of duty by landowners, he stood, in *Fraser's* view, for a 'Church of England Communism' and looked to a regenerated church as 'the spiritual instructor' to reunite

[61] Léon Faucher, *Manchester in 1844: Its Present Condition and Future Prospects* (tr. 1844), 96–105; David Roberts, *Paternalism in Early Victorian England* (1979), 112, and ch. iv, 'The Patriarchy of Sussex', *passim*.

[62] W. C. Lubenow, *The Politics of Government Growth. Early Victorian Attitudes toward State Intervention 1833–1848* (Newton Abbot, 1971), 25–6, 83–8.

[63] Peter Mandler, 'Liberalism and Paternalism. The Whig Aristocracy and the Condition of England, 1830–1852' (Ph.D. dissertation, Harvard Univ., 1984), 554–67.

'the dissevered and mutually repugnant classes'. His 'earnestness, sincerity, and moral energy without parallel' personified the socially-integrating mission of church and aristocracy.[64]

David Urquhart, a younger son of the head of the clan Urquhart of Cromarty, represented another case and a rather different mission. Protectionist M.P. for Stafford in the parliament of 1847, he was an aristocratic populist in the tradition of Sir Francis Burdett, T. S. Duncombe and Feargus O'Connor. To articulate working men, clerks and small businessmen in search of a cause more satisfying than demagogic Chartism or materialistic middle-class radicalism, he held considerable appeal as an independent gentleman who would tell the truth regardless of ridicule. His austere and powerful personality, intensely religious and patriotic as well as publicity-conscious, made him a formidable teacher and prophet. If his claim to have prevented a Chartist insurrection is less than credible, his Foreign Policy movement was a divisive element within Chartism, as he intended it to be: it turned several men such as Robert Lowery, William Cardo of Marylebone and C. D. Collet away from O'Connorism and the programme of the Charter and into collaboration with Urquhart's middle-class disciples to promote his interests in foreign policy. Like Bentinck's, his was a politics of passion and morality. His social gospel of an organic and customary 'Asiatic' medievalism and his turcophilia were probably less attractive than his russophobia and his mission to expose and punish those traitors in high places—Palmerston, Graham, Peel, Prince Albert, all of course free traders—whom he saw as pursuing foreign policies harmful to British interests. Urquhart shared Bentinck's enemies. His constitutional views about the accountability of M.P.s to constituents and of ministers to parliament, his hostility to the 'despotism' of the cabinet and his defence of English municipal institutions against creeping centralisation were close to those held by many protectionists and by Bentinck, even if the latter did not call himself a 'tory of the times of Queen Anne'. Urquhart was not merely an exotic outcrop of protectionism: his activities gave traditionalist politics an additional and popular dimension. By the later 1840s he was laying the groundwork for his Foreign Affairs Committees of the Crimean War and beyond, for a political fief centred on the West Midlands but reaching up to the north (notably Sheffield and Newcastle upon Tyne); and it may well be that the support he obtained from lesser industrial and commercial employers and their workmen

---

[64] [G. H. Francis], 'Lord John Manners', *Fraser's Magazine*, xxxv (Mar. 1847), 321–39. See further Whibley, *Manners*, esp. i. 60–176, for his ideas and pursuit of a responsive paternalism.

was fuelled by the Attwoodian and protectionist outlook of such people, with their suspicions of centralisation and metropolitan liberalism.[65]

Urquhart's campaigns, the attempts by G. F. Young and his National Association for the Protection of British Industry and Capital (1849) to forge links with the industrial protectionism of sections of the London trades (and thus to fish in the promisingly troubled waters of metropolitan Chartism after 1848), and Richard Oastler's parallel activities in the National Philanthropic Association all suggest that Bentinck's hopes for urban support were not ill-founded.[66] Less tangibly, it may well be that protectionism gave political refuge to those Christian men and women who were disturbed, as Jane Garnett has shown, by the moral effects of the unrestrained march of commerce (as revealed in manic speculation and apparently widespread frauds) and who found little or no guidance in the laws of political economy as to how Christians should conduct themselves: R. B. Seeley and the novelist Charlotte Elizabeth Tonna, the leading spirits of the Christian Influence Society, looked to an ideal social order which was protectionist, paternalist and agrarian.[67]

Stafford O'Brien declared waspishly soon after Bentinck's fall that 'Bentinckism is no more. Boom! Boom! Boom! The last echoes of its knell wailed on the last gusts of the last year.'[68] He was wrong. Bentinckism was by no means a lost cause. Of its revival in 1849, John Vincent has remarked that the question is 'why protection was not restored' in that year 'when Parliament talked Protection and voted Free Trade'.[69] Three broad conclusions may be drawn. First, the protectionist movement before and long after 1846 reflected and maintained the cohesion of rural society under its traditional leadership. The speed and skill with which Disraeli's 'men of metal and large-acred squires' responded to the claims of the all-important agricultural middle class—lesser owner-occupiers, tenant farmers substantial as well as marginal, tradesmen and the professional elements serving the landed interest—entailed a politics of mutuality, of mutual deference

[65] See the accounts of him by Olive Anderson, *A Liberal State at War. English Politics and Economics during the Crimean War* (1967), 139–52; Richard Shannon, 'David Urquhart and the Foreign Affairs Committees', in *Pressure from Without in Victorian England*, ed. Patricia Hollis (1974), 239–61; and *Robert Lowery, Radical and Chartist*, ed. Brian Harrison and Patricia Hollis (1979), esp. intro. and 167–8.

[66] See John Belchem, 'Chartism and the Trades, 1848–1850', *E.H.R.*, xcviii (1983), 558–87; and Stewart, *Foundation of the Conservative Party*, 236.

[67] E. J. Garnett, 'Aspects of the relationship between protestant ethics and economic activity in mid-Victorian England' (unpublished D.Phil. thesis, Oxford Univ., 1986), 117–19.

[68] Stafford O'Brien to Manners, 12 Jan. 1848, Whibley, *Manners*, i. 293–4.

[69] *Disraeli, Derby and the Conservative Party*, intro., xiii–iv.

by which the internal strains of rural society were defused and absorbed. Lincoln, the nost notable scalp in the protectionists' belt in 1846, was not far off the mark with his sardonic prediction that 'democracy' would become 'the political principle of the Farmers'. In exceptional cases, as in the South Nottinghamshire bye-election of 1851 to which Lincoln's remarks referred, this 'democracy' was capable of asserting its interests and of reminding its traditional leaders of their duties; but it remained protectionist and socially conservative, as with the 'heavy' agriculturists of Lincolnshire who, in Richard Olney's vivid words, inhaled their conservatism 'from the very furrows that they ploughed'.[70] The identification of protectionist and, later, conservative politics with the existing structure of English land-ownership and land use was to roll back the intermittent threats of major land reform from the late 1840s to the 1860s. A second con-clusion relates to the significance of conflicts within the landowning classes over protection and free trade. The defence by the protectionists of important interests (by no means solely agrarian) which felt endan-gered by free trade was as necessary to the retention of power by the landed classes as a whole as Peelite or whig concessionary strategies. Much had therefore been gained (or retained) by the time the pro-tectionist leaders gave up protection as a lost cause. The 'territorial constitution' which both Bentinck and Peel wanted to uphold had been secured: resistance and concession turned out to be com-plementary operations, 'each-way' bets by which the landed classes could not lose. No doubt, too, the hugely profitable involvement of landowners regardless of party politics in industrial and urban enterprises (a factor emphasised by historians from F. M. L. Thomp-son and David Spring to David Cannadine and John Davies) worked to produce social and economic 'inter-dependence', to dampen any simple conflict between rural and urban ideologies, and to block middle-class radical attempts to undermine landed influence. As Can-nadine has also remarked, such involvement 'in the short term [to the 1880s at least]' gave '*increased* scope for rural, patrician influence on most aspects of urban, industrial life'.[71] Finally, it is worth remarking that the protectionists contributed significantly after 1846 to the evol-ution of 'parliamentary government' conceived of as resting on defined lines of party conflict. In upholding a 'traditionary' politics against 'progressive' liberalism, protectionism formed a vital ideological element in the balance of tensions on which, by W. L. Burn's thesis,

---

[70] Lincoln to Gladstone, 2 Jan. 1851, Newcastle MSS, quoted in J. R. Fisher, 'The Limits of Deference: Agricultural Communities in a Mid-Nineteenth Century Campaign', *Journal of British Studies*, xxi. 1 (1981), 93: Olney, *Lincolnshire Politics*, 249.

[71] *Patricians, power and politics in nineteenth-century towns*, ed. David Cannadine (Leicester, 1982), 3.

the 'Age of Equipoise' rested. The claims of the protectionists to be regarded, along with others, as makers of the mid-Victorian compromise deserve consideration.

ENGLAND AND NORTHERN ITALY IN THE EARLY FOURTEENTH CENTURY: THE ECONOMIC CONTRASTS

By R. H. Britnell

READ 9 DECEMBER 1988

WE know almost as much about the operations of big Italian companies in England as about those in Italy itself during the early fourteenth century. Tuscan trade here engaged some of Europe's most celebrated businesses, attracted by the kingdom's fine wool and the credit-worthiness of her crown and nobility.[1] Historians have sometimes drawn an analogy with international lending from richer to poorer countries in the modern world, both to create a point of contact with their readers and to meet the need for deep-lying explanations. The analogy usually carries the implication that Italy had a more advanced economy than England, and there are authors who say so explicitly. Some use terms designed to describe international economic growth during the last two hundred years, and represent medieval Italy as a pole of development, or a core economy. Others, borrowing the language of power, describe Italy as a dominant economy. Professor Cipolla uses a number of these ideas at once in his observation that 'in the early years of the fourteenth century Florence represented a dominant and developed economy, while England and the kingdom of Naples were two decidedly underdeveloped countries: the periphery, to use Wallerstein's expression'.[2]

The validity of this view needs looking into. Intuitive analogies between the medieval and modern world can distort perspectives or conceal problems, and this one is the more suspect because it contains an element of circular reasoning. The prominence of Italians abroad is explained by the advanced state of their home economy, but is also interpreted as testimony to that advance. By most definitions of economic development it would take more than a few merchant companies to show that one economy was in advance of another. No

[1] E. B. Fryde, 'Italian Maritime Trade with England (c. 1270–c. 1530)', *Recueils de la Société Jean Bodin*, xxxii (1974), 294–303; T. H. Lloyd, *Alien Merchants in England in the High Middle Ages* (Brighton, 1982), 166–203; M. C. Prestwich, 'Italian Merchants in Late Thirteenth and Early Fourteenth Century England', in F. Chiappelli, ed., *The Dawn of Modern Banking*, University of California (Los Angeles, 1979), 77–104.

[2] C. Cipolla, *Il fiorino e il quattrino: la politica monetaria a Firenze nel 1300* (Bologna, 1982), 14.

single method of ranking the economies of northern Italy and England is obviously right, since there is no received wisdom about how to make such distinctions for the fourteenth century. But by taking an eclectic view of economic advance, and comparing a number of different features of the two countries, it should be possible to assess the value of analogies with more recent periods. It is appropriate to involve only Italy north of the kingdom of Naples, since southern Italy is often classified with England as a backward area of Europe. This adjustment has the advantage of bringing the size of the regions to be compared into better balance; north Italy had an area of about 70,000 square miles, as compared with England's 50,000.

The best case for northern Italy's advance relative to England comes from the contrasting economic structures of the two regions. One commonly used index of economic rank in the modern world is the relative importance of non-agricultural employment and incomes. Indeed, the terms industrial and pre-industrial are regularly used as synonyms for advanced and not advanced. By this test northern Italy was unambiguously more advanced than England. In 1300 the share of north Italy's population in cities of over 10,000 inhabitants was at least 16 per cent.[3] In England by contrast, even after accepting Dr Keene's suggestion that London was much bigger than used to be thought, it seems unlikely that the proportion of the population in towns of this size much exceeded 3 per cent.[4] The larger urban share of population in northern Italy implied that a larger percentage of the population was employed outside agriculture. The Florentine catasto of 1427 shows that the bigger the town the larger the share of the population specialised in some non-agricultural occupation.[5] This relationship is easily explained and is relevant in the period before the Black Death both to Italy and England.[6] In the big cities the largest sector of urban employment was in various types of manufacturing. Bonvesin de la Riva in his eulogy of Milan mentions smiths and other metalworkers, weavers of wool, linen, cotton and silk, shoemakers, tanners and tailors.[7] In Florence, whose population in 1338 is esti-

[3] Taking a high estimate of 8m. for the total population of northern Italy and a modest estimate of 1.3m. for population in towns of 10,000 and over: Y. Renouard, *Les Villes d'Italie de la fin du Xe siècle au debut du XIVe siècle*, ed. P. Braunstein (Paris, 2 vols., 1969), ii. 461–2; J. K. Hyde, *Society and Politics in Medieval Italy: the Evolution of Civil Life, 1000–1350* (1973), map 5, p. xxiii.

[4] Taking a modest estimate of 4.5m. for total English population from J. Hatcher, *Plague, Population and the English Economy, 1348–1530* (1977), 68 and a high estimate of 150,000 for population living in towns of 10,000 or more. For London, see D. Keene, 'A New Study of London before the Great Fire', *Urban History Yearbook 1984*, 20.

[5] D. Herlihy and C. Klapisch-Zuber, *Les Toscans et leurs familles* (Paris, 1978), 295.

[6] R. H. Hilton, *A Medieval Society: The West Midlands at the End of the Thirteenth Century* (1966), 185, 189–93.

[7] Bonvesin de la Riva, *De Magnalibus Mediolani*, ed. M. Corti (Milan, 1974), 68–71.

mated at about 110,000, there were 30,000 people dependent on the cloth industry alone, according to Giovanni Villani.[8] In Venice shipbuilding perhaps supported a fifth of the city's households.[9] In addition to manufacturing population, the Italian cities supported large numbers in professional and commercial services—clerks, magistrates, lawyers, teachers, money-changers, retailers, carters.[10] At Bologna in 1294 the city's *Liber matricularum* records over 10,684 guildsmen in a population of some 50,000, and the guild of notaries alone had 1,308 members.[11]

The prominence of Italians abroad is further evidence of the advanced state of the Italian economy in this narrow sense. Italy produced the only merchants who can be thought of as operating on a world scale. Appreciation of the adventurousness of Italians has grown over the years, as historians have come to realise the extent of Genoese and Venetian trade with the Far East.[12] More important, however, for an assessment of the importance of commerce to the Italians is the volume of regular trade they conducted within the Mediterranean world, with the Middle East and with northern and central Europe.[13] The assets of northern Italian merchants, their companies and partnerships, were many times greater than those of English merchants. William de la Pole and his associates were able to topple the ascendancy of Italians as lenders to Edward III at the opening of the Hundred Years War, but the English challenge was confined to this one domestic context.[14] Italy was famous throughout Europe for her merchants and her bankers.[15]

Italy was also in advance of England in the development of its money market. This deserves to be taken seriously as an instance of more advanced economic institutions since a society in which the

[8] C. M. de La Roncière, *Prix et salaires à Florence au XIVᵉ siècle, 1280–1380* (Paris, 1982), 676; Giovanni Villani, *Cronica*, XI, xciv.

[9] G. Luzzatto, *Storia economica di Venezia dall'XI al XVI secolo* (Venice, 1961), 67.

[10] de la Riva, 42–3, 64–9; G. A. Holmes, *Florence, Rome and the Origins of the Renaissance* (Oxford, 1986), 72–4.

[11] A. I. Pini, 'La ripartizione topografica degli artigiani a Bologna nel 1294: un esempio di demografia sociale', in E. Cristiani and others, *Artigiani e salariati: il mondo del lavoro nell'Italia dei secoli XII–XV* (Centro italiano di studi di storia e d'arte, Pistoia, 1984), 199.

[12] M. Balard, 'Les Gênois en Asie centrale et en Extrême-Orient au XIVᵉ siècle: un cas exceptionel?', in *Economies et sociétés au Moyen Age: mélanges offerts à Edouard Perroy* (Paris, 1973), 681–8.

[13] Y. Renouard, *Les hommes d'affaires italiens du Moyen Age*, ed. B. Guillemain (Paris, 1968), 107–216; P. J. Jones, 'La storia economica dalla caduta dall'Impero romano al secolo XIV', in R. Romano and C. Vivanti, eds., *Storia d'Italia dalla caduta dell'Impero romano al secolo XVIII* (Turin, 1974), ii (2), 1681–1740.

[14] E. B. Fryde, *William de la Pole: Merchant and King's Banker* (1988), 87–90, 124–6.

[15] Jones, 'La storia economica', 1740–1.

savings of the rich can be put to commercial use has clear advantages over one where the wealthy have to hoard their money. City dwellers in Italy had long been used to money-changers willing to accept deposits, which they used to make loans.[16] Merchant partnerships too, besides borrowing from local bankers, drew on the savings of wealthier townsmen to invest in international trade and banking.[17] These opportunities meant that townsmen were discouraged from holding large idle balances of cash, though necessarily they also meant that city economies were vulnerable to crises of credit.[18] In England there was no comparable development. There were no money-changers in the cities and there was no native banking system. Banking was discouraged by the scattered nature of wealth in a land whose wealthy families were mostly rural landowners. A few of them employed Italian businessmen as deposit bankers, but this style of investment was unusual. Most of England's wealthiest men kept their money in chests, often in the custody of religious houses.[19] The elder Despenser in 1326 had £1,800 in cash at his manor of Loughborough and a further £1,000 with an agent in Wiltshire. Other treasure was deposited in abbeys in Leicestershire and Surrey.[20]

Boccaccio tells a story that suggests what Italians thought about England in the mid-fourteenth century. The three sons of Tebaldo dei Lamberti, having lost their fortune, went to England to restore it. They lived cheaply in a small house and engaged in usury. When they were wealthy again they returned to Florence, and once more squandered everything. Their luck was then restored by their young London agent Alessandro who was seduced by the king of England's daughter, married her and became earl of Cornwall.[21] Boccaccio's tale suggests that it was easier to live cheaply in England than in Florence, chiefly because there were fewer temptations. It also implies that England was a better place than Tuscany to be lending money. There is little evidence relating to interest rates in England, and none

[16] F. C. Lane and R. C. Mueller, *Money and Banking in Medieval and Renaissance Venice, i: Coins and Moneys of Account* (Baltimore, 1985), 79–89; T. W. Blomquist, 'The Dawn of Banking in an Italian Commune: Thirteenth Century Lucca', in Chiappelli, 57–8, 62–4; D. Herlihy, *Medieval and Renaissance Pistoia: The Social History of an Italian Town, 1200–1430* (New Haven, 1967), 161.

[17] A. Sapori, 'Le compagnie mercantili toscane del dugento e dei primi del trecento', in idem, *Studi di storia economica* (3rd edn., Florence, 1955), ii. 805–7.

[18] Cipolla, 16–18.

[19] M. C. Prestwich, *Edward I* (1988), 403.

[20] E. B. Fryde, 'The Deposits of Hugh Despenser the Younger with Italian Bankers', *Ec.H.R.*, 2nd ser., iii (1951), 358.

[21] G. Boccaccio, *Decameron*, second day, third tale. An approximate historical parallel is the departure of Castruccio Castracani for London after the expulsion of his family from Lucca in 1301: L. Green, *Castruccio Castracani: a Study on the Origins and Character of a Fourteenth-Century Italian Despotism* (Oxford, 1986), 42–5.

relating to petty money lending. Italian lenders to the English crown took their rewards in commercial advantages rather than through any calculable return on their loans, so that evidence from this quarter too is thin.[22] It seems to be the case, though, that Italian communes could attract voluntary loans at 15 per cent or less in normal times, whereas the few rates of return calculated for English royal borrowing in this period range upwards from 26 per cent.[23] The fact that interest rates were higher outside northern Italy is often attributed to higher risks.[24] But this was only one of the relevant causes, and the precocious development of the money market in Tuscany makes a more satisfying explanation for the low rates of interest prevailing there.

The property market in northern Italy may similarly be judged more advanced than that in England, in the sense that landlords were more free from customary constraints. This is notably the case with agricultural land, much of which was owned by city-dwellers. Customary tenure of the English sort was disappearing in northern Italy. Tenures in the villages there were contractual, and gave the landlord control over the way in which his tenants worked the land. There were two main forms of such contracts. Some landlords preferred a lease at a fixed rent in money or in kind.[25] But crop-sharing leases were an increasingly well-favoured arrangement and around Pistoia they rose to nearly half the total of new contracts in the second quarter of the fourteenth century. In the Sienese countryside it seems that over three-quarters of sublet properties already had contracts of this kind in 1316.[26] These contracts commonly stipulated, amongst other conditions, that the tenant was to pay half his crop in rent, though other proportions were known.[27] The determination of landlords to secure supplies from their estates meant, paradoxically, that tenants'

[22] Prestwich, 'Italian Merchants', 88–91; A. Sapori, 'La compagnia dei Frescobaldi in Inghilterra', in idem, *Studi*, ii. 872–8.

[23] C. Violante, *Economia, società, istituzioni a Pisa nel medioevo: saggi e ricerche* (Bari, 1980), 122; W. M. Bowsky, *Le finanze del Comune di Siena, 1287–1355* (Florence, 1975), 264–5; R. W. Kaeuper, *Bankers to the Crown: The Riccardi of Lucca and Edward I* (Princeton, 1973), 120–1; E. B. Fryde, 'Loans to the English Crown, 1328–31', *E.H.R.*, lxx (1955), 209; E. B. Fryde, 'Financial Resources of Edward III in the Netherlands, 1337–40', *Revue Belge de Philologie et d'Histoire*, xlv (1967), 1155.

[24] A. Sapori, 'Il concetto di "usura"', in idem, *Studi*, i. 187; idem, 'I mutui e la proprietà fondiaria', in idem, *Studi*, i. 197–8; C. Cipolla, *Money, Prices and Civilization in the Mediterranean World* (Princeton, 1956), 63.

[25] M. Montanari, *Campagne medievali: strutture produttive, rapporti di lavoro, sistemi alimentari* (Turin, 1984), 91–3; E. Occhipinti, *Il contado milanese nel secolo XIII: l'amministrazione della proprietà fondiaria del Monastero Maggiore* (Bologna, 1982), 178–83.

[26] Herlihy, *Pistoia*, 136; L. A. Kotel'nikova, *Mondo contadino e città in Italia dall'XI al XIV secolo* (Bologna, 1975), 289.

[27] P. J. Jones, 'From Manor to Mezzadria: A Tuscan Case-Study in the Medieval Origins of Modern Agrarian Society', in N. Rubinstein, ed., *Florentine Studies: Politics and Society in Renaissance Florence* (Evanston, 1968), 222–5.

obligations were less monetised in northern Italy than in England.[28] All the same, Marxist historians have classified crop-sharing contracts as transitional between feudalism and capitalism,[29] and we may agree that they were more responsive to changes in land values than English customary tenures. The freer land market in northern Italy also had effects on the lay-out of properties. Landlords and tenants there had gone further than those in England in reconstructing the landscape into compact farms, particularly in the more fertile regions where the advantages of consolidating holdings in this way were greatest.[30]

Both in liberal and in Marxist tradition one index of economic modernisation is the size, wealth and influence of the middle classes. The large urban population of northern Italy, with their merchants, bankers, lawyers and other professional men, suggests strongly that a larger share of the population belonged to the middling ranks of wealth than in England. This is true even of a city like Padua whose long-distance trade was inconspicuous.[31] The middle classes in this sense can be defined loosely as those between the rent-paying peasantry or the artisan class and the land-owning aristocracy. In England the ranks of families in this category were comparatively thin both in the countryside and in all but the largest towns. In Italy, by contrast, this sort of wealth was prominent amongst the politically organised *popolo* of city politics. In a few cities the *popolo* was even sufficiently powerful to take up cudgels against the aristocracy and to win brief spells of political dominance.[32] The prominence of middling ranks in Italy was partly the result of the greater opportunities for commercial profit there. Another reason was the large number of different administrations employing staff in a politically fragmented land. In part, too, middling urban incomes came from past investments in property that yielded rents.[33] The commercialisation of land in Italy probably had the effect that the balance of advantage had tipped even more in favour of property-owners than it had done in England. Information currently available about rents in the two countries is too disconnected to show the differences clearly, but some leasehold rents cited for Italy look high by English standards. Around Pistoia new leasehold rents averaged the equivalent of 5.8 bushels per acre between 1301 and 1350, and this would be equivalent to about 3s. 6d. per acre in

---

[28] Kotel'nikova, 19–110; G. Pinto, *La Toscana nel tardo medioevo: ambiente, economia rurale, società* (Florence, 1982), 275–81; D. J. Osheim, *An Italian Lordship: The Bishopric of Lucca in the Late Middle Ages* (Berkeley and Los Angeles, 1977), 101, 152–3.

[29] Kotel'nikova, 281–4.

[30] Jones, 'From Manor to Mezzadria', 222, 234–5.

[31] J. K. Hyde, *Padua in the Age of Dante* (Manchester, 1966), 37–8, 91–190.

[32] J. Larner, *Italy in the Age of Dante and Petrarch, 1216–1380* (1980), 113–25.

[33] Sapori, 'I mutui e la proprietà fondiaria', 191–213; G. Cherubini, *Signori, contadini, borghesi: ricerche sulla società italiana del basso medioevo* (Florence, 1974), 302–8.

sterling even when prices in England were low.[34] High rents benefited property-owning families at the expense of tenants. The prominence of commercial, professional and rentier families of a middling kind in northern Italy affected the demand for goods and services sufficiently for this to count as a secondary explanation of urban growth. It was such demand that made it possible for Florence in the 1330s to accommodate 600 notaries, 60 physicians and surgeons and 100 dealers in spices.[35]

In all the respects considered so far—the occupational structure of the economy, the workings of the money market, the management of property and the size of the middle classes—there has been a good case for saying that northern Italy was more advanced than England. But there are other comparisons between the two countries where the differences normally expected between more and less advanced economies are slight, ambiguous or non-existent. First place may be given to examining methods of production. Given the more developed markets in capital and property in Italy, technology and organisation there might be expected to be more advanced than in England, and in some instances they were. But on closer inspection the evidence is so localised that it is far from decisive. The perceptible differences were less clear-cut than those between developed and developing economies in the modern world, less marked in fact than those to be found between the advanced economies themselves.

In agriculture there was little, if any, technological gap. It is true that for reasons of climate and terrain Italian farmers had more variety of crops. Near the cities they were also able to benefit from a more organised trade in night soil. The rotations in some lower-lying arable lands were intensive, fallowing was exceptionally infrequent and an unusually large share of the available land was under crops.[36] In some cases these methods were detrimental to the soil, so that their status as agrarian advance is dubious.[37] But, in fact, the advanced husbandry of Italy had close parallels in England. In eastern Norfolk, north and east Kent and coastal Sussex rotations were as intensive as

---

[34] Herlihy, *Pistoia*, 134–5. Southern English wheat prices for the period are listed in J. Z. Titow, *English Rural Society, 1200–1350* (1969), 98–9. For some English leasehold rents, see E. Miller and J. Hatcher, *Medieval England: Rural Society and Economic Change, 1086–1348* (1978), 45–6.

[35] Villani, *Cronica*, XI, xciv.

[36] D. Herlihy, 'Santa Maria Impruneta: a Rural Commune in the Late Middle Ages', in Rubinstein, 252–3; P. J. Jones, 'Medieval Agriculture in its Prime: Italy', in M. M. Postan, ed., *The Cambridge Economic History of Europe, i: The Agrarian Life of the Middle Ages* (2nd edn., Cambridge, 1966), 375; Pinto, 119–20; S. R. Epstein, *Alle origini della fattoria toscana* (Florence, 1986), 154.

[37] G. Cherubini, *L'Italia rurale del basso medioevo* (Rome–Bari, 1984), 27–8.

those in Lombardy.[38] It is doubtful whether high farming was any less representative of England than of Italy, since in both countries it depended on very special local circumstances. Only in restricted areas of northern Italy could intensive farming be attempted at all. As in England, complex rotations were local variants of practices that were less impressive. Much of northern Italy was poor, hilly land where cultivation meant the simple alternation of rye and fallow, or a triennial rotation of winter-sown crop, spring-sown crop and fallow. Infertile lands were cultivated by a loosely patterned infield–outfield regime even in the countryside around Siena. Techniques of working the soil were little changed from Roman times.[39] And in northern Italy a normal wheat yield was about four units harvested for every one sown, much the same as in England.[40] There is no suggestion here of the sort of differences in agriculture that have distinguished advanced from less advanced economies in modern times.

Despite the more developed land market a large part of the land in Italy was still in the hands of small producers many of whom were not motivated primarily by commercial incentives. It is simply not known whether in this respect Italy was any more advanced than England. At Chieri in Piedmont a catasto of 1311 records that only 40 per cent of the land was in units of fifty acres or more. The 2,081 recorded possessors of land held an average of ten acres each, and over half of them had less than five acres. Such small units were also characteristic of the cultivated slopes of the Alps and Appennines.[41] In Impruneta in Tuscany, too, evidence from notarial cartularies between 1276 and 1300 suggests that only about a quarter of the land was in the hands of big landlords, the remaining three-quarters being in the hands of small owners, who included most heads of household in the parish.[42] Sienese catasto records of 1316 show 15,000 properties around the city, of which 6,500 were let out and about 8,500 were

[38] B. M. S. Campbell, 'Agricultural Progress in Medieval England: some Evidence from Eastern Norfolk', *Ec.H.R.*, 2nd ser., xxxvi (1983); P. F. Brandon, 'Farming Techniques: South-Eastern England', in H. E. Hallam, ed., *The Agrarian History of England and Wales, ii: 1042–1350* (Cambridge, 1988), 317–325.

[39] C. Rotelli, *Una campagna medievale: storia agraria del Piemonte fra il 1250 e il 1450* (Turin, 1973), 101–2; F. Panero, *Terra in concessione e mobilità contadina: le campagne fra Po, Sesia e Dora Baltea (secoli XII e XIII)* (Bologna, 1984), 142–5; Pinto, 120n.; Epstein, 154; Cherubini, *L'Italia rurale*, 25–7.

[40] Jones, 'Medieval Agriculture in its Prime: Italy', 377; Cherubini, *Signori, contadini, borghesi*, 89; Pinto, 124; Montanari, 62–3; Cherubini, *L'Italia rurale*, 12–13; Rotelli, 103–4; Epstein, 154n.; J. Z. Titow, *Winchester Yields: a Study in Medieval Agricultural Productivity* (Cambridge, 1972), 14; D. Farmer, 'Grain Yields on Westminster Abbey Manors', *Canadian Journal of History*, xviii (1983), 335.

[41] Rotelli, 127, 329; Cherubini, *Signori, contadi, borghesi*, 100–2.

[42] Herlihy, 'Santa Maria Impruneta', 257.

cultivated by their owners.[43] Even the compact *poderi* of the Tuscan countryside included some miniscule holdings; all but one of those of the Hospital of San Gallo around Florence were smaller than fifteen acres.[44] The labour on small farms such as these was supplied chiefly by the occupying family in both England and Italy. The cultivation of larger units depended upon the existence of wage labour in both countries, and it would be difficult to make any contrast between them on this account.[45] In these respects Italian agriculture cannot confidently be described as more capitalist than that in England.

In the towns themselves the organisation of the larger industries was sometimes more complex than in the equivalent industries in England. At a time when England's urban industries showed few signs of mercantile involvement, some at least of those in northern Italy were taking a more capitalist direction and wage-earners were becoming more dependent upon employers. This was the system of production known to English historians as putting-out. For example, the *lanaiuoli* took responsibility for channelling Florentine woollen cloth through the various stages of its production by subcontracting work to different specialised workers.[46] There was also a greater use of workshop units in some of the textile finishing industries, in the Venetian glass and soap industries and in certain other known contexts.[47] These developments meant that the number of wage-dependent workers in a few Italian cities was large by European standards.[48] On the other hand, this type of more capitalist organisation was characteristic of particular export industries rather than of all manufacturing industry, and it has been cogently argued that Florence was quite exceptional.[49] Most urban industries were carried on in nothing larger than small workshops with a master, a journey-

---

[43] Kotel'nikova, 289.

[44] Pinto, 258–9.

[45] Kotel'nikova, 289, 317–27; L. C. Mauri, ' "Me allogabat in platea": manodopera salariata nelle campagne milanesi alla fine del medioevo', in B. Andreolli and others, *Le prestazioni d'opera nelle campagne italiane del medioevo* (IX Convegno Storico di Bagni di Lucca, Bologna, 1987), 215–20; M. M. Postan, *The Famulus: The Estate Labourer in the XIIth and XIIIth Centuries* (Economic History Review Supplement, 2, Cambridge, 1954), 18–27; Hilton, 137, 165.

[46] F. Melis, *L'economia fiorentina del Rinascimento* (Florence, 1984), 19–21; B. Dini, 'I lavoratori dell'Arte della lana a Firenze nel XIV e XV secolo', in Cristiani and others, 30–2.

[47] F. C. Lane, *Venice, A Maritime Republic* (Baltimore, 1973), 156–65; R. de Roover, *Business, Banking and Economic Thought in Late Medieval and Early Modern Europe* (Chicago, 1974), 47–8; H. Hoshino, *L'Arte della Lana in Firenze nel basso medioevo* (Florence, 1980), 307–12.

[48] G. Cherubini, 'I lavoratori nell'Italia dei secoli XIII–XV: considerazioni storiographiche e prospettive di ricerca', in Cristiani and others, 20.

[49] S. Cohn, 'Florentine Insurrections, 1342–1385, in Comparative Perspective', in R. H. Hilton and T. H. Aston, *The English Rising of 1381* (Cambridge, 1984), 164.

man and an apprentice. Even in the cloth industry there were many small firms rather than a few large ones.[50]

A separate point of comparison between north Italy and England concerns their external trade. Northern Italy can be regarded, with good reason, as an economy in which manufactures and services were exchanged for foodstuffs.[51] The agricultural resources of the country were poor in relationship to its population. Even today a much higher percentage of the land is forest or waste in Italy than in the United Kingdom.[52] The contrast would have been more marked in the earlier fourteenth century when irrigation in the river valleys and the drainage of the marshes was still in its infancy. About 14 per cent of the area of modern Italy has been irrigated or drained since the unification of the country, mostly in the north.[53] In the early fourteenth century well over half the land in north Italy was too mountainous or too wet to be cultivated. The contrast between the poverty of Italy's natural endowment and the intensity of settlement there is a commonplace among historians of agriculture.[54] By 1300, cities had already outgrown reliance on local supplies and depended upon grain from other regions of the Mediterranean, especially Apulia and Sicily. Of the four major cities only Milan, in the middle of the Lombard plain, was supported chiefly by regional agriculture. The ports of Genoa and Venice had such poor hinterlands that they had long depended upon supplies from southern Italy.[55] Dino Compagni the chronicler, in an exordium describing his city, makes the point that for all its populousness Florence too was poorly endowed with land.[56] By the fourteenth century Florence had become so dependent upon grain from the kingdom of Naples that, according to Domenico Lenzi the grain merchant, the city could supply its needs from local sources for only five months of the year in normal years.[57] Amongst the regions of Europe northern Italy was quite exceptionally dependent upon trade for its livelihood.

By contrast some historians have cast England in the role of a modern primary producing country, exporting agricultural com-

[50] L. Zdekauer, *Il mercante senese nel dugento* (Siena, 1925), 25–30; Helihy, *Pistoia*, 172–4; Larner, 194–5.

[51] Cherubini, *Signori, contadini, borghesi*, 90.

[52] The Economist, *The World in Figures* (2nd edn., 1978), 236, 265.

[53] J. M. Houston, *The Western Mediterranean World: An Introduction to its Regional Landscapes* (1964), 151, 438–9.

[54] Pinto, 7; Cherubini, *Signori, contadini, borghesi*, 83–7.

[55] D. Abulafia, 'Southern Italy and the Florentine Economy, 1265–1370', *Ec.H.R.*, 2nd ser., xxxiv (1981), 377–88.

[56] Dino Compagni, *Cronica*, I, i.

[57] *Il libro del biadaiolo: carestia e annona a Firenze dalla metà del '200 al 1348*, ed. G. Pinto (Florence, 1978), 78, 317.

modities in return for imported services and manufactures. But this is at best a half truth. England was indeed an exporter of primary produce; exports of woollen cloth and other manufactures were as yet of little significance.[58] But to classify England's imports as services and manufactures is to misrepresent them. It is impossible to put any exact figure on England's payments for financial services. Dr Fryde suggests that interest payments on the king's debts amounted to £4,000 a year between 1327 and 1337.[59] Loans to private individuals would raise the total figure on Italian receipts from loans some way above this figure. But in these years the average export of wool was 28,629 sacks, which would have earned over £150,000.[60] So interest payments to Italians on the royal debt probably did not exceed 3 per cent of receipts from wool alone, and in addition to wool England was also exporting lead, coal, woolfells and hides. As for the rest of England's imports, the evidence for alien merchants assembled by Dr Lloyd shows that they were not predominantly made up of manufactures except in trade into London. Almost everywhere else the balance was strongly tipped towards materials for local industry and foodstuffs. In the former category come dyes (notably woad) and wood ashes, which were particularly prominent in ports with an industrial hinterland—Southampton, Ipswich and Great Yarmouth. Iron, steel and copper were all imported in an unworked state, and so was timber, especially in ports with prominent ship-building industries. Furs and hides were a standard component of trade with the Baltic. Among foodstuffs the most important was fish, both fresh and salted, a major part of the general merchandise entering the great port of Boston. Salt, too, was commonly imported, and so was some grain.[61] And in this category of non-manufactures it is also admissable to insert wine, which is best regarded as a specialised agricultural product rather like England's own wool. In 1300–1 England imported from Gascony alone about 15,000 tuns of wine to a total value of some £45,000, a figure exceeded in subsequent decades.[62] The Gascon wine trade alone probably exceeded in value England's imports of cloth. The implication of this

[58] E. M. Carus-Wilson, *Medieval Merchant Venturers* (2nd edn., 1967), 241–9.

[59] E. B. Fryde and M. M. Fryde, 'Public Credit with Special Reference to North-Western Europe', in M. M. Postan, E. E. Rich and E. Miller, eds., *The Cambridge Economic History of Europe, iii: Economic Organization and Policies in the Middle Ages* (Cambridge, 1963), 459.

[60] E. M. Carus-Wilson and O. Coleman, *England's Export Trade, 1275–1547* (Oxford, 1963), 43–5. The price of £5.4 a sack is calculated from T. H. Lloyd, *The Movement of Wool Prices in Medieval England* (Ec.H.R. Supplement, 6, Cambridge, 1973), 40–1 (annual means of prices per stone), calculating each sack at 28 stone: E. Power, *The Wool Trade in English Medieval History* (Oxford, 1941), 23.

[61] Lloyd, *Alien Merchants*, 35–60.

[62] M. K. James, *Studies in the Medieval Wine Trade*, ed. E. M. Veale (Oxford, 1971), 9–10, 37.

evidence is that England was not predominantly an importer of other people's manufactures. The kingdom's imports were of the same character as her exports. It is difficult to put these statements into reliable quantitative terms. Between 1327/8 and 1335/6 total cloth imports by aliens, the largest part of the trade, averaged 9,607 cloths, whose value was unlikely to have exceeded one-quarter of the value of the wool exports in these years.[63] This figure represented perhaps only one cloth for every 600 of the population, and it would seem to be a fair inference that most of the cloth worn in England was made in England. It should perhaps be added that imports of manufactures from Italy were negligible.

Another respect in which the differences between northern Italy and England do not correspond to modern international patterns of development and underdevelopment is in the matter of international movements of capital. England's borrowing from Italian bankers was quite unlike the relationships between debtor and creditor nations in the modern world.[64] Borrowing by developing countries is characteristically for investment, in other words to create new sources of income, and it is often associated with the diffusion of technical knowledge and the spread of modern forms of enterprise. Italian lending in England in the early fourteenth century was not of this kind. The financial services offered by Italians were short loans designed to assist in the management of existing sources of income, not to create new ones. Loans to the crown were normally covered by receipts from customs duties.[65] Loans to individuals were sometimes simply advances on sales of wool.[66] Apart from the character of their loans, however, the Italians differed from international lenders in the modern world in the origins of their funds. Today international lending depends upon funds raised in a more advanced economy and flowing into a less advanced one, through the agency of bankers in the advanced economy. Borrowing of this sort creates a return flow of income to the lending country from interest payments and profits. But in the early fourteenth century Italian bankers were resident in England, and it is not evident that their normal activities depended on a flow of funds from abroad. Some at least of the capital with which they operated was drawn from English savings.[67] Trading

[63] Lloyd, *Alien Merchants*, 210–26. The median price for regular coloured cloths was £3 16s. 8d. in 1323–4: E. W. Moore, *The Fairs of Medieval England: An Introductory Study* (Toronto, 1985), 44.

[64] M. M. Postan, 'Italians and the Economic Development of England in the Middle Ages', in idem, *Medieval Trade and Finance* (Cambridge, 1973), 335–41.

[65] Prestwich, 'Italian Merchants', 79.

[66] Kershaw, *Bolton Priory*, 90–3.

[67] Kaeuper, 28; Fryde, 'The Deposits of Hugh Despenser', 347–51; Prestwich, 'Italian Merchants', 95–6.

profits earned in England were an additional source of Italian funds. And the role of the Italians as collectors of papal income, though it may not have had the importance once attributed to it as a source of profit, may be accounted a further source of working capital.[68] As providers of short-term loans in a society without modern economic growth, Italians once established could continue their normal operations from year to year without continuously expanding their capital by drawing from abroad. This explains how a family that was of small account in Italy itself could be big in England. The Ballardi of Lucca pulled no weight in the trade or the politics of their native city, and yet in England they were important enough to be lending to the crown between 1294 and 1314, and after Edward II's accession they were second only to the Bardi in royal esteem.[69]

A comparative study of this kind would ideally take account of incomes and standards of living in England and northern Italy since these are the chief measurement by which economies are ranked in modern discussion. Unfortunately there is no exact way of ranking England and northern Italy by this criterion, and any discussion will be impressionistic. Fortunately there is plenty of information from which clear impressions can be formed.

An opportunity for some direct comparison between the income of England and the income of northern Italy in this period is given by surviving assessments for papal taxation. The evidence here is from the 1290s. England has the record of the sexennial tenth granted by Nicholas IV to Edward I in 1291 and assessed in the winter and spring of 1291–2.[70] From Tuscany there is evidence relating to a triennial tenth which Boniface VIII decreed in the summer of 1295 to finance his war against the Aragonese in Sicily.[71] The collections for 1296, the second year of the three, are well recorded. It is interesting to see that the church of England was more taxable than the church in Italy. A tenth from the whole of Tuscany, with its twelve small dioceses, yielded the equivalent of 10,143 florins in two separate instalments.[72] But in England the equivalent of 15,153 florins was assessed for the tenth in the three south-eastern bishoprics of London, Canterbury and Rochester. Lincoln, the largest English diocese, yielded the equi-

---

[68] Lloyd, *Alien Merchants*, 169–71.

[69] Green, 112–22; Lloyd, *Alien Merchants*, 183–4.

[70] W. E. Lunt, *Financial Relations of the Papacy with England to 1327* (Cambridge, Mass., 1939), 346–65.

[71] *Rationes decimarum Italiae nei secoli XIII e XIV. Tuscia II: Le decime degli anni 1295–1304*, ed. M. Giusti and P. Guidi (Studi e testi 98, Vatican City, 1932), 12.

[72] J. Day, *The Medieval Market Economy* (Oxford, 1987), 138–9. Florins have been valued at 41s. 6d., an average of the rates for June and December 1296: P. Spufford, *Handbook of Medieval Exchange* (Royal Historical Society Guides and Handbooks, 13, 1986), 3.

valent of 29,912 florins from a territory less than half the size of Tuscany and without the benefit of a single major city.[73] This comparison is not wholly appropriate, since the Tuscan figures are of coin actually collected and the English figures are assessments. There were no doubt other major differences between the two sets of figures, and no grand hypothesis can be built upon them. But it would be surprising if concern about poverty was uppermost in Nicholas IV's mind when he prayed for England.

It is important not to prejudge the relative prosperity of England and northern Italy. There may have been more wealth among the propertied classes of Italian society than there was in England, and that may have tipped the balance in favour of average incomes per head in Italy. But the case is not self-evident. It is to be remembered that urban incomes had grown partly at the expense of rural incomes, and that historians of Italy are used to contrasting urban wealth with rural poverty. The Italian rentier classes were characteristically urban. Landed families had moved into the cities, and city dwellers had purchased land from landlords and from peasants.[74] Landed incomes in England were still characteristically rural, so that much of the kingdom's wealth lay in rural areas. This means that it is misleading, to think of the size and wealth of Italian cities as an indicator of higher overall prosperity.

The prominence of town life in northern Italy does not imply that productivity and standards of living were higher there than in England, and the implications could be the very opposite. Such unsophisticated comparison of wage levels as the evidence permits suggest that there can have been no great difference between the two regions in what wages would buy. Between 1320 and 1335 an English labourer in southern England had to work some 40 days to earn a quarter of wheat; in Florence the equivalent was 39 days.[75] Between 1326 and 1332 a master mason can be calculated to have worked 22

[73] W. Stubbs, *The Constitutional History of England*, ii (4th edn., Oxford, 1896), table opp. p. 580. Sterling has been converted at the rate of 2s. 10d. to the florin: Spufford, 198.

[74] E. Fiumi, 'Sui rapporti economici tra città e contado nell'età communale', *Archivo storico italiano*, cxiv (1956), 23, 62–4; idem, 'Fioritura e decadenza dell'economia fiorentina', *Archivo storico italiano*, cxvi (1958), 497–505; Cherubini, *L'Italia rurale*, 65–71; P.J. Jones, 'Economia e società nell'Italia medievale: la leggenda della borghesia', in R. Romano and C. Vivanti, eds., *Storia d'Italia dal feudalesimo al capitalismo* (Turin, 1978), 328–36.

[75] This is calculated on a wage of 2d. a day in England, 4.5 *soldi* a day in Florence: W. Beveridge, 'Wages in the Winchester Manors', *Ec.H.R.*, vii (1936), 42; W. Beveridge, 'Westminster Wages in the Manorial Era', *Ec.H.R.*, 2nd ser., viii (1955), 27; *Il libro del biadaiolo*, 141. The English wheat price (6s. 9d. a quarter) is from Titow, *English Rural Society*, 98. The Florentine wheat price (16 *soldi* a *staio*) is from *Il libro del biadaiolo*, 63–70. Measures have been converted at the rate of 0.73 bushels to the Florentine *staio*: Herlihy, *Pistoia*, xix.

days for a quarter of wheat both in southern England and in Florence.[76] Some calculations by Prof. Farmer show that between 1340 and 1347 a carpenter in England would on average require 33.5 days' work to buy a quarter of wheat. A master carpenter working in Florence between 1340 and 1348 would have to work for 32.6 days to earn the same amount.[77] This evidence suggests that English wage earners would not have been able to improve their lot by emigrating to Italy. This situation contrasts strongly with that in the eighteenth century, when wage rates in England were appreciably higher than those of countries at a comparable state of economic development on the continent.[78]

Doubts about Italy's superiority in this respect are justified by evidence of urban poverty. As in England, wage-earners in Italian city populations are barely distinguishable from paupers because of their vulnerability to shortages of food, and they accounted for a large share of city populations. At Perugia in 1285, 30 per cent of households were classed as propertyless.[79] A comparison between two Sienese taxation assessments, one of 1317–18 and one of 1328, implies that about one-third of the population was propertyless.[80] In hard times almost anyone in this category was likely to go hungry. In 1330, a year of high prices, about a quarter of the population of Florence could be regarded as indigent.[81] The problems of poverty were compounded in northern Italy, as in England, by higher levels of taxation. Rising state budgets, new fiscal devices and an increasingly adverse impact of taxation upon standards of living, are intrinsic to the history of both countries.[82] In the contado of Lucca tax concessions were

[76] This is calculated on a wage of 4d. a day in England, 8.6 *soldi* in Florence: H. Phelps Brown and S. V. Hopkins, *A Perspective of Wages and Prices* (1981), 11; La Roncière, *Prix et salaires*, 280. The wheat price used for Florence (17.25 *soldi* a *staio*) is from *Il libro del biadaiolo*, 66–9. The English price (7s. 4d. a quarter) is from Titow, *English Rural Society*, 98.

[77] D. L. Farmer, 'Crop Yields, Prices and Wages in Medieval England', *Studies in Medieval and Renaissance History* (Vancouver, 1983), 147; La Roncière, *Prix et salaires*, 280, 821. The estimate for Florence is calculated from a daily wage of 6.4 *soldi* and an average wheat price of 19.05 *soldi* a *staio* (average of 1340/1–1347/8, both terms).

[78] E. H. Hunt, *British Labour History, 1815–1914* (1981), 57.

[79] S. R. Blanshei, *Perugia, 1260–1340: Conflict and Change in a Medieval Italian Urban Society* (American Philosophical Society, new ser., lxvi (2), Philadelphia, 1976), 44–5.

[80] Cherubini, *Signori, contadini, borghesi*, 247.

[81] Larner, 204.

[82] Larner, 218–19; C. M. de La Roncière, 'Indirect Taxes or "Gabelles" at Florence in the Fourteenth Century: The Evolution of Tariffs and Problems of Collection', in Rubinstein, 141, 174–82; E. Miller, 'War, Taxation and the English Economy in the Late Thirteenth and Early Fourteenth Centuries', in J. M. Winter, ed., *War and Economic Development* (Cambridge, 1975), 26–7; J. R. Maddicott, *The English Peasantry and the Demands of the Crown, 1294–1341* (Past and Present Supplement, 1, Oxford, 1975), 1–15, 45–75.

having to be granted in the 1330s and 1340s because of impoverishment and depopulation.[83] A Florentine commission appointed to raise 200,000 *lire* in 1338 reported that in 65 parishes of the *contado* the inhabitants were so impoverished that without a lower assessment they would have 'to go begging through the world'. Already many poorer families were said to have sold their possessions because they could not meet the demands placed upon them.[84]

In his history of Pistoia, Herlihy notes a famine in the year 1313, another in 1328–9, a severe epidemic of some sort in 1339–40 which allegedly killed a quarter of the population, and famine again in 1346–7.[85] Such episodes could be matched in all the cities of which we have any demographic record. The most studied town in Italy, from this point of view, is Florence, where the evidence suggests chronic instability during the half century before the Black Death. According to recent estimates by La Roncière, the population of Florence rose at the end of the thirteenth century to a peak it did not subsequently exceed.[86] The Florentine chroniclers record severe famine throughout Tuscany and elsewhere in Italy in 1328–9, and tell of the starving poor who flocked into Florence from other cities, especially Siena, in search of food.[87] A Sienese chronicler describes the poor people from Siena and the *contado*, as well as migrants from elsewhere, who rioted outside the Scala Hospital in their desperation. The city governors were afraid they would sack the city.[88] The famine of 1328–9 was only one of a series of disasters. At Florence the population recovered over the following ten years, chiefly by immigration from the countryside, only to be severely reduced again by famine in 1339–41 and an epidemic in 1340. Recovery was hampered by famine in 1346 and 1347 which was said to have caused the deaths of 4,000 Florentines.[89] The frequency of the disasters that struck Italian cities was in fact greater than in England, where the only major famine in the early fourteenth century was that of 1316–18.[90] It is arguable, indeed, that these dense urban populations were more liable to high mortality

---

[83] C. Meek, *Lucca, 1369–1400: Politics and Society in an Early Renaissance State* (Oxford, 1978), 77–8.

[84] Herlihy, 'Santa Maria Impruneta', 266, 269–70.

[85] Herlihy, *Pistoia*, 105.

[86] La Roncière, *Prix et salaires*, 676.

[87] Villani, *Cronica*, X, cxviii; *Il libro del biadaiolo*, 316–23.

[88] Epstein, 206.

[89] La Roncière, *Prix et salaires*, 628–38; Herlihy and Klapisch-Zuber, 173–6; *Il libro del biadaiolo*, 95–100.

[90] M. M. Postan and J. Z. Titow, 'Heriots and Prices on Winchester Manors', in M. M. Postan, *Essays on Medieval Agriculture and General Problems of the Medieval Economy* (Cambridge, 1973), 150–85; I. Kershaw, 'The Great Famine and Agrarian Crisis in England', in R. H. Hilton, ed., *Peasants, Knights and Heretics* (Cambridge, 1976), 85–132.

from both famines and from epidemics than less crowded populations would have been.[91]

From these observations it may be inferred that the ways in which Italy differed from England were equivalent neither to differences between industrial and preindustrial economies today, nor to differences between colonial powers and colonised peoples in the early modern period. The differences arose chiefly from similar resources of knowledge and similar social attitudes at work in different environments. Northern Italy was better placed than England for merchant enterprise, but resources for agriculture were less favourable. The growth of population and output had consequently depended more upon trading specialisations than they had in England. Many Italian achievements, including some developing techniques of banking, insurance and accountancy, sprang from exceptionally heavy investment in long-distance trade, and it makes undeniable good sense to speak of continuing Italian advance relative to England in this field. But such narrow points of contrast are not what modern comparisons of economic rank and power are all about. The commercial prominence of Italians did not indicate a superior plane of economic welfare in Italy, nor lead in that direction. In comparison with the enormous inequalities between modern economies, any contrast between England and northern Italy in the earlier fourteenth century was trivial. Nor did Italian merchants determine English policies in any respect other than the need to reward their services. England was not dominated by Italians. The concepts of economic backwardness and economic dependence, as they are used to describe international relations today, are here so barely appropriate that they explain little. Economic specialisation, economic ranking and economic domination are all different things, and one of the historian's tasks must be to attempt to distinguish between them in past centuries.

[91] Herlihy and Klapisch-Zuber, 210.

THE ROYAL HISTORICAL SOCIETY
REPORT OF COUNCIL, SESSION 1988-1989

THE Council of the Royal Historical Society has the honour to present the following report to the Anniversary Meeting.

The Government's interventions in educational matters have provided continuing cause for concern over developments at all levels in the study of history. Along with many other scholarly bodies, Council has done its utmost to influence the inquisition into research and publication by the Universities' Funding Council. Council's response to the general invitation to comment on the organization of this 'selectivity exercise' combined forceful criticism with many constructive suggestions, and, later, its nominations of possible advisors to assist the UFC's deliberations were accepted. A submission was also made on the teaching of history in schools to the National Curriculum History Working Group, which is due to report finally late in 1989. On such questions, Council has continued to keep closely in touch with the work of both the History at the Universities Defence Group and Public Sector History. Council regards their activities as an important complement in many ways to the work of the Society and is providing significant financial and other support wherever possible.

While looking forward to the first results of the Historical Association's Young Historian Scheme in connection with the GCSE examinations, Council has also provided advice and assistance, in response to a request from the Council for Industry and Higher Education, with establishing the Cadbury-Schweppes prize for innovative teaching in the humanities. In connection with the Society's own awards, Council has altered the conditions governing the Alexander Prize Essay to make possible entries from among the growing number of mature research students. It has supported the work of the Design Implementation Software History Project at the University of Glasgow, and readily agreed to a suggestion that the Society might like to be represented on the advisory board of the Computers in Teaching Initiative Centre. A further grant has been made from the Robinson Bequest to support publication of a Gainsborough catalogue sponsored by the Dulwich Picture Gallery.

A number of developments have also occurred in the Society's own publishing activities. Council has made arrangements for the *Annual Bibliography of British and Irish History* to be produced in future by

Oxford University Press, beginning with the edition for 1989. In parallel with this departure, Council has also approved proposals from its working party (mentioned in the Report for 1986–1987) for updating and developing the series of *Bibliographies of British History*. Considerable progress has been made by the appointment of a General Editor (Dr J. S. Morrill), Executive Committee and Secretary, with accommodation and computer facilities in Cambridge. The further funding of this project, which will far exceed the Society's own resources, is being actively considered. Council's investigation of the proposal for a series of *Bibliographies of European History*, by comparison, has as yet made little headway.

Council was delighted to note the award to Professor Norman Gash of the C.B.E. in the New Year Honours.

An evening party was held for members and guests in the Upper Hall at University College London on Wednesday, 1 July 1988. 160 acceptances to invitations were received, and it was as usual well-attended.

At the Anniversary Meeting on 18 November 1988 a proposal to increase the annual subscriptions from 1 July 1989 was adopted; Professor F. M. L. Thompson was elected to succeed Dr G. E. Aylmer as President, and the remaining Officers of the Society were re-elected. The Society is, however, still without an Honorary Solicitor.

Council accepted with regret the retirement from the Society's office of Mrs Olive Smith; to mark her long and valuable contribution to its administration over 18 years, an informal presentation was made to her in the Council Room on 14th October 1988.

The representation of the Society upon various bodies was as follows: Professor F. M. L. Thompson on the Joint Anglo-American Committee exercising a general supervision over the production of the *Bibliographies of British History*; Professor G. W. S. Barrow, Mr M. Roper and Professor P. H. Sawyer on the Joint Committee of the Society and the British Academy established to prepare an edition of Anglo-Saxon charters; Professor H. R. Loyn on a committee to promote the publication of photographic records of the more significant collections of British Coins; Professor P. Lasko on the Advisory Council of the reviewing Committee on the Export of Works of Art; Dr G. H. Martin on the Council of the British Records Association; Mr M. R. D. Foot on the Committee to advise the publishers of *The Annual Register*; Professor K. Cameron on the Trust for Lincolnshire Archaeology; Professor W. Doyle on the History at the Universities Defence Group; and Dr A. I. Doyle on the Anthony Panizzi Foundation. Council received reports from its representatives.

Professor E. B. Fryde represents the Society on a committee to regulate British co-operation in the preparation of a new repertory of medieval sources to replace Potthast's *Bibliotheca Historica Medii Aevi*; Professor Glanmor Williams on the Court of the University College of Swansea; Professor A. L. Brown on the University Conference of Stirling University; and Professor C. N. L. Brooke on the British Sub-Commission of the Commission International d'Histoire Ecclé-siastique Comparée. During the year Professor W. Doyle was nominated to represent the Society on the Court of the University of Exeter and Professor N. McCord to the Council of the British Association for Local History. The Society was invited to be represented on both the National Council on Archives and the Computers in Teaching Initiative Centre for History, and Dr Alice Prochaska and Professor W. A. Speck respectively agreed to act on the Society's behalf.

The Vice-Presidents retiring under By-law XVI were Dr G. H. Martin and Professor K. G. Robbins. Professor R. R. Davies and Professor W. A. Speck were elected to replace them. The members of Council retiring under By-law XIX were Professor D. E. D. Beales, Professor R. C. Floud, and Mr G. C. F. Forster and Professor W. A. Speck. Professor M. D. Biddiss, Professor M. Claire Cross, Professor D. K. Fieldhouse and Dr J. S. Morrill were elected to fill the vacancies.

Messrs Davis, Watson and Co., were appointed auditors for the year 1988-9 under By-law XXVIII.

Publications and Papers read

Transactions, Fifth Series, Volume 39, and *Minutes of the Rainbow Circle, 1894-1924*, ed. M. Freeden, (Camden, Fourth Series, Volume 38) went to press during the session and are due to be published in November 1989. The following works were published during the session: *Thomas Starkey: A Dialogue between Pole and Lupset*, ed. T. F. Mayer, (Camden, Fourth Series, Volume 37); and 2 volumes in the STUDIES IN HISTORY series: *James Bryce's 'American Commonwealth', The Anglo-American Background*, by Hugh Tulloch (volume 54); and *Imperial Reaction: The Imperial Aulic Council and Imperial Politics in the Reign of Charles VI*, by Michael Hughes (volume 55).

At the ordinary meetings of the Society the following papers were read:

'Lord George Bentinck and the Protectionists: a lost Cause?', by Dr A. Macintyre (14 October 1988).
'England and Northern Italy in the Early Fourteenth Century: the economic contrasts', by Dr R. H. Britnell (9 December 1988).
'The Comparative Study of Memorial Preaching', by Dr D. d'Avray (27 January 1989).
'Bodin and the development of the French Monarchy', by Professor R. Bonney (3 March 1989).

'Parliament and the shaping of eighteenth-century English social policy' by Miss J. Innes (21 April 1989).

At the Anniversary Meeting on 18 November 1988, the President, Dr G. E. Aylmer, delivered an address on 'Collective mentalities in mid-seventeenth-century England: IV: Cross-currents: Neutrals, Trimmers and others'.

The Whitfield Prize for 1988 was awarded to Dr John Davis for his book *Reforming London, the London Government Problem 1855–1900*, (Oxford University Press).

The Alexander Prize for 1989 was awarded to Dr J. S. A. Adamson for his essay *The Baronial Context of the English Civil War*, which was read to the Society on 19 May 1989.

Membership

Council records with regret the deaths of 21 Fellows, 2 Associates and 2 Corresponding Fellows. Among these Council would mention especially Sir Keith Hancock (an Honorary Vice-President and Corresponding Fellow) and Dr H. Heimpel (a Corresponding Fellow).

The resignations of 10 Fellows, 1 Associate and 8 Subscribing Libraries were received. Professor François Bédarida was elected a Corresponding Fellow. In addition to a further 4 overseas scholars who accepted the President's invitation to become Fellows of the Society, 74 Fellows and 8 Associates were elected and 2 Libraries were admitted. 75 Fellows transferred to the category of Retired Fellow. The membership of the Society on 30 June 1989 comprised 1771 Fellows (including 60 Life Fellows and 178 Retired Fellows), 39 Corresponding Fellows, 151 Associates and 691 Subscribing Libraries (1730, 40, 149 and 697 respectively on 30 June 1988). The Society exchanged publications with 14 Societies, British and foreign.

Finance

At the Anniversary Meeting in November 1988, the Society approved Council's recommendation that the annual subscription be raised. Although this decision has not yet affected the income from subscriptions, the Society has benefitted from an increase in the investment income which reflects both high interest rates and a readjustment in the portfolio. On the side of expenditure, there has been a saving in secretarial and administrative costs, and a large increase in the provision for publications. The outcome has been a fall in the excess of income over expenditure from £36,110 in 1988 to £27,275 in 1989. The increase in subscription income which will be reflected in the accounts for 1989/90 will provide the necessary base for the policy of new initiatives upon which the Society has embarked.

The net current assets of the Society have moved from £12,901 in 1988 to a deficit of £9,182 in 1989. This reflects the decision to reduce current assets held in the form of cash at bank and in hand, and instead to place it on call at the Society's brokers where it is easily realizable.

The Society remains grateful for the bequests it has received in the past, some of which are reflected in the names of prizes, lectures and funds. The decision to publish a new edition of Professor Andrew Browning's 'Reresby Memoirs' was taken in recognition of the contribution made by his legacy to the Society's finances.

Benefactors of the Royal Historical Society:

Mr L. C. Alexander
The Reverend David Berry
Professor Andrew Browning
Mrs W. M. Frampton
Sir George Prothero
Professor T. G. Reddaway
Miss E. M. Robinson
Professor A. S. Whitfield

ROYAL HISTORICAL SOCIETY

Balance Sheet as at 30th June 1989

	Notes	1989 £	1989 £	1988 £	1988 £
Fixed Assets	2		2,700		3,864
Investments	3		666,210		596,198
Current Assets					
Stocks	1(c)	6,007		3,113	
Debtors	4	15,849		11,196	
Cash at Bank and in Hand	5	14,246		38,490	
		36,102		52,799	
Creditors: Amounts falling due within one year	6	45,284		39,898	
Net Current Assets			(9,182)		12,901
			659,728		612,963
Represented by:					
General Fund			611,408		564,121
Miss E. M. Robinson Bequest			26,448		26,539
A. S. Whitfield Prize Fund			13,524		13,452
Studies in History			8,348		8,851
			659,728		612,963

ROYAL HISTORICAL SOCIETY

Income and Expenditure Account for the Year Ended 30th June 1989

GENERAL FUND

	Notes	1989 £	1989 £	1988 £	1988 £
INCOME					
Subscriptions.	7		41,145		42,582
Investment income			64,548		50,551
Royalties and reproduction fees.			441		469
Donations and sundry income			335		927
			106,469		94,529
EXPENDITURE					
Secretarial and Administrative					
Salaries, pensions and national insurance		14,927		22,034	
Printing and stationery		5,105		3,495	
Postage and telephone		3,164		1,963	
Audit and accountancy		2,329		2,875	
Insurance		380		357	
Meetings and travel.		3,584		2,992	
Repairs and renewals		276		1,415	
Depreciation	1(b)	1,164		1,163	
			30,929		36,294
Publications					
Literary director's expenses		225		225	
Publishing costs for the year	8(a)	14,439		(942)	
Provisions for publications in progress	8(b)	29,000		24,000	
Other publication costs	8(c)	701		(575)	
Sales of publications.		(5,616)		(4,393)	
			38,749		18,315
Library and archives	1(d)				
Purchase of books and publications		1,257		936	
Binding		1,226		590	
			2,483		1,526
Other charges					
Centenary Fellowship		5,175		—	
Alexander prize.		100		384	
Prothero lecture		258		100	
Grants		1,000		1,000	
Donations and sundry expenses		—		300	
A level prizes		500		500	
			7,033		2,284
			79,194		58,419
Excess of income over expenditure			27,275		36,110
Surplus on sale of investments			20,012		66,271
			47,287		102,381
Balance brought forward.			564,121		461,740
Balance carried forward.			611,408		564,121

ROYAL HISTORICAL SOCIETY

Income and Expenditure Account for the Year Ended 30th June 1989

SPECIAL FUNDS

MRS E. M. ROBINSON BEQUEST

	1989		1988	
	£	£	£	£
INCOME				
Investment income		909		1,612
Surplus on sale of investments		—		907
		909		2,519
EXPENDITURE				
Grant to Dulwich Picture Gallery.		1,000		500
Excess of income over expenditure for the year.		(91)		2,019
Balance brought forward		26,539		24,520
Balance carried forward.		26,448		26,539

A. S. WHITFIELD PRIZE FUND

INCOME				
Investment income		1,072		1,215
EXPENDITURE				
Prize awarded.	1,000		600	
Advertisement.	—	1,000	227	827
Excess of income over expenditure for the year.		72		388
Balance brought forward.		13,452		13,064
Balance carried forward.		13,524		13,452

STUDIES IN HISTORY

INCOME				
Royalties		2,064		1,631
Investment income.		899		746
		2,963		2,377
EXPENDITURE				
Honorarium	2,750		2,750	
Editor's expenses	716		681	
		3,466		3,431
Excess of expenditure over income for the year.		(503)		(1,054)
Balance brought forward.		8,851		9,905
Balance carried forward.		8,348		8,851

ROYAL HISTORICAL SOCIETY

STATEMENT OF SOURCE AND APPLICATION OF FUNDS FOR THE YEAR ENDED 30TH JUNE 1989

	1989 £	1989 £	1988 £	1988 £
SOURCE OF FUNDS				
Excess of income over expenditure for the year				
General fund		47,287		102,381
Miss E. M. Robinson Bequest.		(91)		2,019
A. S. Whitfield prize fund		72		388
Studies in History fund		(503)		(1,054)
		46,765		103,734
Adjustment for items not involving the movement of funds				
Depreciation	1,164		1,163	
Surplus on sale of investments	(20,012)		(67,178)	
		(18,848)		(66,015)
Total generated from operations		27,917		37,719
Funds from other sources				
Sale of investments		51,744		41,618
		79,661		79,337
APPLICATION OF FUNDS				
Purchase of fixed assets		—	5,027	
Purchase of investments	101,744		61,650	
		101,744		66,677
		(22,083)		12,660
INCREASE/(DECREASE) IN WORKING CAPITAL				
Stock		2,894		2,166
Debtors		4,653		(474)
Creditors		(5,386)		23,723
Liquid funds		(24,244)		(12,755)
		(22,083)		12,660

ROYAL HISTORICAL SOCIETY

Notes to the Accounts for the Year Ended 30th June 1989

1. ACCOUNTING POLICIES
    (a) *Basis of accounting*
        These accounts have been prepared under the historical cost convention.
    (b) *Depreciation*
        Depreciation is calculated by reference to the cost of fixed assets using a straight line basis at rates considered appropriate having regard to the expected lives of the fixed assets.
        The annual rates of depreciation in use are:
        Furniture and equipment   10%
        Computer equipment   25%
        Prior to 1st July 1987 the full cost of fixed assets was written off to General Fund in the year of purchase.
    (c) *Stocks*
        Stock is valued at the lower of cost and net realisable value.
    (d) *Library and archives*
        The cost of additions to the library and archives is written off in the year of purchase.

2. FIXED ASSETS

	Computer Equipment	Furniture and Equipment	Total
	£	£	£
Cost at 1 July 1988	4,407	620	5,027
Additions during year. . . .	—	—	—
Disposals during year	—	—	—
At 30th June 1989	4,407	620	5,027
Depreciation as at 1st July 1988 . .	1,101	62	1,163
Charge for year	1,102	62	1,164
At 30th June 1988	2,203	124	2,327
Net book value			
At 30th June 1988	3,306	558	3,864
At 30th June 1989	2,204	496	2,700

The cost of additions to the library and archives is written off in the year of purchase.
Prior to 1st July 1987 the cost of furniture and equipment was written off in the year of purchase. Items acquired before that date are not reflected in the above figures.

3. INVESTMENTS

	1989 £	1988 £
Quoted securities at cost	576,628	512,735
(market value £1,247,352; 1988 £1,028,349)		
Money at call	89,582	73,463
Short term deposit	—	10,000
	666,210	596,198

4. DEBTORS

	1989 £	1988 £
Sundry debtors	13,294	9,595
Prepayments	2,555	1,601
	15,849	11,196

5. CASH AT BANK AND IN HAND

	1989 £	1988 £
Deposit accounts	11,034	28,475
Current accounts	3,187	9,995
Cash in hand	25	20
	14,246	38,490

6. CREDITORS

	1989 £	1988 £
Sundry creditors .	2,616	7,202
Subscriptions received in advance .	11,598	7,116
Accruals .	2,070	1,580
Provision for publications .	29,000	24,000
	45,284	39,898

7. SUBSCRIPTIONS

	1989 £	1988 £
Current subscriptions .	38,761	38,484
Subscriptions arrears received .	974	2,238
Income tax recovered on covenanted subscriptions	1,410	1,860
	41,145	42,582

8. PUBLICATIONS

(a) Publishing costs for the year

		£	
Transactions, fifth series	Vol. 38	13,987	
Camden, fourth series	Vol. 35	20	
	Vol. 36	14,890	
	Vol. 37	9,542	
		38,439	50,408
Less: Provision brought forward .		24,000	51,350
		14,439	(942)

(b) Provision for publications in progress

Transactions, fifth series	Vol. 39	14,000	
Camden, fourth series	Vol. 38	15,000	
		29,000	24,000

(c) Other publication costs

	1989	1988
Annual *Bibliography*	2,700	1,279
Less: Royalties received	1,999	1,854
	701	(575)

F. M. L. THOMPSON, *President*
M. J. DAUNTON, *Treasurer*

We have audited the accounts on pages 7 to 12 in accordance with approved Auditing Standards.
In our opinion the accounts, which have been prepared under the historical cost convention, give a true and fair view of the Society's affairs at 30th June 1989 and of its surplus and source and application of funds for the year then ended.

118, SOUTH STREET, DORKING
5th September, 1989

DAVIES, WATSON & CO.
Chartered Accountants

THE DAVID BERRY ESSAY TRUST

Balance Sheet as at 30th June 1989

	1989 £	1989 £	1988 £	1988 £
Investments				
483.63 shares in the Charities Official Investment Fund . .		530		530
(Market value £2,795; 1988 £2,007)				
Current assets				
Cash at bank				
deposit account	2,802		2,383	
current account	—		1	
	2,802		2,384	
Creditors: Accounts falling due within one year	372		227	
Net current assets		2,430		2,157
		2,960		2,687
Represented by:				
Accumulated fund		2,960		2,687
Income				
Dividends		267		240
Interest		151		90
		418		330
Expenditure				
Prize	100		—	
Adjudicators' Fee	45		—	
Advertisement	—	145	227	227
Excess of income over expenditure for the year		273		103
Balance brought forward		2,687		2,584
Balance carried forward		2,960		2,687

The late David Berry, by his Will dated 23 April 1926, left £1,000 to provide in every three years a gold medal and prize money for the best essay on the Earl of Bothwell or, at the discretion of the Trustees, on Scottish History of the James Stuarts I to VI, in memory of his father the late Rev. David Berry.

The Trust is regulated by a scheme sanctioned by the Chancery Division of the High Court of Justice dated 23 January 1930, and made in action 1927 A 1233 David Anderson Berry deceased, Hunter and Another V Robertson and Another and since modified by an order of the Charity Commissioners made on 11 January 1978 removing the necessity to provide a medal.

The Royal Historical Society is now the Trustee. The investment held on Capital Account consists of 634 Charities Official Investment Fund shares (Market Value £3,600; 1988 £2,630).

The Trustee will in every second year of the three year period advertise inviting essays.

We have audited the accounts on this page in accordance with approved Auditing Standards.

In our opinion the accounts, which have been prepared under the historical cost convention, give a true and fair view of the Trust's affairs at 30th June 1989 and of its surplus for the year then ended and comply with the provisions of the Trust deed.

118, South Street, Dorking
5th September, 1989

DAVIES, WATSON & CO.
Chartered Accountants

ALEXANDER PRIZE

The Alexander Prize was established in 1897 by L. C. Alexander, F.R.Hist.S. It consists of a silver medal and £100 awarded annually for an essay upon some historical subject. Candidates may select their own subject provided such subject has been previously submitted to and approved by the Literary Director. The essay must be a genuine work of original research, not hitherto published, and one which has not been awarded any other prize. It must not exceed 6,000 words in length and must be sent in on or before 1 November of any year. The detailed regulations should be obtained in advance from the Secretary. Candidates must be under the age of 30.

LIST OF ALEXANDER PRIZE ESSAYISTS (1898-1986)[1]

1898. F. Hermia Durham ('The relations of the Crown to trade under James I').

1899. W. F. Lord, BA ('The development of political parties during the reign of Queen Anne').

1901. Laura M. Roberts ('The Peace of Lunéville').

1902. V. B. Redstone ('The social condition of England during the Wars of the Roses').

1903. Rose Graham ('The intellectual influence of English monasticism between the tenth and the twelfth centuries').

1904. Enid W. G. Routh ('The balance of power in the seventeenth century').

1905. W. A. P. Mason, MA ('The beginnings of the Cistercian Order').

1906. Rachel R. Reid, MA ('The Rebellion of the Earls, 1569').

1908. Kate Hotblack ('The Peace of Paris, 1763').

1909. Nellie Nield, MA ('The social and economic condition of the unfree classes in England in the twelfth and thirteenth centuries').

1912. H. G. Richardson ('The parish clergy of the thirteenth and fourteenth centuries').

1917. Isobel D. Thornely, BA ('The treason legislation of 1531-1534').

1918. T. F. T. Plucknett, BA ('The place of the Council in the fifteenth century').

1919. Edna F. White, MA ('The jurisdiction of the Privy Council under the Tudors').

1920. J. E. Neale, MA ('The Commons Journals of the Tudor Period').

1922. Eveline C. Martin ('The English establishments on the Gold Coast in the second half of the eighteenth century').

1923. E. W. Hensman, MA ('The Civil War of 1648 in the east midlands').

1924. Grace Stretton, BA ('Some aspects of mediæval travel').

1925. F. A. Mace, MA ('Devonshire ports in the fourteenth and fifteenth centuries').

[1] No award was made in 1900, 1907, 1910, 1911, 1913, 1914, 1921, 1946, 1948, 1956, 1969, 1975, 1977, and 1987. The Prize Essays for 1909 and 1919 were not published in the *Transactions*. No Essays were submitted in 1915, 1916 and 1943.

1926. Marian J. Tooley, MA ('The authorship of the *Defensor Pacis*').

1927. W. A. Pantin, BA ('Chapters of the English Black Monks, 1215–1540').

1928. Gladys A. Thornton, BA, PhD ('A study in the history of Clare, Suffolk, with special reference to its development as a borough').

1929. F. S. Rodkey, AM, PhD ('Lord Palmerston's policy for the rejuvenation of Turkey, 1839–47').

1930. A. A. Ettinger, DPhil ('The proposed Anglo-Franco-American Treaty of 1852 to guarantee Cuba to Spain').

1931. Kathleen A. Walpole, MA ('The humanitarian movement of the early nineteenth century to remedy abuses on emigrant vessels to America').

1932. Dorothy M. Brodie, BA ('Edmund Dudley, minister of Henry VII').

1933. R. W. Southern, BA ('Ranulf Flambard and early Anglo-Norman administration').

1934. S. B. Chrimes, MA, PhD ('Sir John Fortescue and his theory of dominion').

1935. S. T. Bindoff, MA ('The unreformed diplomatic service, 1812–60').

1936. Rosamund J. Mitchell, MA, BLitt ('English students at Padua, 1460–1475').

1937. C. H. Philips, BA ('The East India Company "Interest", and the English Government, 1783–4').

1938. H. E. I. Phillips, BA ('The last years of the Court of Star Chamber, 1630–41').

1939. Hilda P. Grieve, BA ('The deprived married clergy in Essex, 1553–61').

1940. R. Somerville, MA ('The Duchy of Lancaster Council and Court of Duchy Chamber').

1941. R. A. L. Smith, MA, PhD ('The *Regimen Scaccarii* in English monasteries').

1942. F. L. Carsten, DPhil ('Medieval democracy in the Brandenburg towns and its defeat in the fifteenth century').

1944. Rev. E. W. Kemp, BD ('Pope Alexander III and the canonization of saints').

1945. Helen Suggett, BLitt ('The use of French in England in the later middle ages').

1947. June Milne, BA ('The diplomacy of John Robinson at the court of Charles XII of Sweden, 1697–1709').

1949. Ethel Drus, MA ('The attitude of the Colonial Office to the annexation of Fiji').

1950. Doreen J. Milne, MA, PhD ('The results of the Rye House Plot, and their influence upon the Revolution of 1688').

1951. K. G. Davies, BA ('The origins of the commission system in the West India trade').

1952. G. W. S. Barrow, BLitt ('Scottish rulers and the religious orders, 1070–1153').

1953. W. E. Minchinton, BSc(Econ) ('Bristol—metropolis of the west in the eighteenth century').

1954. Rev. L. Boyle, OP ('The *Oculus Sacerdotis* and some other works of William of Pagula').

1955. G. F. E. Rudé, MA, PhD ('The Gordon riots: a study of the rioters and their victims').

1957. R. F. Hunnisett, MA, DPhil ('The origins of the office of Coroner').

1958. Thomas G. Barnes, AB, DPhil ('County politics and a puritan *cause célèbre*: Somerset churchales, 1633').

1959. Alan Harding, BLitt ('The origins and early history of the Keeper of the Peace').

1960. Gwyn A. Williams, MA, PhD ('London and Edward I').

1961. M. H. Keen, BA ('Treason trials under the law of arms').

1962. G. W. Monger, MA, PhD ('The end of isolation: Britain, Germany and Japan, 1900–1902').

1963. J. S. Moore, BA ('The Domesday teamland: a reconsideration').

1964. M. Kelly, PhD ('The submission of the clergy').

1965. J. J. N. Palmer, BLitt ('Anglo-French negotiations, 1390–1396').

1966. M. T. Clanchy, MA, PhD ('The Franchise of Return of Writs').

1967. R. Lovatt, MA, DPhil, PhD ('The *Imitation of Christ* in late medieval England').

1968. M. G. A. Vale, MA, DPhil ('The last years of English Gascony, 1451–1453').

1970. Mrs Margaret Bowker, MA, BLitt ('The Commons Supplication against the Ordinaries in the light of some Archidiaconal Acta').

1971. C. Thompson, MA ('The origins of the politics of the Parliamentary middle groups, 1625–1629').

1972. I. d'Alton, BA ('Southern Irish Unionism: A study of Cork City and County Unionists, 1884–1914').

1973. C. J. Kitching, BA, PhD ('The quest for concealed lands in the reign of Elizabeth I').

1974. H. Tomlinson, BA ('Place and Profit: an Examination of the Ordnance Office, 1660–1714').

1976. B. Bradshaw, MA, BD ('Cromwellian reform and the origins of the Kildare rebellion, 1533–34').

1978. C. J. Ford, BA ('Piracy or Policy: The Crisis in the Channel, 1400–1403').

1979. P. Dewey, BA, PhD ('Food Production and Policy in the United Kingdom, 1914–1918').

1980. Ann L. Hughes, BA, PhD ('Militancy and Localism: Warwickshire Politics and Westminster Politics, 1643–1647')'.

1981. C. J. Tyerman, MA ('Marino Sanudo Torsello and the Lost Crusade. Lobbying in the Fourteenth Century').

1982. E. Powell, BA, DPhil ('Arbitration and the Law in England in the Late Middle Ages').

1983. A. G. Rosser, MA ('The essence of medieval urban communities: the vill of Westminster 1200–1540').

1984. N. L. Ramsay, MA, LLB ('Retained Legal Counsel, c. 1275–1475').

1985. George S. Garnett, MA ('Coronation and Propaganda: Some Implications of the Norman Claim to the Throne of England in 1066').

1986. C. J. Given-Wilson ('The King and the Gentry in Fourteenth-Century England').

1988. R. A. W. Rex, MA ('The English Campaign against Luther in the 1520s').

1989. J. S. A. Adamson, BA, PhD ('The Baronial Context of the English Civil War').

DAVID BERRY PRIZE

The David Berry Prize was established in 1929 by David Anderson-Berry in memory of his father, the Reverend David Berry. It consists of a money prize awarded every three years for Scottish history. Candidates may select any subject dealing with Scottish history within the reigns of James I to James VI inclusive, provided such subject has been previously submitted to and approved by the Council of the Royal Historical Society. The essay must be a genuine work of original research not hitherto published, and one which has not been awarded any other prize. The essay should be between 6,000 and 10,000 words, excluding footnotes and appendices. It must be sent in on or before 31 October 1988.

LIST OF DAVID BERRY PRIZE ESSAYISTS (1937-85)[1]

1937. G. Donaldson, MA ('The polity of the Scottish Reformed Church c. 1460-1580, and the rise of the Presbyterian movement').

1943. Rev. Prof. A. F. Scott Pearson, DTh, DLitt ('Anglo-Scottish religious relations, 1400-1600').

1949. T. Bedford Franklin, MA, FRSE ('Monastic agriculture in Scotland, 1440-1600').

1955. W. A. McNeill, MA ('"Estaytt" of the king's rents and pensions, 1621').

1958. Prof. Maurice Lee, PhD ('Maitland of Thirlestane and the foundation of the Stewart despotism in Scotland').

1964. M. H. Merriman ('Scottish collaborators with England during the Anglo-Scottish war, 1543-1550').

1967. Miss M. H. B. Sanderson ('Catholic recusancy in Scotland in the sixteenth century').

1970. Athol Murray, MA, LLB, PhD ('The Comptroller, 1425-1610').

1973. J. Kirk, MA, PhD ('Who were the Melvillians: A study in the Personnel and Background of the Presbyterian Movement in late Sixteenth-century Scotland').

1976. A. Grant, BA, DPhil ('The Development of the Scottish Peerage').

1985. Rev. G. Mark Dilworth ('The Commendator System in Scotland').

1988. J. Goodare ('Parliamentary Taxation in Scotland, 1560-1603').

[1] No essays were submitted in 1940 and 1979. No award was made in 1946, 1952, 1961 and 1982.

WHITFIELD PRIZE

The Whitfield Prize was established by Council in 1976 as a money prize of £400 out of the bequest of the late Professor Archibald Stenton Whitfield: in May 1981 Council increased the prize to £600. Until 1982 the prize was awarded annually to the STUDIES IN HISTORY series. From 1983 the prize, value £600, will be awarded annually to the best work of English or Welsh history by an author under 40 years of age, published in the United Kingdom. The award will be made by Council in the Spring of each year in respect of works published in the preceding calendar year. Authors or publishers should send two copies (non-returnable) of a book eligible for the competition to the Society to arrive not later than 31 December of the year of publication.

LIST OF WHITFIELD PRIZE WINNERS (1977-1987)

1977. K. D. Brown, MA, PhD (*John Burns*).
1978. Marie Axton, MA, PhD (*The Queen's Two Bodies: Drama and the Elizabethan Succession*).
1979. Patricia Crawford, MA, PhD (*Denzil Holles, 1598-1680: A study of his Political Career*).
1980. D. L. Rydz (*The Parliamentary Agents: A History*).
1981. Scott M. Harrison (*The Pilgrimage of Grace in the Lake Counties 1536-7*).
1982. Norman L. Jones (*Faith by Statute: Parliament and the Settlement of Religion 1559*).
1983. Peter Clark (*The English Alehouse: A social history 1200-1830*).
1984. David Hempton, BA, PhD (*Methodism and Politics in British Society 1750-1850*).
1985. K. D. M. Snell, MA, PhD (*Annals of the Labouring Poor*).
1986. Diarmaid MacCulloch, MA, PhD, FSA (*Suffolk and the Tudors: Politics and Religion in an English County 1500-1600*).
1987. Kevin M. Sharpe, MA, DPhil (*Criticism and Compliment: The politics of literature in the England of Charles I*).
1988. J. H. Davis, MA, DPhil (*Reforming London, the London Government Problem 1855-1900*).

THE ROYAL HISTORICAL SOCIETY

(INCORPORATED BY ROYAL CHARTER)

OFFICERS AND COUNCIL—1989

Patron
HER MAJESTY THE QUEEN

President
Professor F. M. L. THOMPSON, MA, DPhil, FSA

Honorary Vice-Presidents

G. E. Aylmer, MA, DPhil, FBA
Professor J. H. Burns, MA, PhD
Professor A. G. Dickens, CMG, MA, DLit, DLitt, LittD, FBA, FSA
Professor G. Donaldson MA, PhD, DLitt, DLitt, FRSE, FBA
Sir Geoffrey Elton, MA, PhD, LittD, DLitt, DLitt, DLit, FBA
Professor P. Grierson, MA, LittD, FBA, FSA
Sir John Habakkuk, MA, FBA
Professor D. Hay, MA, DLitt, FBA, FRSE, Dr h.c. Tours
Professor J. C. Holt, MA, DPhil, DLitt, FBA, FSA
Professor R. A. Humphreys, OBE, MA, PhD, DLitt, LittD, DLitt, DUniv
Miss K. Major, MA, BLitt, LittD, FBA, FSA
Professor D. B. Quinn, MA, PhD, DLit, DLitt, DLitt, DLitt, LLD, DHL,
  Hon FBA
The Hon. Sir Steven Runciman, CH, MA, DPhil, LLD, LittD, DLitt, LitD,
  DD, DHL, FBA, FSA
Sir Richard Southern, MA, DLitt, LittD, DLitt, FBA
Professor C. H. Wilson, CBE, MA, LittD, DLitt, DLitt, DLitt, FBA

Vice-Presidents

Professor R. B. Dobson, MA, DPhil
Professor G. S. Holmes, MA, DLitt, FBA
Miss B. Harvey, MA, BLitt, FBA
Professor W. R. Ward, DPhil
Miss V. Cromwell, MA
Professor P. J. Marshall, MA, DPhil
Professor R. R. Davies, BA, DPhil, FBA
Professor W. A. Speck, MA, DPhil

STANDING COMMITTEES 1988

Finance Committee

PROFESSOR OLIVE ANDERSON
PROFESSOR M. D. BIDDISS
MISS V. CROMWELL
P. J. C. FIRTH
Dr. G. H. MARTIN, CBE
PROFESSOR B. E. SUPPLE, PhD, MA
And the Officers

Publications Committee

C. R. ELRINGTON, MA, FSA
PROFESSOR R. A. GRIFFITHS
MISS B. HARVEY, FBA
PROFESSOR N. McCORD
PROFESSOR D. M. PALLISER
PROFESSOR C. S. R. RUSSELL
PROFESSOR W. A. SPECK
Dr. GILLIAN SUTHERLAND
And the Officers

Library Committee

PROFESSOR OLIVE ANDERSON
Dr J. R. DINWIDDY
PROFESSOR P. J. MARSHALL
PROFESSOR C. S. R. RUSSELL
And the Officers

LIST OF FELLOWS OF THE
ROYAL HISTORICAL SOCIETY

Names of Officers and Honorary Vice-Presidents are printed in capitals.
Those marked* have compounded for their annual subscriptions.

Abramsky, Professor Chimen A., MA, Dept of Hebrew and Jewish Studies, University College London, Gower Street, London WCiE 6BT.

Abulafia, D. S. H., MA, PhD, Gonville and Caius College, Cambridge CB2 1TA.

Acton, E. D. J., PhD, School of History, The University, P.O. Box 147, Liverpool L69 3BX.

Adam, Professor R. J., MA, Easter Wayside, Hepburn Gardens, St Andrews KY16 9LP.

Adams, Professor Ralph J. Q., PhD, Dept of History, Texas A & M University, College Station, Texas 77843–4236, U.S.A.

Adams, S. L., BA, MA, DPhil, 4 North East Circus Place, Edinburgh EH3 6SP.

Adamthwaite, Professor A.P., BA, PhD, 780 King Lane, Leeds LS17 7AU.

Addison, P., MA, DPhil, Dept of History, The University, William Robertson Building, George Square, Edinburgh EH8 9JY.

Ailes, A., MA, 24 Donnington Gardens, Reading, Berkshire RG1 5LY.

Akenson, D. H., BA, PhD, Dept of History, Queen's University, Kingston, Ontario, Canada, K7L 3N6.

Akrigg, Professor G. P. V., BA, PhD, FRSC, #8–2575 Tolmie Street, Vancouver, B.C., Canada, V6R 4M1.

Alcock, Professor L., MA, FSA, 29 Hamilton Drive, Glasgow G12 8DN.

Alder, G. J., BA, PhD, Dept of History, The University, Whiteknights, Reading RG6 2AA.

Alderman, G., MA, DPhil, 172 Colindeep Lane, London NW9 6EA.

Allan, D. G. C., MSc(Econ), PhD, c/o Royal Society of Arts, John Adam Street, London WC2N 6EZ.

Allen, D. F., BA, PhD, School of History, The University, P.O. Box 363, Birmingham B15 2TT.

Allen, D. H., BA, PhD, 105 Tuddenham Avenue, Ipswich, Suffolk IP4 2HG.

Allmand, C. T., MA, DPhil, FSA, 111 Menlove Avenue, Liverpool L18 3HP.

Alsop, J. D., BA, MA, PhD, Dept of History, McMaster University, 1280 Main Street West, Hamilton, Ontario, Canada L8S 4L9.

Altholz, Professor J., PhD, Dept of History, University of Minnesota, 614 Social Sciences Building, Minneapolis, Minn. 55455, U.S.A.

Altschul, Professor M., PhD, Case Western Reserve University, Cleveland, Ohio 44106, U.S.A.

Ambler, R. W., PhD, 37 Cumberland Avenue, Grimsby, South Humberside DN32 0BT.

Anderson, Professor M. S., MA, PhD, 45 Cholmeley Crescent, London N6 5EX.

Anderson, Professor Olive, MA, BLitt, Dept of History, Westfield College, Kidderpore Avenue, London NW3 7ST.

Anderson, R. D., MA, DPhil, 7 North West Circus Place, Edinburgh EH3 6ST.

Anderson, Miss S. P., MA, BLitt, 17–19 Chilworth Street, London W2 3QU.

Andrew, C. M., MA, PhD, Corpus Christi College, Cambridge CB2 1RH.

Anglesey, The Most Hon., The Marquess of, FSA, FRSL, Plas-Newydd, Llanfairpwll, Anglesey LL61 6DZ.

Anglo, Professor S., BA, PhD, FSA, 59 Green Ridge, Withdean, Brighton BN1 5LU.

Angold, M. J., BA, DPhil, 17 Morningside Park, Edinburgh EH10 5HD.

Annan, Lord, OBE, MA, DLitt, DUniv, 16 St John's Wood Road, London NW8 8RE.

Annis, P. G. W., BA, 65 Longlands Road, Sidcup, Kent DA15 7LQ.

Appleby, J. S., Little Pitchbury, Brick Kiln Lane, Great Horkesley, Colchester, Essex CO6 4EU.

Armstrong, Miss A. M., BA, 7 Vale Court, Mallord Street, London SW3.

Armstrong, C. A. J., MA, FSA, Gayhurst, Lincombe Lane, Boars Hill, Oxford OX1 5DZ.

Armstrong, Professor F. H., PhD, Dept of History, University of Western Ontario, London, Ontario, Canada N6A 5C2.

Armstrong, W. A., BA, PhD, Eliot College, The University, Canterbury, Kent CT2 7NS.

Arnstein, Professor W. L., PhD, Dept of History, University of Illinois at Urbana-Champaign, 309 Gregory Hall, Urbana, Ill. 61801, U.S.A.

Artibise, Professor Alan F. J., PhD, Community and Regional Planning, University of British Columbia, 6333 Memorial Road, Vancouver, B.C., Canada, V6T 1W5.

Ashton, Professor R., PhD, The Manor House, Brundall, near Norwich NOR 86Z.

Ashworth, J., BA, MLitt, DPhil, School of English and American Studies, University of East Anglia, Norwich NR4 7TJ.

Ashworth, Professor W., BSc(Econ), PhD, 31 Calton Gardens, Bath, BA2 4QG.

Asquith, Ivon, BA, PhD, 19 Vicarage Lane, New Hinksey, Oxford OX1 4RQ.

Aston, Margaret E., MA, DPhil, Castle House, Chipping, Ongar, Essex CM5 9JT.

Austin, The Rev. Canon, M. R. BD, MA, PhD, 22 Marlock Close, Fiskerton, Nr Southwell, Notts. NG25 0UB.

Axelson, Professor E. V., DLitt, Box 15, Constantia, 7848, S. Africa.

*Aydelotte, Professor W. O., PhD, State University of Iowa, Iowa City, Iowa, U.S.A.

AYLMER, G. E., MA, DPhil, FBA, St Peter's College, Oxford OX1 2DL.

Ayres, P. J., PhD, Dept of English, Monash University, Clayton 3168, Victoria, Australia.

Bahlman, Professor Dudley W. R., MA, PhD, Dept of History, Williams College, Williamstown, Mass. 01267, U.S.A.

Bailie, The Rev. W. D., MA, BD, PhD, DD, 45 Morpra Drive, Saintfield, Co. Down, N. Ireland.

Bailyn, Professor B., MA, PhD, LittD, LHD, Widener J, Harvard University, Cambridge, Mass. 02138, U.S.A.

Baines, A. H. J., PhD, MA, LLB, FSA, FRSA, FSS, Finmere, 90 Eskdale Avenue, Chesham, Bucks. HP5 3AY.

Baker, D., BSc, PhD, MA, BLitt, 21 Valenciennes Road, Sittingbourne, Kent, ME10 1EN.
Baker, J. H., LLD, FBA, St Catharine's College, Cambridge CB2 1RL.
Baker, L. G. D., MA, BLitt, 5 Allendale, Southwater, Horsham, West Sussex RH13 7UE.
Baker, T. F. T., BA, Camden Lodge, 50 Hastings Road, Pembury, Kent.
Ball, A. W., BA, 71 Cassiobury Park Avenue, Watford, Herts. WD1 7LD.
Ballhatchet, Professor K. A., MA, PhD, 12 Park Lane, Richmond, Surrey TW9 2RA.
Banks, Professor J. A., MA, Caldecott House, Kilworth Road, Husbands Bosworth, Lutterworth, Leicestershire LE17 6JZ.
Barber, M. C., BA, PhD, Dept of History, The University, Whiteknights, Reading, Berks. RG6 2AA.
Barber, R. W., MA, PhD, FSA, Stangrove Hall, Alderton, near Woodbridge, Suffolk IP12 3BL.
Barker, A. J., BA, MA, PhD, Dept of History, University of Western Australia, Nedlands, Western Australia 6009.
Barker, Professor T. C., MA, PhD, Minsen Dane, Brogdale Road, Faversham, Kent.
Barkley, Professor The Rev. J. M., MA, DD, 2 College Park, Belfast, N. Ireland.
*Barlow, Professor F., MA, DPhil, FBA, Middle Court Hall, Kenton, Exeter.
Barnard, T. C., MA, DPhil, Hertford College, Oxford OX1 3BW.
Barnes, Miss P. M., PhD, 6 Kings Yard, Kings Ride, Ascot, Berks. SL5 8AH.
Barnett, Correlli, MA, Catbridge House, Rast Carleton, Norwich, Norfolk.
Barratt, Miss D. M., DPhil, The Corner House, Hampton Poyle, Kidlington, Oxford.
Barratt, Professor G. R. de V., PhD, Dept of Russian, Paterson Hall, Carleton University, Ottawa, Canada K1S 5B6.
Barrett, The Rev. P. L. S., The Rectory, Kiln Lane, Otterbourne, Winchester SO21 2EJ.
Barron, Mrs C. M., MA, PhD, 9 Boundary Road, London NW8 0HE.
Barrow, Professor G. W. S., MA, BLitt, DLitt, FBA, FRSE, 12a Lauder Road, Edinburgh EH9 2EL.
Bartlett, Professor C. J., PhD, Dept of Modern History, The University, Dundee DD1 4HN.
Bartlett, Professor R. J., MA, DPhil, Dept of History, University of Chicago, 1126 East 59th Street, Chicago, Illinois 60637, U.S.A.
Bates, D., PhD, School of History and Archaeology, University of Wales, P.O. Box 909, Cardiff CF1 3XU.
Batho, Professor G. R., MA, Fivestones, 3 Archery Rise, Durham DH1 4LA.
Baugh, Professor Daniel A., PhD, Dept of History, McGraw Hall, Cornell University, Ithaca, N.Y. 14853, U.S.A.
Baxter, Professor S. B., PhD, 608 Morgan Creek Road, Chapel Hill, N.C. 27514, U.S.A.
Baylen, Professor J. O., MA, PhD, 45 Saffron Court, Compton Place Road, Eastbourne, E. Sussex, BN21 1DY.
Beachey, Professor R. W., BA, PhD, 1 Rookwood, De La Warr Road, Milford-on-Sea, Hampshire.
Beales, Professor D. E. D., MA, PhD, LittD, Sidney Sussex College, Cambridge CB2 3HU.
Bealey, Professor F., BSc(Econ), Dept of Politics, The University, Taylor Building, Old Aberdeen AB9 2UB.

Bean, Professor J. M. W., MA, DPhil, 622 Fayerweather Hall, Columbia University, New York, N.Y. 10027, U.S.A.

Beardwood, Miss Alice, BA, BLitt, DPhil, 415 Miller's Lane, Wynnewood, Pa, U.S.A.

Beasley, Professor W. G., PhD, FBA, 172 Hampton Road, Twickenham, Middlesex TW2 5NJ.

Beattie, Professor J. M., PhD, Dept of History, University of Toronto, Toronto, Canada, M5S 1A1.

Beauroy, Dr Jacques M., 15 Avenue Marie-Amélie, Chantilly, France 60500.

Bebbington, D. W., MA, PhD, 5 Pullar Avenue, Bridge of Allan, Stirling FK9 4TB.

Beckerman, John S., PhD, 225 Washington Avenue, Hamden, Ct. 06518, U.S.A.

Beckett, I. F. W., BA, PhD, Cottesloe House, The Dene, Hindon, Wiltshire SP3 6EE.

Beckett, Professor J. C., MA, 19 Wellington Park Terrace, Belfast 9, N. Ireland.

Beckett, J. V., BA, PhD, Dept of History, The University, Nottingham NG7 2RD.

Beddard, R. A., MA, DPhil, Oriel College, Oxford OX1 4EW.

*Beer, E. S. de, CBE, MA, DLitt, FBA, FSA, Stoke House, Stoke Hammond MK17 9BN.

Beer, Professor Samuel H., PhD, Faculty of Arts & Sciences, Harvard University, Littauer Center G-15, Cambridge, Mass. 02138, U.S.A.

Belchem, J. C., BA, DPhil, Dept of History, The University, 8 Abercromby Square, Liverpool L69 3BX.

Bell, A., Rhodes House Library, Oxford OX2 7RU.

Bell, P. M. H., BA, BLitt, School of History, The University, P.O. Box 147, Liverpool L69 3BX.

Bellenger, Dominic T. J. A., MA, PhD, Downside Abbey, Stratton-on-the-Fosse, Bath BA3 4RH.

Beloff, Lord, DLitt, FBA, Flat No. 9, 22 Lewes Crescent, Brighton BN2 1GB.

Benedikz, B. S., MA, PhD, Main Library, University of Birmingham, P.O. Box 363, Birmingham B15 2TT.

Bennett, M., MA, 48 Lye Copse Avenue, Farnborough, Hants. GU14 8DX.

Bennett, M. J., BA, PhD, History Dept, University of Tasmania, Box 252C, G.P.O., Hobart, Tasmania 7001, Australia.

Benson, Professor J., BA, MA, PhD, The Polytechnic, Wolverhampton, West Midlands, WV1 1LY.

Bentley, M., BA, PhD, Dept of History, The University, Sheffield S10 2TN.

Berghahn, Professor V. R., MA, PhD, Brown University, Providence, Rhode Island 02912, U.S.A.

Bergin, J., MA, PhD, Dept of History, The University, Manchester M13 9PL.

Bernard, G. W., MA, DPhil, 92 Bassett Green Village, Southampton.

Bhila, Professor H. H. K., BA, MA, PhD, Parliament of Zimbabwe, Box 8055, Causeway, Harare, Zimbabwe.

Biddiss, Professor M. D., MA, PhD, Dept of History, The University, Whiteknights, Reading RG6 2AA.

Bidwell, Brigadier R. G. S., OBE, 8 Chapel Lane, Wickham Market, Woodbridge, Suffolk IP13 0SD.

Bill, E. G. W., MA, DLitt, Lambeth Palace Library, London SE1.

Biller, P. P. A., MA, DPhil, Dept of History, The University, Heslington, York YO1 5DD.

Binfield, J. C. G., MA, PhD, 22 Whiteley Wood Road, Sheffield S11 7FE.

Birch, A., MA, PhD, Dept of History, The University, Hong Kong.

Birke, Professor A. M., DPhil, DPhil-Habil, German Historical Institute, 17 Bloomsbury Square, London WC1A 2LP.

Bishop, A. S., BA, PhD, 44 North Acre, Banstead, Surrey SM7 2EG.

Bishop, T. A. M., MA, 16 Highbury Road, London SW19 7PR.

Black, Professor Eugene C., PhD, Dept of History, Brandeis University, Waltham, Mass. 02154-9110, U.S.A.

Black, J. M. PhD, 38 Elmfield Road, Gosforth, Newcastle, Tyne and Wear NE3 4BB.

Black, R. D., BA PhD, School of History, The University, Leeds LS2 9JT.

Blackbourn, D., MA, PhD, Dept of History, Birkbeck College, Malet Street, London WC1E 7HX.

Blackburn, M. A. S., MA, FSA, Faculty of History, University of Cambridge, West Road, Cambridge CB3 9EF.

Blackwood, B. G., BA, BLitt, DPhil, 4 Knights Close, Felixstowe, Suffolk IP11 9NU.

Blainey, G. N., MA, P.O. Box 257, East Melbourne, Victoria 3002, Australia.

Blake, E. O., MA, PhD, Roselands, Moorhill Road, Westend, Southampton SO3 3AW.

Blake, Lord, MA, FBA, Riverview House, Brundall, Norwich NR13 5LA.

Blakemore, H., PhD, 43 Fitzjohn Avenue, Barnet, Herts, EN5 2HN.

*Blakey, Professor R. G., PhD, c/o Mr Raymond Shove, Order Dept, Library, University of Minnesota, Minneapolis 14, Minn., U.S.A.

Blanning, T. W. C., MA, PhD, Sidney Sussex College, Cambridge CB2 3HU.

Blewett, Hon Dr N., BA, DipEd, MA, DPhil, 68 Barnard Street, North Adelaide, South Australia 5006.

Blinkhorn, RM., BA, AM, DPhil, Dept of History, The University, Bailrigg, Lancaster LA1 4YG.

Board, Mrs Beryl A., The Old School House, Stow Maries, Chelmsford, Essex CM3 6SL.

*Bolsover, G. H., OBE, MA, PhD, 7 Devonshire Road, Hatch End, Middlesex HA5 4LY.

Bolton, Brenda, M., BA, Dept of History, Westfield College, Kidderpore Avenue, London NW3 7ST.

Bolton, Professor G. C., MA, DPhil, Dept of History, University of Queensland, St Lucia, Queensland 4067, Australia.

Bolton, J. L. BA, BLitt, Dept of History, Queen Mary College, Mile End Road, London E1 4NS.

Bond, Professor B. J., BA, MA, Dept of War Studies, King's College London, Strand, London WC2R 2LS.

Bonney, Professor R. J., MA, DPhil, Dept of History, The University, Leicester LE1 7RH.

Bonwick, C. C., MA, PhD, Dept of American Studies, The University, Keele, Staffs. ST5 5BG.

Booker, J. M. L., BA, MLitt, DPhil, Braxted Place, Little Braxted, Witham, Essex CM8 3LD.

Boon, G. C., BA, FSA, FRNS, 43 Westbourne Road, Penarth, S. Glamorgan CF6 2HA.

Borrie, M. A. F., BA, The British Library, Dept of Manuscripts, Great Russell Street, London WC1B 3DG.

Bossy, Professor J. A., MA, PhD, Dept of History, University of York, Heslington, York YO1 5DD.

Bottigheimer, Professor Karl S., Dept of History, State University of New York, Stony Brook, Long Island, N.Y., U.S.A.

Bourne, J. M., BA, PhD., 33 St. John's Road, Selly Park, Birmingham B29 7EP.

Bourne, Professor K., BA, PhD, FBA, London School of Economics, Houghton Street, Aldwych, London WC2A 2AE.

Bowker, Mrs M., MA, BLitt, 14 Bowers Croft, Cambridge CB1 4RP.

Bowyer, M. J. F., 32 Netherhall Way, Cambridge.

*Boxer, Professor C. R., DLitt, FBA, Ringshall End, Little Gaddesden, Berkhamsted, Herts.

Boyce, D. G., BA, PhD, Dept of Political Theory and Government, University College of Swansea, Swansea SA2 8PP.

Boyle, T., Cert.Ed, BA, MPhil, Jersey Cottage, Mark Beech, Edenbridge, Kent TN8 5NS.

Boynton, L. O. J., MA, DPhil, FSA, Dept of History, Westfield College, Kidderspore Avenue, London NW3 7ST.

Brading, D. A., MA, PhD, 28 Storey Way, Cambridge CB3 0DT.

Bradshaw, Rev. B., MA, BD, PhD, Queens' College, Cambridge CB3 9ET.

Brake, Rev. G. Thompson, 61 Westwood Gardens, Hadleigh, Benfleet, Essex SS7 2SH.

Brand, P. A., MA, DPhil, 155 Kennington Road, London SE11.

Brandon, P. F., BA, PhD, Greensleeves, 8 St Julian's Lane, Shoreham-by-Sea, Sussex BN4 6YS.

Breck, Professor A. D., MA, PhD, LHD, DLitt, University of Denver, Denver, Colorado 80208, U.S.A.

Breen, Professor T. H., PhD, Dept of History, North Western University, Evanston, Illinois 60208, U.S.A.

Brentano, Professor R., DPhil, University of California, Berkeley 4, Calif., U.S.A.

Brett, M., MA, DPhil, Robinson College, Cambridge CB3 9AN.

Breuilly, J. J., BA, DPhil, Dept of History, The University, Manchester M13 9PL.

Brewer, J., PhD, University of California—Los Angeles, Center for 17th and 18th Century Studies, 2221B Bunche Hall, Los Angeles, CA 90024-1404, U.S.A.

Bridge, C. R., BA, PhD, History Dept., University of New England, Armidale, N.S.W. 2350, Australia.

Bridge, F. R., PhD, The Poplars, Rodley Lane, Rodley, Leeds.

Bridges, R. C., BA, PhD, Dept of History, University of Aberdeen, King's College, Aberdeen AB9 2UB.

Brigden, Susan, BA, PhD, MA, Lincoln College Oxford, OX1 3DR.

Briggs, Lord, BSc(Econ), MA, DLitt, FBA, Worcester College, Oxford OX1 2HB.

Briggs, J. H. Y., MA, Dept of History, The University, Keele, Staffs. ST5 5BG.

Briggs, R., MA, All Souls College, Oxford OX1 4AL.

Britnell, R. H., MA, PhD, Dept of History, The University, 43–46 North Bailey, Durham, DH1 3EX.

Broad, J., BA, DPhil, Dept of History, Polytechnic of North London, Prince of Wales Road, London NW5 3LB.

Broadhead, P. J., BA, PhD, Dept of History, Goldsmiths' College, Lewisham Way, London SE14 6NW.

Brock, M. G., MA, St George's House, Windsor Castle, Berkshire SL4 1NJ.
Brock, Professor W. R., MA, PhD, 49 Barton Road, Cambridge CB3 9LG.
Brocklesby, R., BA, The Elms, North Eastern Road, Thorne, Doncaster, S. Yorks. DN8 4AS.
Brogan, D. H. V., MA, Dept of History, University of Essex, Wivenhoe Park, Colchester, Essex CO4 3SQ.
*Brooke, Professor C. N. L., MA, LittD, FBA, FSA, Faculty of History, West Road, Cambridge CB3 9EF.
Brooke, Mrs R. B., MA, PhD, c/o Faculty of History, West Road, Cambridge CB3 9EF.
Brooks, C. W., AB, DPhil, Dept of History, The University, 43 North Bailey, Durham, DH1 3EX.
Brooks, Professor N. P., MA, DPhil, Dept of Medieval History, The University, Birmingham B15 2TT.
Brown, Professor A. L., MA, DPhil, Dept of History, The University, Glasgow G12 8QQ.
Brown, The Rev. A. W. G., BA, BD, PhD, The Manse, 28 Quay Road, Ballycastle, Co. Antrim BT54 6BH, N. Ireland.
Brown, G. S., PhD, 1720 Hanover Road, Ann Arbor, Mich. 48103, U.S.A.
Brown, Judith M., MA, PhD, 8 The Downs, Cheadle, Cheshire SK8 1JL.
Brown, K. D., BA, MA, PhD, Dept of Economic and Social History, The Queen's University, Belfast BT7 1NN, N. Ireland.
Brown, Professor M. J., MA, PhD, 350 South Candler Street, Decatur, Georgia 30030, U.S.A.
Brown, P. D., MA, 18 Davenant Road, Oxford OX2 8BX.
Brown, P. R. L., MA, FBA, Hillslope, Pullen's Lane, Oxford.
Brown, T. S., MA, PhD, Dept of History, The University, William Robertson Building, 50 George Square, Edinburgh, EH8 9JY.
Brown, Professor Wallace, PhD, Dept of History, University of New Brunswick, P.O. Box 4400, Fredericton, NB., Canada E3B 5AE.
Bruce, J. M., ISO, MA, FRAeS, 51 Chiltern Drive, Barton-on-Sea, New Milton, Hants. BH25 7JZ.
Brundage, Professor J. A., Dept of History, University of Wisconsin at Milwaukee, Milwaukee, Wisconsin, U.S.A.
Bryson, Professor W. Hamilton, School of Law, University of Richmond, Richmond, Va. 23173, U.S.A.
Buchanan, R. A., MA, PhD, School of Humanities and Social Sciences, The University, Claverton Down, Bath BA2 7AY.
Buckland, P. J. B., MA, PhD, 6 Rosefield Road, Liverpool L25 8TF.
Bueno de Mesquita, D. M., MA, PhD, 283 Woodstock Road, Oxford OX2 7NY.
Buisseret, Professor D. J., MA, PhD, The Newberry Library, 60 West Walton Street, Chicago, Ill. 60610, U.S.A.
Bullock, Lord, MA, DLitt, FBA, St Catherine's College, Oxford OX1 3UJ.
Bullough, Professor D. A., MA, FSA, Dept of Mediaeval History, The University, 71 South Street, St Andrews, Fife KY16 9AJ.
Bumsted, Professor J. M., PhD, St John's College, University of Manitoba, Winnipeg, Mb., Canada R3T 2M5.
Burk, Kathleen M., BA, MA, DPhil, The Long Barn, Towns End, Harwell, Oxon. OX11 0DX.
Burke, U. P., MA, Emmanuel College, Cambridge CB2 3AP.
Burleigh, M., BA, PhD, Dept of International History, London School of Economics, Houghton Street, Aldwych, London WC2A 2AE.

BURNS, Professor J. H., MA, PhD, 6 Chiltern House, Hillcrest Road, London W5 1HL.

Burroughs, P., PhD, Dept of History, Dalhousie University, Halifax, Nova Scotia, Canada B3H 3J5.

Burrow, Professor J. W., MA., PhD, Sussex University, Falmer, Brighton BN1 9QX.

Burt, R., BSc, PhD, Dept of Economic History, Amory Building, University of Exeter, Devon.

Butler, R. D'O., CMG, MA, DLitt, All Souls College, Oxford OX1 4AL.

Byerly, Professor B. F., BA, MA, PhD, Dept of History, University of Northern Colorado, Greeley, Colorado 80631, U.S.A.

Bythell, D., MA, DPhil, Dept of History, University of Durham, 43/46 North Bailey, Durham DH1 3EX.

Cabaniss, Professor J. A., PhD, University of Mississippi, Box No. 253, University, Mississippi 38677, U.S.A.

Callahan, Professor Raymond, PhD, Dept of History, University of Delaware, Newark, Delaware 19716, U.S.A.

Callahan, Professor Thomas, Jr., PhD, Dept of History, Rider College, Lawrenceville, N.J. 08648, U.S.A.

Calvert, Brigadier J. M. (ret.), DSO, MA, MICE, 33a Mill Hill Close, Haywards Heath, Sussex.

Calvert, Professor P. A. R., MA, PhD, AM, Dept of Politics, University of Southampton, Highfield, Southampton SO9 5NH.

Cameron, A., BA, 6 Braid Crescent, Morningside, Edinburgh EH10 6AU.

Cameron, E. K., MA, DPhil, 35 Oaklands, Gosforth, Newcastle upon Tyne NE3 4YP.

Cameron, Professor J. K., MA, BD, PhD, St Mary's College, University of St Andrews, Fife KY16 9JU.

Cameron, Professor K., PhD, FBA, Dept of English, The University, Nottingham NG7 2RD.

Campbell, Professor A. E., MA, PhD, 3 Belbroughton Road, Oxford, OX2 6UZ.

Campbell, G. R., MA, DPhil, Dept of English, The University, Leicester LE1 7RH.

Campbell, J., MA, FBA, Worcester College, Oxford OX1 2HB.

*Campbell, Professor Mildred L., PhD, Vassar College, Poughkeepsie, N.Y., U.S.A.

Campbell, Professor R. H., MA, PhD, Craig, Glenluce, Newton Stewart, Wigtownshire DG8 0NR.

Cannadine, D. N., BA, MA, DPhil, Dept. of History, Fayerweather Hall, Columbia University, New York, NY 10027, USA.

Canning, J. P., MA, PhD, Dept of History, University College of North Wales, Bangor, Gwynedd LL57 2DG.

Cannon, Professor J. A., CBE, MA, PhD, Dept of History, The University, Newcastle upon Tyne NE1 7RU.

Canny, Professor N. P., MA, PhD, Dept of History, University College, Galway, Ireland.

Cant, R. G., MA, DLitt, 3 Kinburn Place, St Andrews, Fife KY16 9DT.

Cantor, Professor N. F., PhD, Dept of History, New York University, 19 University Place, 4th Floor, New York, NY 10003, U.S.A.

Capp, B. S., MA, DPhil, Dept of History, University of Warwick, Coventry, Warwickshire CV4 7AL.

Carey, P. B. R., DPhil, Trinity College, Oxford OX1 3BH.

*Carlson, Leland H., PhD, Huntington Library, San Marino, California 91108, U.S.A.

Carlton, Professor Charles, Dept of History, North Carolina State University, Raleigh, NC 27607, U.S.A.

Carman, W. Y., FSA, 94 Mulgrave Road, Sutton, Surrey.

Carpenter, D. A., MA, DPhil, Dept of History, King's College London, Strand, London WC2R 2LS.

Carpenter, M. Christine, MA, PhD, New Hall, Cambridge CB3 0DF.

Carr, A. D., MA, PhD, Dept of Welsh History, University College of North Wales, Bangor, Gwynedd LL57 2DG.

Carr, Sir Raymond, MA, FBA, Burch, North Molton, South Molton, EX36 3JU.

Carr, W., PhD, 22 Southbourne Road, Sheffield S10 2QN.

Carrington, Miss Dorothy, 3 Rue Emmanuel Arene, 20 Ajaccio, Corsica.

Carter, Jennifer J., BA, PhD, The Old Schoolhouse, Glenbuchat, Strathdon, Aberdeenshire AB3 8TT.

Carwardine, R. J., MA, DPhil, Dept of History, The University, Sheffield S10 2TN.

Casey, J., BA, PhD, School of Modern Languages and European History, University of East Anglia, University Plain, Norwich NR4 7TJ.

Cassels, Professor Alan, MA, PhD, Dept of History, McMaster University, Hamilton, Ontario, Canada L8S 4L9.

Catto, R. J. A. I., MA, Oriel College, Oxford OX1 4EW.

Cazel, Professor Fred A., Jr., Dept of History, University of Connecticut, Storrs, Conn. 06268, U.S.A.

Cell, Professor J. W., PhD, Dept of History, Duke University, Durham, NC 27706, U.S.A.

Cesarani, D., DPhil, 95 Greencroft Gardens, London NW6 3PG.

Chadwick, Professor W. O., OM, KBE, DD, DLitt, FBA, Selwyn Lodge, Cambridge CB3 9DQ.

Challis, C. E., MA, PhD, 14 Ashwood Villas, Headingley, Leeds 6.

Chalmers, C. D., Public Record Office, Ruskin Avenue, Kew, Richmond, Surrey TW9 4DU.

Chamberlain, Muriel E., MA. DPhil, Dept of History, University College of Swansea, Singleton Park, Swansea SA2 7BR.

Chambers, D. S., MA, DPhil, Warburg Institute, Woburn Square, London WC1H 0AB.

Chandaman, Professor C. D., BA, PhD, 23 Bellamy Close, Ickenham, Uxbridge UB10 8SJ.

Chandler, D. G., MA, Hindford, Monteagle Lane, Yateley, Camberley, Surrey.

Chaplais, P., PhD, FBA, FSA, Lew Lodge, Lew, Oxford OX8 2BE.

Chapman, Professor R.A., BA, MA, PhD, FBIM, Dept of Politics, The University, 48 Old Elvet, Durham, DH1 3LZ.

Charles-Edwards, T. M., DPhil, Corpus Christi College, Oxford OX1 4JF.

Charmley, J., MA, DPhil, School of English and American Studies, University of East Anglia, University Plain, Norwich NR4 7TJ.

Chartres, J. A., MA, DPhil, School of Economic Studies, The University, Leeds LS2 9JT.

Chaudhuri, Professor Kirti Narayan, BA, PhD, History Department, S.O.A.S., University of London, Malet Street, London WC1E 7HD.

Cheney, Mrs Mary, MA, 17 Westberry Court, Grange Road, Cambridge CB3 9BG.

Cherry, John, MA, 58 Lancaster Road, London N4.

Chibnall, Mrs Marjorie, MA, DPhil, FBA, 7 Croftgate, Fulbrooke Road, Cambridge CB3 9EG.

Child, C. J., OBE, MA, PhD, 94 Westhall Road, Warlingham, Surrey CR3 9HB.

Childs, J. C. R., BA, PhD, School of History, The University, Leeds LS2 9JT.

Childs, Wendy R., MA, PhD, School of History, The University, Leeds LS2 9JT.

Chitnis, Anand Chidamber, BA, MA, PhD, Dept of History, The University, Stirling FK9 4LA.

Christiansen, E., New College, Oxford OX1 3BN.

Christianson, Professor P. K., PhD, Dept of History, Queen's University, Kingston, Ontario, Canada K7L 3N6.

Christie, Professor I. R., MA, FBA, 10 Green Lane, Croxley Green, Herts. WD3 3HR.

Church, Professor R. A., BA, PhD, School of Social Studies, University of East Anglia, University Plain, Norwich NOR 88C.

Cirket, A. F., 71 Curlew Crescent, Bedford.

Clanchy, M. T., MA, PhD, FSA, 28 Hillfield Road, London NW6 1PZ.

Clapinson, Mrs Mary, MA, Dept of Western Manuscripts, Bodleian Library, Oxford OX1 3BG.

Clark, A. E., MA, 32 Durham Avenue, Thornton Cleveleys, Blackpool FY5 2DP.

Clark, D. S. T., BA, PhD, Dept of History, University College of Swansea, Swansea SA2 8PP.

Clark, J. C. D., MA, PhD, All Souls College, Oxford OX1 4AL.

Clark, P. A., MA, Dept of Economic and Social History, The University, University Road, Leicester LE1 7RH.

Clarke, Howard B., BA, PhD, Room K104, Arts-Commerce-Law Building, University College, Dublin 4, Ireland.

Clarke, P. F., MA, PhD, St John's College, Cambridge CB2 1TP.

Clementi, Miss D., MA, DPhil, Flat 7, 43 Rutland Gate, London SW7 1BP.

Clemoes, Professor P. A. M., BA, PhD, Emmanuel College, Cambridge CB2 3AP.

Cliffe, J. T., BA, PhD, 263 Staines Road, Twickenham, Middx. TW2 5AY.

Clifton, R., DPhil, 58 Mickleton Road, Coventry, West Midlands.

Clive, Professor J. L., PhD, 38 Fernald Drive, Cambridge, Mass. 02138, U.S.A.

Clough, C. H., MA, DPhil, FSA, School of History, The University, P.O. Box 147, Liverpool L69 3BX.

Cobb, H. S., MA, FSA, 1 Child's Way, Hampstead Garden Suburb, London NW11.

Cobban, A. B., MA, PhD, School of History, The University, P.O. Box 147, Liverpool L69 3BX.

Cockburn, Professor J. S., LLB, LLM, PhD, History Dept, University of Maryland, College Park, Maryland 20742, U.S.A.

Cocks, E. J., MA, Middle Lodge, Ardingly, Haywards Heath, Sussex RH17 6TS.

Cohn, H. J., MA, DPhil, Dept of History, University of Warwick, Coventry CV4 7AL.

Cohn, Professor N. R. C., MA, DLitt, FBA, Orchard Cottage, Wood End, Ardeley, Herts. SG2 7AZ.

Coleby, A. M., BA, 24 Lumley Road, Newton Hall, Durham DH1 5NR.

Coleman, B. I., MA, PhD, Dept of History, The University, Exeter EX4 4QH.

Coleman, C. H. D., MA, Dept of History, University College London, Gower Street, London WC1E 6BT.

Coleman, Professor D. C., BSc(Econ.), PhD, LittD, FBA, Over Hall, Cavendish, Sudbury, Suffolk.

Colley, Professor Linda J., BA, MA, PhD, Dept of History, Yale University, PO Box 1504A Yale Station, New Haven, Connecticut 06520-7425, U.S.A.

Collier, W. O., MA, FSA, 34 Berwyn Road, Richmond, Surrey.

Collinge, J. M., BA, 36 Monks Road, Enfield, Middlesex EN2 8BH.

Collini, S. A., MA, PhD, Dept of History, The University, Falmer, Brighton, Sussex BN1 9QX.

Collins, B. W., MA, PhD, The Dean, School of Humanities, The University, Buckingham MK18 1EG.

Collins, Mrs I., MA, BLitt, School of History, The University, P.O. Box 147, Liverpool L69 3BX.

Collinson, Professor P., MA, PhD, FBA, Trinity College, Cambridge, CB2 1TQ.

Colvin, H. M., CBE, MA, FBA, St John's College, Oxford OX1 3JP.

Colyer, R. J., BSc, PhD, Inst. of Rural Sciences, University College of Wales, Aberystwyth, Dyfed.

Congreve, A. L., MA, FSA, Galleons Lap, Sissinghurst, Kent TN17 2JG.

Connell-Smith, Professor G. E., PhD, 7 Braids Walk, Kirkella, Hull, Yorks. HU10 7PA.

Connolly, Sean J., BA, DPhil, Dept of History, University of Ulster, Coleraine, Northern Ireland BT52 1SA.

Constantine, S., BA, DPhil, Dept of History, The University, Bailrigg, Lancaster LA1 4YG.

Contamine, Professor P., DèsL., 12 Villa Croix Nivert, 75015 Paris, France.

Conway, Professor A. A., MA, University of Canterbury, Christchurch 1, New Zealand.

Conway, S. R., BA, PhD, The Bentham Project, Dept of History, University College London, Gower Street, London WC1E 6BT.

Cook, C. P., MA, DPhil, Dept of History, Philosophy and European Studies, The Polytechnic of North London, Prince of Wales Road, London NW5 3LB.

Cooke, Professor, J. J., PhD., Dept of History, University of Mississippi, College of Liberal Arts, University, Miss. 38677, U.S.A.

Coolidge, Professor R. T., MA, BLitt, P.O. Box 4070, Westmount, Quebec, Canada H3Z 2X3.

Cooper, Janet M., MA, PhD, 7 Stonepath Drive, Hatfield Peverel, Chelmsford CM3 2LG.

Cope, Professor Esther S., PhD, Dept of History, Univ. of Nebraska, Lincoln, Neb. 68508, U.S.A.

Copley, A. R. H., MA, MPhil, Rutherford College, The University, Canterbury, Kent CT2 7NX.

Corfield, Penelope J., MA, PhD, Dept of History, Royal Holloway and Bedford New College, Egham Hill, Egham, Surrey TW20 0EX.

Cornell, Professor Paul G., PhD, 202 Laurier Place, Waterloo, Ontario, Canada N2L 1K8.

Corner, D. J., BA, Dept of History, St Salvator's College, The University, St Andrews, Fife KY16 9AJ.

Cornford, Professor J. P., MA, The Brick House, Wicken Bonhunt, Saffron Walden, Essex CB11 3UG.

Cornwall, J. C. K., MA, 1 Orchard Close, Copford Green, Colchester, Essex.

Cosgrove, A. J., BA, PhD, Dept of Medieval History, University College, Dublin 4, Ireland.

Coss, P. R., BA, PhD, 20 Whitebridge Close, Whitebridge Grove, Gosforth, Newcastle upon Tyne NE3 2DN.

Costeloe, Professor M. P., BA, PhD, Dept of Hispanic and Latin American Studies, The University, 83 Woodland Road, Bristol BS8 1RJ.

Countryman, E. F., PhD, Dept of History, University of Warwick, Coventry CV4 7AL.

Cowan, I. B., MA, PhD, Dept of History, University of Glasgow, Glasgow G12 8QQ.

Coward, B., BA, PhD, Dept of History, Birkbeck College, Malet Street, London WC1E 7HX.

Cowdrey, Rev. H. E. J., MA, St Edmund Hall, Oxford OX1 4AR.

Cowie, The Rev. L. W., MA, PhD, 38 Stratton Road, Merton Park, London SW19 3JG.

Cowley, F. G., PhD, 17 Brookvale Road, West Cross, Swansea, W. Glam.

Cox, D. C., BA, PhD, 12 Oakfield Road, Copthorne, Shrewsbury SY3 8AA.

Craig, R. S., BSc(Econ), The Anchorage, Bay Hill, St Margarets Bay, nr Dover, Kent CT15 6DU.

Cramp, Professor Rosemary, MA, BLitt, FSA, Department of Archaeology, 46 Saddler Street, Durham DH1 3NU.

Crampton, R. J., BA, PhD, Rutherford College, The University, Canterbury, Kent CT2 7NP.

Cranfield, L. R., Lot 2, Selby Avenue, Warrandyte, Victoria, Australia 3113.

Craton, Professor M. J., BA, MA, PhD, Dept of History, University of Waterloo, Waterloo, Ontario, Canada N2L 3G1.

Crawford, Patricia M., BA, MA, PhD, Dept of History, University of Western Australia, Nedlands, Western Australia 6009.

*Crawley, C. W., MA, 93 Castelnau, London SW13 9EL.

Cremona, His Hon Chief Justice Professor J. J., KM, DLitt, PhD, LLD, DrJur, 5 Victoria Gardens, Sliema, Malta.

Cressy, D. A., MA, PhD, 231 West Sixth Street, Claremont, Calif. 91711, U.S.A.

Crimmin, Patricia K., MPhil, BA, Dept of History, Royal Holloway and Bedford New College, Egham Hill, Egham, Surrey TW20 0EX.

Crisp, Professor Olga, BA, PhD, 'Zarya', 1 Milbrook, Arbrook Lane, Esher, Surrey.

Croft, J. Pauline, MA, DPhil, Dept of History, Royal Holloway and Bedford New College, Egham Hill, Egham, Surrey TW20 0EX.

Crombie, A. C., BSc, MA, PhD, Trinity College, Oxford OX1 3BH.

Cromwell, Miss V., MA, Arts Building, University of Sussex, Brighton, Sussex BN1 9QN.

Crook, D., MA, PhD, Public Record Office, Chancery Lane, London WC2A 1LR.

Crosby, Professor T. L., Dept of History, Wheaton College, Norton, Mass., 02766 USA.

Cross, Professor M. Claire, MA, PhD, Dept of History, The University, York YO1 5DD.

Crossick, G. J., MA, PhD, Dept of History, University of Essex, Wivenhoe Park, Colchester CO4 3SQ.

Crouch, D. B., PhD, 17c St Johns Grove, Archway, London N19 5RW.

Crowder, Professor Emeritus C. M. D., MA, DPhil, Dept of History, Queen's University, Kingston, Ontario, Canada K7L 3N6.

Crowe, Miss S. E., MA, PhD, 112 Staunton Road, Headington, Oxford.

Crozier, A. J., BA, MA, PhD, Bro Wen, 85 Upper Garth Road, Bangor, Gwynedd LL57 2SS.

Cruickshanks, Eveline G., PhD, 46 Goodwood Court, Devonshire Street, London W1N 1SL.

Cumming, Professor A., MA, DipMA, PGCE, PhD, Carseldine Campus of the Brisbane College of Advanced Education, P.O. Box 284, Zillmere, Queensland 4034, Australia.

Cumming, I., MEd, PhD, 672a South Titirangi Road, Titirangi, Auckland, New Zealand.

Cummins, Professor J. S., PhD, University College London, Gower Street, London WC1E 6BT.

Cumpston, Miss I. M., MA, DPhil, 18 Fuller Street, Deakin, Canberra 2600, Australia.

Cunliffe, Professor M. F., MA, BLitt, DHL, Room 102, T Building, George Washington University, 2110 G. Street N.W., Washington, D.C., 20052, U.S.A.

Currie, C. R. J., MA, DPhil, Institute of Historical Research, Senate House, Malet Street, London WC1E 7HU.

Currie, R., MA, DPhil, Wadham College, Oxford OX1 3PN.

Curry, Anne E., BA, MA, PhD, 5 Melrose Avenue, Reading, Berkshire RG6 2BN.

Curtis, Professor L. Perry, Jr, PhD, Dept of History, Brown University, Providence, R.I. 02912, U.S.A.

*Cuttino, G. P., DPhil, FBA, FSA, 1270 University Dr. N. E., Atlanta, Ga. 30306, U.S.A.

Cuttler, S. H., BPhil, DPhil, 5051 Clanranald →302, Montreal, Quebec, Canada H3X 2S3.

*Dacre, Lord, MA, FBA, Peterhouse, Cambridge CB2 1RD.

Dakin, Professor D., MA, PhD, 20 School Road, Apperley, Gloucester GL19 4DJ.

Dales, Rev. D. J., MA, Hillside, Bath Road, Marlborough, Wiltshire SN8 1NN.

Das Gupta, A., MA, PhD, National Library, Belvedere, Calcutta, India 700027.

DAUNTON, M. J., BA, PhD (*Hon. Treasurer*), Dept of History, University College London, Gower Street, London WC1E 6BT.

Davenport, Professor T. R. H., MA, PhD, Dept of History, Rhodes University, P.O. Box 94, Grahamstown 6140, South Africa.

Davenport-Hines, R. P. T., PhD, BA, 51 Elsham Road, Holland Park, London W14 8HD.

Davidson, R., MA, PhD, Dept of Economic and Social History, The University, 50 George Square, Edinburgh EH8 9JY.

Davies, C. S. L., MA, DPhil, Wadham College, Oxford OX1 3PN.

Davies, I. N. R., MA, DPhil, 22 Rowland Close, Wolvercote, Oxford.

Davies, P. N., MA, PhD, Cmar, Croft Drive, Caldy, Wirral, Merseyside.

Davies, R. G., MA, PhD, Dept of History, The Victoria University of Manchester, Oxford Road, Manchester M13 9PL.

Davies, Professor R. R., BA, DPhil, University College of Wales, Dept of History, Hugh Owen Building, Aberystwyth SY23 3DY.

Davies, Professor Wendy, BA, PhD, Dept of History, University College London, Gower Street, London WC1E 6BT.

*Davis, G. R. C., CBE, MA, DPhil, FSA, 214 Somerset Road, London SW19 5JE.

Davis, J. A., MA, DPhil, Dept of History, University of Warwick, Coventry CV4 7AL.

Davis, Professor J. C., Dept of History, Massey University, Palmerston North, New Zealand.

Davis, J. H., BA, DPhil, 18 Butler Close, Oxford OX2 6JG.

Davis, Professor R. H. C., MA, FBA, FSA, 349 Banbury Road, Oxford OX2 7PL.

Davis, Professor Richard W., Dept of History, Washington University, St Louis, Missouri 63130, U.S.A.

*Dawe, D. A., 46 Green Lane, Purley, Surrey.

Deane, Professor Phyllis M., MA, 4 Stukeley Close, Cambridge CB3 9LT.

de Hamel, C. F. R., BA, DPhil, FSA, Chase House, Perry's Chase, Greenstead Road, Ongar, Essex CM5 9LA.

de la Mare, Miss A. C., MA, PhD, Bodleian Library, Oxford.

Denham, E. W., MA, 4 The Ridge, 89 Green Lane, Northwood, Middx. HA6 1AE.

Dennis, Professor P. J., MA, PhD, Dept of History, University College, University of New South Wales, Australian Defence Force Academy, Campbell, A.C.T. 2600, Australia.

Denton, J. H., BA, PhD, Dept of History, The University, Manchester M13 9PL.

Derry, J. W., MA, PhD, Dept of History, The University, Newcastle upon Tyne NE1 7RU.

Devine, T. M., BA, Viewfield Cottage, 55 Burnbank Road, Hamilton, Strathclyde Region.

Dewey, P. E., BA, PhD, Dept of History, Royal Holloway and Bedford New College, Egham Hill, Egham, Surrey TW20 0EX.

DICKENS, Professor A. G., CMG, MA, DLit, DLitt, LittD, FBA, FSA, Institute of Historical Research, University of London, Senate House, London WC1E 7HU.

Dickinson, Professor H. T., BA, MA, PhD, DLitt, Dept of Modern History, The University, Edinburgh EH8 9YL.

Dickinson, Rev. J. C., MA, DLitt, FSA, Yew Tree Cottage, Barngarth, Cartmel, South Cumbria.

Dickson, P. G. M., MA, DPhil, St Catherine's College, Oxford, OX1 3UJ.

Dilks, Professor D. N., BA, Dept of International History, The University, Leeds LS2 9JT.

Dilworth, Rev. G. M., OSB, MA, PhD, Scottish Catholic Archives, Columba House, 16 Drummond Place, Edinburgh EH3 6PL.

Dinwiddy, J. R., PhD, Dept of History, Royal Holloway and Bedford New College, Egham Hill, Egham, Surrey TW20 0EX.

Ditchfield, G. McC, BA, PhD, Darwin College, University of Kent, Canterbury, Kent CT2 7NY.

Dobson, Professor R. B., MA, DPhil, Professor of Medieval History, Christ's College, Cambridge CB2 3BU.

Dockrill, M. L., MA, BSc(Econ), PhD, Dept of History, King's College London, Strand, London WC2R 2LS.

*Dodwell, Miss B., MA, 30 Eaton Road, Norwich NR4 6PZ.

Dodwell, Professor C. R., MA, PhD, FSA, History of Art Department, The University, Manchester M13 9PL.

Don Peter, The Rt Revd Monsignor W. L. A., MA, PhD, St. John Vianney Seminary, Tudella, Ja-ela, Sri Lanka.

Donahue, Professor Charles, Jr, AB, LLB, Dept of Law, Harvard University, Cambridge, Mass. 02138, U.S.A.

*DONALDSON, Professor G., CBE, MA, PhD, DLitt, DLitt, DUniv, FRSE, FBA, 6 Pan Ha', Dysart, Fife KY1 2TL.

Donaldson, Professor P. S., MA, PhD, Dept of Humanities, 14N-422, Massachusetts Institute of Technology, Cambridge, Mass. 02139, U.S.A.

*Donaldson-Hudson, Miss R., BA, (address unknown).

Donoughue, Lord, MA, DPhil, 1 Sloane Square, London SW1W 8EE.

Doran, Susan M., BA, PhD, Downgate House, 25 Wharf Road, Shillingford, Oxfordshire OX9 8EW.

Dore, R. N., MA, Holmrook, 19 Chapel Lane, Hale Barns, Altrincham, Cheshire WA15 0AB.

Dow, Frances D., MA, DPhil, Dept of History, University of Edinburgh, George Square, Edinburgh EH8 9JY.

Downer, L. J., MA, BA, LLB, 29 Roebuck Street, Red Hill, Canberra 2603, Australia.

Doyle, A. I., MA, PhD, University College, The Castle, Durham.

Doyle, Professor W., MA, DPhil, DrHC, Dept of History, The University, 13–15 Woodland Road, Bristol BS8 1TB.

Driver, J. T., MA, BLitt, PhD, 25 Abbot's Grange, Chester CH2 1AJ.

*Drus, Miss E., MA, 18 Brampton Tower, Bassett Avenue, Southampton SO1 7FB.

Duckham, Professor B. F., MA, Bronllan, Betws Bledrws, near Lampeter, Dyfed SA48 8NY.

Duffy, Michael, MA, DPhil, Dept of History and Archaeology, The University, Queen's Drive, Exeter EX4 4QH.

Duggan, Anne J., BA, PhD, Dept of History, King's College London, Strand, London WC2R 2LS.

Duggan, C., PhD, Dept of History, King's College London, Strand, London WC2R 2LS.

Dugmore, The Rev. Professor C. W., DD, Thame Cottage, The Street, Puttenham, Guildford, Surrey GU3 1AT.

Duke, A. C., MA, Dept of History, The University, Southampton SO9 5NH.

Dumville, D. N., MA, PhD, Dept of Anglo-Saxon, Norse and Celtic, University of Cambridge, 9 West Road, Cambridge CB3 9DP.

Dunbabin, Jean H., MA, DPhil, St Anne's College, Oxford OX2 6HS.

Dunbabin, J. P. D., MA, St Edmund Hall, Oxford OX1 4AR.

Duncan, Professor A. A. M., MA, Dept of History, The University, 9 University Gardens, Glasgow G12 8QQ.

Dunn, Professor R. S., PhD, Dept of History, The College, University of Pennsylvania, Philadelphia, 19104, Pa., U.S.A.

Dunning, R. W., BA, PhD, FSA, Musgrove Manor East, Barton Close, Taunton TA1 4RU.

Durack, Mrs I. A., MA, PhD, University of Western Australia, Nedlands, Western Australia 6009.

Durey, M. J., BA, DPhil, School of Social Inquiry, Murdoch University, Perth, Western Australia 6150.

Durie, A. J., MA, PhD, Dept of Economic History, Edward Wright Building, The University, Aberdeen AB9 2TY.

Durkan, J., MA, PhD, DLitt, Dept of Scottish History, The University, Glasgow G12 8QH.

Durston, C. G., MA, PhD, 49 Percy Street, Oxford.

Dusinberre, W. W., PhD, Dept of History, University of Warwick, Coventry CV4 7AL.

Dutton, D. J., BA, PhD, School of History, The University, P.O. Box 147, Liverpool L69 3BX.

Dyer, C. C., BA, PhD, School of History, The University, P.O. Box 363, Birmingham B15 2TT.

Dykes, D. W., MA, Cherry Grove, Welsh St Donats, nr Cowbridge, Glam. CF7 7SS.

Dyson, Professor K. H. F., BSc(Econ), MSc(Econ), PhD, Undergraduate School of European Studies, The University, Bradford, West Yorkshire BD7 1DP.

Earle, P., BSc(Econ), PhD, Dept of Economic History, London School of Economics, Houghton Street, London WC2A 2AE.

Eastwood, Rev. C. C., PhD, Heathview, Monks Lane, Audlem, Cheshire SW3 0HP.

Eckles, Professor R. B., PhD, P.O. Box 6558. San Antonio, Texas 78209, U.S.A.

Edbury, P. W., MA, PhD, Dept of History, University College, P.O. Box 78, Cardiff CF1 1XL.

Eddy, Rev. J. J., BA, DPhil, History Dept, The Research School of Social Sciences, The Australian National University, GPO Box 4, Canberra, A.C.T. 2601, Australia.

Ede, J. R., CB, MA, Palfreys, East Street, Drayton, Langport, Somerset TA10 0JZ.

Edmonds, Professor E. L., MA, PhD, University of Prince Edward Island, Charlottetown, Prince Edward Island, Canada.

Edwards, Rev. F. O., SJ, BA, FSA, 114 Mount Street, London W1Y 6AH.

Edwards, J. H., MA, DPhil, School of History, The University, P.O. Box 363, Birmingham B15 2TT.

Edwards, O. D., BA, Dept of History, William Robertson Building, The University, George Square, Edinburgh EH8 9YL.

Ehrman, J. P. W., MA, FBA, FSA, The Mead Barns, Taynton, Nr Burford, Oxfordshire OX8 5UH.

Eisenstein, Professor Elizabeth L., PhD, 82 Kalorama Circle N.W., Washington D.C. 20008, U.S.A.

Eldridge, C. C., PhD, Dept of History, Saint David's University College, Lampeter, Dyfed SA48 7ED.

Eley, G. H., BA, DPhil, MA, MA, Dept of History, University of Michigan, Ann Arbor, Michigan 48109, U.S.A.

Elliott, Professor J. H., MA, PhD, FBA, The Institute for Advanced Studies, Princeton, New Jersey 08540, U.S.A.

Elliott, Marianne, BA, DPhil, Dept of History, The University, P.O. Box 147, Liverpool L69 3BX.

Ellis, G. J., MA, DPhil, Hertford College, Oxford OX1 3BW.

Ellis, R. H., MA, FSA, Cloth Hill, 6 The Mount, London NW3.

Ellis, S. G., BA, MA, PhD, Dept of History, University College, Galway, Ireland.

Ellsworth, Professor Edward W., AB, AM, PhD, 27 Englewood Avenue, Brookline, Mass. 02146, U.S.A.

Ellul, M., BArch, DipArch, 'Pauline', 55 Old Railway Road, Birkirkara, Malta.

Elrington, C. R., MA, FSA, Institute of Historical Research, Senate House, Malet Street, London WC1E 7HU.

ELTON, Professor Sir Geoffrey, MA, PhD, LittD, DLitt, DLitt, DLit, FBA, 30 Millington Road, Cambridge CB3 9HP.

Elvin, L., FSA, FRSA, 10 Almond Avenue, Swanpool, Lincoln LN6 0HB.

*Emmison, F. G., MBE, PhD, DUniv, FSA, 8 Coppins Close, Chelmsford, Essex CM2 6AY.

Emsley, C., BA, MLitt, Arts Faculty, The Open University, Walton Hall, Milton Keynes MK7 6AA.

Emsley, K., MA, LlM, 34 Nab Wood Drive, Shipley, West Yorkshire BD18 4EL.

Emy, Professor H. V., PhD, Dept of Politics, Monash University, Wellington Road, Clayton, Melbourne 3146, Australia.

English, Barbara A., MA, PhD, FSA, Centre of Regional and Local History, Loten Building, The University, Hull, HU6 7RX.

Erickson, Charlotte, J., PhD, 8 High Street, Chesterton, Cambridge CB4 1NG.

*Erith, E. J., Holyport Lodge, The Green, Holyport, Maidenhead, Berkshire SL6 2JA.

Erskine, Mrs A. M., MA, BLitt, FSA, 44 Birchy Barton Hill, Exeter EX1 3EX.

Etherington, N. A., PhD, BA, Dept of History, University of Western Australia, Nedlands, Western Australia 6009.

Evans, Mrs A. K. B., PhD, FSA, White Lodge, 25 Knighton Grange Road, Leicester LE2 2LF.

Evans, E. J., MA, PhD, Dept of History, Furness College, University of Lancaster, Bailrigg, Lancaster LA1 4YG.

Evans, Gillian R., PhD, Fitzwilliam College, Cambridge CB2 3HU.

Evans, R. J., MA, DPhil, School of European Studies, University of East Anglia, Norwich NR4 7TJ.

Evans, R. J. W., MA, PhD, FBA, Brasenose College, Oxford OX1 4AJ.

Everitt, Professor A. M., MA, PhD, FBA, Fieldedge, Poultney Lane, Kimcote, nr Lutterworth, Leicestershire LE17 5RX.

Eyck, Professor U. F. J., MA, BLitt, Dept of History, University of Calgary, 2500 University Drive NW, Calgary, Alberta, Canada T2N IN4.

Fage, Professor J. D., MA, PhD, Hafod Awel, Pennal, Machynlleth, Powis SY20 9DP.

Fairs, G. L., MA, Thornton House, Bear Street, Hay-on-Wye, Hereford HR3 5AN.

Falkus, M. E., BSc(Econ), Dept of History, London School of Economics, Houghton Street, London WC2A 2AE.

Farmer, Professor D. L., 411 Quance Avenue, Saskatoon, Sask., Canada S7H 3B5.

Farmer, D. F. H., BLitt, FSA, 26 Swanston Field, Whitchurch, Pangbourne, Berks. RG8 7HP.

Farr, M. W., MA, FSA, 12 Emscote Road, Warwick.

Fell, Professor C. E., MA, Dept of English, The University, Nottingham NG7 2RD.

Fellows-Jensen, Gillian M., BA, PhD, Københavns Universitets, Institut For Navneforskning, Njalsgade 80, DK-2300 København S, Denmark.

Fenlon, Rev. D. B., BA, PhD, Oscott College, Chester Road, Sutton Coldfield, West Midlands, B73 5AA.

Fenn, Rev. R. W. D., ThD, MA, BD, FSA, FSAScot, The Ditch, Bradnor View, Kington, Herefordshire.

Fennell, Professor J., MA, PhD, 8 Canterbury Road, Oxford OX2 6LU.

Fernandez-Armesto, F. F. R., DPhil, River View, Headington Hill, Oxford.

Feuchtwanger, E. J., MA, PhD, Highfield House, Dean Sparsholt, nr Winchester, Hants.

Fieldhouse, Professor D. K., MA, Jesus College, Cambridge CB5 8BL.

Finer, Professor S. E., MA, All Souls College, Oxford OX1 4AL.

Fines, J., MA, PhD, 119 Parklands Road, Chichester.

Finlayson, G. B. A. M., MA, BLitt, 11 Burnhead Road, Glasgow G43 2SU.

Fisher, Professor Alan W., PhD, Dept of History, Michigan State University, East Lansing, Michigan 48824, U.S.A.

Fisher, D. J. V., MA, Jesus College, Cambridge CB3 9AD.

Fisher, H. E. Stephen, BSc, PhD, Dept of History, The University, Amory Building, Rennes Drive, Exeter EX4 4RJ.

Fisher, J. R., BA, MPhil, PhD, School of History, The University, P.O. Box 147, Liverpool L69 3BX.

Fisher, R. M., MA, PhD, Dept of History, University of Queensland, St Lucia, Queensland, Australia 4067.

Fishwick, Professor D., BA, MA, DLitt, Dept of Classics, Humanities Centre, University of Alberta, Edmonton, Alberta, Canada T6G 2E6.

Fitch, Dr M. F. B., CBE, HonFBA, FSA, 22 Ave de Budé, 1202 Geneva, Switzerland.

Fitzpatrick, M. H., PhD, 'Garreg-Wen', Bronant, Aberystwyth, Dyfed SY23 4TQ.

Fletcher, Professor A. J., MA, Dept of History, University of Durham, 43/46 North Bailey, Durham, DH1 3EX.

*Fletcher, The Rt Hon. The Lord, PC, BA, LLD, FSA, 51 Charlbury Road, North Oxford OX2 6UX.

Fletcher, R. A., MA, Dept of History, The University, Heslington, York YO1 5DD.

Flint, Professor J. E., MA, PhD, Dalhousie University, Halifax, Nova Scotia, Canada B3H 3J5.

Flint, Valerie I. J., MA, DPhil, Dept of History, The University, Private Bag, Auckland, New Zealand.

Floud, Professor R. C., MA, DPhil, City of London Polytechnic, 117–119 Houndsditch, London EC3A 7BU.

Fogel, Professor Robert W., PhD, Center for Population Economics, University of Chicago, 1101 East 58th Street, Chicago, Illinois 60637, U.S.A.

Foot, M. R. D., MA, BLitt, 45 Countess Road, London NW5 2XH.

Forbes, D., MA, 18 Thornton Close, Girton, Cambridge CB3 0NQ.

Ford, W. K., BA, 48 Harlands Road, Haywards Heath, West Sussex RH16 1LS.

Forster, G. C. F., BA, FSA, School of History, The University, Leeds LS2 9JT.

Foster, Professor Elizabeth R., AM, PhD, 205 Strafford Avenue, Wayne, Pa. 19087, U.S.A.

Foster, R. F., MA, PhD, Dept of History, Birkbeck College, Malet Street, London WC1E 7HX.

Fowler, Professor K. A., BA, PhD, 2 Nelson Street, Edinburgh 3.

Fowler, Professer P. J., MA, PhD, Dept of Archaeology, The University, Newcastle upon Tyne NE1 7RU.

Fox, J. P., BSc(Econ), MSc(Econ), PhD, 98 Baring Road, London SE12 0PT.

Fox, L., OBE, DL, LHD, MA, FSA, FRSL, Silver Birches, 27 Welcombe Road, Stratford-upon-Avon, Warwickshire.

Fox, R., MA, DPhil, Modern History Faculty, The University, Broad Street, Oxford OX1 3BD.

Frame, R. F., MA, PhD, Dept of History, The University, 43 North Bailey, Durham DH1 3HP.

France, J., BA, PhD, 10 Brynfield Road, Langland, Swansea SA3 4SX.

Franklin, M. J., MA, PhD, Wolfson College, Cambridge CB3 9BB.

Franklin, R. M., The Corner House, Eton College, Windsor, Berkshire SL4 6DB.

Fraser, Lady Antonia, 52 Campden Hill Square, London W8.

*Fraser, Miss C. M., PhD, 39 King Edward Road, Tynemouth, Tyne and Wear NE30 2RW.

Fraser, D., BA, MA, PhD, 117 Alwoodley Lane, Leeds, LS17 7PN.

Fraser, Professor Peter, MA, PhD, The Priory, Old Mill Lane, Marnhull, Dorset DT10 1JX.

Freeden, M. S., DPhil, Mansfield College, Oxford OX1 3TF.

French, D. W., BA, PhD, Dept of History, University College London, Gower Street, London WC1E 6BT.

Frend, Professor W. H. C., MA, DPhil, DD, FRSE, FBA, FSA, The Rectory, Barnwell, nr Peterborough, Northants. PE8 5PG.

Fritz, Professor Paul S., BA, MA, PhD, Dept of History, McMaster University, Hamilton, Ontario, Canada.

Frost, A. J., BA, MA, MA, PhD, Dept of History, La Trobe University, Bundoora, Victoria 3083, Australia.

Fryde, Professor E. B., DPhil, Preswylfa, Trinity Road, Aberystwyth, Dyfed SY23 1LU.

Fryde, Natalie M., BA, DrPhil, Schloss Grünsberg, D-8503 Altdorf, Germany.

*Fryer, Professor C. E., MA, PhD (address unknown).

Fryer, Professor W. R., BLitt, MA, 68 Grove Avenue, Chilwell, Beeston, Nottingham NG9 4DX.

Frykenberg, Professor R. E., MA, PhD, 1840 Chadbourne Avenue, Madison, Wis. 53705, U.S.A.

Fuidge, Miss N. M., Flat 3, 17 Cleve Road, London NW6 3RR.

Fulbrook, Mary J. A., MA, AM, PhD, Dept of German, University College London, Gower Street, London WC1E 6BT.

*Furber, Professor H., MA, PhD, c/o History Department, University of Pennsylvania, Philadelphia 4, Pa., U.S.A.

Fussell, G. E., DLitt, 3 Nightingale Road, Horsham, West Sussex RH12 2NW.

Fyrth, H. J., BSc(Econ), 72 College Road, Dulwich, London SE21 7LY.

Gabriel, Professor A. L., PhD, FMAA, CFIF, CFBA, P.O. Box 578, University of Notre Dame, Notre Dame, Indiana 46556, U.S.A.

*Galbraith, Professor J. S., BS, MA, PhD, Dept of History C–004, University of California, San Diego, La Jolla, Calif. 92093, U.S.A.

Gale, Professor H. P. P., OBE, PhD, 38 Brookwood Avenue, London SW13.

Gale, W. K. V., 19 Ednam Road, Goldthorn Park, Wolverhampton WV4 5BL.

Gann, L. H., MA, BLitt, DPhil, Hoover Institution, Stanford University, Stanford, Calif. 94305, U.S.A.

Garnett, G., MA, St John's College, Cambridge CB2 1TP.

Gash, Professor N., CBE, MA, BLitt, FBA, Old Gatehouse, Portway, Langport, Somerset TA10 0NQ.

Gaskell, S. M., MA, PhD, 4 Lings Coppice, Croxted Road, Dulwich, London SE21 8SY.

Geggus, D. P., MA, DPhil, Dept of History, University of Florida, Gainesville, Florida 32611, U.S.A.

Genet, J.-Ph., Agrégé d'Histoire, 147 Avenue Parmentier, Paris 75010, France.

Gentles, Professor I., BA, MA, PhD, Dept of History, Glendon College, 2275 Bayview Avenue, Toronto, Canada M4N 3M6.

Gerlach, Professor D. R., MA, PhD, University of Akron, Akron, Ohio 44325, U.S.A.

Gibbs, G. C., MA, Dept of History, Birkbeck College, Malet Street, London WC1E 7HX.

Gibbs, Professor N. H., MA, DPhil, All Souls College, Oxford OX1 4AL.

Gibson, J. S. W., FSA, Harts Cottage, Church Hanborough, Oxford OX7 2AB.

Gibson, Margaret T., MA, DPhil, School of History, The University, P.O. Box 147, Liverpool L69 3 BX.

Gifford, Miss D. H., PhD, FSA, 1 Pondtail Road, Fleet, nr Aldershot, Hants. GU13 9JW.

Gilbert, Professor Bentley B., PhD, Dept of History, University of Illinois at Chicago Circle, Box 4348, Chicago, Ill. 60680, U.S.A.

Gildea, R. N., MA, DPhil, Merton College, Oxford OX1 4JD.

Gilkes, R. K., MA, 75 Fouracre Road, Downend, Bristol.

Gillespie, J. L., AB, MA, PhD, Dept of History, Notre Dame College of Ohio, 4545 College Road, Cleveland, Ohio 44121, U.S.A.

Gilley, S. W., BA, DPhil, Dept of Theology, University of Durham, Abbey House, Palace Green, Durham DH1 3RS.

Gillingham, J. B., MA, London School of Economics, Houghton Street, Aldwych, London WC2A 2AE.

Ginter, Professor D. E., AM, PhD, Dept of History, Concordia University, 1455 De Maisonneuve Blvd. W., Montreal, Quebec, Canada H3G 1M8.

de Giorgi, Roger, Development House, Floriana, Malta.

Girtin, T., MA, Butter Field House, Church Street, Old Isleworth, Middx.

Glassey, L. K. J., MA, DPhil, Dept of Modern History, The University, Glasgow G12 8QQ.

Gleave, Group Capt. T. P., CBE, RAF (ret.), Willow Bank, River Gardens. Bray-on-Thames, Berks. SL6 2BJ.

*Glover, Professor R. G., MA, PhD, 2937 Tudor Avenue, Victoria, B.C. Canada V8N 1M2.

*Godber, Miss A. J., MA, FSA, Mill Lane Cottage, Willington, Bedford.

*Godfrey, Professor J. L., MA, PhD, 231 Hillcrest Circle, Chapel Hill, N.C., U.S.A.

Goldie, Mark, MA, PhD, Churchill College, Cambridge CB3 0DS.

Golding, B. J., MA, DPhil, Dept of History, The University, Highfield, Southampton SO9 5NH.

Goldsmith, Professor M. M., PhD, Dept of Politics, University of Exeter, Exeter EX4 4RJ.

Goldsworthy, D. J. BA, BPhil, DPhil, Dept of Politics, Monash University, Clayton, Victoria 3168, Australia.

Gollin, Professor A., DLitt, Dept of History, University of California, Santa Barbara, Calif. 93106, U.S.A.

Gooch, John, BA, PhD, Dept of History, The University, Bailrigg, Lancaster LA1 4YG.

Goodman, A. E., MA, BLitt, Dept of Medieval History, The University, Edinburgh EH8 9YL.

Goodspeed, Professor D. J., BA, 164 Victoria Street, Niagara-on-the-Lake, Ontario, Canada.

*Gopal, Professor S., MA, DPhil, 30 Edward Elliot Road, Mylapore, Madras, India.

Gordon, Professor P., BSc(Econ), MSc(Econ), PhD, 241 Kenton Road, Kenton, Harrow HA3 0HJ.

Goring, J. J., MA, PhD, 31 Houndean Rise, Lewes, East Sussex BN7 1EQ.

Gorton, L. J., MA, 41 West Hill Avenue, Epsom, Surrey.

Gosden, Professor P. H. J. H. MA, PhD, School of Education, The University, Leeds LS2 9JT.

Gough, Professor Barry M., PhD, History Dept, Wilfrid Laurier University, Waterloo, Ontario, Canada N2L 3C5.

Gowing, Professor Margaret, CBE, MA, DLitt, BSc(Econ), FBA, Linacre College, Oxford OX1 1SY.

Graham-Campbell, J. A., MA, PhD, FSA, Dept of History, University College London, Gower Street, London WC1E 6BT.

Gransden, Antonia, MA, PhD, DLitt, FSA, 10 Halifax Road, Cambridge CB4 3PX.

Grant, A., BA, DPhil, Dept of History, The University, Bailrigg, Lancaster LA1 4YG.

Grattan-Kane, P., 12 St John's Close, Helston, Cornwall.

Graves, Professor Edgar B., PhD, LLD, LHD, 318 College Hill Road, Clinton, New York 13323, USA.

Gray, Canon D. C., PhD, MPhil, 1 Little Cloister, Westminster Abbey, London SW1P 3PL.

Gray, Professor J. R., MA, PhD, School of Oriental and African Studies, University of London, London WC1E 7HP.

Gray, J. W., MA, Dept of Modern History, The Queen's University, Belfast BT7 1NN, N. Ireland.

Gray, Miss M., MA, BLitt, 68 Dorchester Road, Garstang, Preston PR3 1HH.

Greatrex, Professor Joan G., MA, PhD, The Highlands, Great Doward, Symonds Yat, Herefordshire, HR9 6DY.

Greaves, Professor Richard L., PhD, 910 Shadowlawn Drive, Tallahassee, Florida 32312, U.S.A.

Greaves, Mrs R. L., PhD, 1920 Hillview Road, Lawrence, Kansas 66044, U.S.A.

Green, I. M., MA, DPhil, Dept of Modern History, The Queen's University, Belfast BT7 1NN, N. Ireland.

Green, Judith A., BA, DPhil, Dept of Modern History, The Queen's University, Belfast BT7 1NN, N. Ireland.

Green, Professor Thomas A., BA, PhD, JD, Legal Research Building, University of Michigan Law School, Ann Arbor, Michigan 48109, U.S.A.

Green, Rev. V. H. H., MA, DD, Lincoln College, Oxford OX1 3DR.

Green, Professor W. A., PhD, Dept of History, Holy Cross College, Worcester, Mass. 01610, U.S.A.

Greene, Professor Jack P., Dept of History, The Johns Hopkins University, Baltimore, Md. 21218, U.S.A.

Greengrass, M., MA, DPhil, Dept of History, The University, Sheffield S10 2TN.

Greenhill, B. J., CB, CMG, DPh, FSA, West Boetheric Farmhouse, St Dominic, Saltash, Cornwall PL12 6SZ.

Greenslade, M. W., JP, MA, FSA, 20 Garth Road, Stafford ST17 9JD.

Greenway, D. E., MA, PhD, Institute of Historical Research, Senate House, Malet Street, London WC1E 7HU.

Gregg, E., MA, PhD, Dept of History, University of South Carolina, Columbia, S.C. 29208, U.S.A.

Grenville, Professor J. A. S., PhD, School of History, University of Birmingham, P.O. Box 363, Birmingham B15 2TT.

GRIERSON, Professor P., MA, LittD, FBA, FSA, Gonville and Caius College, Cambridge CB2 1TA.

Grieve, Miss H. E. P., BA, 153 New London Road, Chelmsford, Essex.

Griffiths, Professor R. A., PhD, University College, Singleton Park, Swansea SA2 8PP.

Grimble, I., MA, PhD, 14 Seaforth Lodge, London SW13 9LE.

Grisbrooke, W. J., MA, Jokers, Bailey Street, Castle Acre, King's Lynn, Norfolk PE32 2AG.

*Griscom, Rev. Acton, MA (address unknown).

Gruner, Professor Wolf D., DrPhil, DrPhil. Habil, Pralleweg 7, 2000 Hamburg 67 (Volksdorf), West Germany.

Gupta, Professor P. S., MA, DPhil, E-75 Masjid Moth, New Delhi, 110048, India.

Guth, Professor D. J., Faculty of Law, University of British Columbia, Vancouver, B.C., Canada V6T 1Y1.

Guy, A. J., BA, MA, DPhil, 145 Queens Road, Wimbledon, London SW19 8NS.

Guy, J. A., PhD, Dept of History, The University, 13–15 Woodland Road, Bristol BS8 1TB.

HABAKKUK, Sir John (H.), MA, DLitt, FBA, Jesus College, Oxford OX1, 3DW.

Haber, Professor F. C., PhD, 3110 Wisconsin Avenue NW, #904, Washington, D.C. 20016, U.S.A.

Hackett, Rev. M. B., OSA, BA, PhD, Curia Generalizia Agostiniana, Via S. Uffizio 25, 00193 Rome, Italy.

Hackmann, Willem D., DPhil, Museum of the History of Science, University of Oxford, Broad Street, Oxford OX1 3AZ.

Haddock, B. A., BA, DPhil, Dept of Political Theory and Government, The University, Singleton Park, Swansea, SA2 8PP.

Haffenden, P. S., PhD, 4 Upper Dukes Drive, Meads, Eastbourne, East Sussex BN20 7XT.

Haigh, C. A., MA, PhD, Christ Church, Oxford OX1 1DP.

Haight, Mrs M. Jackson, PhD, 3 Wolger Road, Mosman, N.S.W. 2088, Australia.

Haines, R. M., MA, MLitt, DPhil, FSA, 20 Luttrell Avenue, London SW15 6PF.

Hainsworth, D. R., MA, PhD, Dept of History, University of Adelaide, North Terrace, Adelaide, South Australia 5001.

Hair, Professor P. E. H., MA, DPhil, School of History, The University, P.O. Box 147, Liverpool L69 3BX.

Hale, Professor J. R., MA, FBA, FSA, Dept of History, University College London, Gower Street, London WC1E 6BT.

Haley, Professor K. H. D., MA, BLitt, 15 Haugh Lane, Sheffield S11 9SA.

Hall, Professor Emeritus A. R., MA, PhD, DLitt, FBA, 14 Ball Lane, Tackley, Oxford OX5 3AG.

Hall, B., MA, PhD, FSA, DD (Hon.), 2 Newton House, Newton St Cyres, Devon EX5 5BL.

Hallam, Elizabeth M., BA, PhD, Public Record Office, Chancery Lane, London WC2A 1LR.

Hallam, Professor H. E., MA, PhD, University of Western Australia, Nedlands, Western Australia 6009.

Hamer, Professor D. A., MA, DPhil, History Dept, Victoria University of Wellington, P.O. Box 600, Wellington, New Zealand.

Hamilton, B., BA, PhD, Dept of History, The University, Nottingham NG7 2RD.

Hamilton, Associate Professor J. S., 1912 Sulgrave Avenue, #1, Baltimore, MD 21209, U.S.A.

Hammersley, G. F., BA, PhD, Dept of History, University of Edinburgh, William Robertson Building, George Square, Edinburgh EH8 9JY.

Hamnett, B. R., BA, MA, PhD, Dept of History, University of Strathclyde, McLance Building, 16 Richmond Street, Glasgow G1 1QX.

Hampson, Professor N., MA, Ddel'U, 305 Hull Road, York YO1 3LB.

Hand, Professor G. J., MA, DPhil, Faculty of Law, University of Birmingham, P.O. Box 363, Birmingham B15 2TT.

Handford, M. A., MA, MSc, 6 Spa Lane, Hinckley, Leicester LE10 1JB.

Hanham, H. J., MA, PhD, The Croft, Bailrigg Lane, Bailrigg, Lancaster LA1 4XP.

Harcourt, Freda, PhD, Dept of History, Queen Mary College, Mile End Road, London E1 4NS.

Harding, Professor A., MA, BLitt, School of History, The University, P.O. Box 147, Liverpool L69 3BX.

Harding, The Hon. Mr Justice H. W., BA, LLD, FSA, 39 Annunciation Street, Sliema, Malta.

Haren, M. J., DPhil, 5 Marley Lawn, Dublin 16, Ireland.

Harfield, Major A. G., BEM, Plum Tree Cottage, Royston Place, Barton-on-Sea, Hampshire BH25 7AJ.

Hargreaves, Professor J. D., MA, 'Balcluain', 22 Raemoir Road, Banchory, Kincardineshire AB3 3UJ.

Harkness, Professor D. W., MA, PhD, Dept of Irish History, The Queen's University, Belfast BT7 1NN, N. Ireland.

Harman, Rev. L. W., 72 Westmount Road, London SE9.

Harnetty, P., BA, AM, PhD, Dept of Asian Studies, University of British Columbia, 1873 East Mall, Vancouver, B.C., Canada V6T 1W5.

Harper Marjory-Ann D., MA, PhD, Silverdale, Disblair, Newmachar, Aberdeen AB5 0RN.

Harper-Bill, C., BA, PhD, 15 Cusack Close, Strawberry Hill, Twickenham, Middlesex TW1 4TB.

Harris, G. G., MA, 4 Lancaster Drive, London NW3.

Harris, Mrs J. F., BA, PhD, 30 Charlbury Road, Oxford OX1 3UJ.

Harris, Professor J. R., MA, PhD, Dept of History, The University, P.O. Box 363, Birmingham B15 2TT.

Harrison, B. H., MA, DPhil, Corpus Christi College, Oxford OX1 4JF.

Harrison, C. J., BA, PhD, Dept of History, The University, Keele, Staffs. ST5 5BG.

Harrison, Professor Royden J., MA, DPhil, 4 Wilton Place, Sheffield S10 2BT.

Harriss, G. L., MA, DPhil, FSA, Magdalen College, Oxford OX1 4AU.

Hart, C. J. R., MA, MB, DLitt, Goldthorns, Stilton, Cambs. PE7 3RH.

Hart, M. W., MA, DPhil, Exeter College, Oxford OX1 3DP.

Harte, N. B., BSc(Econ), Dept of History, University College London, Gower Street, London WC1E 6BT.

Hartley, T. E., BA, PhD, Dept of History, The University, Leicester LE1 7RH.

Harvey, Miss B. F., MA, BLitt, FBA, Somerville College, Oxford OX2 6HD.

Harvey, Margaret M., MA, DPhil, St Aidan's College, Durham DH1 3LJ.

Harvey, Professor P. D. A., MA, DPhil, FSA, Dept of History, The University, 43/46 North Bailey, Durham DH1 3EX.

Harvey, Sally P. J., MA, PhD, Swanborough Manor, Swanborough, Lewes, E. Sussex BN7 3PF.

Haskell, Professor F. J., MA, FBA, Trinity College, Oxford OX1 3BH.

Haskins, Professor G. L., AB, LLB, JD, MA, University of Pennsylvania, The Law School, 3400 Chestnut Street, Philadelphia, Pa. 19104 U.S.A.

Haslam, Group Captain E. B., MA, RAF (retd), 27 Denton Road, Wokingham, Berks. RG11 2DX.

Haslam, Jonathan G., BSc(Econ), MLitt, PhD, 1610c Beekman Place NW, Washington, D.C., 20009, U.S.A.

Hasler, Peter W., BA, MA, History of Parliament Trust, Institute of Historical Research, 34 Tavistock Square, London WC1H 9EZ.

Hassall, W. O., MA, DPhil, FSA, The Manor House, 26 High Street, Wheatley, Oxon. OX9 1XX.

Hast, Adele, PhD, 210 Fourth Street, Wilmette, Illinois 60091, U.S.A.

Hastings, M. M., Guilsborough Lodge, Guilsborough, Northamptonshire NN6 8RB.

Hatcher, M. J., BSc(Econ), PhD, Corpus Christi College, Cambridge CB2 1RH.

Hatley, V. A., BA, ALA, 6 The Crescent, Northampton NN1 4SB.

Hatton, Professor Ragnhild M., PhD, Cand.Mag(Oslo), Dr.h.c., 49 Campden Street, London W8.

Havighurst, Professor A. F., MA, PhD, 11 Blake Field, Amherst, Mass. 01002, U.S.A.

Havinden, M. A., MA, BLitt, Dept of Economic History, Amory Building, The University, Exeter EX4 4QH.

Havran, Professor M. J., MA, PhD, Corcoran Dept of History, Randall Hall, University of Virginia, Charlottesville, Va. 22903, U.S.A.

Hawke, Professor G. R., BA, BCom, DPhil, Dept of History, Victoria, University of Wellington, Private Bag, Wellington, New Zealand.

HAY, Professor D., MA, DLitt, FBA, FRSE, Dr. h.c. Tours, 31 Fountainville Road, Edinburgh EH9 2LN.

Hayes, P. M., MA, DPhil, Keble College, Oxford OX1 3PG.

Hayter, A. J., BA, PhD, Chase House, Mursley, N. Bucks. MK17 0RT.

Hayton, D. W., BA, DPhil, 8 Baker Street, Ampthill, Bedford MK45 2QE.

Hazlehurst, Cameron, BA, DPhil, FRSL, 8 Hunter Street, Yarralumla, A.C.T. 2600, Australia.

Heal, Mrs Felicity, PhD, Jesus College, Oxford OX1 3DW.

Hearder, Professor H., BA, PhD, Dept of History, University College, P.O. Box 78, Cardiff CF1 1XL.

Heath, P., MA, Dept of History, The University, Hull HU6 7RX.

Heathcote, T. A., BA, PhD, Cheyne Cottage, Birch Drive, Hawley, Camberley, Surrey.

Heesom, A. J., MA, Dept of History, The University, 43 North Bailey, Durham DH1 3HP.

Hellmuth, Eckhart H., PhD, German Historical Institute, 17 Bloomsbury Square, London WC1A 2LP.

Helmholz, R. H., PhD, LLB, The Law School, University of Chicago, 1111 East 60th Street, Chicago, Ill. 60637, U.S.A.

Hembry, Mrs P. M., BA, PhD, Pleasant Cottage, Crockerton, Warminster, Wilts. BA12 8AJ.

Hempton, D. N., BA, PhD, Dept of Modern History, The Queen's University, Belfast, BT7 1NN, N. Ireland.

Hendy, M. F., MA, 29 Roberts Road, Cambridge, Mass. 02138, U.S.A.

Henning, Professor B. D., PhD, History of Parliament, 34 Tavistock Square, London WC1H 9EZ.

Hennock, Professor E. P., MA, PhD, School of History, University of Liverpool, P.O. Box 147, Liverpool L69 3BX.

Henstock, A. J. M., BA, Nottinghamshire Record Office, County House, Nottingham NG1 1HR.

Heppell, Muriel, BA, MA, PhD, 97 Eton Place, Eton College Road, London NW3 2DB.

Herde, Professor Peter, PhD, Cranachstr. 7, D 8755 Alzenau, F.R. of Germany.

Herrup, Cynthia B., PhD, MA, BSJ, Dept of History, 6727 College Station, Duke University, Durham, N.C. 27708, U.S.A.

Hexter, Professor J. H., PhD, Dept of History, Washington University, Campus Box 1062, One Brookings Drive, St Louis, Missouri 63130-4899, U.S.A.

Hey, D. G., MA, PhD, Division of Continuing Education, The University, Sheffield S10 2TN.

Hicks, M. A., BA, MA, DPhil, Dept of History, King Alfred's College, Winchester Hampshire, SO22 4NR.

Higham, R. A., BA, PhD, Dept of History and Archaeology, University of Exeter, Queen's Building, Queen's Drive, Exeter, Devon.

Highfield, J. R. L., MA, DPhil, Merton College, Oxford OX1 4JD.

Higman, Professor B. W. C., PhD, Dept of History, University of the West Indies, Mona, Kingston 7, Jamaica.

Hill, B. W., BA, PhD, School of English and American Studies, University of East Anglia, University Plain, Norwich NR4 7TJ.

Hill, J. E. C., MA, DLitt, FBA, Woodway House, Sibford Ferris, nr Banbury, Oxfordshire OX15 5RA.

Hill, Professor L. M., AB, MA, PhD, 5066 Berean Lane, Irvine, Calif. 92664, U.S.A.

*Hill, Miss M. C., MA, Crab End, Brevel Terrace, Charlton Kings, Cheltenham, Glos.

*Hill, Professor Rosalind M. T., MA, BLitt, FSA, Westfield College, Kidderpore Avenue, London NW3 7ST.

Hilton, A. J. Boyd, MA, DPhil, 1 Carlyle Road, Cambridge CB4 3DN.

Hilton, Professor R. H., DPhil, FBA, University of Birmingham, P.O. Box 363, Birmingham B15 2TT.

Himmelfarb, Professor Gertrude, PhD, The City University of New York, Graduate Center, 33 West 42 St, New York, NY 10036, U.S.A.

Hind, R. J., BA, PhD, Dept of History, University of Sydney, Sydney, N.S.W. 2006, Australia.

*Hinsley, Professor Sir (Francis) Harry, MA, OBE, FBA, St John's College, Cambridge CB2 1TP.

Hinton, J., BA, PhD, Dept of History, University of Warwick, Coventry CV4 7AL.

Hirst, Professor D. M., PhD, Dept of History, Washington University, Campus Box 1062, One Brookings Drive, St Louis, Missouri 63130-4899, U.S.A.

Hoak, Professor Dale E., PhD, Dept of History, College of William and Mary, Williamsburg, Virginia 23185, U.S.A.

*Hodgett, G. A. J., MA, FSA, 3 Grafton Mansions, Duke's Road, London WC1H 9AB.

Holderness, B. A., MA, PhD, School of Economic and Social Studies, University of East Anglia, Norwich NR4 7TJ.

Holdsworth, Professor C. J., MA, PhD, FSA, 5 Pennsylvania Park, Exeter EX4 6HD.

Hollaender, A. E. J., PhD, FSA, 119 Narbonne Avenue, South Side, Clapham Common, London SW4 9LQ.

Hollis, Patricia, MA. DPhil, 30 Park Lane, Norwich NOR 4TF.

Hollister, Professor C. Warren, MA, PhD, University of California, Santa Barbara, Calif. 93106, U.S.A.

Holmes, Professor Clive A., MA, PhD, Dept of History, McGraw Hall, Cornell University, NY 14853, U.S.A.

Holmes, G. A., MA, PhD, Highmoor House, Weald, Bampton, Oxon. OX8 2HY.

Holmes, Professor G. S., MA, DLitt, FBA, Tatham House, Burton-in-Lonsdale, Carnforth, Lancs.

Holroyd, M. de C. F., 85 St Mark's Road, London W10.

HOLT, Professor J. C., MA, DPhil, DLitt, FBA, FSA, Fitzwilliam College, Cambridge CB3 0DG.

Holt, Professor P. M., MA, DLitt, FBA, Dryden Spinney, South End, Kirtlington, Oxford OX5 3HG.

Holt, The Rev. T. G., SJ, MA, FSA, 114 Mount Street, London W1Y 6AH.

Honey, Professor, J. R. de S., MA, DPhil, Faculty of Education, Kumamoto University, Kumamoto, 860 Japan.

Hopkin, D. R., BA, PhD, Maesgwyn, Llangawsai, Aberystwyth, Dyfed.

Hopkins, E., BA, MA, PhD, 77 Stevens Road, Stourbridge, West Midlands DY9 0XW.

Hoppen, K. T., MA, PhD, Dept of History, The University, Hull HU6 7RX.

Hoppit, J., MA, PhD, Dept of History, University College London, Gower Street, London WC1E 6BT.

Horrox, Rosemary E., MA, PhD, 61–3 High Street, Cottenham, Cambridge CB4 4SA.

Horton, A.V.M., BA, MA, PhD, 180 Hither Green Lane, Bordesley, Worcs. B98 9AZ.

Horwitz, Professor H. G., BA, DPhil, Dept of History, University of Iowa, Iowa City, Iowa 52242, U.S.A.

Houlbrooke, R. A., MA, DPhil, Faculty of Letters and Social Sciences, The University, Whiteknights, Reading RG6 2AH.

Housley, N. J., MA, PhD, Dept of History, The University, Leicester, LE1 7RH.

Houston, R. A., MA, PhD, Dept of Modern History, The University, St Andrews KY16 9AL.

*Howard, C. H. D., MA, 15 Sunnydale Gardens, Mill Hill, London NW7 3PD.

*Howard, Sir Michael, CBE, MC, DLitt, FBA, Apt. B6, 309 St. Ronan Street, New Haven, Connecticut 06511, U.S.A.

Howarth, Mrs J. H., MA, St Hilda's College, Oxford OX4 1DY.

Howat, G. M. D., MA, MLitt, Old School House, North Moreton, Didcot, Oxfordshire OX11 9BA.

Howell, Miss M. E., MA, PhD, 10 Blenheim Drive, Oxford OX2 8DG.

Howell, P. A., MA., PhD, School of Social Sciences, The Flinders University of South Australia, Bedford Park, South Australia 5042.

Howell, Professor R., MA, DPhil, Dept of History, Bowdoin College, Brunswick, Maine 04011, U.S.A.

Howells, B. E., MA, Whitehill, Cwm Ann, Lampeter, Dyfed.

Hoyle, R. W., BA, DPhil, 13 Parker St., Oxford OX4 1TD.

Hudson, Miss A. M., MA, DPhil, Lady Margaret Hall, Oxford OX2 6QA.

Hudson, T. P., MA, PhD, 23 Glenwood Avenue, Bognor Regis, West Sussex, PO22 8BT.

Hufton, Professor Olwen H., BA, PhD, Center for European Studies, Harvard University, 5 Bryant St, Cambridge, Mass. 02138, U.S.A.

Hughes, Ann L., BA, PhD, Dept of History, The University, Manchester M13 9PL.

Hughes, J. Q., MC, MA, BArch, PhD, Dip. Civic Design, 10a Fulwood Park, Liverpool L17 5AH.

Hull, F., BA, PhD, 135 Ashford Road, Bearsted, Maidstone ME14 4BT.

HUMPHREYS, Professor R. A., OBE, MA, PhD, DLitt, LittD, DLitt, DUniv, 5 St James's Close, Prince Albert Road, London NW8 7LG.

Hunnisett, R. F., MA, DPhil, 23 Byron Gardens, Sutton, Surrey SM1 3QG.

Hunt, K. S., PhD, MA, Rhodes University Grahamstown 6140, South Africa.

Hurst, M. C., MA, St John's College, Oxford OX1 3JP.

Hurt, J. S., BA, BSc(Econ), PhD, Sutton House, Madeira Lane, Freshwater, Isle of Wight PO40 9SP.

*Hussey, Professor Joan M., MA, BLitt, PhD, FSA, Royal Holloway and Bedford New College, Egham Hill, Egham, Surrey TW20 0EX.

Hutchinson, J. H., 182 Burton Stone Lane, York YO3 6DF.

Hutton, R. E., BA, DPhil, Dept of History, The University, 13–15 Woodland Road, Bristol BS8 1TB.

Hyams, P. R., MA, DPhil, Pembroke College, Oxford OX1 1DW.

*Hyde, H. Montgomery, MA, DLit, Westwell House, Tenterden, Kent.

Ingham, Professor K., OBE, MA, MA, DPhil, The Woodlands, 94 West Town Lane, Bristol BS4 5DZ.

Ingram Ellis, Professor E. R., MA, PhD, Dept of History, Simon Fraser University, Burnaby, B.C., Canada V5A IS6.

Inkster, Ian, PhD, Dept of Economic History, University of New South Wales, P.O. Box 1, Kensington, N.S.W. 2033, Australia.

Israel, Professor J. I., MA, DPhil, Dept of History, University College London, Gower Street, London WC1E 6BT.

Ives, E. W., PhD, 214 Myton Road, Warwick CV34 6PS.

Jack, Professor R. I., MA, PhD, University of Sydney, Sydney, N.S.W., Australia.

Jack, Mrs S. M., MA, BLitt, Dept of Economic History, University of Sydney, Sydney, N.S.W., Australia.

Jackman, Professor S. W., PhD, FSA, 1065 Deal Street, Victoria, British Columbia, Canada.

Jackson, J. T., PhD, Dept of History, University College of Swansea, Singleton Park, Swansea SA2 7BR.

Jackson, P., MA, PhD, Dept of History, The University, Keele, Staffs. ST5 5BG.

Jacob, Professor Margaret C., Office of the Dean, Lang College, New School for Social Research, 66 West 12th Street, New York, NY 10071, U.S.A.

Jagger, Rev. P. J., MA, MPhil, PhD, St Deiniol's Library, Hawarden, Deeside, Clwyd CH5 3DF.

Jalland, Patricia, PhD, MA, BA, School of Social Inquiry, Murdoch University, Murdoch, Western Australia 6150.

James, Edward, MA, DPhil, FSA, Dept of History, The University, Heslington, York YO1 5DD.

James, M. E., MA, DLitt, FSA, Middlecote, Stonesfield, Oxon. OX7 2PU.

James, R. Rhodes, MP, MA, FRSL, The Stone House, Great Gransden, nr Sandy, Beds.

James, Thomas B., MA, PhD, 35 Alresford Road, Winchester SO23 8HG.

Jansson, Maija, BA, MA, PhD, 117 Glen Parkway, Hamden, Conn. 06517, U.S.A.

Jarrett, J. D., Withiel House, Withiel, nr Bodmin, Cornwall PL30 5NN.

Jeffery, K. J., MA, PhD, Dept of History, University of Ulster, Shore Road, Newtownabbey, Co. Antrim, N. Ireland BT37 0QB.

Jenkins, Professor B. A., PhD, 133 Lorne, Lennoxville, Quebec, Canada.

Jenkins, Professor D., MA, LLM, LittD, Dept of Law, University College of Wales, Adeilad Hugh Owen, Penglais, Aberystwyth SY23 3DY.

Jenkins, T. A., PhD, 50 Harvey Goodwin Gardens, Cambridge CB4 3EZ.

Jennings, J. R., MA, DPhil, Dept of Political Theory and Government, University College of Swansea, Singleton Park, Swansea SA2 8PP.

Jeremy, D. J., BA, MLitt, PhD, Heatherbank, 2 Old Hall Drive, Whaley Bridge, nr. Stockport, Cheshire SK12 7HF.

Jewell, Miss H. M., MA, PhD, School of History, The University, P.O. Box 147, Liverpool L69 3BX.

Johnson, D. J., BA, 41 Cranes Park Avenue, Surbiton, Surrey.

Johnson, Professor D. W. J., BA, BLitt, Dept of History, University College London, Gower Street, London WC1E 6BT.

Johnson, P. A., MA, DPhil, Dept of Economic History, London School of Economics, Houghton Street, London WC2A 2AE.

Johnston, Professor Edith M., MA, PhD, Dept of History, Macquarie Univ., North Ryde, NSW 2113, Australia.

Johnston, Professor S. H. F., MA, Fronhyfryd, Llanbadarn Road, Aberystwyth, Dyfed.

Jones, A. T., MA, PhD, Institut für Historishe Ethnologie, J. W. Goethe-Universitat, Liebigstr. 41, D-6000 Frankfurt am Main, West Germany.

Jones, C. D. H., BA, DPhil, Dept of History and Archaeology, The University, The Queen's Drive, Exeter EX4 4QH.

Jones, Clyve, MA, MLitt, 41 St Catherines Court, London W4 1LB.

Jones, D. J. V., BA, PhD, Dept of History, University College of Swansea, Singleton Park, Swansea SA2 8PP.

Jones, Dwyryd W., MA, DPhil, Dept of History, The University, Heslington, York YO1 5DD.

Jones, Revd F., BA, MSc, PhD, Casa Renate, Carrer des Pinsas 86, Port de Pollença, Mallorca, Spain.

Jones, G. A., MA, PhD, Monks Court, Deddington, Oxford OX5 4TE.

Jones, G. E., MA, PhD, MEd, 130 Pennard Drive, Pennard, Gower, West Glamorgan.

Jones, Professor G. Hilton, PhD, Dept of History, Eastern Illinois University, Charleston, Ill. 61920, U.S.A.

Jones, Greta J., BA, DipHE, PhD, Dept of History, University of Ulster at Jordanstown, Shore Road, Newtownabbey, Co. Antrim BT37 0QB.

Jones, Professor G. W., BA, MA, DPhil, Dept of Government, London School of Economics, Houghton Street, London WC2A 2AE.

Jones, H. E., MA, DPhil, Flat 3, 115–117 Highlever Road, London W10 6PW.

Jones, Professor I.G., MA, DLitt, 12 Laura Place, Aberystwyth, Dyfed SY23 2AU.

Jones, J. D., MA, PhD, Woodlands Cottage, Marvel Lane, Newport, Isle of Wight PO30 3DT.

Jones, Professor J. R., MA, PhD, School of English and American Studies, University of East Anglia, Norwich NOR 30A.

Jones, Professor M. A., MA, DPhil, Dept of History, University College London, Gower Street, London WC1E 6BT.

Jones, Mrs Marian H., MA, Glwysgoed, Caradog Road, Aberystwyth, Dyfed.

Jones, M. C. E., MA, DPhil, FSA, Dept of History, The University, Nottingham NG7 2 RD.

Jones, The Venerable O. W., MA, 10 Golden Cross, West Cross, Swansea SA3 5PE.

Jones, P. J., DPhil, FBA, Brasenose College, Oxford OX1 4AJ.

Jones, Professor W. J., PhD, DLitt, FRSC, Dept of History, The University of Alberta, Edmonton, Canada T6G 2H4.

Jones-Parry, Sir Ernest, MA, PhD, Flat 3, 34 Sussex Square, Brighton, Sussex BN2 5AD.

Jordanova, Ludmilla J., MA, PhD, MA, Dept of History, University of Essex, Wivenhoe Park, Colchester CO4 3SQ.

Judd, D. O., BA, PhD, Dept of History and Philosophy, Polytechnic of North London, Prince of Wales Road, London NW6.

Judson, Professor Margaret A., PhD, 8 Redcliffe Avenue, Highland Park, NJ 08904, U.S.A.

Judt, T. R., St Anne's College, Oxford OX2 6HS.

Jukes, Rev. H. A. Ll., MA, STh, St Catherines, 1 St Mary's Court, Ely, Cambs. CB7 4HQ.

Jupp, P. J., BA, PhD, 42 Osborne Park, Belfast, N. Ireland BT9 6JN.

Kaeuper, Professor R. W., MA, PhD, 151 Village Lane, Rochester, New York 14610, U.S.A.

Kamen, H. A. F., MA, DPhil, Dept of History, The University of Warwick, Coventry CV4 7AL.

Kanya-Forstner, A. S., PhD, Dept of History, York University, 4700 Keele Street, Downsview, Ontario, Canada M3J 1P3.

Kapelle, Asst. Professor, William E., PhD, History Department, Brandeis University, Waltham, Mass. 00254-9110, U.S.A.

Kealey, Professor Gregory S., PhD, Dept of History, Memorial University of Newfoundland, St John's, Newfoundland. Canada A1C 5S7.

Kedward, H. R., MA, MPhil, 137 Waldegrave Road, Brighton BN1 6GJ.

Keefe, Professor Thomas K., BA, PhD, Dept of History, Appalachian State University, Boone, N.C. 28608, U.S.A.

Keegan, J. D. P., MA, The Manor House, Kilmington, nr. Warminster, Wilts. BA12 6RD.

Keeler, Mrs Mary F., PhD, 302 West 12th Street, Frederick, Maryland 21701, U.S.A.

Keen, L. J., MPhil, Dip Archaeol, FSA, 7 Church Street, Dorchester, Dorset.

Keen, M. H. MA, DPhil, Balliol College, Oxford OX1 3BJ.

Keene, D. J., MA, DPhil, 162 Erlanger Road, Telegraph Hill, London SE14 5TJ.

Kellas, J. G., MA, PhD, Dept of Politics, Glasgow University, Adam Smith Building, Glasgow G12 8RT.

Kellaway, C. W., MA, FSA, 18 Canonbury Square, London N1.

Kelly, Professor T., MA, PhD, FLA, Oak Leaf House, Ambleside Road, Keswick, Cumbria CA12 4DL.

Kemp, Miss B., MA, FSA, St Hugh's College, Oxford OX2 6LE.

Kemp, B. R., BA, PhD, 12 Redhatch Drive, Earley, Reading, Berks.

Kemp, The Right Rev. E. W., DD, The Lord Bishop of Chichester, The Palace, Chichester, Sussex PO19 1PY.

Kemp, Lt-Commander P. K., RN, Malcolm's, 51 Market Hill, Maldon, Essex.

Kendle, Professor J. E., PhD, St John's College, University of Manitoba, Winnipeg, Manitoba, Canada R3T 2M5.

Kennedy, J., MA, 14 Poolfield Avenue, Newcastle-under-Lyme, Staffs. ST5 2NL.

Kennedy, Professor P. M., BA, DPhil, Dept of History, Yale University, 237 Hall of Graduate Studies, New Haven, Conn. 06520, U.S.A.

Kent, Professor C. A., DPhil, Dept of History, University of Saskatchewan, Saskatoon, Sask. Canada S7N 0W0.

Kent, Professor J. H. S., MA, PhD, Dept of Theology, University of Bristol, 3–5 Woodland Road, Bristol BS8 1TB.

Kent, Miss M. R., PhD, BA, BA, School of Social Sciences, Deakin University, Geelong, Victoria, Australia 3217.

Kenyon, Professor J. P., PhD, Dept of History, University of Kansas, 3001, Wescoe Hall, Lawrence, Kansas 66045–2130, U.S.A.

Kenyon, J. R., BA, ALA, The Library, National Museum of Wales, Cardiff CF1 3NP.

Kerridge, Professor E. W. J., PhD, 2 Bishops Court, off Church Road, Broughton, Chester CH4 0QZ.

Kettle, Miss A. J., MA, FSA, Dept of Mediaeval History, The University, 71 South Street, St Andrews, Fife KY16 9AL.

Keynes, S. D., MA, PhD, Trinity College, Cambridge CB2 1TQ.

Kido, Takeshi, MA, PhD, Dept of European History, Faculty of Letters, The University, Hongo, Bunkyo-Ku, Tokyo 113, Japan.

Kiernan, Professor V. G., MA, 'Woodcroft', Lauder Road, Stow, Galashiels, Scotland TD1 2QW.

*Kimball, Miss E. G., BLitt, PhD, 200 Leeder Hill Drive, Apt 640, Hamden, Conn. 06517, U.S.A.

King, Professor E. B., PhD, Dept of History, The University of the South, Box 1234, Sewanee, Tennessee 37375, U.S.A.

King, E. J., MA, PhD, Dept of History, The University, Sheffield S10 2TN.

King, P. D., BA, PhD, Dept of History, Furness College, The University, Bailrigg, Lancaster LA1 4YG.

Kinnear, M. S. R., DPhil, History Dept, University College, University of Manitoba, Winnipeg, Manitoba, Canada R3T 2M8.

Kirby, D. P., MA, PhD, Manoraven, Llanon, Dyfed.

Kirby, J. L., MA, FSA, 209 Covington Way, Streatham, London SW16 3BY.

Kirby, M. W., BA, PhD, Dept of Economics, Gillow House, The University, Lancaster LA1 4YX.

Kirk, J., MA, PhD, DLitt, Dept of Scottish History, University of Glasgow, Glasgow G12 8QQ.

Kirk, Linda M., MA, PhD, Dept of History, The University, Sheffield S10 2TN.

Kirk-Greene, A. H. M., MBE, MA, St Antony's College, Oxford OX2 6JF.

Kishlansky, Professor Mark, Dept of History, University of Chicago, 1126 East 59th Street, Chicago, Illinois 60637, U.S.A.

Kitchen, Professor J. Martin, BA, PhD, Dept of History, Simon Fraser University, Burnaby, B.C., Canada V5A 1S6.

Kitching, C. J., BA, PhD, FSA, 11 Creighton Road, London NW6 6EE.

Klibansky, Professor R., MA, PhD, DPhil, FRSC, 608 Leacock Building, McGill University, P.O. Box 6070, Station A, Montreal, Quebec, Canada H3C 3G1.

Knafla, Professor L. A., MA, PhD, Dept of History, University of Calgary, Alberta, Canada.

Knecht, Professor R. J., MA, DLitt, 79 Reddings Road, Moseley, Birmingham B13 8LP.

Knight R. J. B., MA, PhD, 133 Coleraine Road, London SE3 7NT.

Knowles, C. H., PhD, Dept of History, University College, P.O. Box 78, Cardiff CF1 1XL.

Knox, B. A., BA, BPhil, Dept of History, Monash University, Clayton, Victoria, 3168, Australia.

Koch, Hannsjoachim W., BA, DPhil, Dept of History, The University, Heslington, York YO1 5DD.

Kochan, L. E., MA, PhD, 237 Woodstock Road, Oxford OX2 7AD.

Koenigsberger, Dorothy M. M., BA, PhD, 41a Lancaster Grove, London NW3.

Koenigsberger, Professor H. G., MA, PhD, 41a Lancaster Grove, London NW3.

Kohl, Professor Benjamin G., AB, MA, PhD, Dept of History, Vassar College, Poughkeepsie, New York, 12601, U.S.A.

Kollar, Professor Rene M., BA, MDiv, MA, PhD, St Vincent Archabbey, Latrobe, Pa. 15650, U.S.A.

Korr, Charles P., MA, PhD, College of Arts and Sciences, Dept of History, University of Missouri, 8001 Natural Bridge Road, St Louis, Missouri 63121, U.S.A.

Kossmann, Professor E. H., DLitt, Rijksuniversiteit te Groningen, Groningen, The Netherlands.

Kouri, Professor E. I., PhD, Clare Hall, Cambridge CB3 9AL.

Kramnick, Professor I., PhD, Dean's Office, 201 Lincoln Hall, Cornell University, Ithaca, NY 14853, U.S.A.

Kubicek, Professor R. V., BEd, MA, PhD, Dept of History, University of British Columbia, Vancouver, B.C., Canada V6T 1W5.

Kybett, Mrs Susan, McL, 751 West Morrell Street, Jackson, Michigan 49203, U.S.A.

Lake, P., BA, PhD, Dept of History, Royal Holloway and Bedford New College, Egham Hill, Egham, Surrey TW20 0EX.

Lambert, The Hon. Margaret, CMG, PhD. 39 Thornhill Road, Barnsbury Square, London N1 1JS.

Lambert, W. R., BA, PhD, 47 Llandennis Avenue, Cyncoed, Cardiff CF2 6JF.

Lamont, W. M., PhD, Manor House, Keighton Road, Denton, Newhaven, Sussex BN9 0AB.

Lander, J. R., MA, MLitt, FRSC, 5 Withrington Road, London N5 1PN.

Landes, Professor D. S., PhD, Widener U, Harvard University, Cambridge, Mass. 02138, U.S.A.

Landon, Professor M. de L., MA, PhD, Dept of History, The University of Mississippi, University, Mississippi 38677, U.S.A.

Langford, P., MA, DPhil, Lincoln College, Oxford OX1 3DR.

Langhorne, R. T. B., MA, 15 Madingley Road, Cambridge.

Lannon, Frances, MA, DPhil, Lady Margaret Hall, Oxford OX2 6QA.

Lapidge, M., BA, MA, PhD, Dept of Anglo-Saxon, Norse and Celtic, University of Cambridge, 9 West Road, Cambridge CB3 9DP.

Larkin, Professor M. J. M., MA, PhD, Dept of History, The University, George Square, Edinburgh EH8 9JY.

Larner, J. P., MA, Dept of History, The University, Glasgow G12 8QQ.

Lasko, Professor P. E., BA, FSA, 53 Montagu Square, London W1H 1TH.

Latham, R. C., CBE, MA, FBA, Magdalene College, Cambridge CB3 0AG.

Law, J. E., MA, DPhil, Dept of History, University College of Swansea, Swansea SA2 8PP.

Lawrence, Professor C. H., MA, DPhil, Royal Holloway and Bedford New College, Egham Hill, Egham, Surrey TW20 0EX.

Laws, Captain W. F., BA, MLitt, 23 Marlborough Road, St Leonard's, Exeter EX2 4TJ.

Lead, P., MA, 11 Morland Close, Stone, Staffs. ST15 0DA.

Le Cordeur, Professor Basil A., MA, PhD, Dept of History, University of Cape Town, Rondebosch 7700, Republic of South Africa.

Leddy, J. F., MA, BLitt, DPhil, The Leddy Library, University of Windsor, Windsor, Ontario, Canada N9B 3P4.

Lee, Professor J. M., MA, BLitt, Dept of Politics, The University, 12 Priory Road, Bristol BS8 1TU.

Lehmann, Professor H., DPhil, c/o German Historical Institute, 1759 R.St.N.W., Washington D.C., 20009, U.S.A.

Lehmann, Professor J. H., PhD, De Paul University, 25E Jackson Blvd., Chicago, Illinois 60604, U.S.A.

Lehmberg, Professor S. E., PhD, Dept of History, University of Minnesota, 614 Social Sciences, 267 19th Avenue South, Minneapolis, Minn. 55455, U.S.A.

Leinster-Mackay, D. P., MA, MEd, PhD, Dept of Education, University of Western Australia, Nedlands, Western Australia 6009.

Lenman, B. P., MA, LittD, Dept of Modern History, University of St Andrews, St Andrews, Fife KY16 9AL.

Lentin, A., MA, PhD, 57 Maids Causeway, Cambridge CB5 8DE.

Leslie, Professor R. F., BA, PhD, Market House, Church Street, Charlbury, Oxford OX7 3PP.

Lester, Professor M., PhD, Dept of History, Davidson College, Davidson, NC 28036, U.S.A.

Levine, Professor Joseph M., Dept of History, Syracuse University, Syracuse, New York 13210, U.S.A.

Levine, Professor Mortimer, PhD, 529 Woodhaven Drive, Morgantown, West Va. 26505, U.S.A.

Levy, Professor F. J., PhD, University of Washington, Seattle, Wash. 98195, U.S.A.

Lewis, Professor A. R., MA, PhD, History Dept, University of Massachusetts, Amherst, Mass. 01003, U.S.A.

Lewis, Professor B., PhD, FBA, Near Eastern Studies Dept, Jones Hall, The University, Princeton, N.J. 08540, U.S.A.

Lewis, C. W., BA, FSA, University College, P.O. Box 78, Cardiff CF1 1XL.

Lewis, Professor G., MA, DPhil, Dept of History, University of Warwick, Coventry CV4 7AL.

Lewis, P. S., MA, All Souls College, Oxford OX1 4AL.

Lewis, R. A., PhD, Y Berth Glyd, Siliwen Road, Bangor, Gwynedd LL57 2BS.

Lewis, R. Gillian, St Annes College, Oxford OX2 6HS.

Leyser, Professor K., TD, MA, FBA, FSA, All Souls College, Oxford OX1 4AL.
Liddell, W. H., BA, MA, Dept of Extra-Mural Studies, University of London, 26 Russell Square London WC1B 5DG.
Liddle, Peter H., BA, MLitt, Dipity House, 282 Pudsey Road, Bramley, Leeds LS13 4HX.
Lieu, Samuel N. C., MA, DPhil, FSA. 2a Dickinson Square, Croxley Green, Rickmansworth, Herts. WD3 3EZ.
Lindley, K. J., BA, MA, PhD, Dept of History, New University of Ulster, Coleraine, N. Ireland BT52 1SA.
*Lindsay, Mrs H., MA, PhD (address unknown).
Lindsay, Colonel Oliver J. M., MBIM, Brookwood House, Brookwood, nr Woking, Surrey.
Linehan, P. A., MA, PhD, St John's College, Cambridge CB2 1TP.
Lipman, V. D., CVO, MA, DPhil, FSA, 9 Rotherwick Road, London NW11 9DG.
Livermore, Professor H. V., MA, Sandycombe Lodge, Sandycombe Road, St Margarets, Twickenham, Middx.
Lloyd, Professor H. A., BA, DPhil, Dept of History, The University, Cottingham Road, Hull HU6 7RX.
Lloyd, Simon D., BA, DPhil, Dept of History, The University, Newcastle upon Tyne NE1 7RU.
Lloyd, Professor T. O., MA, DPhil, Dept of History, The University, Toronto, Canada, M5S 1A1.
Loach, Mrs J., MA, Somerville College, Oxford OX2 6HD.
Loades, Professor D. M., MA, PhD, Dept of History, University College of North Wales, Bangor, Gwynedd LL57 2DG.
Lobel, Mrs M. D., BA, FSA, Flat 2, Emden House, Barton Lane, Headington, Oxford, Oxon.
Lockie, D. McN., MA, 25 Chemin de la Panouche, Saint-Anne, 06130 Grasse, France.
Lockyer, R. W., MA, 63 Balcombe Street, London NW1 6HD.
Logan, F. D., MA, MSD, Emmanuel College, 400 The Fenway, Boston, Mass. 02115, U.S.A.
Logan, O. M. T., MA, PhD, 18 Clarendon Road, Norwich NR2 2PW.
London, Miss Vera C. M., MA, 55 Churchill Road, Church Stretton, Shropshire SY6 6EP.
Longley, D. A., MA, PhD, Dept of History, Taylor Building, King's College, The University, Old Aberdeen AB9 2UB.
Longmate, N. R., MA, 30 Clydesdale Gardens, Richmond, Surrey.
Loomie, Rev. A. J., SJ, MA, PhD, Fordham University, New York, NY 10458-5159, U.S.A.
Lottes, Professor G., MA, DPhil, DPhil–Habil, Bucher Str. 74, 8500 Nurnberg 10, West Germany.
Loud, G. A., MA, DPhil, School of History, The University, Leeds LS2 9JT.
Louis, Professor William R., BA, MA, DPhil, Dept of History, University of Texas, Austin, Texas 78712, U.S.A.
Lourie, Elena, MA, DPhil, Dept of History, Ben Gurion University of The Negev, P.O. Box 653, Beer Sheva 84 105, Israel.
Lovatt, R. W., MA, DPhil, Peterhouse, Cambridge CB2 1RD.
Lovegrove, D. W., MA, BD, PhD, Dept of Ecclesiastical History, St Mary's College, The University, St Andrews, Fife KY16 9JU.
Lovell, J. C., BA, PhD, Eliot College, University of Kent, Canterbury CT2 7NS.

Lovett, A. W., MA, PhD, 26 Coney Hill Road, West Wickham, Kent BR4 9BX.

Low, Professor D. A., DPhil, PhD, FAHA, FASSA, Clare Hall, Cambridge CB3 9AL.

Lowe, P. C., BA, PhD, The University, Manchester M13 9PL.

Lowe, R., BA, PhD, Dept of Economic and Social History, The University, 13–15 Woodland Road, Bristol BS8 1TB.

Lowerson, J. R., BA, MA, Centre for Continuing Education, University of Sussex, Brighton.

Lowry, M. J. C., BA, MA, PhD, Dept of History, University of Warwick, Coventry CV4 7AL.

Loyn, Professor H. R., MA, FBA, FSA, Dept of History, Westfield College, Kidderpore Avenue, London NW3 7ST.

Lucas, C. R., MA, DPhil, Balliol College, Oxford OX1 3BJ.

Lucas, P. J., MA, PhD, Dept of English, University College, Belfield, Dublin 4, Ireland.

*Lumb, Miss S. V., MA, Torr-Colin House, 106 Ridgway, Wimbledon, London SW19.

Lunn, D. C. J., STL, MA, PhD, 25 Cornwallis Avenue, Clifton, Bristol BS8 4PP.

Lunt, Major-General J. D., MA, Hilltop House, Little Milton, Oxfordshire OX9 7PU.

Luscombe, Professor D. E., MA, PhD, LittD, FBA, FSA, 4 Caxton Road, Broomhill, Sheffield S10 3DE.

Luttrell, A. T., MA, DPhil, 14 Perfect View, Bath BA1 5JY.

Lyman, Professor Richard W., PhD, 56 Pearce Mitchell Place, Stanford, CA 94305, U.S.A.

Lynch, Professor J., MA, PhD, Inst. of Latin American Studies, University of London, 31 Tavistock Square, London WC1H 9HA.

Lynch, M., MA, PhD, Dept of Scottish History, The University, William Robertson Building, 50 George Square, Edinburgh EH8 9YW.

Lyttelton, The Hon. N. A. O., BA, 30 Paulton's Square, London SW3.

Mabbs, A. W., 32 The Street, Wallington, Herts. SG7 6SW.

Macaulay, J. H., MA, PhD, 11 Kirklee Circus, Glasgow G12 0TW.

McBriar, Professor A. M., BA, DPhil, FASSA, Dept of History, Monash University, Clayton, Victoria 3168, Australia.

McCaffrey, J. F., MA, PhD, Dept of Scottish History, The University, Glasgow G12 8QH.

MacCaffrey, Professor W. T., PhD, 745 Hollyoke Center, Harvard University, Cambridge, Mass. 02138, U.S.A.

McCann, W. P., BA, PhD, 41 Stanhope Gardens, Highgate, London N6.

McConica, Professor J. K., CSB, MA, DPhil, University of St Michael's College, 81 St Mary's Street, Toronto, Ontario, Canada M5S 1J4.

McCord, Professor N., BA, PhD, 7 Hatherton Avenue, Cullercoats, North Shields, Tyne and Wear NE30 3LG.

McCracken, Professor J. L., MA, PhD, 196 Tenth Street, Morningside, Durban 4001, South Africa.

MacCulloch, D. N. J., MA, PhD, FSA, Wesley College, Henbury Road, Westbury-on-Trym, Bristol BS10 7QD.

MacCurtain, Margaret B., MA, PhD, Dept of History, University College, Belfield, Dublin 4, Ireland.

McCusker, J. J., MA, PhD, Dept of History, University of Maryland, College Park, Maryland 20742, U.S.A.

MacDonagh, Professor O., MA, PhD, Research School of Social Sciences, Institute of Advanced Studies, Australian National University, P.O. Box 4, Canberra, A.C.T. 2601, Australia.

MacDonald, C. A., MA, DPhil, Dept of History, University of Warwick, Coventry CV4 7AL.

McDowell, Professor R. B., PhD, LittD, Trinity College, Dublin, Ireland.

Macfarlane, A. D. J., MA, DPhil, PhD, King's College, Cambridge CB2 1ST.

Macfarlane, L. J., PhD, FSA, 43 The Spital, Old Aberdeen AB2 3HX.

McGrath, Professor P. V., MA, Dept of History, University of Bristol, 13–15 Woodland Road, Bristol BS8 1TB.

MacGregor, D. R., MA, ARIBA, FSA, 99 Lonsdale Road, London SW13 9DA.

McGregor, J. F., BA, BLitt, Dept of History, University of Adelaide, SA 5001, Australia.

McGurk, J. J. N., BA, MPhil, PhD, Flat 2, 43 Lulworth Road, Birkdale, Southport, Merseyside, Lancs PR8 2JN.

McGurk, P. M., PhD, 11 Ashdon Close, Woodford Green, Essex IG8 0EF.

McHardy, Alison K., MA, DPhil, Dept of History, Taylor Building, King's College, Aberdeen AB9 1FX.

Machin, Professor G. I. T., MA, DPhil, Dept of Modern History, University of Dundee, Dundee DD1 4HN.

MacIntyre, A. D., MA, DPhil, Magdalen College, Oxford OX1 4AU.

MacKay, A. I. K., MA, PhD, Dept of History, The University, Edinburgh EH8 9YL.

McKay, D., BA, PhD, Dept of International History, London School of Economics, Houghton Street, London WC2A 2AE.

McKendrick, N., MA, Gonville and Caius College, Cambridge CB2 1TA.

McKenna, Professor J. W., MA, PhD, Orchard Hill Farm, Sandown Road, P.O. Box 343, N. Danville, N.H. 03819, U.S.A.

MacKenney, R. S., MA, PhD, Dept of History, University of Edinburgh, William Robertson Building, George Square, Edinburgh EH8 9JY.

MacKenzie, J. MacD., MA, PhD, Dept of History, The University, Bailrigg, Lancaster LA1 4YG.

Mackesy, P. G., MA, DPhil, DLitt, FBA, Leochel Cushnie House, Cushnie, Alford, Aberdeenshire AB3 8LJ.

McKibbin, R. I., MA, DPhil, St John's College, Oxford OX1 3JP.

McKinley, R. A., MA, 42 Boyers Walk, Leicester Forest East, Leicester LE3 3LN.

McKitterick, D. J., MA, Trinity College Library, Cambridge CB2 1TQ.

McKitterick, Rosamond D., MA, PhD, Newnham College, Cambridge CB3 9DF.

Maclagan, M., MA, FSA, Trinity College, Oxford OX1 3BH.

McLean, D. A., BA, MA, PhD, Dept of History, King's College London, Strand, London WC2R 2LS.

MacLeod, Professor R. M., AB, PhD, Dept of History, The University of Sydney, Sydney, N.S.W. 2006, Australia.

McLynn, F. J., MA, MA, PhD, 46 Grange Avenue, Twickenham, Middlesex TW2 5TW.

*McManners, Rev. Professor J., MA, DLitt, FBA, All Souls College, Oxford OX1 4AL.

McMillan, J. F., MA, DPhil, Dept of History, The University, Heslington, York YO1 5DD.

MacNiocaill, Professor G., PhD, DLitt, Dept of History, University College, Galway, Ireland.

McNulty, Miss P. A., BA, 84b Eastern Avenue, Reading RG1 5SF.

Madariaga, Professor Isabel de, PhD, 25 Southwood Lawn Road, London N6.

Madden, A. F., McC, DPhil, Nuffield College, Oxford OX1 1NF.

Maddicott, J. R., MA, DPhil, Exeter College, Oxford OX1 3DP.

Maehl, Professor W. H., PhD, The Fielding Institute, 2112 Santa Barbara Street, Santa Barbara, CA 93105, U.S.A.

Maffei, Professor Domenico, MLL, DrJur, Via delle Cerchia 19, 53100 Siena, Italy.

Maguire, W. A., MA, PhD, 18 Harberton Park, Belfast, N. Ireland BT9 6TS.

Mahoney, Professor T. H. D., AM, PhD, MPA, 130 Mt. Auburn Street, #410, Cambridge, Mass. 02138, U.S.A.

*MAJOR, Miss K., MA, BLitt, LittD, FBA, FSA, 21 Queensway, Lincoln LN2 4AJ.

Malcolm, Dr Joyce L., 1264 Beacon Street, Brookline, Mass. 02146, U.S.A.

Mallett, Professor M. E., MA, DPhil, Dept of History, University of Warwick, Coventry CV4 7AL.

Mallia-Milanes, V., BA, MA, PhD, 135 Zabbar Road, Paola, Malta.

Mangan, James A., BA, PhD, PGCE, ACSE, DLC, 39 Abercorn Drive, Hamilton, Scotland.

Manning, Professor A. F., Bosweg 27, Berg en Dal, The Netherlands.

Manning, Professor B. S., MA, DPhil, Dept of History, New University of Ulster, Coleraine, Co. Londonderry, Northern Ireland BT52 1SA.

Manning, Professor R. B., PhD, 2848 Coleridge Road, Cleveland Heights, Ohio 44118, U.S.A.

Mansergh, Professor P. N. S., OBE, MA, DPhil, DLitt, LittD, FBA, St John's College, Cambridge CB2 1TP.

Maprayil, C., BD, LD, DD, MA, PhD, c/o Institute of Historical Research, Senate House, London WC1E 7HU.

Marchant, The Rev. Canon R. A., PhD, BD, Laxfield Vicarage, Woodbridge, Suffolk IP13 8DT.

Marett, W. P., BA, MA, PhD, BSc(Econ), BCom, 20 Barrington Road, Stoneygate, Leicester LE2 2RA.

Margetts, J., MA, DipEd, DrPhil, 5 Glenluce Road, Liverpool L19 3BX.

Markus, Professor Emeritus R. A., MA, PhD, 100 Park Road, Chilwell, Beeston, Nottingham NG9 4DE.

Marquand, Professor D., MA, Dept of Politics and Contemporary History, The University, Salford M5 4WT.

Marriner, Sheila, MA, PhD, Dept of Economic History, University of Liverpool, Eleanor Rathbone Building, Myrtle Street, P.O. Box 147, Liverpool L69 3BX.

Marsh, Professor Peter T., PhD, Dept of History, Syracuse University, Syracuse, New York 13210, U.S.A.

Marshall, J. D., PhD, Brynthwaite, Charney Road, Grange-over-Sands, Cumbria LA11 6BP.

Marshall, Professor P. J., MA, DPhil, King's College London, Strand, London WC2R 2LS.

Martin, E. W., Crossways, Editha Cottage, Black Torrington, Beaworthy, Devon EX21 5QF.

Martin, G. H., CBE, MA, DPhil, Flat 27, Woodside House, Woodside, Wimbledon, London SW19 7QN.

Martin, Professor Miguel, P.O. Box 1696, Zone 1, Panama 1, Republic of Panama.

Martindale, Jane P., MA, DPhil, School of English and American Studies, University of East Anglia, University Plain, Norwich NR4 7TJ.

Marwick, Professor A. J. B., MA, BLitt, Dept of History, The Open University, Walton Hall, Milton Keynes, Bucks MK7 6AA.

Mason, A., BA, PhD, 1 Siddeley Avenue, Kenilworth, Warwickshire CV8 1EW.

Mason, E. Emma, BA, PhD, Dept of History, Birkbeck College, Malet Street, London WC1E 7HX.

Mason, F. K., Beechwood, Watton, Norfolk IP25 6AB.

Mason, J. F. A., MA, DPhil, FSA, Christ Church, Oxford OX1 1DP.

Mate, Professor Mavis E, MA, PhD, Dept of History, University of Oregon, Eugene, OR 97405, U.S.A.

Mather, Professor Emeritus F. C., MA, 69 Ethelburt Avenue, Swaythling, Southampton SO2 3DF.

Mathew, W. M., MA, PhD, School of English and American Studies, University of East Anglia, University Plain, Norwich NR4 7TJ.

Mathias, P., CBE, MA, DLitt, FBA, Downing College, Cambridge, CB2 1DQ.

*Mathur-Sherry, Tikait Narain, BA, LLB, 3/193-4 Prem-Nagar, Dayalbagh, Agra-282005 (U.P.), India.

Matthew, Professor D. J. A., MA, DPhil, Dept of History, The University, Reading RG6 2AA.

MATTHEW, H. C. G., MA, DPhil, (*Literary Director*), St Hugh's College, Oxford OX2 6LE.

Matthews, J. F., MA, DPhil, Queen's College, Oxford OX1 4AW.

Mattingly, Professor H. B., MA, 40 Grantchester Road, Cambridge CB3 9ED.

Le May, G. H. L., MA, Worcester College, Oxford OX1 2HB.

Mayhew, G. J., BA, DPhil, 29 West Street, Lewes, East Sussex BN7 2NZ.

Mayhew, N. J. MA, 101 Marlborough Road, Oxford OX1 4LX.

Mayr-Harting, H. M. R. E., MA, DPhil, St Peter's College, Oxford OX1 2DL.

Mbaeyi, P. M., BA, DPhil, PO Box 6175, Aladinma Post Office, Owerri, Imo State, Nigeria.

Meek, Christine E., MA, DPhil, 3145 Arts Building, Trinity College, Dublin 2, Ireland.

Meek, D. E., MA, BA, Dept of Celtic, University of Edinburgh, David Hume Tower, George Square, Edinburgh EH8 9JX.

Meller, Miss Helen E., BA, PhD, 2 Copenhagen Court, Denmark Grove, Alexandra Park, Nottingham NG3 4LF.

Melton, Professor F. T., BA, MA, PhD, Dept of History, University of North Carolina at Greensboro, 214 McIver Building, Greensboro, NC 27411-5001, U.S.A.

Merson, A. L., MA, Flat 12, Northerwood House, Swan Green, Lyndhurst, Southampton SO4 17DT.

Metcalf, Professor M, History Dept, 614 Social Sciences, 267 19th Avenue South, Minneapolis, Minn 55455, U.S.A.

Mettam, R. C., BA, MA, PhD, Dept of History, Queen Mary College, Mile End Road, London E1 4NS.

Mews, Stuart, PhD, Dept of Religious Studies, Cartmel College, Bailrigg, Lancaster.

Micklewright, F. H. A., PhD, 4 Lansdowne Court, 1 Lansdowne Road, Ridgway, Wimbledon, London SW20.

Middlebrook, Martin, 48 Linden Way, Boston, Lincs. PE21 9DS.

Middleton, R., BA, PhD, Dept of Economic and Social History, University of Bristol, 13–15 Woodland Road, Bristol BS8 1TB.

Midgley, Miss L. M., MA, 84 Wolverhampton Road, Stafford ST17 4AW.

Miller, Professor A., BA, MA, PhD, Dept of History, University of Houston, Houston, Texas, U.S.A.

Miller, E., MA, LittD, 36 Almoners Avenue, Cambridge CB1 4PA.

Miller, Miss H., MA, Top Meadow, Woodchurch Road, Tenterden, Kent, TN30 7AD.

Miller, J., MA, PhD, Dept of History, Queen Mary College, Mile End Road, London E1 4NS.

Milne, A. T., MA, 9 Frank Dixon Close, London SE21 7BD.

Milne, Miss D. J., MA, PhD, King's College, Aberdeen, AB9 1FX.

Milsom, Professor S. F. C., MA, FBA, 113 Grantchester Meadows, Cambridge CB3 9JN.

Minchinton, Professor W. E., BSc(Econ), 53 Homefield Road, Exeter, Devon, EX1 2QX.

Mingay, Professor G. E., PhD, Mill Field House, Selling Court, Selling, nr Faversham, Kent ME13 9RJ.

Mitchell, C., MA, BLitt, LittD, Woodhouse Farmhouse, Fyfield, Abingdon, Berks.

Mitchell, L. G., MA, DPhil, University College, Oxford OX1 4BH.

Mitchison, Professor Rosalind, MA, Great Yew, Ormiston, East Lothian EH35 5NJ.

Miyoshi, Professor Yoko, 1–29–2 Okayama, Meguro, Tokyo 152, Japan.

Moloney, Thomas M., PhD, 9 Treetops, Sydney Road, Woodford Green, Essex IG8 0SY.

Mommsen, Professor Dr W. J., Leuchtenberger Kirchweg 43, 4000 Dusseldorf-Kaiserswerth, West Germany.

Mondey, D. C., 175 Raeburn Avenue, Surbiton, Surrey KT5 9DE.

Money, Professor J., PhD, 912 St Patrick Street, Victoria, B.C., Canada V8S 4X5.

Moody, Professor Michael E., PhD, 2713 Third Street, La Verne, Calif. 91750, U.S.A.

Moore, B. J. S., BA, Dept of Economic and Social History, University of Bristol, 13–15 Woodland Road, Bristol BS8 1TB.

Moore, Professor D. Cresap, 1 Richdale Avenue, #15, Cambridge, Mass. 02140, U.S.A.

Moore, M. J., Dept of History, Appalachian State University, Boone, NC 28608, U.S.A.

Moore, R. I., MA, Dept of History, The University, Sheffield S10 2TN.

Moore, Professor R. J., DLit, PhD, BA, MA, School of Social Sciences, Flinders University of South Australia, Bedford Park, South Australia 5042, Australia.

Morgan, B. G., BArch, PhD, Tan-y-Fron, 43 Church Walks, Llandudno, Gwynedd.

Morgan, D. A. L., Dept of History, University College London, Gower Street, London WC1E 6BT.

Morgan, David R., MA, PhD, Dept of Politics, Roxby Building, The University, P.O. Box 147, Liverpool L69 3BX.

Morgan, K. O., MA, DPhil, FBA, The Queen's College, Oxford OX1 4AW.

Morgan, Miss P. E., 6 The Cloisters, Hereford HR1 2NG.

Morgan, P. T. J., MA, DPhil, Dept of History, University College of Swansea, Singleton Park, Swansea SA2 7BR.

Morgan, Victor F. G., BA, School of English and American Studies, University of East Anglia, Norwick NR4 7TJ.

Morioka, Professor K., BA, 3–12 Sanno 4 Chome, Ota-Ku, Tokyo 143, Japan.

Morrell, J. B., BSc., MA, Dept of European Studies, The University, Bradford, West Yorkshire BD7 1DP.

Morrill, J. S., MA, DPhil, Selwyn College, Cambridge CB3 9DQ.

Morris, The Rev. Professor C., MA, 53 Cobbett Road, Bitterne Park, Southampton SO2 4HJ.

Morris, G. C., MA, King's College, Cambridge CB2 1ST.

Mortimer, R., PhD, 10 Orchard Avenue, Cambridge CB2 4AH.

Mosse, Professor W. E. E., MA, PhD, Dawn Cottage, Ashwellthorpe, Norwich, Norfolk.

Mullins, E. L. C., OBE, MA, Institute of Historical Research, University of London, Senate House, London WC1E 7HU.

Munro, D. J., MA, 65 Meadowcroft, St Albans, Herts. AL1 1UF.

Murdoch, D. H., MA, School of History, The University, Leeds LS2 9JT.

Murray, A., MA, BA, BPhil, University College, Oxford OX1 4BH.

Murray, Athol L., MA, LLB, PhD, 33 Inverleith Gardens, Edinburgh EH3 5PR.

Murray, Professor B. K., PhD, BA, History Department, University of Witwatersrand, Johannesburg, South Africa.

Myatt-Price, Miss E. M., BA, MA, 20 Highfield Drive, Epsom, Surrey KT19 0AS.

Myerscough, J., MA, 39 Campden Street, London W8 7ET.

Myres, J. N. L., CBE, LLD, DLitt, DLit, FBA, FSA, The Manor House, Kennington, Oxford OX1 5PH.

Nef, Professor J. U., PhD, 2726 N Street NW, Washington, DC 20007, U.S.A.

Nelson, Janet L., BA, PhD, Dept of History, King's College London, Strand, London WC2R 2LS.

Neveu, Dr Bruno, 30 rue Jacob, Paris VIᵉ, France.

New, Professor J. F. H., Dept of History, Waterloo University, Waterloo, Ontario, Canada.

Newbury, C. W., MA, PhD, Linacre College, Oxford OX1 3JA.

Newitt, M. D. D., BA, PhD, Queen's Building, University of Exeter, Exeter, Devon EX4 4QH.

Newman, Professor A. N., MA, DPhil, 33 Stanley Road, Leicester.

Newman, P. R., BA, DPhil, 1 Ainsty Farm Cottage, Bilton in Ainsty, York YO5 8NN.

Newman, R. K., BA, MA, DPhil, Dept of History, University College, Swansea SA2 8PP.

Newsome, D. H., MA, LittD, Master's Lodge, Wellington College, Crowthorne, Berks. RG11 7PU.

Nicholas, Professor David, PhD, Dept of History, Clemson University, Clemson, South Carolina 29634–1507, U.S.A.

Nicholas, Professor H. G., MA, FBA, New College, Oxford OX1 3BN.

Nicholls, A. J., MA, BPhil, St Antony's College, Oxford OX2 6JF.

Nicol, Mrs A., MA, BLitt, Public Record Office, Chancery Lane, London WC2A 1LR.

Nicol, Professor D. M., MA, PhD, 16 Courtyards, Little Shelford, Cambridge CB2 5ER.

Nightingale, Pamela, MA, PhD, 20 Beaumont Buildings, Oxford OX1 2LL.
Noakes, J. D., BA, MA, DPhil, Dept of History, The University, Queen's Bldg, Queen's Drive, Exeter EX4 4QH.
Norman, E. R., MA, PhD, Christ Church College, Canterbury, Kent CT1 1QU.

Obolensky, Professor Sir Dimitri, MA, PhD, DLitt, FBA, FSA, Christ Church, Oxford OX1 1DP.
O'Brien, M. G. R., BA, MA, PhD, Magee College, University of Ulster, Northlands Road, Londonderry, Northern Ireland.
O'Brien, P. K., MA, DPhil, BSc(Econ), St Antony's College, Oxford OX2 6JF.
O'Day, A., BA, MA, PhD, Polytechnic of North London, Prince of Wales Road, London NW5.
O'Day, M. R. (Mrs Englander), BA, PhD, 14 Marshworth, Tinkers Bridge, Milton Keynes MK6 3DA.
*Offler, Professor H. S., MA, 28 Old Elvet, Durham DH1 3HN.
O'Gorman, F., BA, PhD, The University, Manchester M13 9PL.
O'Higgins, The Rev. J. SJ, MA, DPhil, Campion Hall, Oxford.
Okey, R. F. C., MA, DPhil, 10 Bertie Road, Kenilworth, Warwickshire CV8 1JP.
Olney, R. J., MA, DPhil, Historical Manuscripts Commission, Quality House, Quality Court, Chancery Lane, London WC2A 1HP.
Orde, Miss A. W., MA, PhD, Dept of History, University of Durham, 43 North Bailey, Durham DH1 3EX.
Oresko, R. C. J., BA, MA, PhD, 53 Bedford Gardens, London W8 7EF.
Orme, Professor N. I., MA, DPhil, DLitt, FSA, Dept. of History and Archaeology, University of Exeter, Exeter, EX4 4QH.
*Orr, J. E., MA, ThD, DPhil, 11451 Berwick Street, Los Angeles, Calif. 90049, U.S.A.
Ó Tuathaigh, M. A. G., MA, Dept of History, University College, Galway, Ireland.
Outhwaite, R. B., MA, PhD, Gonville and Caius College, Cambridge CB2 1TA.
Ovendale, R., MA, DPhil, Dept of International Politics, University College of Wales, Aberystwyth SY23 3DY.
Owen, A. E. B., MA, 35 Whitwell Way, Coton, Cambridge CB3 7PW.
Owen, Mrs D. M., MA, LittD, FSA, 35 Whitwell Way, Coton, Cambridge CB3 7PW.
Owen, G. D., MA, PhD, 21 Clifton Terrace, Brighton, Sussex BN1 3HA.
Owen, J. B., BSc, MA, DPhil, 24 Hurdeswell, Long Hanborough, Oxford OX7 2DH.

Pagden, A. R. D., MA, DPhil, King's College, Cambridge CB2 1ST.
Palgrave, D. A., MA, CChem, FRSC, FSG, 210 Bawtry Road, Doncaster, S. Yorkshire DN4 7BZ.
Palliser, Professor D. M., MA, DPhil, FSA, Dept of History, The University, Hull HU6 7RX.
Palmer, J. G. MA, MSc(Econ), MPhil, 78 Norroy Road, London SW15 1PG.
Palmer, J. J. N., BA, BLitt, PhD, 59 Marlborough Avenue, Hull HU5 3JR.
Palmer, Professor R. C., PhD, Dept of History, The University, Houston, Texas 77204, U.S.A.
Palmer, Sarah, PhD, MA, MA, Dept of History, Queen Mary College, Mile End Road, London E1 4NS.

Paret, Professor P., Inst. for Advanced Study, School of Historical Studies, Princeton, NJ 08540, U.S.A.

Parish, Professor P. J., BA, Institute of U.S. Studies, 31 Tavistock Square, London WC1H 9EZ.

Parker, Professor N. G., MA, PhD, LittD, FBA, Dept of History, University of Illinois, 309 Gregory Hall, 810 South Wright Street, Urbana, Ill. 61801, U.S.A.

Parker, R. A. C., MA, DPhil, The Queen's College, Oxford OX1 4AW.

Parkes, M. B., BLitt, MA, FSA, Keble College, Oxford OX1 3PG.

*Parkinson, Professor C. N., MA, PhD, 45 Howe Road, Onchan, Douglas, Isle of Man.

Parris, H. W., MA, PhD, Warwick House, 47 Guildhall Street, Bury St Edmunds, Suffolk IP33 1QF.

Parry, G. J. R., MA, PhD, History Dept, Victoria University of Wellington, PO Box 600, Wellington, New Zealand.

Parry, J. P., PhD, Peterhouse, Cambridge CB2 1RD.

Patrick, Rev. J. G., MA, PhD, DLitt, 8 North Street, Braunton, N. Devon EX33 1AJ.

Pavlowitch, Stevan K., MA, LEsL, Dept of History, The University, Southampton SO9 5NH.

Payne, Mrs. Ann, BA, 138 Culford Road, London N1 4HU.

Payne, Professor Peter L., BA, PhD, 68 Hamilton Place, Aberdeen AB2 4BA.

Payton, P. J., Lt-Commander, BSc, PhD, 5 Trecarne View, St Cleer, Liskeard, Cornwall.

Paz, Denis G., PhD, Dept of History, Clemson University, Clemson, South Carolina 29634–1507, U.S.A.

Peake, Rev. F. A., DD, DSLitt, 310 Dalehurst Drive, Nepean, Ontario, Canada K2G 4E4.

Pearce, R. D., BA, DPhil, Dept of History, St Martin's College, Lancaster LA1 3JD.

Pearl, Mrs Valerie L., MA, DPhil, FSA, New Hall, Cambridge CB3 0DF.

Peck, Professor Linda L., PhD, Dept of History, Purdue University, University Hall, West Lafayette, Indiana 47907, U.S.A.

Peden, G. C., MA, DPhil, School of History, University of Bristol, 13–15 Woodland Road, Bristol BS8 1TB.

Peek, Miss H. E., MA, FSA, FSAScot, Taintona, Moretonhampstead, Newton Abbot, Devon TQ13 8LG.

Peel, Lynnette J., BAgrSc, MAgrSc, PhD, 49 Oaklands, Hamilton Road, Reading RG1 5RN.

Peele, Miss Gillian R., BA, BPhil, Lady Margaret Hall, Oxford OX2 6QA.

Pelling, Margaret, BA, MLitt, Wellcome Unit for the History of Medicine, University of Oxford, 45–47 Banbury Road, Oxford OX2 6PE.

Pennington, D. H., MA, Balliol College, Oxford OX1 3BJ.

Perkin, Professor H. J., MA, Dept of History, Northwestern University, Evanston, Illinois 60208-2220, U.S.A.

Perry, Norma, BA, PhD, 2 Crossmead Villas, Dunsford Road, Exeter, Devon, EX2 9PU.

Peters, Professor E. M., PhD, Dept of History, University of Pennsylvania, Philadelphia 19174, U.S.A.

Pettegree, A. D. M., MA, DPhil, Dept. of Modern History, St Andrews University, St Andrews, Fife KY16 9AL.

Pfaff, Professor Richard W., MA, DPhil, Dept of History, Hamilton Hall 070A, University of North Carolina, Chapel Hill, NC 27514, U.S.A.

Phillips, Sir Henry (E. I.), CMG, MBE, MA, 34 Ross Court, Putney Hill, London SW15.

Phillips, Assoc. Professor John A., PhD, Dept of History, University of California, Riverside, Calif. 92521, U.S.A.

Phillips, J. R. S., BA, PhD, FSA, Dept of Medieval History, University College, Dublin 4, Ireland.

Phillips, P. T., PhD, Box 46, Dept of History, St Francis Xavier University, Antigonish, Nova Scotia, Canada B2G 1CO.

Phillipson, N.T., MA, PhD, Dept of History, The University George Square, Edinburgh EH8 9JY.

Phythian-Adams, C. V., MA, Dept of English Local History, The University, University Road, Leicester LE1 7RH.

Pierce, Professor G. O., MA, Dept of History of Wales, University College, P.O. Box 95, Cardiff CF1 1XA.

Piggin, F. S., BA, BD, DipEd, PhD, AKC, Dept of History, University of Wollongong, Wollongong, N.S.W. 2500, Australia.

Pitt, H. G., MA, Worcester College, Oxford OX1 2HB.

Platt, Professor C. P. S., MA, PhD, FSA, Dept of History, The University, Southampton SO9 5NH.

Platt, Professor D. C. St M., MA, DPhil, St Antony's College, Oxford OX2 6JF.

Plumb, Sir John, PhD, LittD, FBA, FSA, Christ's College, Cambridge CB2 3BU.

Pocock, Professor J. G. A., PhD, Dept of History, Johns Hopkins University, Baltimore, Md. 21218, U.S.A.

Pogge von Strandmann, H. J. O., MA, DPhil, University College, Oxford OX1 4BH.

Pole, Professor J. R., MA, PhD, St Catherine's College, Oxford OX1 3UJ.

Pollard, A. J., BA, PhD, 22 The Green, Hurworth-on-Tees, Darlington, Co. Durham DL2 2AA.

Pollard, Professor D. S., BSc(Econ), PhD, Abteilung Geschichte, Fakultät für Geschichtswissenschaft und Philosophie, Univer. Bielefeld, Postfach 8640, 4800 Bielefeld 1.

Polonsky, A. B., BA, DPhil, Dept of International History, London School of Economics, Houghton Street, London WC2A 2AE.

Port, Professor M. H., MA, BLitt, FSA, Dept of History, Queen Mary College, Mile End Road, London E1 4NS.

PORTER, A. N., MA, PhD (*Hon. Secretary*), Dept of History, King's College London, Strand, London WC2R 2LS.

Porter, B. E., BSc(Econ), PhD, Merville, Allan Road, Seasalter, Whitstable, Kent CT5 4AH.

Porter, H. C., MA, PhD, Faculty of History, West Road, Cambridge CB3 9EF.

Porter, J. H., BA, PhD, Dept of Economic History, The University, Amory Buildings, Rennes Drive, Exeter EX4 4RJ.

Porter, S., BA, MLitt, PhD, Royal Commission on the Historical Monuments of England, Newlands House, 37–40 Berners Street, London W1P 4BP.

Post, J., MA, PhD, Public Record Office, Chancery Lane, London WC2A 1LR.

Potter, J., BA, MA(Econ), London School of Economics, Houghton Street, London WC2A 2AE.

Powell, W. R., BLitt, MA, FSA, 2 Glanmead, Shenfield Road, Brentwood, Essex CM15 8ER.

Power, M. J., BA, PhD, School of History, The University, P.O. Box 147, Liverpool L69 3BX.
Powicke, Professor M. R., MA,. 67 Lee Avenue, Toronto, Ontario, Canada, M43 2P1.
Powis, J. K. MA, DPhil, Balliol College, Oxford OX1 3BJ.
Prall, Professor Stuart E., MA, PhD, Dept of History, Queens College, C.U.N.Y., 33 West 42nd Street, New York, NY 10036, U.S.A.
Prentis, Malcolm D., BA, MA, PhD, 3 Marina Place, Belrose, New South Wales 2085, Australia.
Prest, W. R., MA, DPhil, Dept of History, University of Adelaide, North Terrace, Adelaide, S. Australia 5001.
Preston, Professor P., MA, DPhil, MA, Dept of History, Queen Mary College, Mile End Road, London E1 4NS.
*Preston, Professor R. A., MA, PhD, Duke University, Durham, N.C., U.S.A.
Prestwich, J. O., MA, 18 Dunstan Road, Old Headington, Oxford OX3 9BY.
Prestwich, Mrs M., MA, St Hilda's College, Oxford OX4 1DY.
Prestwich, Professor M. C., MA, DPhil, Dept of History, The University, 43/46 North Bailey, Durham DH1 3EX.
Price, A. W., PhD, 19 Bayley Close, Uppingham, Leicestershire LE15 9TG.
Price, Rev. D. T. W., MA, St David's University College, Lampeter, Dyfed SA48 7ED.
Price, F. D., MA, BLitt, FSA, Keble College, Oxford OX1 3PG.
Price, Professor Jacob M., AM, PhD, University of Michigan, Ann Arbor, Michigan 48104, U.S.A.
Price, R. D., BA, DLitt, School of Modern Languages & European History, University of East Anglia, Norwich NR4 7TJ.
Prichard, Canon T. J., MA, PhD, Tros-Yr-Afon, Llangwnnadl, Pwllheli, Gwynedd LL53 8NS.
Prins, G. I. T., MA, PhD, Emmanuel College, Cambridge CB2 3AP.
Pritchard, Professor D. G., PhD, 11 Coed Mor, Sketty, Swansea, W. Glam. SA2 8BQ.
Pritchard, R. J., PhD, 28 Star Hill, Rochester, Kent ME1 1XB.
Prochaska, Alice M. S., MA, DPhil, 9 Addison Bridge Place, London W14 8XP.
Pronay, N., BA, School of History, The University, Leeds LS2 9JT.
Prothero, I. J., BA, PhD, The University, Manchester M13 9PL.
Pugh, M. D., BA, PhD, Dept of History, The University, Newcastle upon Tyne NE1 7RU.
Pugh, T. B., MA, BLitt, 28 Bassett Wood Drive, Southampton SO2 3PS.
Pullan, Professor B. S., MA, PhD, FBA, Dept of History, The University, Manchester M13 9PL.
Pulman, M. B., MA, PhD, AB, History Dept, University of Denver, Colorado 80210, U.S.A.
Pulzer, Professor P. G. J., MA, PhD, All Souls College, Oxford OX1 4AL.

Quested, Rosemary K. I., MA, PhD, 30 Woodford Court, Birchington, Kent CT7 9DR.
Quinault, R. E., MA, DPhil, 21 Tytherton Road, London N19.
QUINN, Professor D. B., MA, PhD, DLit, DLitt, DLitt, DLitt, LLD, MRIA, DHL, Hon. FBA, 9 Knowsley Road, Liverpool L19 0PF.
Quintrell, B. W., MA, PhD, School of History, The University, P.O. Box 147, Liverpool L69 3BX.

Raban, Mrs S. G., MA, PhD, Trinity Hall, Cambridge CB2 1TJ.
Rabb, Professor T. K., MA, PhD, Princeton University, Princeton, N.J. 08540, U.S.A.
Radford, C. A. Ralegh, MA, DLitt, FBA, FSA, Culmcott, Uffculme, Cullompton, Devon EX15 3AT.
*Ramm, Miss A., MA, DLitt, Metton Road, Roughton, Norfolk NR11 8QT.
*Ramsay, G. D., MA, DPhil, 15 Charlbury Road, Oxford OX2 6UT.
Ramsden, J. A., MA, DPhil, Dept of History, Queen Mary College, Mile End Road, London E1 4NS.
Ramsey, Professor P. H., MA, DPhil, Taylor Building, King's College, Old Aberdeen AB9 1FX.
Ranft, Professor B. McL., MA, DPhil, 32 Parkgate, Blackheath, London SE3 9XF.
Ransome, D. R., MA, PhD, 10 New Street, Woodbridge, Suffolk IP12 3DU.
Ratcliffe, D. J., MA, BPhil, PhD, Dept of History, The University, 43 North Bailey, Durham DH1 3EX.
Rawcliffe, Carole, BA, PhD, 24 Villiers Road, London NW2.
Rawley, Professor J. A., PhD, Dept of History, University of Nebraska Lincoln, 612 Oldfather Hall, Lincoln, Nebraska 68588-0327, U.S.A.
Ray, Professor R. D., BA, BD, PhD, Dept of History, University of Toledo, 2801 W. Bancroft Street, Toledo, Ohio 43606-3390, U.S.A.
Read, Professor D., BLitt, MA, PhD, Darwin College, University of Kent at Canterbury, Kent CT2 7NY.
Reader, W. J., BA, PhD, 46 Gough Way, Cambridge CB3 9LN.
Reay, B. G., BA, DPhil, Dept of History, University of Auckland, Private Bag, Auckland, New Zealand.
Reed, Michael A., MA, LLB, PhD, 1 Paddock Close, Quorn, Leicester LE12 8BJ.
Reeves, Professor A. C., MA, PhD, Dept of History, Ohio University, Athens, Ohio 45701, U.S.A.
Reeves, Miss M. E., MA, PhD, 38 Norham Road, Oxford OX2 6SQ.
Reid, B. H., MA, PhD, Dept of War Studies, Kings College London, Strand, London WC2R 2LS.
Reid, F., MA, DPhil, 24 Station Road, Kenilworth, Warwickshire CV8 1JJ.
Reid, Professor L. D., MA, PhD, 200 E. Brandon Road, Columbia, Mo. 65201, U.S.A.
Reid, Professor W. S., MA, PhD, University of Guelph, Guelph, Ontario, Canada N1G 2W1.
Rempel, Professor R. A., DPhil, Dept of History, McMaster University, 1280 Main Street West, Hamilton, Ontario, Canada L8S 4L9.
Renold, Miss P., MA, 51 Woodstock Close, Oxford OX2 8DD.
Renshaw, P. R. G., MA, Dept of History, The University, Sheffield S10 2TN.
Reuter, T. A., MA, DPhil, Monumenta Germaniae Historica, Ludwigstrasse 16, 8 München 34, West Germany.
Reynolds, D. J., MA, PhD, Christ's College, Cambridge CB2 3BU.
Reynolds, Miss S. M. G., MA, 26 Lennox Gardens, London SW1X 0DQ.
Richards, J. M., MA, Dept of History, The University, Bailrigg, Lancaster LA1 4YG.
Richards, Rev. J. M., MA, BLitt, STL, St Mary's, Cadogan Street, London SW3 2QR.
Richardson, P. G. L., BA, PhD, 16 Tanner Grove, Northcote, Victoria 3070, Australia.
Richardson, R. C., BA, PhD, Dept of History, King Alfred's College, Winchester.

Richter, Professor M., DrPhil.habil, Universität Konstanz, Postfach 5560, D–7750 Konstanz 1, Germany.

Riden, Philip J., MA, MLitt, Dept of Extramural Studies, University College, P.O. Box 78, Cardiff CF1 1XL.

Ridgard, J. M., PhD, Dennington Place, Dennington, Woodbridge, Suffolk IP13 8AN.

Riley, P. W. J., BA, PhD, 2 Cherry Tree Cottages, Meal Street, New Mills, Stockport SK12 5EB.

Riley-Smith, Professor J. S. C., MA, PhD, Royal Holloway and Bedford New College, Egham Hill, Egham, Surrey TW20 0EX.

Rimmer, Professor W. G., MA, PhD, University of N.S.W., P.O. Box 1, Kensington, N.S.W. 2033, Australia.

Ritcheson, Professor C. R., DPhil, Dept of History, University of Southern California, University Park, Los Angeles 90007, U.S.A.

Ritchie, J. D., BA, DipEd, PhD, 74 Banambila Street, Aranda, ACT 2614, Australia.

Rizvi, S. A. G., MA, DPhil, 7 Portland Road, Summertown, Oxford.

Roach, Professor J. P. C., MA, PhD, 1 Park Crescent, Sheffield S10 2DY.

Robbins, Professor Caroline, PhD, 815 The Chetwynd, Rosemount, Pa. 19010, U.S.A.

Robbins, Professor K. G., MA, DPhil, DLitt, Dept of History, The University, Glasgow G12 8QQ.

Roberts, J. M., MA, DPhil, Merton College, Oxford OX1 4JD.

Roberts, Professor M., MA, DPhil, DLit, FilDr, FBA, 1 Allen Street, Grahamstown 6140, C.P., South Africa.

Roberts, P. R., MA, PhD, FSA, Keynes College, The University, Canterbury, Kent CT2 7NP.

Roberts, Professor R. C., PhD, 284 Blenheim Road, Columbus, Ohio 43214, U.S.A.

Roberts, Professor R. S., PhD, History Dept, University of Zimbabwe, P.O. Box MP 167, Harare, Zimbabwe.

Roberts, Stephen K., BA, PhD, East View, Iron Cross, Salford Priors, Evesham, Worcs. WR11 5SH.

Robertson, J. C., MA, DPhil, St Hugh's College, Oxford OX2 6LE.

Robinson, F. C. R., MA, PhD, Alderside, Egham Hill, Egham, Surrey TW20 0BD.

Robinson, K. E., CBE, MA, DLitt, LLD, The Old Rectory, Church Westcote, Kingham, Oxford OX7 6SF.

Robinson, R. A. H., BA, PhD, School of History, The University, Birmingham B15 2TT.

Robinton, Professor Madeline R., MA, PhD, 210 Columbia Heights, Brooklyn 1, New York, U.S.A.

Robson, Professor Ann P. W., PhD, 28 McMaster Avenue, Toronto, Ontario, Canada M4V 1A9.

Rodger, N. A. M., MA, DPhil, 40 Grafton Road, Acton, London W3.

*Rodkey, F. S., AM, PhD, 152 Bradley Drive, Santa Cruz, Calif., U.S.A.

Rodney, Professor Emeritus W., MA, PhD, 308 Denison Road, Victoria, B.C., Canada V8S 4K3.

Roebuck, Peter, BA, PhD, Dept of History, New University of Ulster, Coleraine, N. Ireland BT48 7JL.

Rogers, Professor A., MA, PhD, FSA, Ulph Cottage, Church Plain, Burnham Market, Kings Lynn, Norfolk PE31 8EL.

Rogers, N. C. T., BA, PhD, Dept of History, York University, 4700 Keele Street, North York, Ontario, Canada M3J 1P3.

Rogister, J. M. J., MA, DPhil, 4 The Peth, Durham DH1 4PZ.
Rolo, Professor P. J. V., MA, The University, Keele, Staffordshire ST5 5BG.
Rompkey, R. G., MA, BEd, PhD, Dept of English, Memorial University, St John's, Newfoundland, Canada A1C 5S7.
Roots, Professor I. A., MA, FSA, Dept of History, University of Exeter, Queen's Building, The Queen's Drive, Exeter EX4 4QH.
Roper, M., MA, Public Record Office, Chancery Lane, London WC2A 1LR.
Rose, Margaret A., BA, PhD, c/o H.P.S. Faculty of Arts University of Melbourne, Parkville, Victoria 3052, Australia.
Rose, Professor P. L., MA, DenHist (Sorbonne), Dept of General History, University of Haifa, Haifa, Israel.
Rosenthal, Professor Joel T., PhD, Dept of History, State University, Stony Brook, New York 11794, U.S.A.
Roseveare, Professor H. G., PhD, King's College London, Strand, London WC2R 2LS.
Roskell, Professor J. S., MA, DPhil, FBA, The University, Manchester M13 9PL.
Rothblatt, Professor Sheldon, PhD, Dept of History, University of California, Berkeley, Calif. 94720, U.S.A.
Rothermund, Professor D., MA, PhD, DPhil Habil, Oberer Burggarten 2, 6915 Dossenheim, West Germany.
Rothney, Professor G. O., MA, PhD, LLD, St John's College, University of Manitoba, Winnipeg, Canada R3T 2M5.
Rothrock, Professor G. A., MA, PhD, Dept of History, University of Alberta, 2–28 Henry Marshall Tory Building, Edmonton, Alberta, Canada T6G 2H4.
Rothwell, V. H., BA, PhD, History Dept, The University, William Robertson Building, George Square, Edinburgh EH8 9JY.
Rousseau, P. H., MA, DPhil, Dept of History, University of Auckland, Private Bag, Auckland, New Zealand.
*Rowe, Miss B. J. H., MA, BLitt, St Anne's Cottage, Winkton, Christchurch, Hants.
Rowe, W. J., DPhil, Rock Mill, Par, Cornwall PL25 2SS.
Rowse, A. L., MA, DLitt, DCL, FBA, Trenarren House, St Austell, Cornwall.
Roy, I., MA, DPhil, FSA, Dept of History, King's College London, Strand, London WC2R 2LS.
Roy, Professor R. H., MA, PhD, 2841 Tudor Avenue, Victoria, B.C., Canada V8N 1L6.
Royle, E., MA, PhD, Dept of History, The University, Heslington, York YO1 5DD.
Rubens, A., FRICS, FSA, 16 Grosvenor Place, London SW1.
Rubini, D. A., DPhil, Temple University, Philadelphia 19122, Penn., U.S.A.
Rubinstein, Professor N., PhD, 16 Gardnot Mansions, Church Row, London NW3.
Rubinstein, Professor W. D., BA, PhD, School of Social Sciences, Deakin University, Victoria 3217, Australia.
Ruddock, Miss A. A., PhD, FSA, Wren Cottage, Heatherwood, Midhurst, W. Sussex GU29 9LH.
Rudé, Professor G. F. E., MA, PhD, 24 Cadborough Cliff, Rye, E. Sussex TN31 7EB.
Rule, Professor John C., MA, PhD, Dept of History, Ohio State University, 230 West 17th Avenue, Colombus, Ohio 43210-1367, U.S.A.
Rule, J. G., MA, PhD, Dept of History, The University, Southampton SO9 5NH.

Rumble, A. R., BA, PhD, Dip Arch Admin., Dept of Palaeography, University of Manchester, Oxford Road. Manchester M13 8PL.

*RUNCIMAN, The Hon. Sir Steven, CH, MA, DPhil, LLD, LittD, DLitt, LitD, DD, DHL, FBA, FSA, Elshieshields, Lockerbie, Dumfriesshire.

Runyan, Professor Timothy J., Dept of History, Cleveland State University, Cleveland, Ohio 44115, U.S.A.

Rupke, N. A., MA, PhD, History of Ideas Unit, Research School of Social Sciences, Australian National University, GPO Box 4, Canberra, ACT 2601, Australia.

Russell, Professor C. S. R., MA, Dept of History, University College London, Gower Street, London WC1E 6BT.

Russell, Mrs J. G., MA, DPhil, St Hugh's College, Oxford OX2 6LE.

Russell, Professor P. E. L. R., MA, FBA, 23 Belsyre Court, Woodstock Road, Oxford OX2 6HU.

Ryan, A. N., MA, School of History, University of Liverpool, P.O. Box 147, Liverpool L69 3BX.

Ryan, Professor S., PhD, Dept of History, Memorial University, St John's Newfoundland, Canada A1C 5S7.

Rycraft, P., BA, Dept of History, The University, Heslington, York YO1 5DD.

Ryder, A. F. C., MA, DPhil, Dept of History, University of Bristol, 13–15 Woodland Road, Queen's Road, Bristol BS8 1TB.

Sachse, Professor W. L., PhD, 193 Main Street, South Dennis, Ma. 02660, U.S.A.

Sainty, Sir John, KCB, MA, 22 Kelso Place, London W8 5QG.

*Salmon, Professor E. T., MA, PhD, 36 Auchmar Road, Hamilton, Ontario, Canada LPC 1C5.

Salmon, Professor J. H. M., MA, MLitt, DLit, Bryn Mawr College, Bryn Mawr, Pa. 19101, U.S.A.

*Saltman, Professor A., MA., PhD, Bar Ilan University, Ramat Gan, Israel.

Salvadori, Max W., Dr Sc, LittD, 36 Ward Avenue, Northampton, Mass. 01060, U.S.A.

Samuel, E. R., BA, MPhil, Flat 4, Garden Court, 63 Holden Road, Woodside Park, London N12 7DG.

Sanderson, Professor G. N., MA, PhD, 2 Alder Close, Englefield Green, Surrey TW20 0LU.

Sar Desai, Professor Damodar R., MA, PhD, Dept of History, University of California, Los Angeles, Calif. 90024, U.S.A.

Saul, N. E., MA, DPhil, Dept of History, Royal Holloway and Bedford New College, Egham Hill, Egham, Surrey TW20 0EX.

Saunders, A. D., MA, FSA, 12 Ashburnham Grove, Greenwich, London SE10 8UH.

Saunders, D. B., MA, DPhil, 19 Albemarle Avenue, Newcastle upon Tyne NE2 3NQ.

Saville, Professor J., BSc(Econ), Dept of Economic and Social History, The University, Hull HU6 7RX.

Sawyer, Professor P. H., MA, Viktoriagatan 18, 441 33 Alingsas, Sweden.

Sayers, Miss J. E., MA, BLitt, PhD, FSA, University College London, Gower Street, London WC1E 6BT.

Scammell, G. V., MA, Pembroke College, Cambridge CB2 1RF.

Scammell, Mrs Jean, MA, Clare Hall, Cambridge.

Scarisbrick, Professor J. J., MA, PhD, 35 Kenilworth Road, Leamington Spa, Warwickshire.

Schofield, A. N. E. D., PhD, 57 West Way, Rickmansworth, Herts. WD3 2EH.

Schofield, R. S., MA, PhD, 27 Trumpington Street, Cambridge CB2 1QA.

Schreiber, Professor Roy E., PhD, Dept of History, Indiana University, P.O.B. 7111, South Bend, Indiana 46634, U.S.A.

Schreuder, Professor D. M., BA, DPhil, Dept of History, The University of Sydney, N.S.W. 2006, Australia.

Schroder, Professor H.-C., DPhil, Technische Hochschule Darmstadt, Institut fur Geschichte, Schloss, 6100 Darmstadt, West Germany.

Schurman, Professor D. McK., MA, MA, PhD, 191 King Street East, Kingston, Ontario, Canada K7L 3A3.

Schweizer, Karl W., MA, PhD, Dept of Humanities, New Jersey Institute of Technology, Newark, NJ 07102, U.S.A.

Schwoerer, Professor Lois G., PhD, 7213 Rollingwood Drive, Chevy Chase, Maryland 20015, U.S.A.

Scott, Dom Geoffrey, MA, PhD, Dip Theol, Douai Abbey, Upper Woolhampton, Reading RG7 5TH.

Scott, H. M., MA, PhD, Dept of Modern History, The University, St Salvator's College, St Andrews, Fife.

Scott, Tom, MA, PhD, School of History, The University, P.O. Box 147, Liverpool L69 3BX.

Scouloudi, Miss I., MSc(Econ), FSA, 82, 3 Whitehall Court, London SW1A 2EL.

Scribner, R. W., MA, PhD, Clare College, Cambridge CB2 1TL.

Seaborne, M. V. J., MA, Penylan, Cilcain Road, Pantymwyn, Mold, Clwyd CH7 5NJ.

Searle, A., BA, MPhil, Dept of Manuscripts, British Library, London WC1B 3DG.

Searle, Professor Eleanor, AB, PhD, 431 S. Parkwood Avenue, Pasadena, . Calif. 91107, U.S.A.

Searle, G. R., MA, PhD, School of English and American Studies, University of East Anglia, University Plain, Norwich NR4 7TJ.

Seaver, Professor Paul S., MA, PhD, Dept of History, Stanford University, Stanford, Calif. 94305, U.S.A.

Seddon, P. R., BA, PhD, Dept of History, The University, Nottingham NG7 2RD.

Sell, Rev. Professor A. P. F., BA, BD, MA, PhD, Dept of Religious Studies, Faculty of Humanities, 2500 University Drive NW, Calgary, Alberta, Canada T2N 1N4.

Sellar, W. D. H., BA, LLB, 6 Eildon Street, Edinburgh EH3 5JU.

Semmell, Professor Bernard, PhD, Dept of History, State University of New York at Stony Brook, NY 11790, U.S.A.

Serjeant, W. R., BA, 51 Derwent Road, Ipswich, Suffolk IP3 0QR.

Seton-Watson, C. I. W., MC, MA, Oriel College, Oxford OX1 4EW.

Shannon, Professor R. T., MA, PhD, Dept of History, University College of Swansea, Swansea SA2 8PP.

Sharpe, J. A., MA, DPhil, Dept of History, The University, Heslington, York YO1 5DD.

Sharpe, K. M., MA, DPhil, Dept of History, University of Southampton, Highfield, Southampton SO9 5NH.

Sharpe, R., MA, PhD, 35 Norreys Avenue, Oxford OX1 4ST.

Shaw, I. P., MA, 3 Oaks Lane, Shirley, Croydon, Surrey CR0 5HP.

Shead, N. F., MA, BLitt, 8 Whittliemuir Avenue, Muirend, Glasgow G44 3HU.

Sheils, W. J., PhD, Goodricke Lodge, Heslington Lane, York YO1 5DD.

Shennan, Professor J. H., PhD, Dept of History, University of Lancaster, Furness College, Bailrigg, Lancaster LA1 4YG.

Sheppard, F. H. W., MA, PhD, FSA, 10 Albion Place, West Street, Henley-on-Thames, Oxon RG9 2DT.

Sherborne, J. W., MA, 26 Hanbury Road, Bristol BS8 2EP.

Sheridan, Professor R. B., BS, MS, PhD, Dept of Economics, University of Kansas, Lawrence, Kansas 66045, U.S.A.

Sherwood, R. E., 22 Schole Road, Willingham, Cambridge CB4 5JD.

Short, K. R. MacD., BA, MA, BD, EdD, DPhil, 89 Bicester Road, Kidlington, Oxford OX5 2LD.

Shukman, H., BA, DPhil, MA, St Antony's College, Oxford OX2 6JF.

Simpson, D. H., MA, Royal Commonwealth Society, 18 Northumberland Avenue, London WC2.

Simpson, G. G., MA, PhD, FSA, Taylor Building, King's College, Old Aberdeen AB9 2UB.

Simpson, M. A., MA, MLitt, Dept of History, University College of Swansea, Singleton Park, Swansea SA2 8PP.

Sinar, Miss J. C., MA, 60 Wellington Street, Matlock, Derbyshire DE4 3GS.

Siney, Professor Marion C., MA, PhD, 1890 East 107th Street, Apt 534, Cleveland, Ohio 44106, U.S.A.

Sked, A., MA, DPhil, Flat 3, Aberdeen Court, 68 Aberdeen Park, London N5 2BH.

Skidelsky, Professor R. J. A., BA, PhD, Tilton House, Selmeston, Firle, Sussex.

Skinner, Professor Q. R. D., MA, FBA, Christ's College, Cambridge CB2 3BU.

Slack, P. A., MA, DPhil, Exeter College, Oxford OX1 3DP.

Slade, C. F., PhD, FSA, 28 Holmes Road, Reading, Berks.

Slater, A. W., MSc(Econ), 146 Castelnau, London SW13 9ET.

Slatter, Miss M. D., MA, 2 Tuscan Close, Tilehurst, Reading, Berks. RG3 6DF.

Slaven, Professor A, MA, BLitt, Dept of Economic History, University of Glasgow, Adam Smith Building, Glasgow G12 8RT.

Slavin, Professor A. J., PhD, College of Arts & Letters, University of Louisville, Louisville, Kentucky 40268, U.S.A.

Slee, P. R. H., PhD, BA, 10 Burghley Lane, Stamford, Lincolnshire.

Smith, A. G. R., MA, PhD, 5 Cargil Avenue, Kilmacolm, Renfrewshire PA13 4LS.

Smith, A. Hassell, BA, PhD, School of English and American Studies, University of East Anglia, Norwich NR4 7TJ.

Smith, B. S., MA, FSA, Historical Manuscripts Commission, Quality House, Quality Court, Chancery Lane, London WC2A 1HP.

Smith, D. M., MA, PhD, FSA, Borthwick Institute of Historical Research, St Anthony's Hall, York YO1 2PW.

Smith, E. A., MA, Dept of History, Faculty of Letters, The University, Whiteknights, Reading RG6 2AH.

Smith, F. B., MA, PhD, Research School of Social Sciences, Institute of Advanced Studies, Australian National University, G.P.O. Box 4, Canberra, A.C.T. 2601, Australia.

Smith, Professor Goldwin A., MA, PhD, DLitt, Wayne State University, Detroit, Michigan 48202, U.S.A.

Smith, I. R., MA, MA, DPhil, Dept of History, University of Warwick, Coventry CV4 7AL.

Smith, J. Beverley, MA, University College, Aberystwyth SY23 2AX.

Smith, Joseph, BA, PhD, Dept of History, The University, Exeter EX4 4QH.
Smith, Julia M. H., MA, DPhil, Dept of History, Trinity College, Hartford, Conn. 06106, U.S.A.
Smith, Professor L. Baldwin, PhD, Northwestern University, Evanston, Ill. 60201, U.S.A.
Smith, Professor P., MA, DPhil, Dept of History, The University, Southampton SO9 5NH.
Smith, Professor R. E. F., MA, Dept of Russian, The University, P.O. Box 363, Birmingham B15 2TT.
Smith, Richard M., BA, PhD, All Souls College, Oxford OX1 4AL.
Smith, R. J., BSc, PhD, Dept of Surveying, Trent Polytechnic Nottingham, Burton Street, Nottingham NG1 4BU.
Smith, R. S., MA, BA, 7 Capel Lodge, 244 Kew Road, Kew, TW9 3JU.
Smith, S., BA, PhD, Les Haies, 40 Oatlands Road, Shinfield, Reading, Berks RG2 9DN.
Smith, Professor T. A., BSc(Econ), Queen Mary College, Mile End Road, London E1 4NS.
Smith, W. H. C., BA, PhD, Erin Lodge, Symons Hill, Falmouth TR11 2SX.
Smith, W. J., MA, 5 Gravel Hill, Emmer Green, Reading, Berks. RG4 8QN.
Smyth, A. P., BA, MA, DPhil, FSA, Keynes College, The University, Canterbury CT2 7NP.
Smyth, Associate Professor D. P., BA, PhD, Dept of History, University of Toronto, Toronto, Canada M5S 1A1.
Snell, L. S., MA, FSA, FRSA, 27 Weoley Hill, Selly Oak, Birmingham B29 4AA.
Snow, Professor V. F., MA, PhD, Dept of History, Syracuse University, 311 Maxwell Hall, Syracuse, New York 13244, U.S.A.
Snyder, Professor H. L., MA, PhD, 5577 Majestic Court, Riverside, Calif. 92506, U.S.A.
Soden, G. I., MA, DD, Buck Brigg, Hanworth, Norwich, Norfolk.
Soffer, Professor Reba N., PhD, 665 Bienveneda Avenue, Pacific Palisades, California 90272, U.S.A.
Soloway, R. A., PhD, Dept of History, Hamilton Hall, The University of North Carolina, Chapel Hill, NC 27515, U.S.A.
Somers, Rev. H. J., JCB, MA, PhD, St Francis Xavier University, Antigonish, Nova Scotia, Canada.
Somerville, Sir Robert, KCVO, MA, FSA, 2 Hunt's Close, Morden Road, London SE3 0AH.
Sommerville, Johann P., MA, PhD, Dept of History, University of Wisconsin-Madison. 3211 Humanities Building, 455 North Park Street, Madison, Wisconsin 53706, U.S.A.
SOUTHERN, Sir Richard (W.), MA, DLitt, LittD, DLitt, FBA, 40 St John Street, Oxford OX1 2LH.
Southgate, D. G., BA, DPhil, The Old Harriers, Bridford, nr Exeter, Devon EX6 7HS.
Spalding, Miss R., MA, 34 Reynards Road, Welwyn, Herts.
Speck, Professor W. A., MA, DPhil, School of History, The University, Leeds LS2 9JT.
Spencer, B. W., BA, FSA, 6 Carpenters Wood Drive, Chorleywood, Herts. WD3 5RJ.
Spiers, E. M., MA, PhD, 170 Alwoodley Lane, Leeds, West Yorkshire LS17 7PF.
Spinks, Rev. B. D., BA, MTh, BD, Churchill College, Cambridge CB3 0DS.

Spinner, Professor T. J. Jr, PhD, Dept of History, University of Vermont, 314 Wheeler House, Burlington, Vermont 05405, U.S.A.

Spooner, Professor F. C., MA, PhD, LittD, FSA, 31 Chatsworth Avenue, Bromley, Kent BR1 5DP.

Spring, Professor D., PhD, Dept of History, Johns Hopkins University, Baltimore, Md. 21218, U.S.A.

Spufford, Mrs H. M., MA, PhD, LittD, Newnham College, Cambridge CB3 9DF.

Spufford, P., MA, PhD, Queens' College, Cambridge CB3 9ET.

Squibb, G. D., QC, FSA, The Old House, Cerne Abbas, Dorset DT2 7JQ.

Stacey, Assistant Professor R. C., BA, MA, PhD, Dept of History, Yale University, New Haven, Connecticut 06520, U.S.A.

Stachura, P. D., MA, PhD, Dept of History, The University, Stirling FK9 4LA.

Stacpoole, Dom Alberic J., OSB, MC, MA, DPhil, Saint Benet's Hall, Oxford OX1 3LN.

Stafford, Pauline A., BA, DPhil, Athill Lodge, St Helen's Lane, Adel, Leeds LS16 8BS.

Stanley, The Hon. G. F. G., MA, BLitt, DPhil, PO Box 790, Sackville, N.B., Canada EoA 3Co.

Stannage, Associate Professor C. T., PhD, Dept of History, University of Western Australia, Nedlands, Australia 6009.

Stansky, Professor Peter, PhD, Dept of History, Stanford University, Stanford, Calif. 94305-2024, U.S.A.

Stapleton, B., BSc, School of Economics, Portsmouth Polytechnic, Locksway Road, Milton, Southsea PO4 8JF.

Starkey, D. R., MA, PhD, 49 Hamilton Park West, London N5 1AE.

Steele, E. D., MA, PhD, School of History, The University, Leeds LS2 9JT.

Steinberg, J., MA, PhD, Trinity Hall, Cambridge CB2 1TJ.

Steiner, Mrs Zara S., MA, PhD, New Hall, Cambridge CB3 0DF.

Stephens, J. N., MA, DPhil, Dept of History, University of Edinburgh, William Robertson Building, George Square, Edinburgh EH8 9JY.

Stephens, W. B., MA, PhD, FSA, 37 Batcliffe Drive, Leeds 6.

Stephenson, Mrs Jill, MA, PhD, Dept of History, University of Edinburgh, William Robertson Building, George Square, Edinburgh EH8 9JY.

Steven, Miss M. J. E., PhD, 3 Bonwick Place, Garran, A.C.T. 2605, Australia.

Stevenson, David, MA, PhD, Dept of International History, London School of Economics, Houghton Street, Aldwych, London WC2A 2AE.

Stevenson, D., BA, PhD, Dept of History, Taylor Building, King's College, Old Aberdeen AB1 0EE.

Stevenson, Miss J. H., BA, c/o Institute of Historical Research, Senate House, Malet Street, London, WC1E 7HU.

Stevenson, J., MA, DPhil, Dept of History, The University, Sheffield S10 2TN.

Stewart, A. T. Q., MA, PhD, Dept of Modern History, The Queen's University, Belfast BT7 1NN.

Stitt, F. B., BA, BLitt, DLitt, 2 Ashtree Close, Little Haywood, Stafford ST18 0NL.

Stockwell, A. J., MA, PhD, Dept of History, Royal Holloway and Bedford New College, Egham Hill, Egham, Surrey TW20 0EX.

Stone, E., MA, DPhil, FSA, Keble College, Oxford OX1 3PG.

Stone, Professor L., MA, Princeton University, Princeton, NJ 08540, U.S.A.

Storey, Professor R. L., MA, PhD, 19 Elm Avenue, Beeston, Nottingham NG9 1BU.

Storry, J. G., The Eyot House, Sonning Eye, Reading RG4 0TN.
Story, Professor G. M., CM, BA, DPhil, FRSC, FSA, 335 Southside Road, St John's Newfoundland, Canada.
Stourzh, Professor G., DPhil, Brechergasse 14, A-1190 Vienna, Austria.
Stow, G. B., PhD, Dept of History, La Salle University, Philadelphia, Pennsylvania 19141, U.S.A.
*Stoye, J. W., MA, DPhil, Magdalen College, Oxford OX1 4AU.
Strachan, H. F. A., MA, PhD, Corpus Christi College, Cambridge CB2 1RH.
Street, J., MA, PhD, Badgers' Wood, Cleveley, Forton, Garstang, Preston PR3 1BY.
Stringer, K. J., BA, MA, PhD, Dept of History, Furness College, The University, Lancaster LA1 4YG.
Strong, Mrs F., MA, Traigh Gate, Arisaig, Inverness-shire PH39 4N1.
Strong, Sir Roy, BA, PhD, FSA, The Laskett, Much Birch, Herefordshire HR2 8HZ.
Stuart, C. H., MA, Christ Church, Oxford OX1 1DP.
Studd, J. R., PhD, Dept of History, The University, Keele, Staffs. ST5 5BG.
Sturdy, D. J., BA, PhD, Dept of History, New University of Ulster, Coleraine, N. Ireland BT52 1SA.
Supple, Professor B. E., BSc(Econ), PhD, MA, St Catharine's College, Cambridge CB2 1RL.
Sutcliffe, Professor A. R., MA, DU, Dept of Economic and Social History, The University, 21 Slayleigh Avenue, Sheffield S10 3RA.
Sutherland, Gillian, MA, DPhil, MA, PhD, Newnham College, Cambridge CB3 9DF.
Swanson, R. N., MA, PhD, School of History, The University, P.O. Box 363, Birmingham B15 2TT.
Swanton, Professor M. J., BA, PhD, FSA, Queen's Building, The University, The Queen's Drive, Exeter EX4 4QH.
Swart, Professor K. W., PhD, LittD, University College London, Gower Street, London WC1 6BT.
Sweet, D. W., MA, PhD, Dept of History, The University, 43 North Bailey, Durham DH1 3NP.
Sweetman, J., MA, PhD, 98 Kings Ride, Camberley, Surrey GU15 4LN.
Swenarton, M. C., BA, PhD, 10d Barnsbury Terrace, London N1 1JH.
Swift, R. E., PhD, MA, BA, 23 Deansway, Tarvin, nr Chester, Cheshire CH2 8LX.
Swinfen, D. B., MA, DPhil, 14 Cedar Road, Broughty Ferry, Dundee.
Sydenham, Professor Emeritus M. J., PhD, Dept of History, Carleton University, Ottawa, Canada K1S 5B6.
Syrett, Professor D., PhD, 329 Sylvan Avenue, Leonia, NJ 07605, U.S.A.
Szechi, D., BA, DPhil, History Dept, 7030 Haley Center, Auburn University, Alabama 36849-5207, U.S.A.

Taft, Barbara, PhD, 3101, 35th Street, Washington, D.C. 20016, U.S.A.
Talbot, C. H., PhD, BD, FSA, 47 Hazlewell Road, London SW15.
Tamse, Coenraad Arnold, DLitt, De Krom, 12 Potgieterlaan, 9752 Ex Haren (Groningen), The Netherlands.
Tanner, J. I., CBE, MA, PhD, DLitt, Flat One, 57 Drayton Gardens, London SW10 9RU.
Tanner, Rev. N. P., Bth, MA, DPhil, Campion Hall, Oxford OX1 1QS.
Tarling, Professor P. N., MA, PhD, LittD, University of Auckland, Private Bag, Auckland, New Zealand.

Tarn, Professor J. N., B.Arch, PhD, FRIBA, Dept of Architecture, The University, Leverhulme Building, Abercromby Square, P.O. Box 147, Liverpool L69 3BX.

Taylor, Arnold J., CBE, MA, DLitt, FBA, FSA, Rose Cottage, Lincoln's Hill, Chiddingfold, Surrey GU8 4UN.

Taylor, Professor Arthur J., MA, School of History, The University, Leeds LS2 9JT.

Taylor, Rev. Brian, MA, FSA, The Rectory, The Flower Walk, Guildford GU2 5EP.

Taylor, J., MA, School of History, The University, Leeds LS2 9JT.

Taylor, J. W. R., 36 Alexandra Drive, Surbiton, Surrey KT5 9AF.

Taylor, P. M., BA, PhD, School of History, The University, Leeds LS2 9JT.

Taylor, R. T., MA, PhD, Dept of Political Theory and Government, University College of Swansea, Swansea SA2 8PP.

Taylor, W., MA, PhD, FSAScot, 25 Bingham Terrace, Dundee.

Teichova, Professor Alice, BA, PhD, University of East Anglia, University Plain, Norwich NR4 7TJ.

Temperley, H., BA, MA, PhD, School of English and American Studies, University of East Anglia, University Plain, Norwich NR4 7TJ.

Temple, Nora C., BA, PhD, Dept of History, University College, P.O. Box 78, Cardiff CF1 1XL.

Terraine, J. A., 74 Kensington Park Road, London W11 2PL.

Thacker, A. T., MA, DPhil, Flat 1, 6 Liverpool Road, Chester, Cheshire.

Thackray, Professor Arnold W., PhD, E. F. Smith Hall D-6, University of Pennsylvania, Philadelphia 19104, PA, U.S.A.

Thane, Patricia M., BA, PhD, 5 Twisden Road, London NW5 1DL.

Thirsk, Mrs I. Joan, PhD, FBA, 1 Hadlow Castle, Hadlow, Tonbridge, Kent TN11 0EG.

Thistlethwaite, Professor F., CBE, DCL, LHD, 15 Park Parade, Cambridge CB5 8AL.

Thomas, Professor A. C., MA, DipArch, FSA, HonMRIA, Lambessow, St Clement, Truro, Cornwall.

Thomas, D. O., MA, PhD, Orlandon, 31 North Parade, Aberystwyth, Dyfed SY23 2JN.

Thomas, E. E., BA, The Shippen, Pilgrim's Way, Westhumble, Dorking, Surrey RH5 6AW.

Thomas of Swynnerton, Lord, MA, 29 Ladbroke Grove, London W11 3BB.

Thomas, J. H., BA, PhD, School of Social and Historical Studies, Portsmouth Polytechnic, Bellevue Terrace, Southsea, Portsmouth PO5 3AT.

Thomas, Sir Keith, MA, DLitt, FBA, Corpus Christi College, Oxford OX1 4JF.

Thomas, Professor P. D. G., MA, PhD, Dept of History, Hugh Owen Building, University College of Wales, Aberystwyth SY23 2AU.

Thomas, W. E. S., MA, Christ Church, Oxford OX1 1DP.

Thomis, Professor M. I., MA, PhD, University of Queensland, St Lucia, Brisbane 4067, Australia.

Thompson, A. F., MA, Wadham College, Oxford OX1 3PN.

Thompson, C. L. F., BA, Colne View, 69 Chaney Road, Wivenhoe, Essex.

Thompson, Mrs D. K. G., MA, Wick Episcopi, Upper Wick, Worcester WR2 5SY.

Thompson, D. M., MA, PhD, Fitzwilliam College, Cambridge CB3 0DG.

Thompson, E. P., MA, Wick Episcopi, Upper Wick, Worcester WR2 5SY.

THOMPSON, Professor F. M. L., MA, DPhil, FBA, (*President*) Institute of Historical Research, Senate House, London WC1E 7HU.

Thompson, I. A. A., MA, PhD, PhD, Dept of History, The University, Keele, Staffs. ST5 5BG.

Thompson, J. A., MA, PhD, St Catharine's College, Cambridge CB2 1RL.

Thompson, Rev. J., BA, BD, MTh, PhD, 27 Ravenhill Park, Belfast BT6 0DE.

Thompson, R. F., MA, School of English and American Studies, University of East Anglia, Norwich NR4 7TJ.

Thomson, J. A. F., MA, DPhil, The University, Glasgow G12 8QQ.

Thomson, R. M., MA, PhD, Dept of History, University of Tasmania, Box 252C, GPO, Hobart, Tasmania 7001, Australia.

Thorne, C. G., MA, DLitt, FBA, School of European Studies, University of Sussex, Falmer, Brighton BN1 9QN.

Thornton, Professor A. P., MA, DPhil, University College, University of Toronto, Toronto, Canada, M5S 1A1.

Throup, D. W., MA, PhD, MSc, 232 Church Plantations, Keele, Staffordshire ST5 5AX.

*Thrupp, Professor S. L., MA, PhD, 57 Balsam Lane, Princeton, New Jersey 08540, U.S.A.

Thurlow, The Very Rev. A. G. G., MA, FSA, 2 East Pallant, Chichester, West Sussex PO19 1TR.

Tite, C. G. C., BA, MA, PhD, 12 Montagu Square, London W1H 1RB.

Todd, Associate Professor Margo, AB, MA, PhD, Dept of History, Vanderbilt University, Nashville, TN 37235, U.S.A.

Tomizawa, Professor Reigan, MA, DLitt, Dept of History, Kansai University, 3–10–12 Hiyoshidai, Taksukishi, Osaka 569, Japan.

Tomkeieff, Mrs O. G., MA, LLB, 88 Moorside North, Newcastle upon Tyne NE4 9DU.

Tomlinson, H. C., BA, DPhil, The Cathedral School, Old College, 29 Castle Street, Hereford HR1 2NN.

Tonkin, J. M., BA, BD, PhD, Dept of History, University of Western Australia, Nedlands, Western Australia 6009.

Townshend, C. J. N., MA, DPhil, Dept of Modern History, The University, Keele, Staffs. ST5 5BG.

Trainor, L., BA, PhD, History Dept, University of Canterbury, Private Bag, Christchurch, New Zealand.

Trebilcock, R. C., MA, Pembroke College, Cambridge CB2 1RF.

Tsitsonis, S. E., PhD, 31 Samara Street, Paleo Psyhico (15452), Athens, Greece.

Tuck, J. A., MA, PhD, Dept of History, The University, 13–15 Woodland Road, Bristol BS8 1TB.

Turnbull, Professor Constance M., BA, PhD, 36 Stoneleigh Avenue, Coventry, CV5 6BZ.

Turner, Mrs Barbara D. M. C., BA, 27 St Swithuns Street, Winchester, Hampshire.

Turner, G. L'E., FSA, DSc, The Old Barn, Mill Street, Islip, Oxford OX5 2SY.

Turner, J. A., MA, DPhil, 31 Devereux Road, London SW11 6JR.

Turner, Professor Ralph V., MA, PhD, History Department, Florida State University, Tallahassee, Florida 32306-2029, U.S.A.

Tyacke, N. R. N., MA, DPhil, 1a Spencer Rise, London NW5.

Tyerman, C. J., MA, DPhil, Exeter College, Oxford OX1 3DP.

Ugawa, Professor K., BA, MA, PhD, Minami-Ogikubo, 1-chome 25-15, Suginami-Ku, Tokyo 167, Japan.

Underdown, Professor David, MA, BLitt, DLitt, Dept of History, Yale University, P.O. Box 1504A, Yale Station, New Haven, Conn. 06520, U.S.A.
Upton, A. F., MA, 5 West Acres, St Andrews, Fife KY16 9UD.

Vaisey, D. G., MA, FSA, 12 Hernes Road, Oxford.
Vale, M. G. A., MA, DPhil, St John's College, Oxford OX1 3JP.
Van Caenegem, Professor R. C., LLD, PhD, Veurestraat 47, B9821 Gent-Afsnee, Belgium.
Van Houts, Elisabeth, DLitt, Girton College, Cambridge CB3 0JG.
Van Roon, Professor Ger, Dept of Contemporary History, Vrije Universiteit, Amsterdam, Koningslaan 31–33, The Netherlands.
Vann, Professor Richard T., PhD, Dept of History, Wesleyan University, Middletown, Conn. 06457, U.S.A.
*Varley, Mrs J., MA, FSA, 164 Nettleham Road, Lincoln.
Vaughan, Sir (G) Edgar, KBE, MA, 9 The Glade, Sandy Lane, Cheam, Sutton, Surrey SM2 7NZ.
Veale, Elspeth M., BA, PhD, 31 St Mary's Road, Wimbledon, London SW19 7BP.
Véliz, Professor C., BSc, PhD, Dept. of Sociology, La Trobe University, Melbourne, Victoria 3083, Australia.
Vessey, D. W. T. C., MA, PhD, Dept of Classics, King's College London, Strand, London WC2R 2LS.
Vile, Professor M. J. C., Boston University, 43 Harrington Gardens, Kensington, London SW7 4JU.
Vincent, D. M., BA, PhD, Dept of History, The University, Keele, Staffs ST5 5BG.
Vincent, Professor J. R., MA, PhD, Dept of History, The University, 13 Woodland Road, Bristol BS8 1TB.
Virgoe, R., BA, PhD, School of English and American Studies, University of East Anglia, Norwich NR4 7TJ.

Waddell, Professor D. A. G., MA, DPhil, Dept of History, University of Stirling, Stirling FK9 4LA.
*Wagner, Sir Anthony (R.), KCVO, MA, DLitt, FSA, College of Arms, Queen Victoria Street, London EC4.
Waites, B. F., MA, FRGS, 6 Chater Road, Oakham, Leics. LE15 6RY.
Walford, A. J., MA, PhD, FLA, 45 Parkside Drive, Watford, Herts WD1 3AU.
Walker, Rev. Canon D. G., DPhil, FSA, University College of Swansea, Swansea SA2 8PP.
Walker, G., BA, PhD, Dept of English, University of Queensland, St Lucia, Brisbane, Queensland 4067, Australia.
Walker, Professor Sue S., MA, PhD, History Department, Northeastern Illinois University, Chicago, Illinois 60625, U.S.A.
Walkowitz, Professor Judith R., PhD, 133 W. 17th Street, Apt 5D, New York, NY 10011, U.S.A.
Wallace, Professor W. V., MA, Institute of Soviet and East European Studies, University of Glasgow, 9–11 Southpark Terrace, Glasgow G12 8LQ.
Waller, P. J., BA, MA, Merton College, Oxford OX1 4JD.
Wallis, Miss H. M., OBE, MA, DPhil, FSA, 96 Lord's View, St John's Wood Road, London NW8 7HG.
Wallis, P. J., MA, 43 Briarfield Road, Newcastle upon Tyne NE3 3UH.
Walne, P., MA, FSA, County Record Office, County Hall, Hertford.

Walton, J. K., BA, PhD, Dept of History, Furness College, The University, Lancaster LA1 4YG.

Walvin, J., BA, MA, DPhil, Dept of History, The University, Heslington, York YO1 5DD.

Wang, Professor Rong-tang, BA, Dept of History, Liaoning University, Shen-yang, People's Republic of China.

Wangermann, Professor E., MA, DPhil, Institut f. Geschichte, Universität Salzburg, A-5020 Salzburg, Mirabellplatz 1, Germany.

Wanklyn, M. D., BA, MA, PhD, Dept of Arts, The Polytechnic, Wulfruna Street, Wolverhampton, West Midlands.

Ward, Jennifer, C., MA, PhD, 51 Hartswood Road, Brentwood, Essex CM14 5AG.

Ward, Professor W. R., DPhil, 21 Grenehurst Way, The Village, Petersfield, Hampshire GU31 4AZ.

Warner, Professor G., MA, Arts Faculty, The Open University, Walton Hall, Milton Keynes MK7 6AA.

Warren, A. J., MA, DPhil, Vanbrugh Provost's House, 1 Bleachfield, Heslington, York YO1 5DD.

Warren, Professor W. L., MA, DPhil, FRSL, Dept of Modern History, The Queen's University, Belfast, N. Ireland BT7 1NN.

Washbrook, D. A., BA, MA, PhD, 29 Gretna Road, Green Lane, Coventry, West Midlands.

Wasserstein, Professor B. M. J., MA, DPhil, Dept of History, Brandeis University, Waltham, Mass. 02254, U.S.A.

Wasserstein, D. J., MA, DPhil, Dept of Semitic Languages, University College, Belfield, Dublin 4, Ireland.

*Waters, Lt-Commander D. W., RN, FSA, Jolyons, Bury, nr Pulborough, W. Sussex.

Wathey, A. B., MA, DPhil, Dept of Music, University of Lancaster, Bailrigg, Lancaster LA1 4YN.

Watkin, The Rt Rev. Abbot Aelred, OSB, MA, FSA, St Benet's, Beccles, Suffolk NR34 9NR.

WATSON, Professor A. G., MA, DLit, BLitt, FSA (*Hon Librarian*), University College London, Gower Street, London WC1E 6BT.

Watson, D. R., MA, BPhil, Dept of Modern History, The University, Dundee DD1 4HN.

Watt, Professor D. C., MA, London School of Economic, Houghton Street, London WC2A 2AE.

Watt, Professor D. E. R., MA, DPhil, St John's House, University of St Andrews, c/o 71 South Street, St Andrews KY16 9QW.

Watt, Professor J. A., BA, PhD, Dept of History, The University, Newcastle upon Tyne NE1 7RU.

Watts, D. G., MA, BLitt, 34 Greenbank Crescent, Bassett, Southampton SO1 7FQ.

Watts, M. R., BA, DPhil, Dept of History, The University, University Park, Nottingham NG7 2RD.

Webb, Professor Colin de B., BA, MA, University of Natal, PO Box 375, Pietermaritzburg 3200, S. Africa.

Webb, J. G., MA, 11 Blount Road, Pembroke Park, Old Portsmouth, Hampshire PO1 2TD.

Webb, Professor R. K., PhD, 3309 Highland Place NW, Washington, D.C. 20008, U.S.A.

Webster (A.) Bruce, MA, FSA, 5 The Terrace, St Stephens, Canterbury.

Webster, C., MA, DSc, FBA, Corpus Christi College, Oxford OX1 4JF.

Wedgwood, Dame (C.) Veronica, OM, DBE, MA, LittD, DLitt, LLD, Whitegate, Alciston, nr Polegate, Sussex.

Weinbaum, Professor M., PhD, 133–33 Sanford Avenue, Flushing, N.Y. 11355, U.S.A.

Weinstock, Miss M. B., MA, 26 Way View Crescent, Broadway, Weymouth, Dorset.

Wellenreuther, H., PhD, 33 Merkel Str., 34 Gottingen, Germany.

Wells, R. A. E., BA, DPhil, Dept of Humanities, Brighton Polytechnic, Falmer, Brighton, Sussex.

Wende, Professor P. P., DPhil, Historisches Seminar der Johann Wolfgang Goethe-Universtat, Senckenberganlage 31, Postfach 11 19 32, D–6000 Frankfurt am Main 11, West Germany.

Wendt, Professor Bernd Jurgen, DrPhil, Beim Andreasbrunnen 8, 2 Hamburg 20, West Germany.

Wernham, Professor R. B., MA, Marine Cottage, 63 Hill Head Road, Hill Head, Fareham, Hants.

*Weske, Mrs. Dorothy B., AM, PhD, Oakwood, Sandy Spring, Maryland 20860, U.S.A.

West, Professor F. J., PhD, Pro Vice Chancellor's Office, Deakin University, Victoria 3217, Australia.

Weston, Professor Corinne C., PhD, 200 Central Park South, New York, NY 10019, U.S.A.

Whaley, Joachim, MA, PhD, Gonville and Caius College, Cambridge CB2 1TA.

Whatley, C. A., BA, PhD, Dept of Modern History, The University, Dundee DD1 4HN.

White, Rev. B. R., MA DPhil, 55 St Giles', Regent's Park College, Oxford OX1 2LB.

White, G. J., MA, PhD, Chester College, Cheyney Road, Chester CH1 4BJ.

Whiteman, Miss E. A. O., MA, DPhil, FSA, Lady Margaret Hall, Oxford OX2 6QA.

Whiting, J. R. S., MA, DLitt, 15 Lansdown Parade, Cheltenham, Glos.

Whiting, R. C., MA, DPhil, School of History, The University, Leeds LS2 9JT.

Whittam, J. R., MA, BPhil, PhD, Dept of History, University of Bristol, 13–15 Woodland Road, Bristol BS8 1TB.

Wickham, C. J., MA, DPhil, School of History, The University, P.O. Box 363, Birmingham B15 2TT.

Wiener, Professor J. H., BA, PhD, Dept of History, City College of New York, Convent Avenue at 138th Street, NY 10031, U.S.A.

Wiener, Professor M. J., PhD, Dept of History, Rice University, Houston, Texas 77251, U.S.A.

Wilkie, Rev. W., MA, PhD, Dept of History, Loras College, Dubuque, Iowa 52001, U.S.A.

Wilks, Professor M. J., MA, PhD, Dept of History, Birkbeck College, Malet Street, London WC1E 7HX.

*Willan, Professor T. S., MA, DPhil, 3 Raynham Avenue, Didsbury, Manchester M20 0BW.

Williams, D., MA, PhD, DPhil, University of Calgary, Calgary, Alberta, Canada T2N 1N4.

Williams, Daniel T., BA, PhD, Dept of History, The University, Leicester LE1 7RH.

Williams, Sir Edgar (T.), CB, CBE, DSO, MA, 94 Lonsdale Road, Oxford OX2 7ER.

Williams, (Elisabeth) Ann, BA, PhD, 77 Gordon Road, Wanstead, London E11 2RA.

Williams, Gareth W., MA, MSc(Econ), MA, Dept of History, Hugh Owen Building, University College of Wales, Aberystwyth SY23 3DY.

Williams, Professor Glanmor, MA, DLitt, 11 Grosvenor Road, Swansea SA2 0SP.

Williams, Professor Glyndwr, BA, PhD, Dept of History, Queen Mary College, Mile End Road, London E1 4NS.

Williams, Professor G. A., MA, PhD, 66 De Burgh Street, Cardiff CF1 8LD.

Williams, J. A., MA, BSc(Econ), 44 Pearson Park, Hull, HU5 2TG.

Williams, J. D., BA, MA, PhD, 56 Spurgate, Hutton Mount, Brentwood, Essex CM13 2JT.

Williams, Patrick L, BA, PhD, 30 Andover Road, Southsea, Hants. PO4 9QG.

Williams, P. H., MA, DPhil, New College, Oxford OX1 3BN.

Williams, T. I., MA, DPhil, 20 Blenheim Drive, Oxford OX2 8DG.

Williamson, P. A., PhD, Dept of History, The University, 43/46 North Bailey, Durham DH1 3EX.

Willmott, H. P. MA, 13 Barnway, Englefield Green, Egham, Surrey TW20 0QU.

WILSON, Professor C. H., CBE, MA, LittD, DLitt, DLitt, DLitt, FBA, Jesus College, Cambridge CB5 8BL.

Wilson, Sir David M., MA, LittD, FilDr, DrPhil, FBA, FSA, The Director's Residence, The British Museum, London WC1B 3DG.

Wilson, H. S., BA, BLitt, Dept of History, The University, Heslington, York YO1 5DD.

Wilson, R. G., BA, PhD, University of East Anglia, School of Social Studies, University Plain, Norwich NR4 7TJ.

Wilson, Professor T. G., MA, DPhil, Dept of History, University of Adelaide, Adelaide, South Australia.

Winch, Professor D. N., PhD, BSc(Econ), FBA, University of Sussex, Brighton BN1 9QN.

Winks, Professor R. W. E., MA, PhD, 648 Berkeley College, Yale University, New Haven, Conn. 06520, U.S.A.

Winstanley, M. J., BA, MA, Dept of History, Furness College, The University, Bailrigg, Lancaster LA1 4YG.

Winter, J. M., BA, PhD, Pembroke College, Cambridge CB2 1RF.

Wiswall, Frank L., Jr., BA, JuD, PhD, Meadow Farm, Castine, Maine 04421 U.S.A.

Withrington, D. J., MA, MEd, Dept of History, University of Aberdeen, Taylor Building, King's College, Old Aberdeen AB9 2UB.

Wong, John Yue-Wo, BA, DPhil, Dept of History, University of Sydney, N.S.W., Australia 2006.

*Wood, Rev. A. Skevington, PhD, 17 Dalewood Road, Sheffield S8 0EB.

Wood, Diana, BA, PhD, 8 Bartlemas Close, Oxford OX4 2AE.

Wood, I. N., MA, DPhil, School of History, The University, Leeds LS2 9JT.

Wood, Mrs S. M., MA, BLitt, Greengables, Eardisley, Herefordshire HR3 6PQ.

Woolf, Professor, S. J., MA, DPhil, Dept of History, University of Essex, Wivenhoe Park, Colchester CO4 3SQ.

Woolrych, Professor A. H., BLitt, MA, DLitt, FBA, Patchetts, Caton, Lancaster LA2 9QN.

Wootton, Professor D. R. J., Dept of Political History, University of Victoria, PO Box 1700, Victoria, B.C., Canada V8W 2Y2.

WORDEN, A. B., MA, DPhil (*Literary Director*), St Edmund Hall, Oxford OX1 4AR.

Wordie, James R., MA, PhD, St. Andrew's Hall, Redlands Road, Reading, Berks. RG1 5EY.

Wormald, B. H. G., MA, Peterhouse, Cambridge CB2 1RD.

Wormald, C. Patrick, MA, 60 Hill Top Road, Oxford OX4 1PE.

Wormald, Jennifer, MA, PhD, St Hilda's College, Oxford OX4 1DY.

Wortley, Rev. Professor J. T., MA, PhD, DD, History Dept, University of Manitoba, Winnipeg, Manitoba, Canada R3T 2N2.

Wright, A. D., MA, DPhil, School of History, The University, Leeds LS2 9JT.

Wright, C. J., MA, PhD, 8 Grove Road, East Molesey, Surrey KT8 9JS.

Wright, D. G., BA, PhD, Dip Ed. 9 Victoria Park, Shipley, West Yorkshire BD18 4RL.

Wright, Professor E., MA, Institute of United States Studies, 31 Tavistock Square, London WC1H 9EZ.

Wright, Rev. Professor J. Robert, DPhil, General Theological Seminary, 175 Ninth Avenue, New York, NY 10011, U.S.A.

Wright, Professor Maurice W., BA, DPhil, Dept of Government, Dover Street, Manchester M13 9PL.

Wrightson, K., MA, PhD, Jesus College, Cambridge CB5 8BL.

Wrigley, C. J., BA, PhD, Dept of History, The University, University Park, Nottingham NG7 2RD.

Wroughton, J. P., MA, 6 Ormonde House, Sion Hill, Bath BA1 2UN.

Yale, D. E. C., MA, LLB, FBA, Christ's College, Cambridge CB2 3BU.

Yates, W. N., MA, Kent Archives Office, County Hall, Maidstone, Kent ME14 1XH.

Yorke, Barbara A. E., BA, PhD, King Alfred's College of Higher Education, Sparkford Road, Winchester SO22 4NR.

Youings, Professor Joyce A., BA, PhD, 5 Silver Street, Thorberton, Exeter EX5 5LT.

Young, J. W., BA, PhD, Dept of International History, London School of Economics, Houghton Street, London WC2A 2 AE.

Young, K. G., BSc(Econ), MSc, PhD, (address unknown).

Young, Mrs Susan H. H., BA, 78 Holland Road, Ampthill, Beds. MK45 2RS.

Youngs, Professor F. A., Jr, 2901 South Carolina Avenue, New Orleans, Louisiana 70118-4391, U.S.A.

Zagorin, Professor P., PhD, Dept of History, College of Arts and Science, University of Rochester, River Campus Station, Rochester, NY 14627, U.S.A.

Zeldin, T., MA, DPhil, St Antony's College, Oxford OX2 6JF.

Zeman, Zbynek A. B., MA, DPhil, St Edmund Hall, Oxford OX1 4AR.

Ziegler, P. S., FRSL, 22 Cottesmore Gardens, London W8.

ASSOCIATES OF THE
ROYAL HISTORICAL SOCIETY

Abela, Major A. E., MBE, 21 Borg Olivier Street, Sliema, Malta.
Addy, J., MA, PhD, 66 Long Lane, Clayton West, Huddersfield, HD8 9PR.
Aitken, Rev. Leslie R., MBE, 36 Ethelbert Road, Birchington, Kent CT7 9PY.
Ayrton, M. McI., 134 Iffley Road, Hammersmith, London W6 0PE.
Ayton, A. C., BA, Dept of History, The University, Cottingham Road, Hull HU6 7RX.

Begley, M. R., 13 Adelaide Avenue, King's Lynn, Norfolk PE30 3AH.
Birchenough, Mrs F. J., 6 Cheyne Walk, Bramblefield Estate, Longfield, Kent.
Bird, E. A., 29 King Edward Avenue, Rainham, Essex RN13 9RH.
Blackwood, B., FRIBA, FRTPI, FSAScot, DipTP, Dip Con Studies, Ebony House, Whitney Drive, Stevenage SG1 4BL.
Bottomley, A. F., BA, MA, Eversley School, Southwold, Suffolk IP18 6AH.
Boyes, J. H., 129 Endlebury Road, Chingford, London E4 6PX.
Bratt, C., 65 Moreton Road, Upton, Merseyside L49 4NR.
Bryant, W. N., MA, PhD, College of S. Mark and S. John, Derriford Road, Plymouth, Devon.
Bussey, G. R., 64 Pampisford Road, Purley, Surrey CR2 2NE.
Butler, Mrs M. C., MA, 4 Castle Street, Warkworth, Morpeth, Northumberland NE65 0UW.

Cairns, Mrs W. N., MA, Alderton House, New Ross, Co. Wexford, Ireland.
Carter, F. E. L., CBE, MA, FSA, 8 The Leys, London N2 0HE.
Cary, Sir Roger, Bt, BA, 23 Bath Road, London W4.
Chandra, Shri Suresh, MA, MPhil, BE Havelock Road Colony, Lucknow 226001, India.
Chappell, Rev. M. P., MA, St Luke's Vicarage, 37 Woodland Ravine, Scarborough YO12 6TA.
Clifton, Dr Gloria C., BA, 55 The Ridgway, Sutton, Surrey SM2 5JX.
Cobban, A. D., 11 Pennyfields, Warley, Brentwood, Essex CM14 5JP.
Condon, Miss M. M., BA, 56 Bernard Shaw House, Knatchbull Road, London NW10.
Cooksley, P. G., 4 Ellerslie Court, Beddington Gardens, Wallington, Surrey SM6 0JD.
Cowburn-Wood, J. O. BA, MEd, The Dolphins, 131 King Edward Road, Onchan, Isle of Man.
Cox, A. H., Winsley, 11a Bagley Close, West Drayton, Middlesex.
Creighton-Williamson, Lt-Col. D., 1 The Pines, Westend Lane, Hucclecote, Gloucester GL3 3SH.

d'Alton, Ian, MA, PhD, 30 Kew Park Avenue, Lucan, Co. Dublin, Ireland.
Daniels, C. W., MEd, Culford School, Bury St Edmunds, Suffolk IP28 6TX.
Davies, G. J., BA, PhD, FSA, 16 Melcombe Avenue, Weymouth, Dorset DT4 7TH.

Davies, P. H., BA, Erskine House, Homesfield, Erskine Hill, London NW11 6HN.

Davis, J. M., BA, MA, MSc, 6 Ellerslie Court, Gladstone Road, Crowborough, East Sussex TN6 1PL.

Davis, Virginia G., BA, PhD, Dept of History, Westfield College, Kidderpore Avenue, London NW3 7ST.

Denton, Barry, 10 Melrose Avenue, Off Bants Lane, Northampton NN5 5PB.

Downie, W. F., BSc, CEng, FICE, FINucE, MIES, 10 Ryeland Street, Strathaven, Lanarkshire ML10 6DL.

Dowse, Rev. I. R., 23 Beechfield Road, Hemel Hempstead HP1 1PP.

Edgell, The Revd H. A. R., SB, StJ, Horning Vicarage, Norwich NR12 8PZ.

Elliott, Rev. W., BA, 8 Lea View, Cleobury Mortimer, Kidderminster, Worcs. DY14 8EE.

Enoch, D. G., BEd, MEd, Treetops, 14 St David's Road, Miskin, Pontyclun CF7 8PW.

Filletti, The Hon. Mr. Justice J. A., LlD, BA, 6 Balluta Buildings, St Ignatius Street, St Julian's, Malta.

Firth, P. J. C., 59 Springfield Road, London NW8 0QJ.

Fitzgerald, R., PhD, BA, 32 Kynaston Road, Enfield, Middlesex EN2 0DB.

Foster, J. M., MA, 3 Marchmont Gardens, Richmond, Surrey TW10 6ET.

Franco de Baux, Don Victor, KCHS, KCN, Flat 2, 28 St Stephen's Avenue, London W12 8JH.

Frazier, R. Ll., BA, Dept of History, The University, Nottingham NG7 2RD.

Freeman, Miss J., 5 Spencer Close, Stansted Mountfitchet, Essex.

Granger, E. R., Bluefield, Blundall Road, Blofield, Norfolk NR13 4LB.

Green, P. L., MA, 9 Faulkner Street, Gate Pa, Tauranga, New Zealand.

Grosvenor, Ian D., BA, 69 Church Road, Moseley, Birmingham B13 9EB.

Gurney, Mrs S. J., 'Albemarle', 13 Osborne Street, Wolverton, Milton Keynes MK12 5HH.

Guy, Rev. J. R., BA, Selden End, Ash, nr Martock, Somerset TA12 6NS.

Hall, P. T., Accrington and Rosendale College, Sandy Lane, Accrington, Lancs. BB5 2AW.

Hamilton-Williams, D. C., BSc, SRN, MRSH, 6 Faraday Avenue, East Grinstead, West Sussex RH19 4AX.

Hanawalt, Professor Barbara A., MA, PhD, Dept of History, University of Minnesota, Minneapolis, MN 55455, U.S.A.

Hawkes, G. I., BA, MA, PhD, Linden House, St Helens Road, Ormskirk, Lancs.

Hawtin, Miss U. G., BA, PhD, FSAScot, FRSAI, Honey Cottage, 5 Clifton Road, London SW19 4QX.

Henderson-Howat, Mrs A. M. D., 9 Capel Court, The Burgage, Prestbury, Cheltenham, Glos GL52 3EL.

Hendrie, A. W. A., BA, ACP, Sandy Ridge, Amberley Road, Storrington, West Sussex RH20 4JE.

Hillman, L. B., BA, 18 Creswick Walk, Hampstead Garden Suburb, London NW11 6AN.

Hoare, E. T., 70 Addison Road, Enfield, Middlesex.

Hodge, Mrs G., 85 Hadlow Road, Tonbridge, Kent.

Hope, R. B., MA, MEd, PhD, 5 Partis Way, Newbridge Hill, Bath, Avon BA1 3QG.

Jackson, A., BA, 14 Latimer Lane, Guisborough, Cleveland.

James, T. M., BA, MA, PhD, 36 Heritage Court, Boley Park, Lichfield, Staffs. WS14 9ST.

Jarvis, L. D., Middlesex Cottage, 86 Mill Road, Stock, Ingatestone, Essex.

Jennings, T. S., GTCL, The Willows, 54 Bramcote Road, Loughborough LE11 2AS.

Jermy, K. E., MA, Cert. Archaeol., CEng, MIM, FISTC, AIFA, FRSA, 5 Far Sandfield, Churchdown, Gloucester GL3 2 JS.

Jerram-Burrows, Mrs L. E., Parkanaur House, 88 Sutton Road, Rochford, Essex.

Johnston, F. R., MA, 15 Lon Y Waun, Abergele, Clwyd LL22 7EU.

Johnstone, H. F. V., 119 Kingsbridge Road, Parkstone, Poole, Dorset BH14 8TL.

Jones, Rev. D. R., BA, MA, Chaplain's Office, St George's Church, HQ Dhekelia, British Forces Post Office 58.

Jones, Dr N. L., Dept of History & Geography, Utah State University, UMC 07, Logan, Utah 84322, U.S.A.

Kadish, Sharman I. DPhil, 126 Broadfields Avenue, Edgware, Middlesex HA8 8SS.

Keast, W. J., MPh, BA, Ziba View, 39 St George's Road, Barbican, East Looe, Cornwall.

Keir, Mrs G. I., BA, BLitt, 17 Battlefield Road, St Albans Herts. AL1 4DA.

Kennedy, M. J., BA, Dept of Medieval History, The University, Glasgow G12 8QQ.

Kilburn, T., BSocSc, MA, Pineacres, Grove Lane, Hackney, Matlock, Derbyshire DE4 2QF.

Knight, G. A., BA, PhD, DAA, MIInfSc, 17 Lady Frances Drive, Market Rasen, Lincs. LN8 3 JJ.

Land, N., BA, DPSE(History), FRSA, FRGS, FCollP, 44 Lineholt Close, Oakenshaw South, Redditch, Worcs.

Leckey, J. J., MSc(Econ), LCP, FRSAI, Vestry Hall, Ballygowan, Co. Down, N. Ireland BT23 6HQ.

Lee, Professor M. du P., PhD, Douglass College, Rutgers University, New Brunswick, NJ 08903, U.S.A.

Lewin, Mrs J., MA, 3 Sunnydale Gardens, Mill Hill, London NW7.

Lewis, J. B., MA, CertEd, FRSA, 93 Five Ashes Road, Westminster Park, Chester CH4 7QA.

McDowell, W. H., MA, MSc, BA, 13 Saughtonhall Avenue, Edinburgh EH12 5RJ.

McErlean, J. M. P., MA, PhD, Dept of History, York University, Downsview, Ontario, Canada M3J 1P3.

McIntyre, Miss S. C., BA, DPhil, West Midlands College of Higher Education, Walsall, West Midlands.

McKenna, Rev. T. J., P.O. Box 979, Queanbeyan, NSW 2620, Australia.

McLeod, D. H., BA, PhD, Dept of Theology, The University, P.O. Box 363, Birmingham B15 2TT.

Meatyard, E., BA, DipEd, Guston, Burial Lane, Church Lane, Llantwit Major, S. Glam. CF6 9ZZ.

Metcalf, D. M., MA, DPhil, 40 St Margaret's Road, Oxford OX2 6LD.

Mileham, Major (Rtd) P. J. R., 16 Grovely View, Wilton, Wiltshire SP2 0NA.

Morris, A. R., BSc(Econ), MA, Woolpit End, Duke of Kent School, Ewhurst, Surrey GU6 7NS.
Munson, K. G., 'Briar Wood', 4 Kings Ride, Seaford, Sussex BN25 2LN.

Nagel, L. C. J., BA, (address unknown).
Newman, L. T., MSc, DIC, CEng, 60 Hurford Drive, Thatcham, Newbury, Berks. RG13 4WA.
Noonan, J. A., BA, MEd, HDE, St Patrick's Comprehensive School, Curriculum Development Centre, Shannon, Co. Clare, Ireland.

Oggins, R. S., PhD, Dept of History, State University of New York, Binghamton 13901, U.S.A.
Osborne, Irving M., BEd, Adv.DipEd, FRSA, FRGS, FCollP, 169 Goodman Park, Slough SL2 5NR.

Pam, D. O., 44 Chase Green Avenue, Enfield, Middlesex EN2 8EB.
Paton, L. R., 49 Lillian Road, Barnes, London SW13.
Paulson, E., BSc(Econ), 11 Darley Avenue, Darley Dale, Matlock, Derbys. DE4 2GB.
Perry, E., FSAScot, 11 Lynmouth Avenue, Hathershaw, Oldham OL8 3 ES.
Perry, K., MA, 14 Highland View Close, Colehill, Wimborne, Dorset.
Powell, Mrs A. M., 129 Blinco Grove, Cambridge CB1 4TX.
Priestley, Captain E. J., MA, MPhil, 7 Inverleith Place, Edinburgh EH3 5QE.

Raspin, Miss A., London School of Economics, Houghton Street, London WC2A 2AE.
Rees, Rev. D. B., BA, BD, MSc(Econ), PhD, 32 Garth Drive, Liverpool L18 6HW.
Reid, N. H., MA, c/o Cayman Islands Museum Office, Government Admin. Building, George Town, Grand Cayman, British West Indies.
Rendall, Miss J., BA, PhD, Dept of History, University of York, Heslington, York YO1 5DD.
Richards, N. F., PhD, 376 Maple Avenue, St Lambert, Prov. of Quebec, Canada J4P 2S2.
Roberts, S. G., MA, DPhil, 23 Beech Avenue, Radlett, Herts. WD7 7DD.
Rosenfield, M. C., AB, AM, PhD, Box 395, Mattapoisett, Mass. 02739, U.S.A.
Russell, Mrs E., BA, c/o Dept of History, University College London, Gower Street, London WC1E 6BT.

Sabben-Clare, E. E., MA, 4 Denham Close, Abbey Hill Road, Winchester SO23 7BL.
Sainsbury, F., 16 Crownfield Avenue, Newbury Park, Ilford, Essex.
Scannura, C. G., MA, 1/11 St Dominic Street, Valletta, Malta.
Scott, The Rev. A. R., MA, BD, PhD, Sunbeam Cottage, 110 Mullalelish Road, Richhill, Co Armagh, N. Ireland BT61 9LT.
Sellers, J. M., MA, 9 Vere Road, Pietermaritzburg 3201, Natal, S. Africa.
Shores, C. F., ARICS, 40 St Mary's Crescent, Hendon, London NW4 4LH.
Sorensen, Mrs M. O., MA, 8 Layer Gardens, London W3 9PR.
Sparkes, I. G., FLA, 124 Green Hill, High Wycombe, Bucks.
Starr, C. R., 63 Abbey Gardens, London W6 8QR.
Sygrave, I., BA, PGCE, MCollP, 52 Burgoyne Road, Haringey, London N4 1AE.

Teague, D. C., ARAeS, MIMM, 52 Beresford Street, Stoke, Plymouth PL2 3AL.

Thomas, D. L., BA, Public Record Office, Chancery Lane, London WC2A 1LR.

Thomas, Miss E. J. M., BA, 8 Ravenscroft Road, Northfield End, Henley-on-Thames, Oxon., RG9 2DH.

Thompson, L. F., Colne View, 69 Chaney Road, Wivenhoe, Essex.

Tracy, J. N., BA, MPhil, PhD, 239 George Street, Fredericton, N.B., Canada E3B 1J4.

Tudor, Victoria M., BA, PhD, 33 Convent Close, Hitchin, Herts. SG5 1QN.

Waldman, T. G., MA, 620 Franklin Bldg./I6, University of Pennsylvania, Philadelphia, Pa. 19104, U.S.A.

Walker, J. A., 1 Sylvanus, Roman Wood, Bracknell, Berkshire RG12 4XX.

Wall, Rev. J., BD, MA, PhD, 10 Branksome Road, Norwich NR4 6SN.

Ward, R. C., BA, MPhil, 192 Stortford Hall Park, Bishop's Stortford, Herts. CM23 5AS.

Warren, Ann K., PhD, Dept of History, Case Western Reserve University, Cleveland, Ohio 44106, U.S.A.

Warrillow, E. J. D., MBE, FSA, Hill-Cote, Lancaster Road, Newcastle, Staffs.

Weise, Selene H. C., PhD, 22 Hurd Street, Mine Hill, New Jersey 07801, U.S.A.

Welbourne, D. J., 57 West Busk Lane, Otley, West Yorkshire LS21 3LY.

Westlake, R. A., 53 Claremont, Malpas, Newport, Gwent NP9 6PL.

Whittaker, Rev. (Rtd) G. H., MA, 1 Ash Grove, Ilkley, West Yorkshire LS29 8EP.

Wickham, David E., MA, 116 Parsonage Manorway, Belvedere, Kent.

Wilkinson, F. J., 40 Great James Street, Holborn, London WC1N 3HB.

Williams, A. R., BA, MA, 5 Swanswell Drive, Granley Fields, Cheltenham, Glos. GL51 6LL.

Williams, C. L. Sinclair, ISO, The Old Vicarage, The Green, Puddletown, nr Dorchester, Dorset.

Williams, G., FLA, 32 St John's Road, Manselton, Swansea SA5 8PP.

Williams, P. T., FSAScot, FRSA, FFAS, Bryn Bueno, Whitford Street, Holywell, Clwyd, North Wales.

Wilson, A. R., BA, MA, 80 Apedale Road, Wood Lane, Bignall End, Stoke-on-Trent ST7 8PH.

Windrow, M. C., West House, Broyle Lane, Ringmer, nr Lewes, Sussex.

Winterbottom, D. O., MA, BPhil, Clifton College, Bristol BS8 3JH.

Wood, A. W., A.Dip.R, 11 Blessington Close, London SE13 5ED.

Woodall, R. D., BA, Bethel, 7 Wynthorpe Road, Horbury, nr Wakefield, Yorks. WF4 5BB.

Worsley, Miss A. V., BA, 3d St George's Cottages, Glasshill Street, London SE1.

Young, Assoc., Professor M. B., BA, MA, PhD, Dept of History, Illinois Wesleyan University, Bloomington, Illinois 61702, U.S.A.

Zerafa, Rev. M. J., St Dominic's Priory, Valletta, Malta.

CORRESPONDING FELLOWS

Ajayi, Professor J. F. Ade, University of Ibadan, Ibadan, Nigeria, West Africa.

Bédarida, Professor F., 13 rue Jacob, Paris 75006, France.
Berend, Professor T. Ivan, Hungarian Academy of Sciences, 1361 Budapest V, Roosevelt-tèr 9, Hungary.
Bischoff, Professor B., DLitt, 8033 Planegg C., Ruffini-Allee 27, München, West Germany.
Boorstin, Daniel J., MA, LLD, 3541 Ordway Street, N.W., Washington, DC 20016, U.S.A.
Boyle, Monsignor Leonard E., OP, Biblioteca Apostolica Vaticana, Vatican City, Rome, Italy.

Cipolla, Professor Carlo M., University of California, Berkeley Campus, Berkeley, Calif. 94720, U.S.A.
Constable, Giles, PhD, School of Historical Studies, The Institute for Advanced Study, Princeton, NJ 08540, U.S.A.
Crouzet, Professor F. M. J., 6 rue Benjamin Godard, 75016 Paris, France.

Duby, Professor G., Collège de France, 11 Place Marcelin-Berthelot, 75005 Paris, France.

Garin, Professor Eugenio, via Francesco Crispi 6, 50129 Firenze F, Italy.
Gieysztor, Professor Aleksander, Polska Akademia Nauk, Wydzial I Nauk, Rynek Starego Miasta 29/31, 00–272 Warszawa, Poland.
Giusti, Rt Rev. Mgr M., JCD, Archivio Segreto Vaticano, Vatican City, Italy.
Glamann, Professor K., DPhil, DLitt, The Carlsberg Foundation, H.C. Andersens Boulevard 35, 1553 København, V, Denmark.
Gopal, Professor S., MA, DPhil, Centre for Historical Studies, Jawaharlal Nehru University, New Mehrauli Road, New Delhi-110067, India.
Guenée, Professor Bernaerd, 8 rue Huysmans, 75006 Paris, France.

Hanke, Professor L. U., PhD, E8 Amity Pl., Amhurst, MA 01002, U.S.A.

Inalcik, Professor Halil, PhD, The University of Ankara, Turkey.
Inglis, Professor K. S., DPhil (History Dept) The Research School of Social Sciences, The Australian National University, GPO Box 4, Canberra, ACT 2601, Australia.

Klingenstein, Professor Grete, Paniglgasse 19 A/31, A-1040 Wien IV, Austria.
Kossmann, Professor E. H., DLitt, Rijksuniversiteit te Groningen, Groningen, The Netherlands.
Kuttner, Professor S., MA, JUD, SJD, LLD, Institute of Medieval Canon Law, University of California, Berkeley, Calif. 94720, U.S.A.

Ladurie, Professor E. B. LeRoy, Collège de France, 11 Place Marce-linBerthelot, 75005 Paris, France.

Leclercq, The Rev. Dom Jean L., OSB, Abbaye St-Maurice, L-9737 Clervaux, Luxembourg.

McNeill, Professor William H., 1126 East 59th Street, Chicago, Illinois 60637, U.S.A.
Maruyama, Professor Masao, 2–44–5 Higashimachi, Kichijoji, Musashinoshi, Tokyo 180, Japan.
Michel, Henri, 12 Rue de Moscou, 75008 Paris, France.
Morgan, Professor Edmund S., Department of History, P.O. Box 1504A Yale Station, New Haven, Conn. 06520-7425, U.S.A.

Peña y Cámara, J. M. de la, Avenida Reina, Mercedes 65, piso 7-B, Seville 12, Spain.
Prawer, Professor J., Department of Medieval History, Hebrew University, Il-Jerusalem, Israel.

Slicher van Bath, Professor B. H., Gen. Fouldesweg 113, Wageningen, The Netherlands.

Thapar, Professor Romila, Dept of Historical Studies, Jawaharlal Nehru University, New Mehrauli Road, New Delhi-110067, India.
Thorne, Professor S. E., MA, LLB, LittD, LLD, FSA, Law School of Harvard University, Cambridge, Mass. 02138, U.S.A.

Van Houtte, Professor J. A., PhD, FBA, Termunkveld, Groeneweg, 51, Egenhoven, Heverlee, Belgium.
Verlinden, Professor C., PhD, 3 Avenue du Derby, 1050 Brussels, Belgium.

Wang, Professor Juefei, Nanjing University, China.
Wolff, Professor Philippe, Édifici Roureda Tapada, 2ª,7, Santa Coloma (Principality of Andorra), France.
Woodward, Professor C. Vann, PhD, Yale University, 104 Hall of Graduate Studies, New Haven, Conn. 06520, U.S.A.

Zavala, S., LLD, Montes Urales 310, Mexico 10, D.F., Mexico.

TRANSACTIONS AND PUBLICATIONS

OF THE

ROYAL HISTORICAL SOCIETY

The publications of the Society consist of the *Transactions*, supplemented in 1897 by the *Camden Series* (formerly the Camden Society, 1838–97); since 1937 by a series of *Guides and Handbooks* and, from time to time, by miscellaneous publications. The Society also began in 1937 an annual bibliography of *Writings on British History*, for the continuation of which the Institute of Historical Research accepted responsibility in 1965; it publishes, in conjunction with the American Historical Association, a series of *Bibliographies of British History*.

List of series published

The following are issued in collaboration with the distributor/publisher indicated:

Annual Bibliography of British and Irish History	
All titles	Harvester Press
Bibliographies of British History	
All except 1485–1603, 1714–1789	Oxford University Press
1485–1603, 1714–1789	Harvester Press
Camden Series	
Old Series and New Series	Johnson Reprint
Third and Fourth Series*	Boydell and Brewer
Guides and Handbooks	
Main Series*	Boydell and Brewer
Supplementary Series*	Boydell and Brewer
Miscellaneous titles	Boydell and Brewer
Studies in History	
All titles	Boydell and Brewer
Transactions of the Royal Historical Society	
Up to *Fifth Series*, Vol. 19	Kraus Reprint
Fifth Series, Vol. 20 onwards*†	Boydell and Brewer
Writings on British History	
Up to 1946	Dawson Book Service
1946–1974	Instititute of Historical Research

Members' entitlements

Fellows and Subscribing Libraries receive free copies of new volumes of series marked*.

Corresponding Fellows, Retired Fellows and Associates receive free copies of new volumes of this series marked†.

Terms for members' purchase of individual titles are listed below.

Methods of Ordering Volumes

Institute of Historical Research—an invoice will be sent with volume.

In all other cases pre-payment is required. If correct price is not known, a cheque made payable to the appropriate supplier, in the form 'Not exceeding £   ' may be sent with the order. Otherwise a pro-forma invoice will be sent.

LIST OF TITLES
ARRANGED BY DISTRIBUTOR

BOYDELL & BREWER

Address for orders: P.O. Box 9, Woodbridge, Suffolk IP12 3DF.

Camden Third Series: All titles now available; a list can be sent on request. Prices range from £19.50 for original volumes to £35 for the largest reprinted volumes. (£14.62–£26.25 to Members).

Camden Fourth Series: The following titles are available price £15. (£11.25 to Members) unless otherwise indicated:

1. Camden Miscellany, Vol. XXII: 1. Charters of the Earldom of Hereford, 1095–1201. Edited by David Walker. 2. Indentures of Retinue with John of Gaunt, Duke of Lancaster, enrolled in Chancery, 1367–99. Edited by N. B. Lewis. 3. Autobiographical memoir of Joseph Jewell, 1763–1846. Edited by A. W. Slater. 1964. £35.00.
2. Documents illustrating the rule of Walter de Wenlock, Abbot of Westminster, 1283–1307. Edited by Barbara Harvey. 1965.
3. The early correspondence of Richard Wood, 1831–41. Edited by A. B. Cunningham. 1966. £35.00.
4. Letters from the English abbots to the chapter at Cîteaux, 1442–1521. Edited by C. H. Talbot. 1967.
5. Select writings of George Wyatt. Edited by D. M. Loades. 1968.
6. Records of the trial of Walter Langeton, Bishop of Lichfield and Coventry (1307–1312). Edited by Miss A. Bearwood. 1969.
7. Camden Miscellany, Vol. XXIII: 1. The Account Book of John Balsall of Bristol for a trading voyage to Spain, 1480. Edited by T. F. Reddaway and A. A. Ruddock. 2. A Parliamentary diary of Queen Anne's reign. Edited by W. A. Speck. 3. Leicester House politics, 1750–60, from the papers of John second Earl of Egmont. Edited by A. N. Newman. 4. The Parliamentary diary of Nathaniel Ryder, 1764–67. Edited by P. D. G. Thomas. 1969.
8. Documents illustrating the British Conquest of Manila, 1762–63. Edited by Nicholas P. Cushner. 1971.
9. Camden Miscellany, Vol XXIV: 1. Documents relating to the Breton succession dispute of 1341. Edited by M. Jones. 2. Documents relating to the Anglo-French negotiations, 1439. Edited by C. T. Allmand. 3. John Benet's Chronicle for the years 1400 to 1462. Edited by G. L. Harriss. 1972.
10. Herefordshire Militia Assessments of 1663. Edited by M. A. Faraday. 1972.
11. The early correspondence of Jabez Bunting, 1820–29. Edited by W. R. Ward. 1972.
12. Wentworth Papers, 1597–1628. Edited by J. P. Cooper, 1973.
13. Camden Miscellany, Vol. XXV: 1. The Letters of William, Lord Paget. Edited by Barrett L. Beer and Sybil Jack. 2. The Parliamentary Diary of John Clementson, 1770–1802. Edited by P. D. G. Thomas. 3. J. B. Pentland's Report on Bolivia, 1827. Edited by J. V. Fifer, 1974.
14. Camden Miscellany, Vol. XXVI: 1. Duchy of Lancaster Ordinances, 1483. Edited by Sir Robert Somerville. 2. A Breviat of the Effectes

devised for Wales. Edited by P. R. Roberts. 3. Gervase Markham, The Muster-Master. Edited by Charles L. Hamilton. 4. Lawrence Squibb, A Book of all the Several Offices of the Court of the Exchequer (1642). Edited by W. H. Bryson. 5. Letters of Henry St John to Charles, Earl of Orrery, 1709–11. Edited by H. T. Dickinson. 1975.

15. Sidney Ironworks Accounts, 1541–73. Edited by D. W. Crossley. 1975.
16. The Account-Book of Beaulieu Abbey. Edited by S. F. Hockey. 1975.
17. A calendar of Western Circuit Assize Orders, 1629–48. Edited by J. S. Cockburn. 1976.
18. Four English Political Tracts of the later Middle Ages. Edited by J.-Ph. Genet. 1977.
19. Proceedings of the Short Parliament of 1640. Edited by Esther S. Cope in collaboration with Willson H. Coates. 1977.
20. Heresy Trials in the Diocese of Norwich, 1428–31. Edited by N. P. Tanner. 1977.
21. Edmund Ludlow: A Voyce from the Watch Tower (Part Five: 1660–1662). Edited by A. B. Worden. 1978.
22. Camden Miscellany, Vol. XXVII: 1. The Disputed Regency of the Kingdom of Jerusalem, 1264/6 and 1268. Edited by P. W. Edbury. 2. George Rainsford's *Ritratto d'Ingliterra* (1556). Edited by P. S. Donaldson. 3. The Letter-Book of Thomas Bentham, Bishop of Coventry and Lichfield, 1560–1561. Edited by Rosemary O'Day and Joel Berlatsky. 1979.
23. The Letters of the Third Viscount Palmerston to Laurence and Elizabeth Sulivan, 1804–63. Edited by Kenneth Bourne. 1979.
24. Documents illustrating the crisis of 1297–98 in England. Edited by M. Prestwich. 1980.
25. The Diary of Edward Goschen, 1900–1914. Edited by C. H. D. Howard. 1980.
26. English Suits before the Parlement of Paris, 1420–36. Edited by C. T. Allmand and C. A. J. Armstrong. 1982.
27. The Devonshire Diary, 1759–62. Edited by P. D. Brown and K. W. Schweizer. 1982.
28. Barrington Family Letters, 1628–1632. Edited by A. Searle. 1983.
29. Camden Miscellany XXVIII: 1. The Account of the Great Household of Humphrey, first Duke of Buckingham, for the year 1452–3. Edited by Mrs M. Harris. 2. Documents concerning the Anglo-French Treaty of 1550. Edited by D. L. Potter. 3. *Vita Mariae Reginae Anglie*. Edited by D. MacCulloch. 4. Despatch of the Count of Feria to Philip II, 1558. Edited by S. L. Adams and M. J. Rodriguez-Salgado. 1983.
30. Gentlemen of Science: Early correspondence of the British Association for the Advancement of Science. Edited by A. W. Thackray and J. B. Morrell. 1984.
31. Reading Abbey Cartularies, Vol. I. Edited by B. R. Kemp. 1986.
32. The Letters of the First Viscount Hardinge of Lahore to Lady Hardinge and Sir Walter and Lady James 1844–1847. Edited by Bawa Satinder Singh. 1986.
33. Reading Abbey Cartularies, Vol. II. Edited by B R. Kemp. 1987. £19.50.
34. Camden Miscellany, Vol. XXIX: 1. Computus Rolls of the English Lands of the Abbey of Bec (1272–1289). Edited by Marjorie Chibnall. 2. Financial Memoranda of the Reign of Edward V. Edited by Rosemary Horrox. 3. A collection of several speeches and treatises of the late Treasurer Cecil. Edited by Pauline Croft. 4. John Howson's Answers to Archbishop Abbot's Accusations, 1615. Edited by Nicholas Cranfield

and Kenneth Fincham. 5. Debates in the House of Commons 1697–1699. Edited by D. W. Hayton. 1987. £19.50.

35. The Short Parliament (1640) Diary of Sir Thomas Aston. Edited by Judith D. Maltby. 1988.

36. Swedish Diplomats at Cromwell's Court, 1655–1656. Edited by M. Roberts.

37. Thomas Starkey: A Dialogue between Pole and Lupset. Edited by T. F. Mayer.